Advances in Higher Education and Professional Development (AHEPD) Book Series

Jared Keengwe
University of North Dakota, USA

ISSN:2327-6983
EISSN:2327-6991

Mission

As world economies continue to shift and change in response to global financial situations, job markets have begun to demand a more highly-skilled workforce. In many industries a college degree is the minimum requirement and further educational development is expected to advance. With these current trends in mind, the **Advances in Higher Education & Professional Development (AHEPD) Book Series** provides an outlet for researchers and academics to publish their research in these areas and to distribute these works to practitioners and other researchers.

AHEPD encompasses all research dealing with higher education pedagogy, development, and curriculum design, as well as all areas of professional development, regardless of focus.

Coverage

- Adult Education
- Assessment in Higher Education
- Career Training
- Coaching and Mentoring
- Continuing Professional Development
- Governance in Higher Education
- Higher Education Policy
- Pedagogy of Teaching Higher Education
- Vocational Education

IGI Global is currently accepting manuscripts for publication within this series. To submit a proposal for a volume in this series, please contact our Acquisition Editors at Acquisitions@igi-global.com or visit: http://www.igi-global.com/publish/.

I0868993

The Advances in Higher Education and Professional Development (AHEPD) Book Series (ISSN
701 E. Chocolate Avenue, Hershey, PA 17033-1240, USA, www.igi-global.com. This series is composed of titles available for purchase individually; each title is edited to be contextually exclusive from any other title within the series. For pricing and ordering information please visit http://www.igi-global.com/book-series/advances-higher-education-professional-development/73681. Postmaster: Send all address changes to above address. © © 2022 IGI Global. All rights, including translation in other languages reserved by the publisher. No part of this series may be reproduced or used in any form or by any means – graphics, electronic, or mechanical, including photocopying, recording, taping, or information and retrieval systems – without written permission from the publisher, except for non commercial, educational use, including classroom teaching purposes. The views expressed in this series are those of the authors, but not necessarily of IGI Global.

Titles in this Series

For a list of additional titles in this series, please visit: http://www.igi-global.com/book-series/advances-higher-education-professional-development/73681

Handbook of Research on Practices for Advancing Diversity and Inclusion in Higher Education
Eleni Meletiadou (London Metropolitan University, UK)
Information Science Reference • © 2022 • 451pp • H/C (ISBN: 9781799896289) • US $270.00

Self-Care and Stress Management for Academic Well-Being
Karis L. Clarke (Clark Atlanta University, USA)
Information Science Reference • © 2022 • 302pp • H/C (ISBN: 9781668423349) • US $215.00

Preparing Agriculture and Agriscience Educators for the Classroom
Andrew C. Thoron (Abraham Baldwin Agricultural College, USA) and R. Kirby Barrick (University of Florida, USA (retired))
Information Science Reference • © 2022 • 381pp • H/C (ISBN: 9781668434208) • US $215.00

Formative and Shared Assessment to Promote Global University Learning
José Sánchez-Santamaría (Universidad de Castilla-La Mancha, Spain)
Information Science Reference • © 2022 • 335pp • H/C (ISBN: 9781668435373) • US $215.00

New Models of Higher Education: Unbundled, Rebundled, Customized, and DIY
Aaron M. Brower (University of Wisconsin Extended Campus, USA) and Ryan J. Specht-Boardman (University of Wisconsin Extended Campus, USA)
Information Science Reference • © 2022 • 425pp • H/C (ISBN: 9781668438091) • US $240.00

Contributions of Historically Black Colleges and Universities in the 21st Century
Anisah Bagasra (Kennesaw State University, USA) Alison Mc Letchie (South Carolina State University, USA) and Jonathan Wesley (Southern New Hampshire University, USA)
Information Science Reference • © 2022 • 330pp • H/C (ISBN: 9781668438145) • US $215.00

Handbook of Research on Opening Pathways for Marginalized Individuals in Higher Education
Stephanie P. Huffman (Missouri State University, USA) Denise D. Cunningham (Missouri State University, USA) Marjorie Shavers (Missouri State University, USA) and Reesha Adamson (Missouri State University, USA)
Information Science Reference • © 2022 • 400pp • H/C (ISBN: 9781668438190) • US $270.00

IGI Global
PUBLISHER of TIMELY KNOWLEDGE

701 East Chocolate Avenue, Hershey, PA 17033, USA
Tel: 717-533-8845 x100 • Fax: 717-533-8661
E-Mail: cust@igi-global.com • www.igi-global.com

Published in the United States of America by
IGI Global
Information Science Reference (an imprint of IGI Global)
701 E. Chocolate Avenue
Hershey PA, USA 17033
Tel: 717-533-8845
Fax: 717-533-8661
E-mail: cust@igi-global.com
Web site: http://www.igi-global.com

Copyright © 2022 by IGI Global. All rights reserved. No part of this publication may be reproduced, stored or distributed in any form or by any means, electronic or mechanical, including photocopying, without written permission from the publisher. Product or company names used in this set are for identification purposes only. Inclusion of the names of the products or companies does not indicate a claim of ownership by IGI Global of the trademark or registered trademark.

Library of Congress Cataloging-in-Publication Data

Names: Saura, José Ramón, 1992- editor.
Title: Teaching innovation in university education : case studies and main practices / José Ramón Saura, Editor.
Description: Hershey, PA : Information Science Reference, [2022] | Includes bibliographical references and index. | Summary: "In this digital era, this book can be used as a sourcebook on study cases focused on teaching innovation methodologies as well as on the identification of new technologies that will help the development of initiatives and practices focused on teaching innovation at universities"-- Provided by publisher.

Identifiers: LCCN 2022007246 (print) | LCCN 2022007247 (ebook) | ISBN 9781668444412 (hardcover) | ISBN 9781668444450 (paperback) | ISBN 9781668444429 (ebook)
Subjects: LCSH: Educational innovations--Case studies. | Educational technology--Study and teaching (Higher)--Case studies. | Education, Higher--Computer-assisted instruction--Case studies. | Universities and colleges--Case studies.
Classification: LCC LB1027 .T343 2022 (print) | LCC LB1027 (ebook) | DDC 378.1/7344678--dc23
LC record available at https://lccn.loc.gov/2022007246
LC ebook record available at https://lccn.loc.gov/2022007247

This book is published in the IGI Global book series Advances in Higher Education and Professional Development (AHEPD) (ISSN: 2327-6983; eISSN: 2327-6991)

British Cataloguing in Publication Data
A Cataloguing in Publication record for this book is available from the British Library.

All work contributed to this book is new, previously-unpublished material. The views expressed in this book are those of the authors, but not necessarily of the publisher.

For electronic access to this publication, please contact: eresources@igi-global.com.

Teaching Innovation in University Education:

Case Studies and Main Practices

Jose Ramon Saura
Rey Juan Carlos University, Spain

A volume in the Advances in Higher Education and Professional Development (AHEPD) Book Series

IGI Global
PUBLISHER of TIMELY KNOWLEDGE

Table of Contents

Section 2

Detailed Table of Contents

This work aims to analyze and explain the didactic strategies used to achieve meaningful learning. It begins under the assumption that meaningful learning is created if students are given freedom and confidence. In this situation, they can find their own answers and develop their knowledge, both in the classroom and in practical life. The method used is an analytical-descriptive one of the reviews of the literature of the main authors who have given rise to this approach, its elements, and the didactic strategies used. It is concluded that the design and implementation of didactic strategies focused on meaningful learning with the application of active didactic methodologies and strategies in meaningful learning processes depending on the context in which it takes place. They obtain better results in the training of professionals.

Due to the digital transformation, universities have had to renew the didactic strategies used by teachers so that they can comply with the teaching-learning process. The implementation of practices in social networks has been essential to adapt to the skills of the new generation of digital students. The main objective of this chapter is to analyze how social networks and user-generated content can be used by university teachers as tools that foster innovation. For this, a review of the literature and different sources is carried out that allows for laying the foundations of the research. In addition, the chapter provides information on the main platforms used in the different educational experiences. With the data obtained, it is possible to understand how these social interaction tools can contribute to teaching innovation and, therefore, to the significant improvement of the learning results of higher education students.

Section 2

Section 2 compiles the main case studies that analyze the implementation of teaching innovation practices in universities. Likewise, it presents in-depth case studies of teaching innovation in different subjects and academic themes.

This chapter presents an overview of the development and implementation of a student-centered teaching approach, namely the Student-Led Instructor Facilitated Guided-Inquiry Learning (SLIFGIL), in an undergraduate chemistry laboratory course. SLIFGIL is a hybrid approach to teaching and is based on the science writing heuristic (SWH) approach used in the laboratory settings. The SWH approach has been used for two decades in school and college science classrooms. Prior studies have reported the effectiveness of the SWH approach in improving student academic performance and conceptual understanding. Though the SWH approach has its strengths, student participation in collaborative group work and continued reliance on the instructor to step in to guide the flow of laboratory activities and facilitate student learning was observed to be a challenge by the first author. To address these challenges, SLIFGIL approach was developed to shift the ownership of learning to the students. In this chapter, an overview of the SLIFGIL approach and results on its effectiveness are presented.

This chapter describes a new interdisciplinary course introduced at Indiana University South Bend. The course is designed for students of any majors to meet their general education requirement on 'the natural world' subject. The course topics are divided into three parts. First, using 'information' as the main thread, this course connects physical information, chemical information, biological information, and social information. Second, using basic computing model and information entropy, this course generalizes information and information theory. Third, information is correlated to cutting-edge computing topics such as quantum computing, complexity, and uncertainty. The main objective of this course is to provide an outline of information theory to students using an interdisciplinary approach.

What is special about the German-speaking education system is that there are two types of higher education institutions. While classical universities do academic teaching, so-called universities of applied sciences (UAS) focus more on practical training for the labour market. This chapter presents the experiences of two professors with practice-integrated teaching at two UAS that ensure employability to a large extent. The common setting of the four courses presented is that students work on real business cases, practical challenges, and real fields of innovation. Methodologically, design think and SCRUM are used. It is described for these cases how the design of the course contributes to students developing innovative and digital approaches for real companies. The chapter concludes with a compilation of good practices that emerged from experiences. These can serve as input for other teachers to design their own practice-integrated courses.

This chapter reflects on teaching practice in an undergraduate induction session introducing agile methodology-based product (e.g., software, paper-aircraft) development and project management. The induction session took place in a paper-aircraft design and development workshop at the City, University of London. The central theme of the teaching practice is step-by-step exercise-oriented (i.e., constructivism) product development activities and the contextual relationship with the distributed software production business processes. Students worked in development teams to understand and appreciate how to capture requirements, design, and build products following agile methodology. Initially, the workshop instructor introduced the different software development process models, activities, and comparative challenges to the students. In addition, students track their progress within the team structure and collaborate with classroom-based teaching and learning activities. Finally, a set of questionaries helped get students' feedback on the appropriateness of agile methodology in product development activities through classroom-based exercises.

This study describes an experience carried out at a university that combines problem-based learning and the use of information and communication technologies (ICT). The activity pursues to deepen the learning of a subject with complex and singular content, taking as a reference the study of real cases. Specifically, the aim is to develop knowledge about the different sectoral accounting standards that are applied in the preparation of companies' financial information. The student checks for himself the usefulness of accounting knowledge to understand the financial situation of real companies. The results show a generalized improvement in student motivation and in results obtained in the subject. It demonstrates how in complex subjects that are less attractive to students active methodologies can be used to connect with them. They learn to take advantage of the resources offered by ICT to access information of great relevance in the business world.

This research will focus on a specific case of teaching innovation involving the use of the "hashtag" phenomenon on the digital platform Twitter by students as a measure of educational improvement. The objective, therefore, is to analyze how this system acts a teaching innovation measure in the educational development of university students. This experience puts into practice the use of social networks as platforms for publication and analysis of relevant news in university students. The sample analyzed is composed of accounting and finance students enrolled in the subjects of Financial Management and Working Capital Management at the Universidad Rey Juan Carlos in three different campuses, where the teaching innovation system was only applied in two of the campus, and results were compared. The purpose, therefore, is to observe and analyze how this innovation system affects the group and what results are obtained in comparison with the group that did not apply it.

This chapter describes the process of designing, developing, and implementing a gamification strategy in a Production Management course. The online tool Genially was used for this purpose. The strategy of using gamification as a learning method allows students not only to acquire and enhance their learning but also to develop competencies and capabilities such as problem solving, teamwork, communication, information management, and critical thinking. It also incentivizes learning self-regulation in an attractive way, thanks to the potential of games to influence the behavior and motivation of students. This chapter lists the steps required to develop and implement gamification in the classroom, describes the implementation of gamification in a specific course, and discusses the results of the experience.

The current model of higher education uses digital technologies for learning. One of the major applications is their use for online examinations. However, the validity of these exams is questioned, suggesting the commitment of dishonest practices by students. This research analyses whether self-deception behaviours negatively influence the students' learning performance. First, the authors carry out an identical midterm test to the same students in an online environment and in a face-to-face environment, and exam marks are compared. Second, they carry out a regression analysis where they introduce a dummy variable that reflects the changes on the midterm exam mark and analyse how that variable influences on student learning. Data from 230 students from three different courses in business are used. The findings show that students have a higher mark in the online exam than in the face-to-face exam, suggesting for dishonest behaviours. Also, those students who had a dishonest behaviour in the midterm exam have a lower performance in the final exam, suggesting the existence of self-deception.

Educational methodology evolves over time in search of an improvement in the student's learning process, taking into account a practical aspect in its path towards teaching. This chapter presents the service-learning methodology in which, while the learner offers a service to the community in order to improve it, the student learns moral values as well as the basic competences of the educational field. Service-learning is a method for linking educational success and social commitment, since learning brings quality to the service provided and service gives meaning to learning. This study analyses the case of the Sagrado Corazón of Pamplona School as a result of the application of the service-learning methodology within the school's educational programme.

Preface

Teaching innovation has become a key factor in the education industry (Bordogna et al., 1993). Innovation drives the adoption of new technologies and teaching methods (Saura et al., 2022). In a context in which data has positioned itself as a fundamental variable for decision-making, the evolution of teaching and learning models should be able to adapt to a new digital age (Grewal et al., 2022). Innovation and teaching must be combined as concepts and themes that jointly seek academic excellence (Dias et al., 2021).

The university and higher education industries should be understood as areas for the validation of knowledge (Hockings, 2005). University communities should encourage the promotion of future practices and uses of new teaching techniques that can maintain student motivation and encouraging learning by adapting to the needs of the present data-based era (Foster and Yaoyuneyong, 2016).

In this way, there are many teaching initiatives that have been developed in the last decade to promote teaching innovation in universities and higher education institutions (Lantz, 2010). In these ecosystems, both teachers/students and professionals or practitioners who take part in university teaching are active agents that cause positive experiences linked to teaching innovation strategies (Saura et al., 2022a).

At the same time, the development of the Internet and the use of new technologies have allowed teachers around the world to adapt their teaching innovation strategies in different ways (Virdun et al., 2013). Both the use of tools for teleworking, collaborative environments, the use of artificial intelligence, automated analysis of structured environments, flexible and digital methodologies, among others, have been initiatives developed in the last decade. Although it is true, the COVID-19 pandemic has caused many universities and higher education centers to adapt their innovation strategies to a new era focused on data (Ribeiro-Navarrete et al., 2021; Saura et al., 2022b).

Innovation in the education industry is not only a concept linked to teaching, but also covers multiple areas from the internal organization of universities and higher education centers to the training of teachers and students (Zhang et al., 2012), internal and external communication, the teaching culture and philosophy, or the adaptation of infrastructures, to an era in which Big Data (Saura et al., 2021), the Internet of Things (IoT) (Saura et al., 2021a), or data-centric decision-making are key elements for the development of innovation in general, and specifically, in the education industry (Yock et al., 2011).

In this context, this book aims to collect case studies of applications of different teaching innovation methodologies and approaches. In this way, the readers of this book will be able to apply the techniques and case studies developed to date. In addition, this book will allow them to understand the adoption of new methodological approaches that can be applied in the future.
Therefore, the secondary objectives of this edited book are presented as follow:

- To create knowledge in relation to teaching innovation processes and methodologies

- To identify perspectives of analysis of teaching innovation strategies
- To understand the main actions of teaching innovation through case studies
- To explore the use of new technologies and innovation at the university
- To identify future lines for the development of teaching innovation practices in the university ecosystem

In this way, Chapter 1 has the objective of identifying the main methodologies applied in higher education institutions. The article analyzes the main methodologies that use teaching innovation in the educational ecosystems. For this, they carry out a literature review in which the main characteristics of the identified teaching methodologies are classified. Active and reflective learning or the adaptability of flexible groups in real contexts are highlighted.

Likewise, Chapter 2 analyzes and identifies the main teaching innovation strategies after the COVID-19 pandemic. In this study, a systematic literature review is developed and the main practices of both students and teachers linked to teaching innovation are identified. The development of examples and case studies are proposed. In the results, the authors demonstrated what are the advantages and disadvantages of an innovative ecosystem focused on and adapted post COVID-19 education.

In Chapter 3, the main teaching strategies used by teachers for the development of useful learning processes are explained. In this way, teaching innovation linked to knowledge and practical processes in the classroom are proposed and discussed. An analytical method is described using a systematic literature review. The authors define the design and implementation of didactic strategies centered on useful methodologies.

In Chapter 4, the main teaching innovation methodologies developed in universities and linked to social networks are presented. In this way, the main digital tools are presented in which the content generated by the user in social networks participates as a fundamental base. Its main uses and strategies applied to the future of teaching innovation at the university are defined and conceptualized.

Chapter 5 presents the development and implementation of a student-centered model to improve teaching in which a guide for instructors is developed in an undergraduate chemistry laboratory course. The authors present a hybrid approach to teaching focused on the writing method is presented. The application of this new method is proposed as an innovation to improve the results and performance of the students and instructors. The results also discuss the effectiveness of the presented model and link it to the development of teaching innovation.

Chapter 6 describes and uses a new interdisciplinary method at Indiana University South Bend. In this study, the division of the contents into three parts is proposed, focusing on the quality of the information, on the development of computational models and on the correlation of these issues linked to the concepts of quantum computing, complexity and uncertainty. The main objectives of this study are to propose teaching methods that use innovation and information theory to studies with an interdisciplinary approach.

In Chapter 7, models and good practices are presented in the teaching innovation ecosystem at social science universities in Germany. In this way, experiences of two professors are presented for the analysis of cases linked to business, practical challenges as well as the different fields of innovation. In this way, the study proposes the methodological development of Design Thinking to understand a conglomerate of good practices that arise from the experiences presented in the study.

Chapter 8 develops a reflection for the use of agile practices as a methodology linked to product development and management. The study proposes step by step the development of a workshop at the University of London. The students worked in teams to solve the challenges proposed by the teacher. In this study, the different outlets are collected in addition to proposal for creating knowledge by working with agile methodologies focused on the development of teaching innovation.

In Chapter 9, active methodologies are presented in which learning elements are combined through problems and the use of information and communication technologies. In this way, this study proposes the development of knowledge creation linked to the accounting sector in relation to the financial interests of companies. In this case, students use their knowledge of accounting to understand real situations in the financial environment. Through this teaching innovation of real cases, the authors indicate contributions linked to teaching innovation in this area of research.

Chapter 10 proposes the use of hashtags in the social network Twitter in order to use this new digital channel to interact between students and teachers and therefore increasing the engagement. The study presents contributions linked to the accounting and finance areas with the aim of proposing the development of new lines of research linked to teaching innovation.

Chapter 11 presents the gamification technology, a process for design, development and implementation in subjects related to production management. In this study, the authors use a branching tool as a teaching method that allows students to acquire knowledge and develop skills in relation to their problem-solving, teamwork, and critical thinking skills. Likewise, this study develops a guide for the implementation of gamification in university classrooms.

In Chapter 12, the development of a model applied to higher education and focused on the use of digital technologies for teaching is proposed. In this way, the applications to take online exams are analyzed. In addition, the concept of self-deception behavior is analyzed to understand how it can negatively affect students in their learning processes. In this way, the authors analyze how these variables can influence the online learning of students in digital environments.

Chapter 13 proposes the use of the service-learning approach to improve the teaching process and drive innovation in higher education institutions. Likewise, this study develops this methodology to examine the improvement of ethical and moral values of studies in this field. In an exploratory way, this study proposes the analysis of a case in which this methodology is applied. Finally, the authors present the contributions of the study to teaching innovation.

Chapter 14 discusses the use of case studies as a traditional methodology. They indicate that, if this is adopted, it can be understood as a method of teaching innovation. Also, students use new methodologies and tools with the aim of increasing discussions related to case studies. In this way, this study indicates the steps of a group of teachers to implement this methodology in their classes, encountering some difficulties. In addition, the evaluation of three different methods is proposed to centralize the understanding of the case studies in relation to positive results. These actions have been applied to university-level business schools.

In Chapter 15, the use of the case is presented pedagogically. This study identifies different concepts linked to the "case" as a method and explores the different pieces to develop pedagogical exercises in educational institutions. Finally, a logical reasoning of the main concepts and definitions linked to the theory and different tricks and ideas to improve it effectively is presented and discussed.

Finally, it should be noted that this book can be used by teachers at any level of education. Although it is true, the contents are mainly linked to the university ecosystem, they can be understood from different education levels. In any case, the methods proposed on teaching innovation as well as the case studies discussed can help teachers to improve their teaching practices and to develop new learning models both focused on the traditional and digital atmosphere. This fact allows practitioners to increase the quality of their teaching innovation methods to boost knowledge and critical use of these innovations.

Jose Ramon Saura
Rey Juan Carlos University, Spain

REFERENCES

Bordogna, J., Fromm, E., & Ernst, E. W. (1993). Engineering education: Innovation through integration. *Journal of Engineering Education*, *82*(1), 3–8. doi:10.1002/j.2168-9830.1993.tb00065.x

Dias, G. P., Barbosa, B., Santos, C. A., Pinheiro, M. M., Simões, D., & Filipe, S. (2021). Between promises and pitfalls: The impact of mobility on the internationalization of higher education. *Journal of Further and Higher Education*, *45*(1), 79–94. doi:10.1080/0309877X.2020.1735321

Foster, J., & Yaoyuneyong, G. (2016). Teaching innovation: Equipping students to overcome real-world challenges. *Higher Education Pedagogies*, *1*(1), 42–56. doi:10.1080/23752696.2015.1134195

Grewal, R., Meyer, R., & Mittal, V. (2022). Education and Marketing: Decision Making, Spending, and Consumption. *JMR, Journal of Marketing Research*, *59*(1), 1–10. doi:10.1177/00222437211068091

Hockings, C. (2005). Removing the barriers? A study of the conditions affecting teaching innovation. *Teaching in Higher Education*, *10*(3), 313–326. doi:10.1080/13562510500122149

Lantz, M. E. (2010). The use of 'clickers' in the classroom: Teaching innovation or merely an amusing novelty? *Computers in Human Behavior*, *26*(4), 556–561. doi:10.1016/j.chb.2010.02.014

Ribeiro-Navarrete, S., Saura, J. R., & Palacios-Marqués, D. (2021). Towards a new era of mass data collection: Assessing pandemic surveillance technologies to preserve user privacy. *Technological Forecasting and Social Change*, *167*, 120681. doi:10.1016/j.techfore.2021.120681 PMID:33840865

Saura, J. R., Palacios-Marqués, D., & Ribeiro-Soriano, D. (2021). How SMEs use data sciences in their online marketing performance: A systematic literature review of the state-of-the-art. *Journal of Small Business Management*, 1–36. doi:10.1080/00472778.2021.1955127

Saura, J. R., Palacios-Marqués, D., & Ribeiro-Soriano, D. (2022a). Exploring the boundaries of Open Innovation: Evidence from social media mining. *Technovation*, 102447. Advance online publication. doi:10.1016/j.technovation.2021.102447

Saura, J. R., Ribeiro-Soriano, D., & Iturricha-Fernández, A. (2022). Exploring the challenges of remote work on Twitter users' sentiments: From digital technology development to a post-pandemic era. *Journal of Business Research*, *142*(March), 242–254. doi:10.1016/j.jbusres.2021.12.052

Saura, J. R., Ribeiro-Soriano, D., & Palacios-Marqués, D. (2021a, July 15). Setting privacy "by default" in social IoT: Theorizing the challenges and directions in Big Data Research. *Big Data Research*, *25*, 100245. doi:10.1016/j.bdr.2021.100245

Saura, J. R., Ribeiro-Soriano, D., & Palacios-Marqués, D. (2022b). Assessing behavioral data science privacy issues in government artificial intelligence deployment. *Government Information Quarterly*, *101679*. Advance online publication. doi:10.1016/j.giq.2022.101679

Virdun, C., Gray, J., Sherwood, J., Power, T., Phillips, A., Parker, N., & Jackson, D. (2013). Working together to make Indigenous health care curricula everybody's business: A graduate attribute teaching innovation report. *Contemporary Nurse, 46*(1), 97–104. doi:10.5172/conu.2013.46.1.97 PMID:24621295

Yock, P. G., Brinton, T. J., & Zenios, S. A. (2011). Teaching biomedical technology innovation as a discipline. *Science Translational Medicine, 3*(92). doi:10.1126/scitranslmed.3002222

Zhang, Y., Liang, R., & Ma, H. (2012). Teaching innovation in computer network course for undergraduate students with packet tracer. *IERI Procedia, 2*, 504–510. doi:10.1016/j.ieri.2012.06.124

Section 1

Section 1 compiles the main contributions that analyze the processes and teaching innovation methodologies applied in the university and higher education ecosystems.

Chapter 1
Main Innovative Methodologies Currently Being Applied in Higher Education

Ana Lacárcel
University of Murcia, Spain

José Manuel Vera Zaragoza
University of Murcia, Spain

Francisco Javier S. Lacárcel
University of Alicante, Spain

ABSTRACT

New learning techniques and technologies cause a further increase in innovation in methodological areas in higher education. This chapter analyzes the most relevant innovation methodologies in educational fields through a systematic literature review. Afterwards, a classification is made in which they are divided according to their main characteristics in which the authors distinguish competence learning, ICT, active and reflexive learning, flexible groups, and real contextualization.

INTRODUCTION

Despite the continuous advances in science, technology or communication that today's society enjoys, we live immersed in situations of continuous change accentuated by the gaps created by inequalities, poverty and even discrimination and current social fragmentation. However, both knowledge and learning constitute the most powerful weapons in the renewal processes required by this globalized society in which education plays an essential role.

Currently, as referenced in the paper from the United Nations Educational Scientific and Cultural Organization through its guidance for policy-makers (2021), the current situation due to COVID-19 crisis has widely implied a need for educational innovation in a very short period of time due to the fact that traditional educational contexts such as face-to-face education have moved towards educational

DOI: 10.4018/978-1-6684-4441-2.ch001

Copyright © 2022, IGI Global. Copying or distributing in print or electronic forms without written permission of IGI Global is prohibited.

contexts based on Information and Communication Technologies (hereinafter ICT). In addition, it is important to refer to the international commitment to comply with The Global Education 2030 Agenda, which specifically highlights the commitment to comply with the Sustainable Development Goal (SDG) number 4 related to obtaining an inclusive and equitable quality education in order to promote lifelong learning for all the citizens (Saura et al., 2022). This objective is specified in specific goals related to the achievement of learning skills, which requires a transformation of education supported by technology, innovation and associations produced suddenly during these years.

It is important to highlight that all innovation in the educational context has a certain influence on society as a whole due to the fact that it requires the collaboration of all the intervening stakeholders, where it is necessary to allocate a series of resources for its development, that is, A climate of consensus must be produced to favor innovation (García, 1996; Saura et al., 2022a). It is undeniable that human beings have always tended to evolve in all aspects that surround them, including the way in which they acquire knowledge, and in this time of globalization, this evolution in the way people learn is directly related to the information revolution produced by the use of ICT In addition, it is essential that teachers maintain their interest in acquiring new knowledge related to teaching to develop the ability to innovate in the teaching-learning process and that this motivation to learn is transferred directly to their students (Montico, 2004; Rodríguez et al., 2009).

Sometimes, educational innovation in higher education, that is, in the context of universities, is considered an utopian purpose since this context tends to be still dominated by a large part of the conservative sector of the current society. Due to the fact that higher education is directly linked to the labor market, one of its main concerns should be preparing responsible citizens capable of assuming and facing the challenges that it demands (Saura et al., 2022b). Therefore, it is essential that this innovative trend be developed in all dimensions of the educational institution (Sanchez Ibañez, 2008). Thus, in this paper, the term educational innovation will be assumed as the way in which changes are produced in the teaching-learning process with the aim of improving the learning outcome, taking into account that it must respond to needs, be effective, efficient and whose results are capable of being maintained over time, the context in which said innovation occurs being essential (García-Peñalvo, 2015).

The objective of this paper is to know the main innovative methodologies that are implemented in higher education based on their common elements that characterize them. Consequently, to address these objectives, a systematic review of the literature has been carried out based on the terms Educational Methodology and Teaching Method. The databases consulted were Web of Science and Scopus. Continuing the criteria from vom Brocke et al. (2015), this methodology allows us to study a lot of different aspects and determine the common characteristics of the educational methodologies used in higher education.

The remainder of this paper is structured into four sections. First, a theoretical framework is presented with information on the characteristics and needs of innovative methodologies in higher education. Secondly, the methodology used to address the proposed research objective is detailed, followed by an analysis of the results obtained with a particular focus on the characterization of the particularities of said methodologies. Finally, the last section draws conclusions and outlines directions of future research.

BACKGROUND

Both teaching and educational practices linked to Higher Education have undergone a major paradigm shift linked to the creation and configuration of the European Higher Education Area (EHEA) over the last twenty years (De Miguel Díaz, 2005). This is conceived as a framework for communication and international work for the improvement, updating and compliance with quality guarantees of European university studies. Thus, as referred in De Miguel Díaz (2006) and Romero López (2017), the inclusion of this framework meant not only changes in the structuring of the study plans or the inclusion of the European Credit Transfer System (ECTS) in the different universities, but it involved the adoption of new ways of conceiving the learning process at a higher level and therefore the inclusion of new methodologies for both teaching and learning (Saura et al., 2022c).

In this sense, learning skills, changes in the roles of teachers and students, the incorporation of ICT, as well as the adoption of new teaching strategies are some of the changes that, although At present, they are assumed as essential or natural, they continue to constitute elements of change and improvement within the field of educational innovation. However, it is important to refer to the learning process as a process that must follow a specific and organized structure so that students are able to interrelate the new information received with the existing ones through previous studies or obtained from of experience (Vygotsky, 1978, as cited in Roigh-vila et al., 2017).

Although it is sometimes considered that the main purpose of educational innovation is to be able to offer quality education (Rimari, 2002), methodological renewal at different educational levels involves promoting positive attitudes both at the classroom level and in relation to the educational community., the promotion of updated solutions that respond to educational problems and difficulties connected with reality and the achievement of educational practices in accordance with the particularities of the students.

Competence and Reflexive Learning

The European convergence process leads to the promotion of the acquisition of a competence learning by students that provides them the skills, abilities and abilities of citizens capable of applying the knowledge they have learned throughout their formal education to real contexts and other non-formal contexts, including the different work environments. As referred to in De Miguel Díaz (2006), the acquisition of skills related to the construction of professional profiles linked to Higher Education degrees implies the necessary adaptation of teaching methods in addition to a broad curricular reform. Thus, said conversion process needs a great methodological structuring that guarantees learning of competencies in accordance with the needs of society.

Competence-based learning methodologies go beyond the mere transmission and acquisition of knowledge and imply a change related to the teaching methodologies with the purpose that the applied methodologies focus on the way in which the student learns and place him in the center of the learning process. As stated in the paper of the Commission of the European Communities (2000), it is intended that teaching methods cover many areas of interest and needs that focus on the user, in this case the student. This teaching approach is based on the fact that the learning of the youngest students as children acquires significant learning by a natural investigation about the world around them. This way of working is what guarantees active learning (Schwartz & Pollishuke, 1995) in which the learners experience and interact with the people and elements of their environment, living a significant experience that guarantees the acquisition of knowledge.

Reflection and sharing of knowledge with the rest of their classmates, motivated by the fact of taking risks in the process of solving the problem posed, ensures lasting, integrated and non-rote learning. In addition, with these approaches, students must participate in a critical observation and decision-making process, due to the fact that feeling at the center of the teaching-learning process raises their self-esteem and satisfies their desire for greatness (see Figure 1). In relation to this, the most current psychopedagogical approaches based on Neurodidactics defend the idea that the achievement of lasting learning is linked to both positive and negative emotions generated during its acquisition (Caine & Caine, 1994; Cantó-Domenech, 2015)

Figure 1. Student role in active learning
Note. Own elaboration.

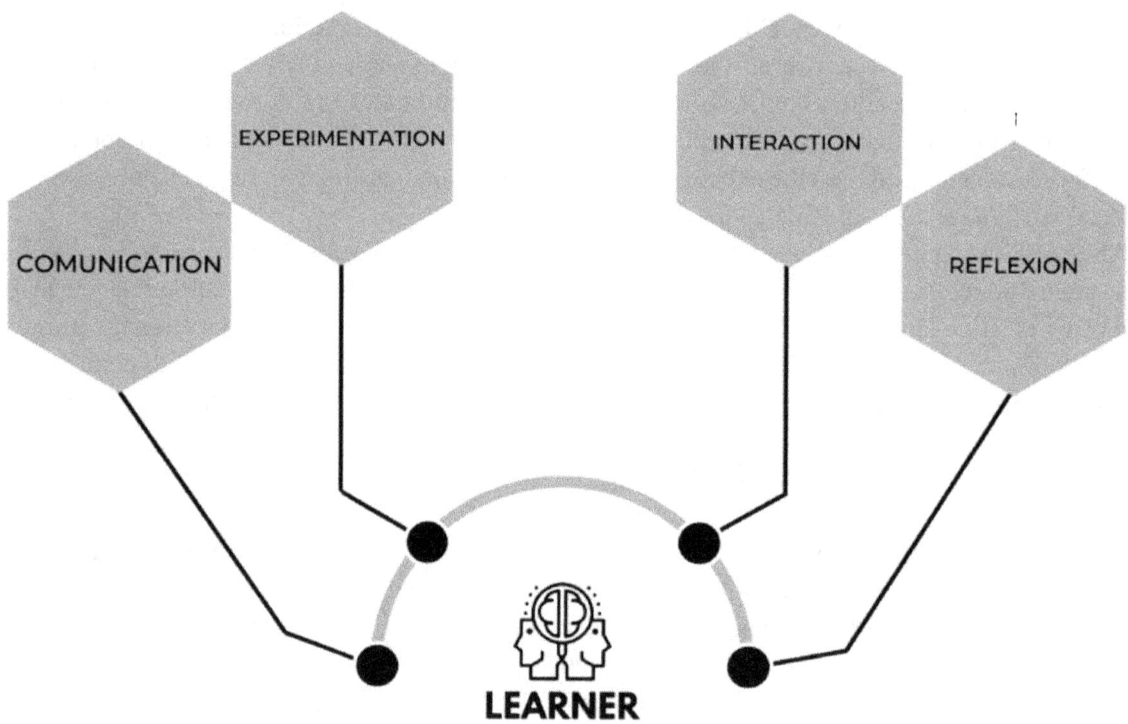

Innovative Methodologies

For authors such as De Miguel Díaz (2006), Huber (2008), Salinas Ibañez (2008), the methodological change required through the European Higher Education Area (EHEA) requires an optimal organization of academic activity through the inclusion of new methodologies in which special attention is paid to the organizational modalities, the didactic methods used, as well as the forms of evaluation. Thus, strategies such as the revitalization of traditional face-to-face master classes, the inclusion of ICT or the promotion of autonomous work by students in class, are some of the main points that the new methodologies include, favoring a better attitude, higher performance and deeper learning for students (Gargallo, 2008).

As García-Peñalvo (2015) refers, educational innovation is defined as the way in which changes are produced in the teaching-learning process with the aim of improving learning results, taking into account specific needs and context. These changes must be able to introduce improvements and be maintained over time (Salinas, 2004), therefore the context in which such innovation occurs is essential and it is essential that educational innovation involves intentional, relevant and properly planned processes.

(Fullan, 1994, according to Salinas, 2008; Aguiar et al., 2019; de León, 2005). That is why the area in which improvements are to be implemented can be used to classify the actions that imply innovation in education. In this paper, special attention will be paid to innovation methodologies applied from the perspective of teachers and their teaching, that is, in a pedagogical and technological context based on the availability of digital resources (Salinas, 2008; Saura et al., 2022d).

The approaches that allow the classification of educational methodologies are very varied, some refer to the way in which the contents are treated, such as methodologies focused on theory and others to the process of learning acquisition, such as those focused on practice through problem solving (De Miguel Díaz, 2006). However, it is considered that both methodological aspects must be implicit in any applied methodology since both the consideration of practice and work through projects are usually related to the skills that are intended to be acquired in higher education.

In this section, it is assumed the perspective of Huber (2008) in which innovative methodologies must allow students to be able to apply their learning to real contexts that must be linked to both the context and the environment of the learners. In relation to the learning acquisition process, it is interesting to refer to deductive and inductive methodologies. During the application of the former, the teacher explains to the students the content they have to learn in an expository manner, with the intention that they draw the consequences, ideas and conclusions to build their learning. However, if the teacher uses an inductive methodology, the students are the center of their own learning, since they acquire knowledge by solving a series of problems or challenges. Within the latter, Problem-Based Learning (PBL) or the Gamification of learning could be included (Prieto et al., 2014).

One of the best known forms of educational innovation is the application of ICT, however, as Fullan and Stiegelbauer (1991) refer, a methodological renewal does not only imply the inclusion of new materials or resources, but also involves assuming new paradigms of teaching in both teachers and students and changes in the organization of teaching and learning processes. This is why in this article it is considered that any innovative action must include changes in both the way of teaching and learning (Angulo, 1990). Some of the changes that ICTs produce in the educational system are related to the forms of communication between teachers and students, the possibilities of information management and communication between students, as well as the creation of virtual learning environments in which students can manage their learning processes by themselves. In this sense, the application of ICT contributes to the development of learning methodologies such as Distance Learning (DL) and Flipped Learning (FL). These are methodologies in which both deductive and inductive learning are combined (Prieto et al., 2014), in which the study of theoretical content is transferred outside the classroom, promoting the development of autonomous study by the student, while class time is used to carry out activities that favor cooperative learning supervised by teachers (Bergmann 2012).

Flexible Groups

Although the creation of flexible groups is usually associated with the teaching and learning process in Primary or Secondary Education, this organizational strategy within the classroom aims to cover and attend to all students based on their learning rhythms and specific characteristics. They are normally known by the name of heterogeneous or homogeneous groupings since, depending on the learning objectives, competence homogeneity will be sought or, on the contrary, the competence weaknesses of each student will be complemented with the strengths of the rest (Castle et al., 2005).

In addition, this kind of strategy is a motivation strategy to students due to the fact that they can form working groups with their classmates to achieve their common objectives. It is why this strategy is useful to attend to the individualities and needs of the students. Some possible flexible group configurations can be: whole-class meetings, teacher-led small groups, student-led small groups, partners and individual (one-on-one instruction) (Hoffman, 2002). The choice of grouping considered depends on the learning objectives and the characteristics of the group of students.

METHODOLOGY

The methodology applied in this research is a Systematic Literature Review (SLR). With it, the research questions can be identified and extracted through the contribution of other authors. For the development of the methodology, two databases have been used; Web of Science and Scopus. The choice of these two databases is mainly due to the remarkable insights of their articles and their impact factor (Saura et al., 2021).

The methodology has been developed through the PRISMA diagram, following the following steps; In the first place, keywords have been identified in order to obtain the results to carry out our research. Next, search filters have been used on title, abstract and keywords to find articles as precisely as possible. The Figure 2 below and Table 1 provide more details on the terms chosen and the number of results obtained.

Figure 2. Identification of Terms, Application of Filters and Databases
Note. Own elaboration

In Table 1 it can be seen the average of the databases; Web of Science and Scopus have found a total of 352 articles, in which some articles have been considered inconclusive because they are not directly related to the objectives of the research, in Figure 3 this process is more specifically addressed.

Table 1. Potential results of databases

Databases	Number of Results	Number of potential results
Scopus	102	5
Web of Science	240	12
Total	**352**	**17**

Source: Own elaboration.

In the process of the Systematic Literature Review, the aforementioned structure has been used: PRISMA Diagram. Figure 3 represents the total process that has been developed for the selection process of the results obtained in this investigation.

Figure 3. PRISMA diagram
Source: Own elaboration.

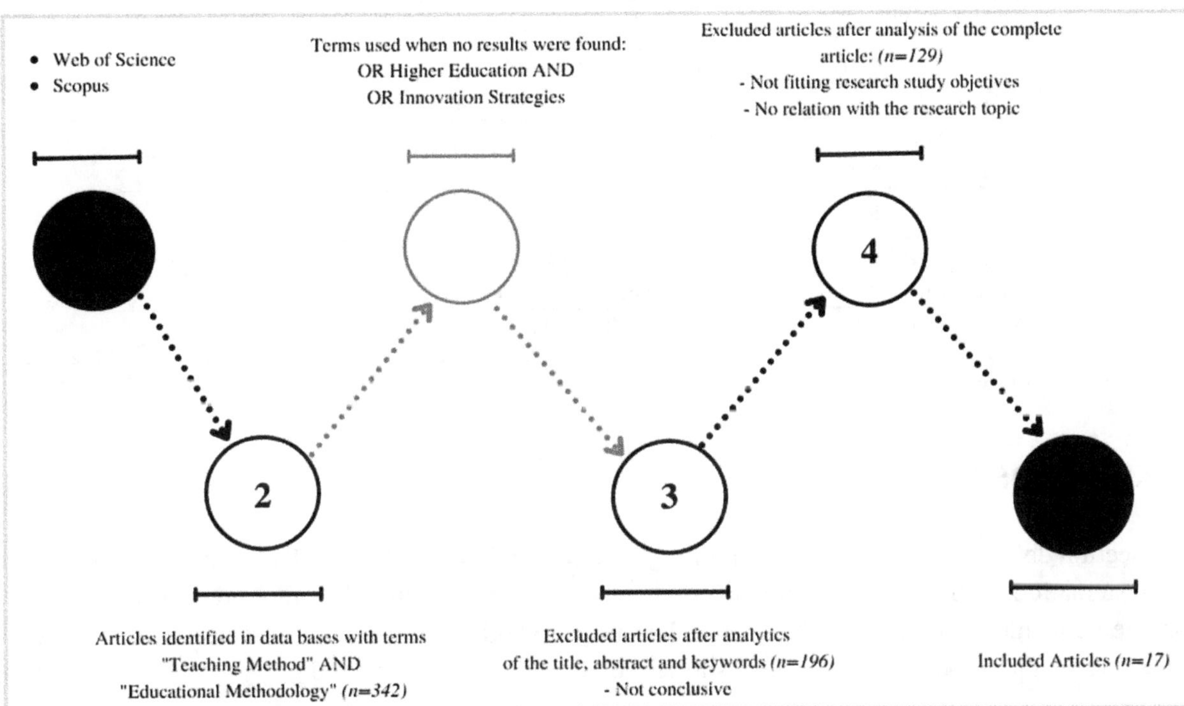

Figure 3 shows the process by which articles have been found and analyzed in the databases; Web of Science and Scopus. The articles that have been identified are all in English mainly through the use of the terms; "Teaching Method" AND "Educational Methodology" and when we have not found enough conclusive articles we have complemented with the use of "Higher Education" OR "Innovation Strategies". Next, articles that were not directly related to the research objectives through their title, abstract or keywords have been excluded. Then, the articles in which a complete analysis of all their content has been carried out because they do not respond to the objective of the study. Finally, 17 articles have been chosen for the results. Therefore, the following Table 2 shows the articles that have provided the research with results, identifying their chosen journal and database (Saura et al., 2021a).

Table 2. Authors, journal, and source of included articles

Authors	Journal	WOS	Scopus
Peisachovich et al. (2019)	Innovations in Education and Teaching International	X	
Castedo et al. (2019)	Computer Applications in Engineering Education	X	
Pérez-Aldeguer, (2017)	Foro de Educación	X	
Mujiyanto et al. (2021)	Journal of e-Learning and Knowledge Society		X
Rodríguez et al. (2019)	Revista de Currículum y Formación del Profesorado	X	
Oliva et al. (2019)	Texto Livre: Linguagem e Tecnologia	X	
Garrido et al. (2021)	Higher Education Theory and Practice		X
Manero et al. (2011)	Revista de Educación	X	
Moravcová & Mad'arová, (2016)	International Scientific Days	X	
Larionova et al. (2021)	Journal Society, Culture & Language		X
Vieira et al. (2020)	IEEE Transactions on Education		X
Castro-Schez et al. (2014)	Journal of Network and Computer Applications	X	
Rogado et al. (2010)	Springer	X	
Panfeng, (2015)	International Conference on Social Science and Higher Education		
Chaturvedi, (2021)	Journal of Dental Education		X
Bozzi et al. (2021)	Education Sciences	X	
Mayo-Cubero, (2021)	Asia Pacific Media Educator		X

Source: Own elaboration.

ANALYSIS OF RESULTS

This section defines the results obtained through the research methodology. The data obtained through the Systematic Literature Review are aimed at improving the student's learning process, these can be considered as methodologies, techniques or learning strategies. However, in research it is called by a generic term: "Methodologies". Table 3 shows the results we have achieved.

Table 3. Innovation Methodologies

Methodologies	Definition
Simulated-person (SP)	Methodology that offers real-world simulations to promote the development skills and meet learning objectives.
Flipped Classroom (FC)	Blended learning in which theoretical contents are presented to the student outside the classroom to encourage learners' autonomous work and leaving time within the classroom for the student to carry out practical tasks under the supervision of the teacher.
Service Learning	As a result of service learning, students learn more about the community and themselves while fulfilling a need in the community and meeting classroom or degree requirements.
Gamification	Methodology based on increasing the motivation of students by presenting the contents and tasks through playing games in specific contexts and obtaining rewards .
Mobile learning	Educational strategy by which mobile devices are used as an instrument to access and manage the knowledge that is present on the network with the purpose of solving problems and regulating self-learning.
Reading circle	Language learning methodology in which small groups of students debate and speak about different topics to improve and connect all aspects of literacy.
Peer-to-peer learning Cooperative learning	Methodology that promotes work in small groups of learners who work together in a coordinated way to solve any problem or learning task
Triangulation in Teaching Method (TTM)	Methodology in which the evaluation implies collecting evidence of the students' learning results through three different sources that are interviews, direct observation and another product or evaluation instrument
Content and Language Integrated Learning (CLIL)	Approach where students learn specific subjects through a second language
Problem Based Learning (PBL)	Didactic technique characterized by promoting self-directed learning and critical thinking aimed at solving contextualized problems in real situations of interest and that respond to a specific learning objective
Distance Learning	Approach to instructing students online in which talks and learning materials are sent over online
Neurodidactics Model	Discipline that improves teaching and learning processes considering the way the human brain works in relation to the acquisition of knowledge
Computational Thinking	Learning approach in which problems and tasks are solved through a computational approach and using the discipline's own tools to process, create and analyze data
Blended Learning	Combination of virtual or online learning and face-to-face education led by a teacher
Massive Open Online Course (MOOC)	Online methodology that offers open and large-scale interactive courses to build a specific community of knowledge in which teachers and learners contribute to the teaching and learning process
Universal Design for Learning (UDL)	Teaching approach with the purpose of attending the large variety of learners' necessities through considering afective, recognition and strategic networks
Seminar method	Group methodology in which a specific problem situation is offered for a relative experts students that receive a guided interaction

Source: Own elaboration.

It could be said that the methodologies included in this review are configured around a common factor related to the type of learning that they all seek. In this sense, and as reflected in Table 4, the inclusion of ICT, reflective learning in search of skills acquisition, as well as the formation of flexible groups that favor cooperative work and the contextualization of knowledge in real contexts these are some of the peculiarities of the so-called innovative methodologies (Saura et al., 2021b).

Far from the search for traditional learning focused on the rote reproduction of content, it is observed that all approaches have the purpose of obtaining reflexive, competence and permanent learning that implies that the student positions himself as the main protagonist of his knowledge, promoting his autonomous work and the teacher acquiring only the role of guide in the teaching and learning process (Ausubel, 1983). In this sense, considering the students' background, interests, previous experiences, knowledge and skills will ensure that all methodological strategies selected by teachers are effective (Bower, 1992; Baker et al., 2010).

On the other hand, it is important to highlight the fact that the use of ICT is usually considered as a characteristic element of any innovative methodology, even considering its mere inclusion as such. However, an educational methodology is made up of a systematic and organized set of tasks, provision of resources and strategies that responds to specific learning objectives (de León, 2005) and, as derived from the review carried out in this work, they are not always strictly necessary, although they may be convenient. In this sense, methodologies such as Gamification or Play-based Learning tend to involve the use of ICT, however, the good results offered by this approach are not necessarily linked to the inclusion of ICT, but to the correct configuration. of the reward system based on the interests of the students and obtaining motivation in them (Deterding et al., 2011; Goshevski et al., 2017, Wang et al., 2016).

Table 4. Main characterístic of innovative methodologies gathered

Methodology	TIC	Competencial learning	Active and reflexive learning	Flexible groups	Real contextualization
Simulated-person (SP)	X	X	X		X
Flipped Classroom (FC)	X	X	X		
Service Learning		X	X		X
Gamification		X	X		
Mobile learning	X		X		
Reading circle		X	X	X	
Peer-to-peer learning		X	X	X	
Triangulation in Teaching Method (TTM)		X			
Content and Language Integrated Learning (CLIL)		X	X		
Problem Based Learning (PBL)		X	X		
Distance Learning	X	X	X		
Neurodidactics Model		X	X		
Computational Thinking	X	X	X		
Blended Learning	X	X	X		
Massive Open Online Course (MOOC)	X	X			
Universal Design for Learning (UDL)	X	X	X		X
Seminar method		X	X	X	

Source: Own elaboration.

One aspect to note is that most of the methodological approaches reflected in Table 4 do not present the need for flexible working groups involving teamwork and taking advantage of the peer tutoring process. This is again a methodological principle which is sometimes shared by different methodologies and which emphasizes the role of the learner as the responsible and protagonist of his/her learning process. However, the methodologies included and associated with higher education present to a greater extent an autonomous and individual work of the student, who organizes and manages his/her learning process but, as it has been found through this methodology, does not benefit from teamwork.

In addition, it is found that most of the methodologies reflected in Table 4 do not ensure good transferability of theoretical and practical contents by the students. For this, the contextualization of the contents learned in real and familiar situations for the students is fundamental. In this sense, although on many occasions, the work of this competence is justified with the use of simulators that bring students closer to other realities, but this does not necessarily imply that the contents are worked in a structured way and not in a reflexive way. It should not be forgotten that one of the purposes of education is the comprehensive development of responsible citizens who are capable of finding a decent job.

Finally, it is considered important to highlight the low presence of express references to the use of work through the formation of flexible groups of students in higher education (see Table 4) classrooms. From this chapter, teamwork is considered essential for the development of both academic and cross-cutting skills related to personal values.

CONCLUSION

In this article, 17 innovative methodologies that are currently being applied in higher education have been obtained. Then, the results have been classified according to their aspects and functionalities, in which they have been classified in; 8 methodologies related to Technology of the information and communication (ICTs), 3 linked to flexible groups involving teamwork and coordination, 3 with real contextualization, 16 directly related to active and reflective learning and finally all of them, are linked to competence learning.

The results obtained allow us to answer the research objective formulated in the introduction of the article; to know the main innovative methodologies that are implemented in higher education according to their common elements. In this way, we could say that a large percentage of innovative methodologies are directly linked to ICTs. Besides, although the functionalities of most of the methodologies are said to be linked to active and reflective learning and competence learning in the student education process, no clear connection has been found between this way of working and the development of competences that allow and facilitate students to transfer the contents studied to real situations.

In this sense, due to the fact that 16 innovative methodologies are related to active and reflective learning and competence learning, it is essential to consider that it could be interesting to develop some research in this area of education, to discover all the advantages and disadvantages that this kind of methodologies could offer to children. In a first view, it could improve some skills like working in a team, communication, creativity, concentration and some abilities related to the world around them (Aliaga & Sachalk, 2010).

Finally, the analysis of innovative methodologies in higher education and the production of articles such as this one have important implications in educational practice and in the learning results obtained by students. Perhaps, the detailed study of the strengths and weaknesses of the different educational methodologies would help in the design of new hybrid methodologies capable of combining the strengths of each one and ensuring the achievement of significant learning.

REFERENCES

Aguiar, B., Velazquez, R., & Aguiar, J. (2019). *Teaching innovation and use of ICT in Higher Education* [Innovación docente y empleo de las TIC en la Educación Superior]. Academic Press.

Aliaga, C., & Schalk, A. (2010). E2: Early employability and entrepreneurship. Two major challenges in higher education in Chile [E2: Empleabilidad temprana y emprendimiento. Dos grandes desafíos en la formación superior en Chile]. *Calidad en la Educación*, (33), 319–337. doi:10.31619/caledu.n33.145

Angulo, F. (1990). Action research and curriculum: a new perspective in educational research [Investigación-acción y currículum: una nueva perspectiva en la investigación educativa]. *Investigación en la escuela, 11*, 39-50.

Ausubel, D. (1983). Teoría del aprendizaje significativo. *Fascículos de CEIF, 1*, 1–10.

Baker, R. S., D'Mello, S. K., Rodrigo, M. M. T., & Graesser, A. C. (2010). Better to be frustrated than bored: The incidence, persistence, and impact of learners' cognitive–affective states during interactions with three different computer-based learning environments. *International Journal of Human-Computer Studies*, *68*(4), 223–241. doi:10.1016/j.ijhcs.2009.12.003

Bergmann, J. & Sams, A. (2012). *Flip your classroom: reach every student in every class every day.* Academic Press.

Berne Manero, C., Lozano Chavarria, P., & Marzo Navarro, M. (2011). Innovation in university teaching through the TTM method. *Revista de Educacion*, (355), 605–619. doi:10.4438/1988-592X-RE-2010-355-117

Bower, G. H. (1992). How might emotions affect learning? In S.-Å. Christianson (Ed.), *The handbook of emotion and memory: Research and theory* (pp. 3–31). Lawrence Erlbaum Associates, Inc.

Bozzi, M., Raffaghelli, J. E., & Zani, M. (2021). Peer Learning as a Key Component of an Integrated Teaching Method: Overcoming the Complexities of Physics Teaching in Large Size Classes. *Education Sciences*, *11*(2), 67. doi:10.3390/educsci11020067

Caine, R. N., & Caine, G. (1994). *Making connections. Teaching and the human brain.* Innovative Learning Publication.

Cantó-Domenech, J. (2015). Results of the implementation of neurodidactics in early childhood education classrooms [Resultados de la implementación de la neurodidáctica en las aulas de educación infantile]. *Opción*, *31*(5), 189–199.

Castedo, R., López, L. M., Chiquito, M., Navarro, J., Cabrera, J. D., & Ortega, M. F. (2019). Flipped classroom—Comparative case study in engineering higher education. *Computer Applications in Engineering Education*, *27*(1), 206–216. doi:10.1002/cae.22069

Castle, S., Deniz, C. B., & Tortora, M. (2005). Flexible grouping and student learning in a high-needs school. *Education and Urban Society*, *37*(2), 139–150. doi:10.1177/0013124504270787

Castro-Schez, J. J., Redondo, M. A., Jurado, F., & Albusac, J. (2014). Experience applying language processing techniques to develop educational software that allow active learning methodologies by advising students. *Journal of Network and Computer Applications*, *41*, 65–79. doi:10.1016/j.jnca.2013.10.011

Chaturvedi, S., Elmahdi, A. E., Abdelmonem, A. M., Haralur, S. B., Alqahtani, N. M., Suleman, G., Sharif, R. A., Gurumurthy, V., & Alfarsi, M. A. (2021). Predoctoral dental implant education techniques—Students' perception and attitude. *Journal of Dental Education*, *85*(3), 392–400. doi:10.1002/jdd.12453 PMID:33067837

de León, P. C. (2005). *Educational innovation* [La innovación educativa]. Ediciones Akal.

De Miguel Díaz, M. (2005). *Teaching modalities focused on the development of competences. Guidelines to promote methodological change in the European Higher Education Area* [Modalidades de enseñanza centradas en el desarrollo de competencias. Orientaciones para promover el cambio metodológico en el Espacio Europeo de Educación Superior] (Proyecto EA2005-0118). Servicio de Publicaciones: Universidad de Oviedo. Recuperado de http://www.mec.es/univ/proyectos2005/EA 2005-0118.pdf

De Miguel Díaz, M. (2006). Methodologies to optimise learning: second objective of the European Higher Education Area [Metodologías para optimizar el aprendizaje: segundo objetivo del Espacio Europeo de Educación Superior]. *Revista interuniversitaria de formación del profesorado, 57*, 71-92.

Deterding, S., Dixon, D., Khaled, R., & Nacke, L. (2011). From game design elements to gamefulness: Defining gamification. In *15th International Academic MindTrek Conference: Envisioning Future Media Environments* (pp. 9-15). New York, NY: ACM.

Fullan, M., & Stiegelbauer, S. (1991). *The New Meaning of Educational Change*. Casell.

García, C. M. (1996). *Educational innovation, counselling and professional development* (Vol. 124). Ministerio de Educación.

García-Peñalvo, F. J. (2015). Map of trends in Educational Innovation [Mapa de tendencias en Innovación Educativa]. *Education in the Knowledge Society, 16*(4), 6-23.

Gargallo, B. (2008). Teaching styles and evaluation of university professors and their influence on the ways of learning of their students [Estilos de docencia y evaluación de los profesores universitarios y su influencia sobre los modos de aprender de sus estudiantes]. *Revista Española de Pedagogía*, *241*, 425–445.

Goshevski, D., Veljanoska, J., & Hatziapostolou, T. (2017, September). A review of gamification platforms for higher education. In *Proceedings of the 8th Balkan Conference in Informatics* (pp. 1-6). 10.1145/3136273.3136299

Hoffman, J. (2002). Flexible grouping strategies in the multiage classroom. *Theory into Practice*, *41*(1), 47–52. doi:10.120715430421tip4101_8

Huber, G. L. (2008). Active learning and methods of teaching [Aprendizaje activo y metodologías educativas]. *Tiempos de cambio universitario en, 59*.

Kitchenham, B., & Charters, S. (2007). Guidelines for conducting systematic literature reviews in software engineering [Pautas para realizar revisiones sistemáticas de literatura en ingeniería de software]. *Ingeniería*, *2*, 1051–1052. doi:10.1145/1134285.1134500

Larionova, I., Kapysheva, G., Chzhan, Y., Fedossova, S., & Rovnyakova, I. (2021). Modelling of Teaching Korean as a Second Foreign Language in Higher Education using CLIL (An Example of Educational Program Disciplines). *International Journal of Society, Culture & Language*, *9*(2), 98–113.

Magaña, J. R., Ferreirapinto, J., Blair, M., & Mata, A. (1992). Pedagogy of consciousness taking for the prevention of HIV/AIDS. *Revista Latinoamericana de Psicología*, *24*(1-2), 97–108.

Mayo-Cubero, M. (2021). Teaching innovation experience for COVID-19 times: A case study on blended learning of television journalism courses with moodle. *Asia Pacific Media Educator*, *31*(2), 178–194. doi:10.1177/1326365X211048619

Montico, S. (2004). Motivation in the university classroom: A pedagogical need? [La motivación en el aula universitaria:¿ una necesidad pedagógica?]. *Ciencia, Docencia y Tecnología*, *15*(29), 105–112.

Moravcová, L., & Maďarová, L. (2016). *Neurodidactics and its utilization in the field of language teaching*. International Scientific Days.

Mujiyanto, J., Nurkamto, J., & Hartono, R. (2021). The impact of online instruction integrated with Brain Based Teaching to EFL Students with Different Motivation Level. *Journal of e-Learning and Knowledge Society*, *17*(2), 66-73.

Oliva, H. A. (2016). Gamification as a methodological strategy in the university educational context [La gamificación como estrategia metodológica en el contexto educativo universitario]. *Realidad y Reflexión, 16*(44), 108-118.

Oliva, M. F. R., Fernández, R. J., & Ponce, H. H. (2019). Analysis of the implementation of an educational program based on the mobile learning methodology [Análisis de la implementación de un programa educativo basado en la metodología mobile learning]. *Texto Livre. Linguagem e Tecnologia*, *12*(2), 172–201. doi:10.17851/1983-3652.12.2.172-201

Panfeng & Zhao. (2015). *Discussion on Teaching Method of Electronic Technology based on MOOC*. Academic Press.

Pérez-Aldeguer, S. (2017). Las artes escénicas como metodología educativa en la educación superior. *Foro de Educación*, *15*(22). Advance online publication. doi:10.14516/fde.587

Prieto, A., Díaz, D., & Santiago, R. (2014). Inductive Methodologies: The challenge of teaching through questioning and challenges [Metodologías Inductivas: El desafío de enseñar mediante el cuestionamiento y los retos]. *Innovations in Education and Teaching International*, *56*(1), 46–56. doi:10.1080/14703297.2017.1399808

Rodríguez, D. V., Mezquita, J. M. M., & Vallecillo, A. I. G. (2019). Innovative methodology based on educational gamification: Test type evaluation with the Quizizz tool. Teaching staff [Metodología innovadora basada en la gamificación educativa: evaluación tipo test con la herramienta Quizizz. Profesorado]. *Revista de Currículum y Formación del Profesorado*, *23*(3), 363–387. doi:10.30827/profesorado.v23i3.11232

Rodríguez, S., Núñez, J. C., Valle, A., Blas, R., & Rosario, P. (2009). Teacher self-efficacy, teacher motivation and teaching strategies [Auto-eficacia docente, motivación del profesor y estrategias de enseñanza]. *Escritos de Psicología (Internet), 3*(1), 1–7.

Rogado, A. B. G., Conde, M. J. R., Migueláñez, S. O., Riaza, B. G., & Peñalvo, F. J. G. (2010, May). Efficiency assessment of a blended-learning educational methodology in engineering. In *International Conference on Technology Enhanced Learning* (pp. 148-155). Springer. 10.1007/978-3-642-13166-0_22

Roig-Vila, R., Antolí Martínez, J. M., Blasco Mira, J. E., Lledó Carreres, A., & Pellín Buades, N. (2017). *Collaborative networks around university teaching* [Redes colaborativas en torno a la docencia universitaria]. Academic Press.

Romero López, M. A. (2017). European higher education area-driven educational innovation. *Procedia: Social and Behavioral Sciences, 237*, 1505–1512. doi:10.1016/j.sbspro.2017.02.237

Ruiz Garrido, A., Vélez Rivera, R., Leal Orellana, P., & Quintiliano Scarpelli, D. (2021). *Characterization of the Educational Innovation Process: Teaching Concerns and Results in the Teaching and Learning Process in a Chilean University Over 5 Years.* doi:10.33423/jhetp.v21i15.4892

Salinas, J. (2004). Teaching innovation and use of ICT in university education. Journal of University and Knowledge Society (RUSC) [Innovación docente y uso de las TIC en la enseñanza universilavtaria. Revista de Universidad y Sociedad del Conocimiento (RUSC)]. *UOC, 1*(1).

Salinas, J. (2008). *Educational innovation and use of ICT* [Innovación educativa y uso de las TIC]. Universidad Internacional de Andalucía.

Saura, J. R., Dwivedi, Y. K., & Palacios-Marqués, D. (2022d). Online User Behavior and User-Generated Content. *Frontiers in Psychology, 13*, 895467. Advance online publication. doi:10.3389/fpsyg.2022.895467 PMID:35548513

Saura, J. R., Palacios-Marqués, D., & Ribeiro-Soriano, D. (2021). How SMEs use data sciences in their online marketing performance: A systematic literature review of the state-of-the-art. *Journal of Small Business Management*, 1–36. doi:10.1080/00472778.2021.1955127

Saura, J. R., Palacios-Marqués, D., & Ribeiro-Soriano, D. (2022a). Exploring the boundaries of Open Innovation: Evidence from social media mining. *Technovation*, 102447. Advance online publication. doi:10.1016/j.technovation.2021.102447

Saura, J. R., Ribeiro-Soriano, D., & Iturricha-Fernández, A. (2022). Exploring the challenges of remote work on Twitter users' sentiments: From digital technology development to a post-pandemic era. *Journal of Business Research, 142*(March), 242–254. doi:10.1016/j.jbusres.2021.12.052

Saura, J. R., Ribeiro-Soriano, D., & Palacios-Marqués, D. (2021a, July 15). Setting privacy "by default" in social IoT: Theorizing the challenges and directions in Big Data Research. *Big Data Research, 25*, 100245. doi:10.1016/j.bdr.2021.100245

Saura, J. R., Ribeiro-Soriano, D., & Palacios-Marqués, D. (2021b). Using data mining techniques to explore security issues in smart living environments in Twitter. *Computer Communications, 179*, 285–295. doi:10.1016/j.comcom.2021.08.021

Saura, J. R., Ribeiro-Soriano, D., & Palacios-Marqués, D. (2022b). Assessing behavioral data science privacy issues in government artificial intelligence deployment. *Government Information Quarterly, 101679*. Advance online publication. doi:10.1016/j.giq.2022.101679

Saura, J. R., Ribeiro-Soriano, D., & Palacios-Marqués, D. (2022c). Adopting digital reservation systems to enable circular economy in entrepreneurship. *Management Decision*. doi:10.1108/MD-02-2022-0190

Schwartz, S., & Pollishuke, M. (1995). *Active Learning: A Student-Centered Classroom Organization* (Vol. 134). Narcea Ediciones.

Trujillo, F. (2015). *Project-based learning. Infant, Primary and Secondary* [Aprendizaje basado en proyectos. Infantil, Primaria y Secundaria]. MECD & INTEF.

UNESCO. (n.d.). *International Bureau of Education. Competency-based approach* [Oficina Internacional de educación. Enfoque por competencias]. Consultado el 2 de abril de 2018 en http://www.ibe.unesco.org/es/temas/enfoque-por-competencias

UNESCO. (2021). *AI and education: Guidance for policy-markers*. UNESCO publishing.

vom Brocke, J., Simons, A., Riemer, K., Niehaves, B., Plattfaut, R., & Cleven, A. (2015). Standing on the shoulders of giants: Challenges and recommendations of literature search in information systems research. *Communications of the Association for Information Systems, 37*(1), 9. doi:10.17705/1CAIS.03709

Wang, A. I., Zhu, M., & Sætre, R. (2016). The effect of digitizing and gamifying quizzing in classrooms. In *Proceedings of the 10th European Conference on Games Based Learning*. University of the West of Scotland.

Chapter 2
University Teaching Innovation in the COVID-19 Dra:
A Systematic Literature Review

Paula González-Padilla
Rey Juan Carlos University, Spain

Thais González-Torres
Rey Juan Carlos University, Spain

Ignacio Danvila-del-Valle
Universidad Complutense de Madrid, Spain

ABSTRACT

This case study is based on contextualizing and responding to some dichotomies in education at all levels, focusing specifically on the university level and how the education system in general, and teachers in particular, can and should innovate in order to offer quality education to students. These students have been adapting to the latest technological advances. This chapter gives as an example case studies where it is demonstrated that these technological advances are not the exclusive focus on which educational innovation should be based.

1. INTRODUCTION

One of the fundamental pillars for global progress is education. Education is a right possessed by all citizens and should be used as a tool that favors advancement, progress and improvement at all levels. However, it is important to be aware that education, as in many other areas, must be updated and adapted to current times. In this way, students will be able to have access to a more current education and their contribution in the future will have much greater value than if they continue to be taught in the traditional way, i.e., without taking into account technological and ideological changes and without taking advantage of new methodologies that have proven to be effective in education (gamification).

DOI: 10.4018/978-1-6684-4441-2.ch002

Copyright © 2022, IGI Global. Copying or distributing in print or electronic forms without written permission of IGI Global is prohibited.

With this in mind, it is important to identify which factors have an impact on education. This study will take into account some of the most relevant ones, from teachers, the tools used, the evaluation and work processes, and even the governmental institutions that are in charge of configuring the contents that teachers will teach and students will study. All this contextualized, moreover, with the current reality that determines all processes in society: the global pandemic of COVID-19 (Saura et al., 2022).

The pandemic posed a global challenge, obviously also for the sector under study, since the containment measures adopted by the different countries led to the closure of educational centers at all levels (Montes & Andrés, 2021). In the specific case of Spain, education went from one day to the next, from being taught in face-to-face mode to being taught online, with the consequent challenge that this entails, both for institutions and teachers, as well as for students and their adaptation to the new model, and also for families, who had to cover the needs of devices for each child, in addition to the attention and care during school hours.

One of the characteristics that occurred as a result of the pandemic and the actions that were carried out, such as the confinement and its consequent distance education, is the immediacy with which it was necessary to act. This is what happens in emergency situations, and it is so because it is not possible to plan in advance, so we proceed to act and apply practices that have not been previously planned, or not in that context and with all the variables that occurred. One of the consequences of this rapid adaptation is, precisely, the also rapid acceptance by the faculty (Bond, Bedenlier, Marín, & Händel (2021), when previously it could be more critical with this type of modalities, and now it is already an accepted and potentially valued trend in higher education so that it stays and has long-term effects.

It is also important to take into account and know the role of university students in this whole process. From their environment, lifestyles, interests and concerns to have an approach to all educational strata and offer a better education being a more effective way to transfer knowledge. Currently, the use and implementation of technology as a key element for educational innovation cannot be left aside (Saura et al., 2022a). Technology can be used in different ways when talking about education and, depending on how, when and by whom it is used, we can achieve insights or results that make a difference.

On the other hand, a term that has been trending in recent years is innovation. The definition of educational innovation contemplates various aspects: technology, didactics, pedagogy, processes and people. An educational innovation implies the implementation of a significant change in the teaching-learning process. It must incorporate a change in materials, methods, content or in the contexts involved in teaching (Ferreira, Altamirano, Ortega & González, 2019). The perceived difference should be related to the quality of novelty of the improved element, the value contribution of the improved element to the teaching-learning process and the relevance that the proposed innovation will bring to the educational institution and external stakeholders.

The world is changing at an ever-increasing pace and education is no exception. The speed required to respond to new challenges in the education sector forces institutions to be better informed about trends in order to anticipate changes and stay one step ahead (Díaz & Gómez, 2009). The nature of innovation also considers how the type of innovation might affect access to education, implementation plans, educational practice and the experience of the end user, who in most cases are the students.

Many companies and organizations base their work methodologies on innovation, and for many of them, innovation is part of the organizational culture. In these environments, it has been seen how the integration of innovation or creativity has led to different, disruptive and incredibly revealing results.

Returning to the topic of education, how can innovation be used in education, is technology the main driver of educational innovation? If so, how can it be harnessed in the education system? What is the role of teachers in bringing innovation to the classroom? What are the main skills that teachers need to have in innovative education? What is the role of students and what are the benefits of them receiving this type of education? Is it worth it? What impact can students receiving this type of education have in the future on a social, corporate, digital, etc. level? What are the changes that need to take place to move from "traditional" education to innovative education?

Considering the above statements, the aim of the present study is to shed light on the importance of innovation within the field of education. Furthermore, in relation to the importance of the issues discussed, the present study aims to answer the following research questions: RQ1. What are the patterns and hot topics in the field?; RQ2. What are the main challenges and future research agenda?

It should be noted that the originality of this study lies in a review of the relevant scientific literature focused on educational innovation techniques by educational institutions, an area that has not yet been studied in depth. An important contribution is that our results provide significant implications for educational institutions, and for society in general, as well as filling a gap in the literature.

The rest of this paper is structured as follows. Section 2 reviews the theoretical framework on the concept of educational innovation techniques and their current context, specifically in the educational setting. Section 3 then presents the methodology. In Section 4, the results are presented, followed by a discussion in Section 5. Finally, Section 6 presents the conclusions.

2. THEORETICAL FRAMEWORK

When we talk about innovation we always tend to associate it with technology, and although it is true that it occupies an important part of the basic concept, it is also true that in terms of innovation in education there are many other variables and factors that are determinant at the moment of determining a dynamic or learning as innovative. It can therefore be said that technology and the use of digital tools are not the panacea for the changes in education that societies seem to be demanding today (Saura et al., 2022b). The use of technology helps, but many of the changes needed by today's educational systems do not depend exclusively on it, but it is important that they are based on substantial transformations in the dynamics and management of the relationships that have to do with the teaching-learning synergy (Espinosa & Cartagena, 2021).

As already detailed, innovation is a permanent, original process, and with an intention to find a substantial improvement in this particular case, in the education sector, both in the field of quality as such, to forms of learning and how this affects students. To find the optimal and effective method and point it is necessary to have clear objectives about what, how and why you want to educate, and therefore, to find the changes that need to be made to achieve these objectives. If this point of effectiveness is really found, we would be facing a very important step that directly affects the quality of life of both this generation and, of course, future generations. As Francesc Pedró, director of Unesco's International Institute for Higher Education in Latin America and the Caribbean (IESALC) points out: "It is innovation if it adds value to learning".

The subject that concerns us in this study must also be contextualized taking into account the latest events that have shaken the world today, affecting all sectors including the educational system. The COVID-19 pandemic has forced governments to take measures in terms of the pre-established dynamics in education (Moreno-Correa, 2020; Saura et al., 2021), since in order to avoid the spread of the virus, schools and universities were closed for months, urging an online education with the corresponding effect of leaving without receiving that education those students who did not possess either devices such as computers, tablets, or mobiles, or those who did not have a network to connect to. All of these pose a challenge, both for teachers and institutions, as well as for the students themselves, and even today, there are effects on these dynamics (Satorre, 2021).

In a short time, methodologies had to be adapted to migrate to a more digital system, and although one part is positive since much progress has been made in this aspect in a short time, as mentioned above, it also represents a turning point or a gap between those who can follow and join this new paradigm and those who for reasons, especially economic, are left out of the system, forming part of the already known digital divide (Saura et al., 2021a). This new reality adds to the previous need to advance and innovate in terms of the application of changes in education and pedagogy.

The emergency situation following the pandemic has also provided an opportunity for student interaction and engagement within online education and are already a key pedagogical element in the development of classes, also putting the focus on the creation of a good learning environment along with the dynamics of content communication that have to have a basis of clarity to ensure a good cognitive presence (Ní Shé, Farrell, Brunton, Costello, Donlon, Trevaskis, & Eccles, 2019).

A study on the learning experience categorized (Buckley, Stone, Farrell, Glynn, Lowney, & Smyth, 2021) recommendations to ensure a good future within education, on the one hand taking into account the development of the curriculum within an online framework, considering teaching as the key point, valuing the need for commitment, and giving the importance it requires to the aspect of constant evaluation of the process. In this way the authors propose recommendations for the improvement of the student experience, where we find: strategies to enhance a learning community in online spaces, develop and nurture the teaching, social and cognitive presence, the incorporation of an ethic of care in the curriculum, teaching, learning and evaluation, and finally, clarity in the design of a sustainable system of effective communication.

The challenge for higher education institutions has been relevant for the continuous learning also of these new dynamics that are generated between the protagonists, in this case the interaction between student and teacher, as well as the relationship between teaching and learning itself (Garcez, Silva, & Franco, 2022). For all this, the so-called academic entrepreneurship has been key to the success of this transformation, and digital technology has some characteristics that have been decisive for this evolution. Its editable, recombinable, reprogrammable, and constant content-generating nature has allowed the development of ecosystems distributed around the world that have required different business skills, innovation processes, and specific governance structures. Therefore, the disruptive role played by digital transformation in this whole context is important, as it can empower digital academic entrepreneurship (Rippa & Secundo, 2019).

3. METHODOLOGY

A systematic literature review ensures that the synthesis of research is conducted in a rigorous, transparent and reproducible manner (Gomezelj, 2016). The documents were initially retrieved from the Web of Science (WoS) bibliographic database, which is one of the most relevant in the field of Social Sciences. We have followed a keyword search of the literature. With this method, the researchers' subjectivity in data collection is excluded (Saura et al., 2022c). The research query included articleS published in peer-reviewed journals included in the WoS database. The search terms were 'teaching innovation', 'covid

19', 'higher education', and 'university'. The search took into consideration works published within the period 2020 (since the pandemic outbreak) until nowadays, according to the protocol of Table 1.

We ran our query in the WoS database in February 2022. The number of documents obtained was 584. We have reviewed the title, abstract, and keywords to verify these documents are related to the topic. In some cases of doubt, the full text was read. All the documents not treating teaching innovation in university related to the pandemic were excluded. The resultant sample contained 568 documents.

Table 1. Search protocol and results.

Database	Web of Science (WoS)	
Data range	2020- 2022	
Search date	February 2022	
Search terms	*'teaching innovation'* AND 'university' *OR* 'higher education' *AND 'covid 19'*	
Initial number of documents	6172	
Filtered process	WoS categories: – Education and educational research Inclusion criteria – Articles	Duplicates Author not identified Not related to the topic
Final number of documents	568	

In order to identify the thematic organization or knowledge structure of the research topic, the relational technique of bibliographic coupling is applied. This technique assumes that two documents have a thematic connection if they share the intellectual base, in other words, the references they cite. Accordingly, the more shared references, the stronger the thematic relationship between two documents (Kessler, 1963; Zupic & Čater, 2015). Aiming at presenting the information in a more visual way, we have adopted a bibliometric mapping approach, using the VOS-Viewer software (Van Eck & Waltman, 2010; Saura et al., 2021b).

4. BIBLIOGRAPHIC COUPLING RESULTS

Applying the bibliographic coupling technique and using the threshold of 15 documents, we got seven groups containing thirty-eight documents. In Figure 1, we represent the network. The nodes represent the references, the larger the number of citations per document, the larger the node size. Coupling relationships are represented by the links between the nodes. The strength of the link between the nodes is illustrated by its thickness. Following the association strength normalization method used by the VOS-Viewer, we have identified seven clusters (see Figure 1).

Figure 1. Bibliographic coupling of documents

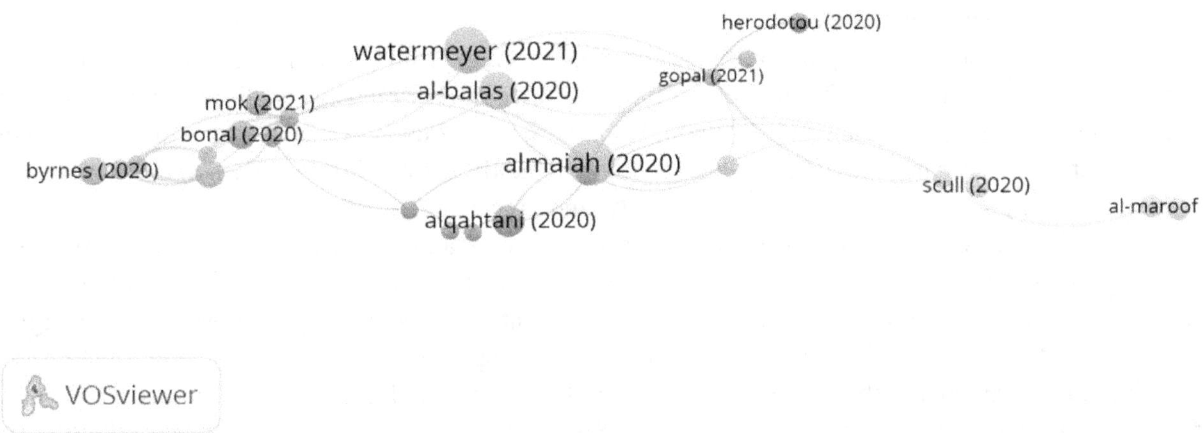

The red and orange clusters encompass studies that mainly address challenges in the remote teaching process. Because of the pandemic outbreak in early 2020, universities had to tackle a sudden shift in their organization of the teaching process, in particular adaptations to the remote teaching-learning system. Considering that a digital educational environment differs from conventional teaching methods, these have been extraordinary circumstances with no time for preparation, thus affecting the readiness of e-learning execution (Almazova, Krylova, Rubtsova, & Odinokaya, 2020; García-Alberti, Suárez, Chiyón & Mosquera Feijoo, 2021). Following Alqahtani & Rajkhan (2020), the readiness of e-learning execution was crucial in boosting the educational process during the COVID-19 pandemic.

Within this context, research has placed particular emphasis on addressing critical factors and challenges that affect online learning in the higher education context. Among the main ones are the university electronic environment and support: psychological, methodological, and technological – related to the budget for purchasing advanced technologies as well as the lack of technical support–. Academic staff readiness is also highlighted as an important factor hindering the implementation of the efficient online education process.

The main challenges faced are related to the lack of technical knowledge, negative attitudes, course integration with technology, and the lack of motivation. In this regard, there are studies calling for teachers' professional development programs to increase their computer literacy level and minimize the negative impact of the rapid changes in the educational process. Finally, students' readiness for online learning is also needed to ensure efficient online education (Almazova et al., 2020; Alqahtani & Rajkhan, 2020; Joshi, Vinay & Bhaskar, 2020). In this vein, the work of García-Alberti et al. (2021) suggests that there is a lack of research addressing how to support distance-learning students to overcome their lack of motivation and difficulty in understanding some applied courses and remotely oriented work.

The green cluster contains quantitative empirical studies examining health sciences university students' perceptions of the effectiveness of remote learning during the COVID-19 pandemic. The epidemic outbreak and resulting suspension of clinical training, pose unique challenges to medical students' education considering the relevance of domains that require superior psychomotor, communication, and cognitive skills (Khalaf, El-Kishawi, Moufti & Al Kawas, 2020; Byrnes, Civantos, Go, McWilliams & Rajasekaran, 2020). Diverse scholars affirm that the issue of how health sciences students have adjusted to exclusive e-learning has not yet been explored (Byrnes et al., 2020; Puljak, Čivljak, Haramina, Mališa, Čavić, Klinec & Ivanišević, 2020).

In doing so, most studies explore attitudes and concerns regarding the complete switch to e-learning during the epidemic outbreak. This includes, for example, a comparison between distance and classroom learning (Amir, Tanti, Maharani, Wimardhani, Julia, Sulijaya & Puspitawati, 2020), an investigation on the self-perceived preparedness of graduates (Hattar, AlHadidi, Sawair, Alraheam, El-Ma'aita & Wahab, 2021), or the application of a final online exam (Khalaf et al., 2021).

The yellow cluster comprises documents exploring digital readiness from different perspectives during the coronavirus pandemic in the higher education sector. Hong & Kim (2018, p. 304) define digital readiness as "technology-related knowledge, skills, and attitudes and competencies for using digital technologies to meet educational aims and expectations in higher education".

Within this framework, the research addresses higher education digital readiness under the premise that the sector was not well prepared for the challenge of the disruption caused by the pandemic (e.g. Scull, Phillips, Sharma & Garnier, 2020). Scholars have also examined digital readiness for teachers and students to participate in the real-time online learning implemented during the Covid-19 outbreak. As an example, Händel, Stephan, Gläser-Zikuda, Kopp, Bedenlier & Ziegler (2020) explore the preparedness of higher education students for emergency distance learning in terms of technology equipment availability, prior experiences with e-learning, and skills for digital learning. On the other hand, Al-Maroof, Salloum, Hassanien & Shaalan (2020) focus on understanding the effect of the pandemic on the adoption by students and teachers of a specific tool: Google Meet.

The purple cluster mainly addresses student satisfaction with remote learning during the COVID-19 pandemic. The work of Dinh & Nguyen (2020) revealed that the main problems faced by students with their participation in online courses are the Internet access quality and the quality of sound. Gopal, Singh & Aggarwal (2021) detected that for educational management, the essential factors to have a high level of satisfaction and performance for online courses are: the quality of instructors, the course design, prompt feedback, and expectation of students positively impact students' satisfaction and further student's satisfaction positively impact students' performance.

Dark and pale blue clusters are quite related since the main articles are focused on university educators' remote teaching perspectives, practices, and future adoption intentions. In this regard, most of them explore dysfunctionalities and disturbances resulting from online migration and how it affected their pedagogical roles and their personal lives (e.g. Watermeyer, Crick, Knight & Goodall, 2021; O'Brien, Adamakis, O'Brien, Onofre, Martins, Dania & Costa, 2020; Müller, Goh, Lim & Gao, 2021).

In a study on quality and educational innovation in continuing teacher training, qualitatively evaluating educational centers (Iglesias, Lozano & Roldán, 2018) the results show the need for teachers to receive ongoing training according to their interests and needs, focused in most cases on methodological educational innovations. The knowledge and assessment of the conceptions and beliefs of the participating teachers about educational innovation and their continuing education is of interest in order to advance towards an improvement in the professional development of teachers.

As mentioned above, the object of the study is to answer two specific questions about educational innovation, and it is here where the first answer is given to what the main techniques are used in educational innovation (RQ1), determining that the most used ones are:

- Project-learned based: this is a technique in which the student is placed as the center and protagonist of his or her own learning, equating in importance the acquisition of skills and attitudes with the acquisition of knowledge itself. This type of methodological learning focuses its importance on the learning path itself, and on the deepening of each of the students in the process that they carry out at the research level, being the actors in seeking and finding solutions to the problems they are presented with. The student assumes the main role, is assigned a project to develop autonomously, being able to collaborate with their peers also promoting a collaborative work environment and leaving the role of the teacher as that of an advisor or guide.

- Gamification: consists of the application of principles and techniques based on games to other types of less playful activities, such as teaching. In this technique, games are used to motivate learning and create more enjoyable study environments and situations where communication and student relationships are improved. It promotes perseverance and it is important to highlight that it promotes in a dynamic and stimulating way the participation of young students. Gamification is widely used at the labor level in areas such as human resources or marketing, so it is also very favorable to apply it in higher education that are related to these sectors, as it can be part of the daily life of the now students and future workers.
- Flipped classroom: in this case it is a logical evolution of the role of the teacher as a result of new technological advances, which have democratized teaching and given access to a multitude of information and knowledge to anyone with a device and an internet connection. Thus we see how the teacher no longer acts as a simple transmitter but gets involved and proposes activities and asks questions to students in order to encourage exploration and application of ideas from them, reversing the traditional teaching model and putting the students themselves as the main actors.

On the other hand, responding to whether these tools can be an added value for future generations (RQ2), it can be categorically stated that yes. Although this is not the only determining factor, the use of technology in the classroom should not be overlooked, since it is a catalytic factor. It is one of the elements that contribute and encourage teachers to be more up-to-date, to connect more with their students, and to prepare them for the challenges of the working world and the constant changes that are occurring rapidly at all levels. Despite these positive aspects, it must be taken into account that the integration of technologies in universities can be a slow and even difficult process in some cases and anticipating this possible gap will make them more prepared to solve and seek other equally valid resources (Saura et al., 2022d). All of this will result in more creative, problem-solving, and multi-skilled future professionals (Renz & Hilbig, 2020).

DISCUSSION AND CONCLUSION

It is now more than two years since the terrible coronavirus entered our lives, substantially altering the way we live and relate to each other. In the field of university teaching (as well as in non-university education and in many other jobs), the way of working changed in just a few days. Teachers and students went from face-to-face teaching to telematic teaching (in many cases, without the knowledge or the necessary means to carry out this new task effectively).

Everyone quickly had to learn to use tools that had been unknown or little used before the pandemic began. The teaching programme was reworked and adapted to the new situation. Alternative assessment tests were devised so that students did not lose the academic year. Digital platforms or Virtual Campuses were used for teaching classes or for academic tutorials. In many cases, the academic calendar was extended in order to be able to deliver the initially planned syllabuses.

Due to the health situation, it was necessary to use a new teaching methodology that led to the emergence of innovative teaching practices. It is in this context that the present work is developed.

Specifically, the main objective of our research is to carry out an in-depth review of the literature on university teaching innovation since the advent of COVID-19, using bibliometric methods of bibliographic linkage. We believe that there are few studies that have analysed this issue, and most of those that have done so were carried out at the beginning of the pandemic, without the perspective that the passage of these two years has given us.

Our research aims to offer a complete and current vision, although we are aware that we are analysing a changing reality that evolves at great speed. For this reason, we wish to be cautious in the interpretation of the results obtained, as these correspond to the time in which we carried out the study.

Our work shows that the study of university teaching innovation practices in times of COVID-19 is a subject that has been little analysed (due to the short time that has elapsed since the beginning of the pandemic) in the academic and business literature. The analysis of the published articles leads us to affirm that we are facing a challenging topic, on which new research can be developed, focusing on issues that have been little studied until now. In this line, our research aims to open up new perspectives.

Specifically, our work aims to understand the patterns and current topics in this field, as well as the main challenges and future lines of research that we will face.

With regard to the first question posed *(What are the current patterns and clichés in the field?*), we must begin by pointing out that the speed and urgency with which in a few days it was necessary to move from a face-to-face system to an online one, led to a general acceptance by the teaching staff of the use of technological instruments. We were faced with a new and unexpected situation and telematic means appeared to be the only solution that facilitated teaching.

If it had been a planned action, there might have been greater opposition from teachers to the change of methodology, but in this case, there was no other possible alternative. At the same time, from the beginning of the pandemic, a vast majority of students accepted the use of innovative, technology-based educational practices as the best means of knowledge transfer.

The main educational innovation techniques employed in this period are threefold:

- **Project-learned based**: This technique focuses on the importance of learning. The learner plays the main role and should be the protagonist of his or her own learning.
- **Gamification:** This technique uses games to make learning attractive and to motivate learners.
- **Flipped classroom:** The student takes on a leading role through study and research, while the teacher ceases to be a mere transmitter of knowledge and proposes initiatives or asks questions to the students so that they can reason.

In response to the second question *(What are the main challenges and the future research agenda?*), numerous studies point out that the education sector was not prepared for the challenge of disruption caused by the pandemic. Alongside technological development, the implementation of new pedagogical methods is essential. In the new situation, teachers must have a set of competences and skills that enable them to keep students' attention and motivate them.

For this reason, in-service training for teachers must be implemented, as greater preparation and commitment is now demanded of teachers. Specifically, teachers should be provided with training focused on methodological aspects and educational innovation practices, with the aim of adapting to the reality of each moment and keeping students excited through agile and attractive classes.

Therefore, in the current situation, one of the main challenges is to train and enthuse teachers and students with the tools of e-learning. In many cases, resistance to change, lack of technical knowledge or demotivation will have to be overcome.

A second challenge that will determine the educational agenda in the coming years is to create a suitable electronic environment at the University. In other words, if technological tools are to be implemented, all students and teachers must have access to them. University budgets will have to include items that make it possible for all teachers and students to acquire advanced technologies. In addition, it will be necessary to provide technical support and psychological and methodological support.

The development of teaching innovation projects is key to the successful implementation of new digital methodologies that improve teaching quality. The studies analysed show that we are faced with an opportunity to improve learning techniques and dynamics and the way knowledge is transmitted.

Practical Implications

The results of this study may be of interest to academics and researchers as well as to managers of educational institutions. Scholars of innovative teaching practices at the university may appreciate our study as a rigorous review of the main papers published on this topic during COVID-19. Such a review can help to understand the evolution of research in this field.

In addition, our research can help to analyse the technological tools most commonly used in this period, as well as to provide a glimpse of innovative teaching practices that may remain after the pandemic has been fully defeated.

This work can also be useful for managers of public and private university institutions. The results obtained can guide decision-making on the implementation of new teaching methods that improve the quality of university education. Likewise, it may be useful to know which methodologies contribute to the improvement of teaching in specific situations and which are appropriate in any scenario.

In this way, it will be possible to implement innovative teaching techniques that improve the transmission of knowledge and the ways in which students learn.

Limitations and Future Research

Of course, the present study has some limitations, which are listed below. The main limitation of the work derives from the short time that has elapsed since the beginning of the pandemic to the present day. For this reason, there is no research on this subject prior to 2020. We have tried to minimise this limitation by carrying out a rigorous and exhaustive search for articles. Specifically, we obtained 584 documents, of which 568 were used after studying the title, abstract and keywords. We consider this to be a good number, considering the short time that has elapsed.

A second limitation comes from the database chosen, in our case Web of Science (WoS). Although it is one of the most relevant in the field of Social Sciences and undoubtedly the most prestigious, the choice of this database may lead to the omission of some relevant papers.

Thirdly, the choice of the bibliographic linkage technique has some advantages, previously acknowledged, and some disadvantages. We have tried to minimize these disadvantages, but we are aware that it is not possible to avoid them completely.

With regard to possible lines of future research, these are determined by the limitations outlined above. Only two years have passed since the start of the pandemic and most of the published work dates from the beginning of the pandemic. It seems clear that these studies will need to be replicated in a few years' time, when the pandemic is completely over and normality is 100% restored. At that time, it will be possible to analyze which instruments and mechanisms were only used because of the forced lack of presence and which should remain, as they improved the quality of the university education system.

REFERENCES

Al-Maroof, R. S., Salloum, S. A., Hassanien, A. E., & Shaalan, K. (2020). Fear from COVID-19 and technology adoption: The impact of Google Meet during Coronavirus pandemic. *Interactive Learning Environments*, 1–16. doi:10.1080/10494820.2020.1830121

Almazova, N., Krylova, E., Rubtsova, A., & Odinokaya, M. (2020). Challenges and opportunities for Russian higher education amid COVID-19: Teachers' perspective. *Education Sciences*, *10*(12), 368. doi:10.3390/educsci10120368

Alqahtani, A. Y., & Rajkhan, A. A. (2020). E-learning critical success factors during the covid-19 pandemic: A comprehensive analysis of e-learning managerial perspectives. *Education Sciences*, *10*(9), 216. doi:10.3390/educsci10090216

Amir, L. R., Tanti, I., Maharani, D. A., Wimardhani, Y. S., Julia, V., Sulijaya, B., & Puspitawati, R. (2020). Student perspective of classroom and distance learning during COVID-19 pandemic in the undergraduate dental study program Universitas Indonesia. *BMC Medical Education*, *20*(1), 1–8. doi:10.118612909-020-02312-0 PMID:33121488

Arnal de Rincón, J., & Latorre, M. (1994). *Educational Research Fundamentals and Methodology* [Investigación Educativa Fundamentos y Metodología]. Editorial Labor SA.

Bond, M., Bedenlier, S., Marín, V. I., & Händel, M. (2021). Emergency remote teaching in higher education: Mapping the first global online semester. *International Journal of Educational Technology in Higher Education*, *18*(1), 1–24. doi:10.118641239-021-00282-x PMID:34778537

Buckley, K., Stone, S., Farrell, A. M., Glynn, M., Lowney, R., & Smyth, S. (2021). Learning from student experience: Large, higher education classes transitioning online. *Irish Educational Studies*, *40*(2), 399–406. doi:10.1080/03323315.2021.1916566

Byrnes, Y. M., Civantos, A. M., Go, B. C., McWilliams, T. L., & Rajasekaran, K. (2020). Effect of the COVID-19 pandemic on medical student career perceptions: A national survey study. *Medical Education Online*, *25*(1), 1798088. doi:10.1080/10872981.2020.1798088 PMID:32706306

Chetty, S. (1996). The case study method for research in small-and medium-sized firms. *International Small Business Journal*, *15*(1), 73–85. doi:10.1177/0266242696151005

Díaz, J. T., & Gómez, J. I. A. (2009). Professional development of teachers in the face of the new challenges of information and communication technologies in schools [Desarrollo profesional docente ante los nuevos retos de las tecnologías de la información y la comunicación en los centros educativos]. *Pixel-Bit. Revista de medios y educación*, (34), 31-47.

Dinh, L. P., & Nguyen, T. T. (2020). Pandemic, social distancing, and social work education: Students' satisfaction with online education in Vietnam. *Social Work Education*, *39*(8), 1074–1083. doi:10.1080/02615479.2020.1823365

Eisenhardt, K. M. (2020). Theorizing from cases: A commentary. In *Research methods in international business* (pp. 221–227). Palgrave Macmillan. doi:10.1007/978-3-030-22113-3_10

Espinosa, M. P. P., & Cartagena, F. C. (2021). Advanced technologies to meet the challenge of educational innovation [Tecnologías avanzadas para afrontar el reto de la innovación educativa]. *RIED. Revista Iberoamericana de Educación a Distancia*, *24*(1), 33–53.

Ferreira, A. C., Altamirano, M., Ortega, M. D. L. Á. L., & González, O. A. G. (2019). Learning analytics and educational neurosciences: New challenges in technological integration [Analítica del aprendizaje y las neurociencias educativas: nuevos retos en la integración tecnológica]. *Revista Iberoamericana de Educación*, *80*(1), 31–54.

Garcez, A., Silva, R., & Franco, M. (2022). Digital transformation shaping structural pillars for academic entrepreneurship: A framework proposal and research agenda. *Education and Information Technologies*, *27*(1), 1159–1182. doi:10.100710639-021-10638-5 PMID:34248387

García-Alberti, M., Suárez, F., Chiyón, I., & Mosquera Feijoo, J. C. (2021). Challenges and experiences of online evaluation in courses of civil engineering during the lockdown learning due to the COVID-19 pandemic. *Education Sciences*, *11*(2), 59. doi:10.3390/educsci11020059

Gersick, C. J. (1988). Time and transition in work teams: Toward a new model of group development. *Academy of Management Journal*, *31*(1), 9–41.

Gomezelj, D. O. (2016). A systematic review of research on innovation in hospitality and tourism. *International Journal of Contemporary Hospitality Management*, *28*(3), 516–558. doi:10.1108/IJCHM-10-2014-0510

Gopal, R., Singh, V., & Aggarwal, A. (2021). Impact of online classes on the satisfaction and performance of students during the pandemic period of COVID 19. *Education and Information Technologies*, *26*(6), 6923–6947. doi:10.100710639-021-10523-1 PMID:33903795

Hamel, G., & Prahalad, C. K. (1993). Strategy as stretch and leverage. *Harvard Business Review*, *71*(2), 75–84. PMID:10124635

Händel, M., Stephan, M., Gläser-Zikuda, M., Kopp, B., Bedenlier, S., & Ziegler, A. (2020). Digital readiness and its effects on higher education students' socio-emotional perceptions in the context of the COVID-19 pandemic. *Journal of Research on Technology in Education*, 1–13.

Hattar, S., AlHadidi, A., Sawair, F. A., Alraheam, I. A., El-Ma'aita, A., & Wahab, F. K. (2021). Impact of COVID-19 pandemic on dental education: Online experience and practice expectations among dental students at the University of Jordan. *BMC Medical Education, 21*(1), 1–10. doi:10.118612909-021-02584-0 PMID:33685451

Hong, A. J., & Kim, H. J. (2018). College students' digital readiness for academic engagement (DRAE) scale: Scale development and validation. *The Asia-Pacific Education Researcher, 27*(4), 303–312. doi:10.100740299-018-0387-0

Iglesias Martínez, M. J., Lozano Cabezas, I., & Roldán Soler, I. (2018). *Educational quality and innovation in continuous teacher training: a qualitative study in two educational centers* [La calidad e innovación educativa en la formación continua docente: un estudio cualitativo en dos centros educativos]. Academic Press.

Joshi, A., Vinay, M., & Bhaskar, P. (2020). Impact of coronavirus pandemic on the Indian education sector: Perspectives of teachers on online teaching and assessments. *Interactive Technology and Smart Education*.

Kessler, M. M. (1963). Bibliographic coupling between scientific papers. *American Documentation, 14*(1), 10–25. doi:10.1002/asi.5090140103

Khalaf, K., El-Kishawi, M., Moufti, M. A., & Al Kawas, S. (2020). Introducing a comprehensive high-stake online exam to final-year dental students during the COVID-19 pandemic and evaluation of its effectiveness. *Medical Education Online, 25*(1), 1826861. doi:10.1080/10872981.2020.1826861 PMID:33000704

Kidder, L. H. (1982). *Face validity from multiple perspectives*. New Directions for Methodology of Social & Behavioral Science.

Martínez & Piedad. (2006). The case study method: methodological strategy of scientific research [El método de estudio de caso: estrategia metodológica de la investigación científica]. *Pensamiento & Gestión, 20*, 165-193.

Montes, C. P., & Andrés, S. M. (2021). The teaching modalities in the new normal for the 2020-21 academic year in Spanish public universities [Las modalidades de enseñanza en la nueva normalidad para el curso 2020-21 en las universidades públicas españolas]. *IJERI: International Journal of Educational Research and Innovation*, (15), 273-290.

Moreno-Correa, S. M. (2020). Educational innovation in the times of the Coronavirus [La innovación educativa en los tiempos del Coronavirus]. *Salutem Scientia Spiritus, 6*(1), 14–26.

Müller, A. M., Goh, C., Lim, L. Z., & Gao, X. (2021). Covid-19 emergency elearning and beyond: Experiences and perspectives of university educators. *Education Sciences, 11*(1), 19. doi:10.3390/educsci11010019

Ní Shé, C., Farrell, O., Brunton, J., Costello, E., Donlon, E., Trevaskis, S., & Eccles, S. (2019). *Teaching online is different: critical perspectives from the literature*. Dublin City University. 10.

O'Brien, W., Adamakis, M., O'Brien, N., Onofre, M., Martins, J., Dania, A., Makopoulou, K., Herold, F., Ng, K., & Costa, J. (2020). Implications for European Physical Education Teacher Education during the COVID-19 pandemic: A cross-institutional SWOT analysis. *European Journal of Teacher Education, 43*(4), 503–522. doi:10.1080/02619768.2020.1823963

Puljak, L., Čivljak, M., Haramina, A., Mališa, S., Čavić, D., Klinec, D., Aranza, D., Mesarić, J., Skitarelić, N., Zoranić, S., Majstorović, D., Neuberg, M., Mikšić, Š., & Ivanišević, K. (2020). Attitudes and concerns of undergraduate university health sciences students in Croatia regarding complete switch to e-learning during COVID-19 pandemic: A survey. *BMC Medical Education, 20*(1), 1–11. doi:10.118612909-020-02343-7 PMID:33167960

Renz, A., & Hilbig, R. (2020). Prerequisites for artificial intelligence in further education: Identification of drivers, barriers, and business models of educational technology companies. *International Journal of Educational Technology in Higher Education, 17*(1), 1–21. doi:10.118641239-020-00193-3

Rippa, P., & Secundo, G. (2019). Digital academic entrepreneurship: The potential of digital technologies on academic entrepreneurship. *Technological Forecasting and Social Change, 146*, 900–911. doi:10.1016/j.techfore.2018.07.013

Sánchez, F. J. S., & Sarabia, F. (1999). *Methodology for research in marketing and business management* [Metodología para la investigación en marketing y dirección de empresas]. Ediciones Pirámide.

Satorre Cuerda, R. (2021). *New educational challenges in higher education in the face of the COVID-19 challenge* [Nuevos retos educativos en la enseñanza superior frente al desafío COVID-19]. Academic Press.

Saura, J. R., Dwivedi, Y. K., & Palacios-Marqués, D. (2022d). Online User Behavior and User-Generated Content. *Frontiers in Psychology, 13*, 895467. Advance online publication. doi:10.3389/fpsyg.2022.895467 PMID:35548513

Saura, J. R., Palacios-Marqués, D., & Ribeiro-Soriano, D. (2021). How SMEs use data sciences in their online marketing performance: A systematic literature review of the state-of-the-art. *Journal of Small Business Management*, 1–36. doi:10.1080/00472778.2021.1955127

Saura, J. R., Palacios-Marqués, D., & Ribeiro-Soriano, D. (2022a). Exploring the boundaries of Open Innovation: Evidence from social media mining. *Technovation*, 102447. Advance online publication. doi:10.1016/j.technovation.2021.102447

Saura, J. R., Ribeiro-Soriano, D., & Iturricha-Fernández, A. (2022). Exploring the challenges of remote work on Twitter users' sentiments: From digital technology development to a post-pandemic era. *Journal of Business Research, 142*(March), 242–254. doi:10.1016/j.jbusres.2021.12.052

Saura, J. R., Ribeiro-Soriano, D., & Palacios-Marqués, D. (2021a, July 15). Setting privacy "by default" in social IoT: Theorizing the challenges and directions in Big Data Research. *Big Data Research, 25*, 100245. doi:10.1016/j.bdr.2021.100245

Saura, J. R., Ribeiro-Soriano, D., & Palacios-Marqués, D. (2021b). Using data mining techniques to explore security issues in smart living environments in Twitter. *Computer Communications, 179*, 285–295. doi:10.1016/j.comcom.2021.08.021

Saura, J. R., Ribeiro-Soriano, D., & Palacios-Marqués, D. (2022b). Assessing behavioral data science privacy issues in government artificial intelligence deployment. *Government Information Quarterly, 101679*. Advance online publication. doi:10.1016/j.giq.2022.101679

Saura, J. R., Ribeiro-Soriano, D., & Palacios-Marqués, D. (2022c). Adopting digital reservation systems to enable circular economy in entrepreneurship. *Management Decision*. doi:10.1108/MD-02-2022-0190

Scull, J., Phillips, M., Sharma, U., & Garnier, K. (2020). Innovations in teacher education at the time of COVID19: An Australian perspective. *Journal of Education for Teaching*, *46*(4), 497–506. doi:10.1080/02607476.2020.1802701

Shaw, E. (1999). A guide to the qualitative research process: Evidence from a small firm study. *Qualitative Market Research*, *2*(2), 59–70. doi:10.1108/13522759910269973

Van Eck, N., & Waltman, L. (2010). Software survey: VOSviewer, a computer program for bibliometric mapping. *Scientometrics, 84*(2), 523-538.

Watermeyer, R., Crick, T., Knight, C., & Goodall, J. (2021). COVID-19 and digital disruption in UK universities: Afflictions and affordances of emergency online migration. *Higher Education*, *81*(3), 623–641. doi:10.100710734-020-00561-y PMID:32836334

Yin, R. K. (2011). *Applications of case study research*. Sage.

Zupic, I., & Čater, T. (2015). Bibliometric methods in management and organization. *Organizational Research Methods*, *18*(3), 429–472. doi:10.1177/1094428114562629

Chapter 3
Didactic Strategies for Meaningful Learning

José G. Vargas-Hernández
https://orcid.org/0000-0003-0938-4197
Tecnológico Mario Molina Unidad Zapopan, Mexico

Myrna Tovar Vergara
https://orcid.org/0000-0003-1247-9998
Tecnológico Mario Molina Unidad Zapopan, Mexico

ABSTRACT

This work aims to analyze and explain the didactic strategies used to achieve meaningful learning. It begins under the assumption that meaningful learning is created if students are given freedom and confidence. In this situation, they can find their own answers and develop their knowledge, both in the classroom and in practical life. The method used is an analytical-descriptive one of the reviews of the literature of the main authors who have given rise to this approach, its elements, and the didactic strategies used. It is concluded that the design and implementation of didactic strategies focused on meaningful learning with the application of active didactic methodologies and strategies in meaningful learning processes depending on the context in which it takes place. They obtain better results in the training of professionals.

INTRODUCTION

Changes in the historical evolutionary process of education are relevant factors that influence the economic, social, political, and environmental development of peoples. In the evolution of educational models, the constant is the characterization of the need to give meaning to values and attitudes that guide the generation and development of ideas, projects, strategies and programs that allow the reproduction and preservation of the material and social conditions that they facilitate the contemplation and incorporation of the human being to his concrete reality from a comprehensive perspective of inclusive and meaningful learning.

DOI: 10.4018/978-1-6684-4441-2.ch003

Copyright © 2022, IGI Global. Copying or distributing in print or electronic forms without written permission of IGI Global is prohibited.

The dynamic forms and processes of learning have undergone transformations over time at the service of human development (Apodaca-Orozco, Ortega-Pipper, Verdugo-Blanco, and Reyes-Barribas, 2017) that have resulted in significant learning advances that attribute responsibilities in a shared way for the achievement of goals based on the self-care of people and with a clear tendency of protagonist recognition of the beneficiaries of these processes (Lillo, 2014). The rote learning of disciplinary concepts with traditional approaches have been exceeded by the expectations that students have, and the demands made by the economic, labor, social, political, cultural reality, etc.

The methodological approaches that support the didactic strategies applied in learning have always been under the traditional approaches to teaching as absolute models in university systems, which, to be implemented, repress culture, language, history, traditions, customs, and the practices of the peoples. These types of learning have not been significant because there is no correspondence with the cultural traits of the peoples (Arnold and Yapita, 2000).

Over time, the development of higher education has been perfected in all fields of knowledge, but in health, with the implementation of curricular reforms based on pedagogy and science related to education that are necessary and indispensable to confront the paradigms. In meaningful learning, different paradigms are presented because the teacher goes from being the person in charge and protagonist of the students' learning to whom their process is planned and organized in the form of self-regulation so that they choose and decide on their behavior, as promoters and architects of their own learning (Garrote Rojas, Garrote Rojas, and Jiménez Fernández, 2016). Through essential changes in study plans and programs, progress is made in achieving curricular flexibility, meaningful learning, the incorporation of new ethical values and modern technologies (Vergara, Travieso & Crespo, 2014).

The different pedagogical and didactic models are relevant to the extent that they promote a vision in which the student is considered the center of active and meaningful learning (Espejo Leupin, 2016, p. 17). There are several meaningful learning models that use creative learning and that define all forms of learning methods that involve students in meaningful teaching-learning processes (Bonwell, and Eison, 1991).

For meaningful learning to be guaranteed with the significant results of the experiences that students have that requires their motivations, interests and actions as a subject with their own content, a permanent relationship with the content of previous knowledge and the link with new knowledge in their environment connected with local problems and global trends, in such a way that opportunities and solutions to problems are identified (Beck, Sollbrekke, Sutphen and Fremstad, 2015). Part of the meaningful learning experiences are the involvement of students in discursive and disciplinary activities instead of just being receptive (Almulla MA. 2020).

There are few studies focused on strengthening the training processes of teachers, to improve the teaching-learning processes through the design and implementation of didactic strategies in environments focused on meaningful learning.

In this work, the objective of which is to analyze and explain the didactic strategies used to achieve significant learning, first a conceptualization is carried out and then the elements or components are analyzed and finally a detailed analysis is made in the delimitation and design of the didactic strategies that are implemented for the achievement of the best results in meaningful learning.

The need and motivation of this study is only a scope regarding the importance of teaching strategies used by teachers in the classroom through learning activities that promote meaningful learning and favor knowledge in students of higher and essential education today. day in the industry. In Higher Education, the Educational Model of the XXI Century (MESXXI) mentions: Didactic strategies are integrated sets of activities designed by the teacher that, in addition to generating creative spaces, favor the achievement of learning and give meaning to the didactic relationship, these they must be adjusted to the educational objectives and contents and connected to the real context.

On the other hand, it puts into practice and evaluates the didactic strategies, and ensures that the research of the actors of the teacher-student education is promoted, that the specific and generic competences indicated in the professional profile are reached and developed; the use of various methods, techniques aimed at solving problems and developing projects, practices and experiments is encouraged; investigations and consultations are carried out by accessing various sources of information and the use of new information and communication technologies is incorporated, in accordance with the nature of the skills to be developed. (Acosta et al., 2012).

This leads to the need to incorporate real strategies in the activities promoted in the classroom that derive from the teacher-student didactic relationship, and generate significant learning applied to real situations, and promote the formulation of research projects. We are in a changing context and the school-society gear deserves to pay particular attention to the needs of the latter and the professional training of students. This leads to proposing the need to generate a repository of didactic strategies and that teachers make use of it, seeking to create classroom environments that promote meaningful learning in higher education students, without leaving behind that meaningful learning in students brings knowledge in its present and future life, in turn, the knowledge society considers that it adds value to organizations (Fidalgo et al., 2014).

CONCEPTUALIZATION

Meaningful learning is a strategy for the implementation of teaching-learning processes based on the reality of practice that promotes student autonomy to achieve the maximum result. Quality education implies prioritizing the understanding and use of new learning content based on the reality of the context (Galdames, Walqui & Gustafson, 2011). Knowledge and experiences that are identified and related to community activities such as actions, images and use of objects that help to develop meanings and concepts, contribute to generating significant learning (Julca, 2000).

Meaningful learning is defined as the non-arbitrary substantive incorporation of new concepts, propositions, and knowledge in the non-arbitrary frame of reference of the cognitive structure. Meaningful learning goes beyond the realm of cognition, due to contextualization supported by the possibilities of sharing meaning. The meaningful learning design has as specification the significance of learning with the creation of cognitive-constructivist conceptual activities based on contextual problems of the students and using the environment as a learning resource (Suyatno 2009). The meaningful learning process implies that the learner understands the meanings of the new learning content, connecting with the new concepts and propositions, expanding, reorganizing, and reconstructing the existing cognitive structure (Ausubel, 1963; Ausubel et al., 1978).

Student learning must be a significant assimilation, with potentially significant materials and content, with logical meanings relevant to the cognitive structure and where the main objective is to have the intention to learn significantly.

Meaningful learning is described as learning that has the purpose of building knowledge based on students' experiences, feelings, and interactions with other students (Scott, & Friesen, 2013). Deep meaningful learning is of an elevated level of thought and development that is conducted through intellectual involvement in questioning, critical thinking, problem solving and metacognitive skills that are oriented to the construction of meanings through patterns of recognition and association concepts (Mystakidis, 2021).

The concept of meaningful learning is consistent with constructivism where students build their knowledge with their experiences by making meaningful connections between new experiences and content already acquired. In meaningful learning, students use their knowledge to learn new concepts, solve problems, and transfer their knowledge to new situations and problems. Students learn meaningfully when they relate new knowledge to existing knowledge. It is a process of relating the added information with the concepts already contained in the cognitive structure (Dahar, 2011). For meaningful learning to occur, new concepts must be integrated into the existing knowledge structure, connecting existing concepts with the new knowledge (Fletcher, & Chróinín, 2021; Bao, Koenig, 2019).

Meaningful learning theory and epistemology is humanistic constructivism. The concept of meaningful learning has a greater integration with constructivism as a combination of human learning psychology and knowledge production epistemology (Novak, 1990; Mintzes, and Wandersee, 2000). Cognitive learning theory is the basis for developing meaningful learning as a process for the acquisition of new meaning, assuming a set of tools potentially for meaningful learning tasks (Ausubel, 1978).

To be meaningful, the content to be studied is assimilated and related to the previously acquired knowledge, which is why it is a process that is associated with the added information in relevant concepts contained in the cognitive structure and connects them to produce the understanding of the environment. Students must understand the situation to solve the problem in a way that is meaningful to them (Ausubel, 1978; Sriraman 2010).

Meaningful learning is achieved with the theoretical-practical aspects can conduct simultaneously. Meaningful learning provides skills to be creative and innovative. Students have access to knowledge, skills, and attitudes to solve problems. For teachers, understanding meaningful learning is valuable to apply to all levels of education.

As a theory, meaningful learning accommodates the demand for teaching-learning processes achieved through the application of knowledge in authentic contexts. Meaningful learning is related to contextual learning supported by problems and situations. For meaningful learning to happen is to relate learning to context problems. Students need to understand the situation to solve the problem in such a way that it is a meaningful learning (Sriraman 2010). Therefore, having activities, creativity and innovation are relevant factors to create meaningful learning outcomes.

The assimilation of learning theory defines meaningful learning as the substantive incorporation of new knowledge or propositions in the hierarchical frame of reference of the cognitive structure (Ausubel, 1963; Ausubel et al., 1978). Student learning must be a meaningful assimilation, with potentially significant materials and content, with logical meanings relevant to the cognitive structure and where the main objective is to have the intention to learn meaningfully.

The concept of meaningful learning is polysemic and inserted in the socio-cultural reality and with a future perspective proposed by the same society. This conception of meaningful learning is related to the educational practices of the teaching-learning processes that have migrated from approaches that focus on transmitting disciplinary theoretical knowledge to more dynamic practices where the student adopts a more autonomous role of meaningful learning. The construction of meaningful learning is the mark of higher education achieved through sustained critical discourse (Ausbel, 1961) linked with teaching methods that result in the ability to identify and analyze the structure to connect existing concepts with new ones (Jonassen, 2003; Mystakidis, Berki, Valtanen, 2019).

Ausubel developed the theory of cognitive psychology as a branch of psychology to include scientific studies of mental symptoms in the acquisition of knowledge in the way in which humans obtain knowledge, the way in which added information is assimilated and assumes that the knowledge is the result of human construction. If students relate the information to the knowledge they already have, they obtain meaningful learning that has more advantages than learning by heart. Therefore, learning can vary from memorized to meaningful learning where information is delivered to students to identify, select, and learn the findings (Novak, and Gowin, 2006).

There is no homogeneous, uniform approach to teaching and learning that has been nurtured with complementary theories and their applications that provide a rationale for the promotion of academic and social skills that contribute to meaningful learning, such as the development of social cooperation and communication (Sharan, 2015). Hanani (2020) explores the meaningful learning of the millennial generation that provides students with the formation of creative, critical, and innovative thinking skills and that can be achieved by various methods, including active learning, collaborative learning, cooperative learning, problem-based learning, etc.

Meaningful learning for millennials is a process that adds experiences through their problems contained in their environments that makes students understand and relate the content according to Gowin (1990) the process is significant when there is interaction between students, educators and content that enables understanding of learning by sharing meanings. Meaningful learning is the interaction of students, educators, and content with innovative concepts and without eliminating scientific values (Moreira, 2011). Meaningful learning prepares millennials to respond appropriately to the competition of the information age.

Meaningful teaching-learning processes encourage the student to compare the new knowledge they acquire with that previously acquired and support students in the construction of personal knowledge structures (Wang et al., 2014). The quality and quantity of the student's previous knowledge allows diverse types of associations to be made with the added content, which gives rise to various levels of meaningful learning (Wang, J., Shimada, Oi, Ogata, & Tabata, 2020)

The concept of meaningful learning varies among students who can understand what is learned in daily experiences and teachers use different contexts such as activation, connection to reality and the creation of intercultural contexts to apply the learning contents in the school. Teachers have different concepts of meaningful learning that can be inspired by the educational aligned with theoretical notions to create the contexts and environments establishing the objectives for or with their students, even though their practices are not always clearly linked to the concepts and theories, so it is not possible to find consistent patterns.

Meaningful learning takes place in contexts that are recognized to create learning environments in which students can interact (Van Oers 1998; Lui and Bonner 2016; Verschafel and Greer 2013). Practices such as dialogue, collaboration, independent work, and experiential learning support meaningful learning (Polman, Hornstra, & Volman, 2021). Collaborative processing promotes meaningful learning because the student understands the meaning of each concept and discovers its similarities, dependencies, and contrasts.

Cultural and social assumptions about the nature of responsible learning imply that students authentically participate in the activities of the teaching-learning process (Hammer et al., 2012). The assumption that learning takes place in meaningful learning environments considers that students' motivation and understanding is shared by different theoretical approaches to meaningful learning (Loyens and Gijbels 2008; Mayer 2004; Wardekker et al. 2012). Meaningful learning is created under the assumption that, if students are given freedom and confidence, they can find their own answers and develop their knowledge, both in the classroom and in practical life.

Meaningful learning is a characteristic of education (Oostdam et al. 2007), but little is known what teachers do to achieve it in their students, how they interpret and establish it depending on their personal points of view, but it is also reflected of the educational concept that creates meaningful learning environments in accordance with its pedagogical concept and philosophy. This develops the context to create meaningful learning environments.

The concept of meaningful learning has different meanings in practice. In relation to the teaching-learning processes, this goes beyond the mere application of knowledge and practice within a context that gives meaning to students, but little is known about teachers what practices they do in their meaningful learning process for the students. Teachers have different perceptions of what is meaningful learning based on different theoretical-conceptual notions and pedagogical practices that contribute and with varied objectives depending on what students understand that must be learned creating an oriented inter-curricular context.

The inclusive concepts are entities of the cognitive structure that allow meaningful learning with new elements that form categories through systems of representation of reality that integrate knowledge into the structure of the subject (Ausubel, 1968). The model of human cognitive architecture based on the theory of cognitive load of instruction in an intrinsic, extrinsic, and pertinent way of the elements of interactive information and the time required for meaningful learning (Romero Juárez, 2020).

The notion that emphasizes the cognitive processes by which students incorporate knowledge into their existing knowledge structures is meaningful learning, despite the context to be performed, cognitive, socio-constructivist and sociocultural learning theories differ in the types of context meanings emerging. The cognitive approach emphasizes the existence of a cognitive structure in which the learner learns, meaning that meaningful learning emerges in the context of what he already knows, in such a way that teachers need to prepare the environment in such a way that it offers relationships to the structures. preexisting cognitive structures that are used as anchors to deliver added content in the cognitive structure (Ausubel 1968).

In socio-constructivist approaches they emphasize social interaction, communication, and collaboration to create meaningful learning contexts (Roelofs and Terwel 1999; Roelofs et al. 2003). Sociocultural approaches define social learning as the participation of students in social practices (Van Oers 1998), rather than in contexts focused on tasks in solving specific problems but in participation in social practices (Volman and Ten Dam, 2015).

The teacher enables significant learning in his students by producing relationships between previous organizers that, as cognitive bridges, establish inclusive concepts and new materials organized so that relationships with prior knowledge and what should be learned are produced. Machine learning is different from meaningful learning because it only involves memorization by repetition without recognition of meaning and little contributes to modifying the cognitive structure of students, who have diverse backgrounds of prior knowledge, in quality and quantity to make associations between the old and new knowledge giving rise to the occurrence of various levels of meaningful learning (Novak 1993).

Meaningful learning makes it possible to solve the challenges of the environment with the recognition of a new world order by the new generations that demand quality education and pedagogical innovation, training spaces, didactics, curricular content, evaluation, teacher training, etc. (Vincent-Lancrin et al., 2019).

The promotion of inclusive education in the entire academic community must be done from a participation of meaningful learning, close to the integral quality approaches of the educational system that is valued by society as a right in relation to people and the type of society that you want to achieve (UNESCO and OREALC, 2007). Inclusive education requires a conceptual resignification of creation and development of common learning spaces delimited by special conditions under models of teaching and evaluation of significant learning, from humanistic perspectives that respond to the socio-cultural historical complexity to train quality students, capable of develop all their human potential, which remains and culminates in their training (Rosano, 2007).

Meaningful learning is globalizing learning, which relates through knowledge construction schemes, sequence the use of previous learning to provoke the significant generation of knowledge. For meaningful learning, the conditions must be met that the curricular contents of studies lead to meaningful learning based on psych pedagogical bases and that the student has interest and an attitude of motivation for the attitudes, abilities, skills, competencies, and capacities of the subject. that learns. Compliance with the acquisition of significant learning corresponds to the development of analysis and synthesis skills and abilities.

Constructivism is a theoretical current that considers knowledge as an active process of transformation of the human being that is integrated into their own structures of knowledge (Aznar, 1992; Carretero, 1993; Gómes and Gargallo, 1993) in an emotional-affective and semantic that give meaning to learning.

ELEMENTS OF MEANINGFUL LEARNING

Among the elements of the construction of an inclusive education with significant learning is the sensitization of the actors directly more involved in the teaching-learning processes, teachers, and students, who conduct the substantive functions of teaching, research and socio-economic projection validated by the results (Arizabaleta et al., 2016).

Teachers have new roles as facilitators, advisers, and administrators rather than as teachers. The teacher is conceived as a learner in the process of their own training with the support of historical-cultural components and content that are essential to promote meaningful learning. Create and maintain learning environments that involve students in meaningful learning activities that have social presence, learning presence and cognitive presence as components (Valverde Berrocoso, Garrido-Arroyo, Burgos-Videla, and Morales-Cevallos, 2020; Arbaugh, 2013; Thomas, West, Borup, 2017; Shea, Bidjerano, 2009; Joo, Lim, Kim, 2011; Joksimovic, Gasevic, Kovanovic, Adesope, Hatala, 2014; Shea, Bidjerano, 2012; Kozan, Caskurlu, 2018; Rubin, Fernandes, Avgerinou, 2013; Kim, Kwon, Cho, 2011; Zhan, Mei, 2013; Borup, West, Graham, 2012; Ke, 2010).

The role of the teacher is to adapt the teaching-learning processes to the educational profile of the students to empower their will and action in the generation of meaningful learning. In the meaningful teaching-learning process, the teacher ceases to be the protagonist and responsible according to the behaviorist theory to become the planner and organizer of the work of his students, whom he must motivate in their interest in the subject.

Meaningful learning uses processes of organization, elaboration, and introduces critical concepts and principles of content. Learning experiences that use thinking skills with prior structures have been associated with deep understanding of content and long-term retention of meaningful learning (Kay, and Kibbl, 2016). Transformative learning implies the construction of learning processes through meaningful, integrative, and democratic interaction and active involvement in the construction of meaningful knowledge processes that facilitate positive attitudes and skills. The meaningful learning process is facilitated with collaborative, interactive, investigative, and high-level thinking activities (Tsimane, Downing, 2019).

Teachers who offer meaningful learning experiences to their students consider constructive, active, intentional, cooperative, authentic, and relational as attributes for their design (Howland, Jonassen, Marra, 2011; Mystakidis, 2019). Meaningful learning requires tasks linked to authentic experiences. It is cooperative and relational because they occur naturally in knowledge-building communities, emotionally involving learners in designs that link theory and practice with experiences where teachers and students express themselves (Kostiainen, Ukskoski, Ruohotie-Lyhty, Kauppinen, Kainulainen, Mäkinen, 2018).

The cultural identity of the teacher in her community is inherent because it is the mediator between the knowledge, knowledge, traditions, and customs that are integrated with the new knowledge to generate meaningful and quality learning. Cultures have a large amount of knowledge, knowledge, experiences and practices on certain trades and issues that can be used in the socio-intercultural teaching-learning processes for the development of community identity and meaningful learning. The committed teacher is always up to date with new knowledge in all fields of human knowledge.

The teacher is responsible for the development of his class, the maker of pedagogical knowledge and his own teaching practice; his professional academic training must promote critical, reflective, and innovative teaching-learning processes for meaningful learning in students (Araujo & Moraima 2006). Greater involvement in reflecting on the relationships between knowledge concepts increases the generation of meaningful learning (Nesbit & Adesope, 2013).

Responsibility for the complex functions of the teacher requires more than the simple transmission of information, the use of affective and cognitive processes that contribute to the meaningful learning of students. The teacher must have the ability to integrate technology, pedagogy, and disciplinary content, to build knowledge and facilitate meaningful learning. These activities contribute to self-assessment processes to identify the appropriation of new knowledge and changes in skills as strategies for evaluating the meaningful teaching-learning process, to improve (Del Campo, 2000; Delgado & Oliver, 2010).

This model aims to make the student competent with capacities to face current demands with the acquisition of significant knowledge in accordance with the different contexts in which they will have their professional development. The use of capacities based on multiple intelligences with an axiological approach contributes to the development of meaningful learning. The individual capacities perceived to organize and execute the courses of action required to obtain meaningful learning represent a construct of motivation to achieve different forms of performance (Bandura, 1986, p. 391).

Motivation and learning attitude are two factors to consider in creating meaningful learning. Making learning meaningful improves students' motivation to learn. Meaningful learning improves student motivation and achievement (Loyens and Gijbels 2008; Van Rijk et al. 2017). Evaluative judgments of self-efficacy such as capacity to perform a function demonstrate significant changes in learning and self-efficacy after instruction. Pedagogical and didactic interventions that are more connected to the individual needs of students have a greater chance of achieving better performance in meaningful learning.

Meaningful learning environments relate students' needs and interests to their learning and make their experience worthwhile beyond school (Newman et al. 1996; Roelofs and Terwel 1999; Van Oers 2009). Self-evaluating judgments about self-efficacy in teaching-learning processes must be realistic to demonstrate significant changes in learning after instruction (Graham, Harris, and Mason 2005).

The operational and differentiated educational planning allows the extrapolation in different dimensions of the realization of didactic activities with significant learning proposed in the study program with the vision of turning them into innovative, creative, and fair actors. Selecting the topic by coupling the contents to the socioeconomic context and establishing the learning objectives of knowledge, attitudes, skills, and capacities that one wishes to develop, are necessary elements for a more meaningful learning. The essential elements for the meaningful learning of a specific topic are its multidimensional reality, its historical-cultural background, its socioeconomic environment, characteristics, approaches, values, principles, material, and didactic strategies, etc.

Knowledge of a broad vocabulary by teachers and students facilitates the understanding of readings, learning materials, communications in the classroom, and promotes meaningful learning (Pun and Jin 2021). The experience that results from the need to learn to review academic works provides the opportunity for teachers and students about the characteristics of effective writing as meaningful instructional learning (Chen, Zhang, Wang, Zhang, 2021; MacArthur, 2015, 2018). The command of the language used in the teaching-learning processes is critical to conduct oneself in academic activities and achieve superior performance in meaningful learning, and cognitive differences should be considered based on individual characteristics and differences, such as gender. (Zhang, Mi 2010) Chen, Wang, Zou, Lin, Xie 2019).

In classes, teachers put into practice active and participatory methodologies for students to reflect and use the knowledge learned as knowledge-generating subjects through meaningful learning. Thus, the variables that most influence the generation of meaningful knowledge are the role of the teacher and practical activities.

The correct use of technological tools and knowledge of active methodologies allow the construction and consolidation of meaningful learning, such as problem-based learning, the flipped classroom and case studies, among other methodologies. For example, teachers must demonstrate a broad conceptual proficiency in the flipped classroom, its implementation process in the classroom, accompanying students in the various stages of the teaching-learning process, considering that the student is the protagonist of the educational model.

DIDACTIC STRATEGIES FOR MEANINGFUL LEARNING

Teachers introduce learning strategies in accordance with instructional objectives for the achievement of meaningful learning. The stimulation, motivation, development, and promotion of academic and scientific activities at an early age, based on a diagnosis, the interventions and participation of teachers are determined, and didactic strategies are formulated to strengthen meaningful learning in research. The participation and interventions of teachers in the activities of the teaching-learning process through didactic strategies must be aimed at achieving meaningful learning.

The meaningful learning approach requires a teacher who, beyond the traditional approach, uses the most proactive, creative, and innovative teaching strategies, ethically committed in his or her guiding performance that assumes changes in the environment, understands reality and visualizes the challenges of opportunities. In this way, the implementation of innovative didactic strategies that transform pedagogical and didactic practices aimed at building meaningful learning is relevant.

Different teaching strategies can be used to increase the quality of teaching-learning processes with meaningful results. The didactic material to be used in the strategies of a meaningful teaching-learning process must motivate considering the learning styles, the aesthetics of the design, the style, the purpose of the communication (Morales, 2020). The contents of the subjects that students consider complex require, in addition to proficiency in the subject, the training of teachers in educational strategies that aim to promote meaningful learning to effectively transmit knowledge.

The interaction in collective works as a didactic strategy between people who are the same facilitates the construction and the natural acquisition of knowledge, abilities and skills that give rise to meaningful learning. The blended and blended learning model is a strategy that provides students with opportunities that help them obtain deeper and more complex levels of meaningful learning (Patrick and Sturgis 2015; Şentürk, 2021).

The design of virtual education didactic strategies with B-learning modality tools to strengthen meaningful learning with the support of active learning methods in training close to the reality of practice and with an increase in student autonomy. Virtual education with the use of information and communication technologies facilitates the use of tools in the educational process that favor the development of meaningful learning (Guerrero Castañeda, Rojas Morales, Villafañe Aguilar, 2019). Information and communication technologies as part of a didactic strategy have a positive impact on meaningful teaching-learning processes where the more the use of ICTs is used in learning, the better the learning results of the students (Al -Ansi, Suprayogo, and Abidin 2019).

The development of skills and knowledge of didactic strategies to be implemented through information and communication technologies through communication platforms is essential for students to achieve meaningful learning (Flores et al. 2020). Interactive learning activities (Wu et al. 2017) as didactic strategies contribute to improving meaningful teaching-learning processes with the development of skills through the creation of online learning communities from home and with the practice of authentic tasks in face-to-face sessions, discussion groups, presentations and with direct questions to the instructor online.

The acquisition of methodologies and didactics for the creation of e-learning and blended learning (b-learning) strategies, facilitate the generation of virtual learning modalities that allow metacognition and meaningful learning. The use of augmented reality and neuro-didactics as recreational tools allow the design and optimization of the use of didactic strategies for significant learning processes through brain and sensory stimulation of emotions and imagination, which affect meaningful learning from a motivating perspective.

Meaningful learning, reception and discovery environments, and individual differences influence prior knowledge on learning effectiveness. The environment integrates discovery learning to encourage active engagement in meaningful learning. Using a framework of the meaningful learning environment using a machine-guided ontology, Wang et al. (2017) develop a visualization support system that helps the ebook user to identify and understand the concepts and relate them to their cognitive structure, which results in a better environment for receiving meaningful learning.

Reception and discovery learning are two diverse types of meaningful learning environments (Ausubel et al., 1978; Novak & Cañas, 2008). In the receiving learning environment, relationships are explicitly provided on the map for transmission to the student, while, in the discovery learning environment type, relationships between knowledge are identified student autonomy (Ausubel et al., 1978). To encourage meaningful learning, cognitive maps and connections help students organize and structure their own frames of reference (Novak & Cañas, 2008).

In the meaningful learning environment, conceptual maps, knowledge, and knowledge topics are provided to the student so that they associate the content elements, definitions, and explanations of knowledge, with the provided structure (Chu et al., 2011; Novak & Cañas, 2008; Lee & Segev, 2012; O'Donnell et al., 2002; Wang et al. 2020).

Concept maps are an effective learning tool and because it provides an additional resource to make it meaningful, it allows feedback to students and offers a means of evaluating the performance of meaningful learning (Baliga, Walvekar, Mahantshetti 2021; Daley, Tower 2010).

The development of foreign language skills in the inverted room, the group of students working with the platform including the learning strategies, contribute to the achievement of cognitive learning results, obtain more significant learning in grammar, speaking, reading, and writing. In the same way, Kostaris, Sergis, Sampson, Giannakos, and Pelliccione (2017) have revealed that meaningful learning in the inverted room contributes to greater involvement and motivation in information and communication. Self-regulated meaningful learning strategies affect the performance of abilities, skills, and abilities in favor of groups working in the inverted room model (Öztürk, Çakıroğlu, 2021).

However, the research results are not conclusive in terms of improving students' meaningful learning in such a way that allows them better knowledge and autonomy in their professional training, although it was shown that in virtual education, as much or more is learned than in the traditional way. In virtual learning, students do not always have prior experience, but it is more effective than with traditional learning. The achievement of meaningful learning depends on the student's experience in the use of virtuality after conducting training activities in any type of technological tool.

In contrast, other research results show that students have learning difficulties to achieve meaning in computer courses taught under the inverted room strategy compared to traditional methods, due to time constraints and that they soon become angry (Cabı 2018).

Active engagement avoids the erosion of curiosity and willingness to explore as in the case of the meaningful reception learning environment, which also serves as an assessment tool that encourages building learning using meaningful learning strategies. The broad connections made between learning tasks, instruction, and assessment feedback support students in achieving meaningful learning. Connective feedback helps students navigate through blended and blended learning that connects new learning tasks and different instructional modules that helps make sense of assessment results (Wang, Tlili, Lehman, et al. 2021).

CONCLUSION

Traditional learning styles centered on the teacher and through memorization are only replaced by meaningful learning that focuses more on student participation. The application of active didactic methodologies and strategies that achieve the implementation of significant learning processes depending on the context in which it takes place, obtains better results in the training of professionals. It is in this sense that no didactic method and strategy is adequate for all contexts. For example, case studies in which students analyze specific situations presented to arrive at an experiential conceptualization and find effective solutions, allows content and learning to be more meaningful.

The results of academic performance as indicators of the significant learning achieved by students in virtual environments are favorable even though they are not always optimal due to multiple factors. The generation of meaningful teaching-learning processes is subject to the complexity of the subject, to the design of the virtual didactic strategy. The advantages of meaningful learning design are that it eliminates the tendency to passive learning because students organize their learning activities, improves collaboration in the group, working together to stimulate the ability to think and the ability to understand the content.

The results of research on the impact of information and communication technologies on meaningful learning are not entirely conclusive, although it has been shown that, in virtual learning, although students do not have previous experiences and knowledge, they achieve greater effectiveness than with the traditional learning system. The student's previous experience and knowledge about the use of virtual education is related to their meaningful learning.

The results show that more must be paid in the process of teaching interaction, based on the analysis of the subjects, formulating anticipated didactic strategies that impact meaningful learning and the development of student skills; research ability, ability to learn, adapt to new situations, generate innovative ideas. Theoretical implications for education at a higher level is constantly challenged derived from the changing and competitive context (Fidalgo et al., 2014), which implies that in teaching practice it is essential to reflect on the didactic intention in a clear and specific way in planning and implementation. of didactic strategies in the classroom environment that favors meaningful learning, helping to generate the value of essential knowledge in higher education and in industries.

Practical implications for education it makes reflection indispensable; regarding the choice of the teaching staff, their academic training, professional experience, teacher training and assignment to teach the respective subject; analyze and evaluate their work in their teaching practice through didactic planning and selection of didactic strategies and suitable learning activities focused on the achievement of significant learning, where the student relates theoretical aspects to practical and real situations; and the results that generate knowledge in the students and provide an answer or solution to the problems raised and in real contexts.

Questions are being opened to conduct future lines of research on the cognitive capacities of recovery, understanding, analysis and application of knowledge (Marzano and Kendall 2007) should be applied for each specific competence and to assess the profile of the teacher in the achievement of meaningful learning. In future research on meaningful learning, conceptualization must consider the diversity of practices with which teachers attempt to create environments.

REFERENCES

Al-Ansi, A., Suprayogo, I. & Abidin, M. (2019). *Impact of Information and Communication Technology (ICT) on Different Settings of Learning Process in Developing Countries.*. doi:10.5923/j.scit.20190902.01

Almulla, M. A. (2020, July). The Effectiveness of the Project-Based Learning (PBL) Approach to Engage Students in Learning. *SAGE Open, 10*(3). Advance online publication. doi:10.1177/2158244020938702

Apodaca-Orozco, G. U. G., Ortega-Pipper, L. P., Verdugo-Blanco, L. E., & Reyes-Barribas, L. E. (2017). Modelos educativos: un reto para la educación en salud. *Ra Ximhai, 13*(2), 77-86.

Araujo, M., & Campos, M. (2006). La praxis pedagógica en la educación física y los estilos de enseñanza predominantes en los docentes de educación básica. *Revista EDUCARE-UPEL-IPB-Segunda Nueva Etapa 2.0, 10*(3).

Arbaugh, J. B. (2013). Does academic discipline moderate CoI-course outcomes relationships in online MBA courses? *Internet High. Educ, 2013*(17), 16–28. doi:10.1016/j.iheduc.2012.10.002

Arizabaleta, S. L., & Ochoa, A. F. (2016). Hacia una educación superior inclusiva en Colombia. *Pedagogía y saberes*, (45), 41-52.

Arnold, D. Y., & Yapita, J. D. (2000). *El rincón de las cabezas: Luchas textuales, educacion y Tierras en los Andes*. La Paz, Bolivia: Instituto de Lengua y Cultura aymara IICA.

Ausubel, D. (1963). *The psychology of meaningful verbal learning*. Grune & Stratton.

Ausubel, D. (1978). *Educational Psychology: A Cognitive View*. Holt, Rinehart and Winston.

Ausubel, D., Novak, J., & Hanesian, H. (1978). *Educational psychology: A cognitive view*. Holt, Rinehart & Winston.

Ausubel, D. P. (1961). In Defense of Verbal Learning. *Educational Theory*, *1961*(11), 15–25. doi:10.1111/j.1741-5446.1961.tb00038.x

Ausubel, D. P. (1968). *Educational psychology. A cognitive view*. Holt Rinehart and Winston.

Aznar, P. (1992). *Constructivismo y educación*. Tirant lo Blanch.

Baliga, S. S., Walvekar, P. R., & Mahantshetti, G. J. (2021). Concept map as a teaching and learning tool for medical students. *Journal of Education and Health Promotion*, *10*(1), 35. doi:10.4103/jehp.jehp_146_20 PMID:33688544

Bandura, A. (1986). *Social Foundations of Thought and Action: A Social Cognitive Theory*. Prentice Hall.

Bao, L., & Koenig, K. (2019). Physics education research for 21st century learning. *Discip Interdscip Sci Educ Res*, *1*(1), 2. doi:10.118643031-019-0007-8

Beck, E., Sollbrekke, T., Sutphen, M., & Fremstad, E. (2015). When mere knowledge is not enough: The potential of building as self-determination, co-determination, and solidarity. *Higher Education Research & Development*, *34*(3), 445–457. doi:10.1080/07294360.2014.973373

Bonwell, C. C., & Eison, J. A. (1991). Active Learning: Creating Excitement in the Classroom. *ASHE-ERIC Higher Education Report*, *1*(1).

Borup, J., West, R. E., & Graham, C. R. (2012). Improving online social presence through asynchronous video. *Internet High. Educ.*, *2012*(15), 195–203. doi:10.1016/j.iheduc.2011.11.001

Cabı, E. (2018). The impact of the flipped classroom model on students'academic achievement. *International Review of Research in Open and Distance Learning*, *19*(3), 203–221. doi:10.19173/irrodl.v19i3.3482

Carretero, M. (1993). *Constructivismo y educación*. Luis Vives.

Chen, Wang, Zou, Lin, & Xie. (2019). Effects of caption and gender on junior high students' EFL learning from iMap-enhanced contextualized learning. *PLOS ONE Students' challenges and learning strategies*.

Chen, J., Zhang, L. J., Wang, X., & Zhang, T. (2021). Impacts of Self-Regulated Strategy Development-Based Revision Instruction on English-as-a-Foreign-Language Students' Self-Efficacy for Text Revision: A Mixed-Methods Study. *Frontiers in Psychology*. https://www.frontiersin.org/article/10.3389/fpsyg.2021.670100 DOI=10.3389/fpsyg.2021.670100

Chu, K. K., Lee, C. I., & Tsai, R. S. (2011). Ontology technology to assist learners' navigation in the concept map learning system. *Expert Systems with Applications, 38*(9), 11293–11299. doi:10.1016/j.eswa.2011.02.178

Dahar, R. W. (2011). *Teori belajar dan pembelajaran*. Erlangga.

Daley, B. J., & Torre, D. M. (2010). Concept maps in medical education: An analytical literature review. *Medical Education, 44*(5), 440–448. doi:10.1111/j.1365-2923.2010.03628.x PMID:20374475

Del Campo, S. (2000). *Análisis del manejo de la autoevaluación de los alumnos por parte de los profesores que imparten cursos transferidos con el nuevo modelo de rediseño creado en la misión del ITESM para el año 2005 en el campus Cd. Juárez* (Tesis de maestría, Instituto Tecnológico y de Estudios Superiores de Monterrey). https://repositorio.tec.mx/bitstream/handle/11285/628762/EGE00000007633.pdf?sequence=1

Delgado, A. M., & Oliver, R. (2010). Interacción entre la evaluación continua y la autoevaluación formativa: La potenciación del aprendizaje autónomo. *Revista de Docencia Universitaria, 4*, 2-13. https://revistas.um.es/redu/article/view/92581

Espejo Leupin, R. M. (2016). ¿Pedagogía activa o métodos activos? El caso del aprendizaje activo en la universidad. *Revista Digital de Investigación en Docencia Universitaria, 10*(1), 16. doi:10.19083/ridu.10.456

Fidalgo-Blanco, Á., Sein-Echaluce, M. L., & García-Peñalvo, F. J. (2014). Espirales de conocimiento en la innovación docente en educación superior. *Revista Internacional de Gestión del Conocimiento (IJKM), 10*(4), 16-37. doi:10.4018/ijkm.2014100102

Fletcher, T. & Chróinín, D. N. (2021). Pedagogical principles that support the prioritisation of meaningful experiences in physical education: conceptual and practical considerations. *Physical Education and Sport Pedagogy*. doi:10.1080/17408989.2021.1884672

Flores, G., De Alba, R., & Caicedo, E. (2020). Recomendaciones básicas de competencias docentes para la modalidad no escolarizada en tiempos de la pandemia. *Humanidades, Tecnología y Ciencia, del instituto Politécnico Nacional, 22*(25). http://revistaelectronica-ipn.org/ResourcesFiles/Contenido/23/HUMANIDADES_23_000877.pdf

Galdames, V., Walqui, A., & Gustafson, B. (2011). *Enseñanza de la lengua indígena como Lengua Materna*. PROEIB Andes.

Garrote Rojas, D., Garrote Rojas, C., & Jiménez Fernández, S. (2016). Factores Influyentes en Motivación y Estrategias de Aprendizaje en los Alumnos de Grado REICE. *Revista Iberoamericana sobre Calidad, Eficacia y Cambio en Educación, 14*(2), 31-44.

Gómes, C., & Gargallo, B. (1993). Las bases de una concepción constructivista de la educación. Implicaciones pedagógicas. In *Construcción humana y procesos de estructuración: propuestas de intervención pedagógica* (pp. 35–65). Quiles Artes Gráficas.

Gowin, D. B. (1990). *Educating* (2nd ed.). Cornell University Press.

Graham, S., Harris, K. R., & Mason, L. (2005). Improving the writing performance, knowledge, and self-efficacy of struggling young writers: The effects of self-regulated strategy development. *Contemporary Educational Psychology*, *30*(2), 207–241. doi:10.1016/j.cedpsych.2004.08.001

Guerrero Castañeda, A., Rojas Morales, C., & Villafañe Aguilar, C. (2019). Impacto de la Educación Virtual en Carreras de Pregrado del Área de Ciencias de la Salud. Una Mirada de las Tecnologías Frente a la Educación. Trabajo de Grado presentado como requisito parcial para optar al título de: Especialización en Docencia Universitaria Línea de Investigación: Monografía Universidad Cooperativa de Colombia Facultad de Educación Especialización en docencia universitaria.

Hammer, D., Goldberg, F., & Fargason, S. (2012). Responsive teaching and the beginnings of energy in a third-grade classroom. *Review of Science, Mathematics, and ICT Education*, *6*(1), 51–72.

Hanani, N. (2020). Meaningful Learning Reconstruction for Millennial: Facing competition in the information technology era. *IOP Conference Series. Earth and Environmental Science*, *469*(1), 012107. doi:10.1088/1755-1315/469/1/012107

Howland, J. L., Jonassen, D. H., & Marra, R. M. (2011). *Meaningful Learning with Technology* (4th ed.). Pearson.

Joksimovic, S., Gasevic, D., Kovanovic, V., Adesope, O., & Hatala, M. (2014). Psychological characteristics in cognitive presence of communities of inquiry: A linguistic analysis of online discussions. *Internet High. Educ*, *22*, 1–10. doi:10.1016/j.iheduc.2014.03.001

Jonassen, D. H. (2003). *Learning to Solve Problems with Technology: A Constructivist Perspective* (2nd ed.). Merrill.

Joo, Y. J., Lim, K. Y., & Kim, E. K. (2011). Online university students' satisfaction and persistence: Examining perceived level of presence, usefulness, and ease of use as predictors in a structural model. *Computers & Education*, *2011*(57), 1654–1664. doi:10.1016/j.compedu.2011.02.008

Julca, F. (2000). *Uso de las lenguas quechua y castellano en la escuela urbana: Un estudio de caso* (Tesis de maestría). Cochabamba: Universidad Mayor de San Simón – Bolivia. Recuperado de http://bvirtual.proeibandes.org/bvirtual/docs/tesis/proeib/Tesis_Felix_Julca.pd

Kay, D., & Kibbl, J. (2016). Learning theories 101: Application to everyday teaching and scholarship. *Advances in Physiology Education*, *40*(1), 17–25. doi:10.1152/advan.00132.2015 PMID:26847253

Ke, F. (2010). Examining online teaching, cognitive, and social presence for adult students. *Computers & Education*, *2010*(55), 808–820. doi:10.1016/j.compedu.2010.03.013

Kim, J., Kwon, Y., & Cho, D. (2011). Investigating factors that influence social presence and learning outcomes in distance higher education. *Computers & Education*, *2011*(57), 1512–1520. doi:10.1016/j.compedu.2011.02.005

Kostaris, C., Sergis, S., Sampson, D. G., Giannakos, M. N., & Pelliccione, L. (2017). Investigating the potential of the flipped classroom model in K-12 ICT teaching and learning: An action research study. *Journal of Educational Technology & Society*, *20*(1), 261–273.

Kostiainen, E., Ukskoski, T., Ruohotie-Lyhty, M., Kauppinen, M., Kainulainen, J., & Mäkinen, T. (2018). Meaningful learning in teacher education. *Teaching and Teacher Education, 2018*(71), 66–77. doi:10.1016/j.tate.2017.12.009

Kozan, K., & Caskurlu, S. (2018). On the Nth presence for the Community of Inquiry framework. *Computers & Education, 2018*(122), 104–118. doi:10.1016/j.compedu.2018.03.010

Lee, J. H., & Segev, A. (2012). Knowledge maps for e-learning. *Computers & Education, 59*(2), 353–364. doi:10.1016/j.compedu.2012.01.017

Lillo, V. (2014). Salud Y Educación: Dos Vocaciones Al Servicio De Los Derechos Humanos. *Revista Médica Clínica Las Condes, 25*(2), 357–362. doi:10.1016/S0716-8640(14)70047-1

Loyens, S. M. M., & Gijbels, D. (2008). Understanding the efects of constructivist learning environments: Introducing a multi-directional approach. *Instructional Science, 36*(5-6), 351–357. doi:10.100711251-008-9059-4

Lui, A. M., & Bonner, S. M. (2016). Preservice and inservice teachers' knowledge, beliefs, and instructional planning in primary school mathematics. *Teaching and Teacher Education, 56*, 1–13. doi:10.1016/j.tate.2016.01.015

MacArthur, C. A. (2015). Instruction in evaluation and revision. In Handbook of Writing Research. New York, NY: Guilford Publications.

MacArthur, C. A. (2018). Evaluation and revision. In S. Graham, C. A. Charles, M. Hebert, & J. Fitzgerald (Eds.), *Best Practices in Writing Instruction* (pp. 287–308). Guilford Publications.

Mayer, R. E. (2004). Should there be a three-strikes rule against pure discovery learning? *The American Psychologist, 59*(1), 14–19. doi:10.1037/0003-066X.59.1.14 PMID:14736316

Mintzes, J., & Wandersee, J. (2000). Reforma e Inovação no Ensino da Ciência: uma visão construtivista. In Ensinando Ciência para a compreensão – uma visão construtivista. Plátano Edições Técnicas.

Morales-Cevallos, M. B. (2020). Trends in Educational Research about e-Learning: A Systematic Literature Review (2009–2018). *Sustainability, 12*(12), 5153. doi:10.3390u12125153

Moreira, M. A. (2011). Why Concepts, Why Meaningful Learning, Why Collaborative Activities and Why Concept Maps? *Aprendizagem Significativa em Revista/Meaningful Learning Review, 6*(3), 5.

Mystakidis, S. (2019). Motivation Enhanced Deep and Meaningful Learning with Social Virtual Reality. University of Jyväskylä.

Mystakidis, S. (2021). Deep Meaningful Learning. *Encyclopedia, 2021*(1), 988–997. doi:10.3390/encyclopedia1030075

Mystakidis, S., Berki, E., & Valtanen, J.-P. (2019). The Patras Blended Strategy Model for Deep and Meaningful Learning in Quality Life-Long Distance Education. *Electron. J. e-Learning, 17*, 66–78.

Nesbit, J. C., & Adesope, O. O. (2013). Concept maps for learning: Theory, research, and design. In G. Schraw, M. T. McCrudden, & D. Robinson (Eds.), *Current perspectives on cognition, learning, and instruction. Learning through visual displays* (pp. 303–328). Information Age Publishers.

Newman, F. M., Marks, H. M., & Gamoran, A. (1996). Authentic pedagogy and student performance. *American Journal of Education, 104*(4), 280–312. doi:10.1086/444136

Novak, J. (1990). Human Construtivism: A Unification of Psychological and Epistemological Phenomena in Meaning Making. *Dalam Fourth North American Conference on Personal Construct Psychology*, 15.

Novak, J. D. (1993). A view on the status of Ausubel's assimilation theory of learning. In *Proceedings of the third international seminar on misconceptions and educational strategies in science and mathematics*. Misconceptions Trust.

Novak, J. D., & Cañas, A. J. (2008). *The theory underlying concept maps and how to construct them.* Technical report IHMC CmapTools 2006-01 Rev 01-2008.

Novak, J. D., & Gowin, D. (2006). *Learning How to Learn.* Cambridge University Press.

O'Donnell, A. M., Dansereau, D. F., & Hall, R. H. (2002). Knowledge maps as scaffolds for cognitive processing. *Educational Psychology Review, 14*(1), 71–86. doi:10.1023/A:1013132527007

Oostdam, R. J., Peetsma, T. T. D., & Blok, H. (2007). *Het nieuwe leren in basisonderwijs en voortgezet onderwijs nader beschouwd* [New learning in primary and secondary education reconsidered]. SCO-Kohnstamm Instituut.

Öztürk, M., & Çakıroğlu, Ü. (2021). Flipped learning design in EFL classrooms: Implementing self-regulated learning strategies to develop language skills. *Smart Learn. Environ.*, *8*(1), 2. doi:10.118640561-021-00146-x

Patrick, S., & Sturgis, C. (2015). *Maximizing competency education and blended learning: Insights fromexperts.* Vienna: iNACOL.

Polman, J., Hornstra, L., & Volman, M. (2021). The meaning of meaningful learning in mathematics in upper-primary education. *Learning Environments Research, 24*(3), 469–486. doi:10.100710984-020-09337-8

Pun, J., & Jin, X. (2021, May 7). Student challenges and learning strategies at Hong Kong EMI universities. *PLoS One, 15 / 16*(5), e0251564. Advance online publication. doi:10.1371/journal.pone.0251564

Pun, J., & Jin, X. (2021). Student challenges and learning strategies at Hong Kong EMI universities. *PLoS One, 16*(5), e0251564. doi:10.1371/journal.pone.0251564 PMID:33961675

Roelofs, E., & Terwel, J. (1999). Constructivism and authentic pedagogy: State of the art and recent developments in the Dutch national curriculum in secondary education. *Journal of Curriculum Studies, 31*(2), 201–227. doi:10.1080/002202799183232

Roelofs, E., Visser, J., & Terwel, J. (2003). Preferences for various learning environments: Teachers' and parents' perceptions. *Learning Environments Research, 6*(1), 77–110. doi:10.1023/A:1022915910198

Romero Juárez, M. G. (2020). *Enseñanza de programación de estructuras de datos aplicando estrategias didácticas basadas en la teoría de carga cognitiva.* Tesis de maestría en informática y tecnologías computacionales-Universidad Autónoma de Aguascalientes. Centro de Ciencias Básicas. Repositorio bibliográfico. http://hdl.handle.net/11317/1857

Rosano, S. (2007). *La cultura de la diversidad y la educación inclusiva*. Recuperado de http://benu. edu.mx/wp-content/uploads/2015/03/La_cultura_de_la_diversidad_y_la_educacion_inclusiva.pdf

Rubin, B., Fernandes, R., & Avgerinou, M. D. (2013). The effects of technology on the Community of Inquiry and satisfaction with online courses. *Internet High. Educ*, *2013*(17), 48–57. doi:10.1016/j.iheduc.2012.09.006

Scott, D., & Friesen, S. (2013). Inquiry-Based Learning: A Review of the Research Literature. *Alberta Education*, *1*, 1–29.

Şentürk, C. (2021). Effects of the blended learning model on preservice teachers' academic achievements and twenty-first century skills. *Education and Information Technologies*, *26*(1), 35–48. doi:10.100710639-020-10340-y PMID:33020691

Sharan, Y. (2015). *Meaningful Learning in the Co-operative Classroom. Education 3-13: International Journal of Primary, Elementary and Early Years Education, 43(1), 83-94.*

Shea, P., & Bidjerano, T. (2009). Community of inquiry as a theoretical framework to foster "epistemic engagement" and "cognitive presence" in online education. *Computers & Education*, *2009*(52), 543–553. doi:10.1016/j.compedu.2008.10.007

Shea, P., & Bidjerano, T. (2012). Learning presence as a moderator in the community of inquiry model. *Computers & Education*, *2012*(59), 316–326. doi:10.1016/j.compedu.2012.01.011

Sriraman. (2010). *Theories of Mathematics Education*. Springer-Verlag Berlin Heidelberg.

Suyatno. (2009). *Menjelajah Pembelajaran Inovatif.* Bumi Aksara.

Thomas, R. A., West, R. E., & Borup, J. (2017). An analysis of instructor social presence in online text and asynchronous video feedback comments. *Internet and Higher Education*, *2017*(33), 61–73. doi:10.1016/j.iheduc.2017.01.003

Tsimane, T. A., & Downing, Ch. (2019). Transformative learning in nursing education: A concept analysis. *International Journal of Nursing Sciences, 7*(1), 91-98, https://www.sciencedirect.com/science/article/pii/S2352013219301760

Valverde-Berrocoso, J., Garrido-Arroyo, M. C., Burgos-Videla, C., & Morales-Cevallos, M. B. (2020). Trends in Educational Research about e-Learning: A Systematic Literature Review (2009–2018). *Sustainability*, *2020*(12), 5153. doi:10.3390u12125153

Van Oers, B. (1998). From context to contextualizing. *Learning and Instruction*, *8*(6), 473–488. doi:10.1016/S0959-4752(98)00031-0

Van Oers, B. (2009). Developmental education: Improving participation in cultural practices. In M. Fleer, M. Hedegaard, & J. Tudge (Eds.), *Childhood studies and the impact of globalization: Policies and practices at global and local levels* (pp. 213–229). Routledge.

Van Rijk, Y., Volman, M., de Haan, D., & van Oers, B. (2017). Maximizing meaning: Creating a learning environment for reading comprehension of informative texts from a Vygotskian perspective. *Learning Environments Research*, *20*(1), 77–98. doi:10.100710984-016-9218-5

Vergara, I., Travieso, N., & Crespo, M. (2014). Dinámica del proceso enseñanza-aprendizaje de la Química en tecnología de la salud. *Educación Médica Superior*, *28*(2), 272–281.

Verschafel, L., & Greer, B. (2013). Mathematics education. In J. M. Spector, M. D. Merrill, J. Elen, & M. J. Bishop (Eds.), *Handbook of research on educational communications and technology* (pp. 553–563). Springer. doi:10.1007/978-1-4614-3185-5_43

Vincent-Lancrin, S., Urgel, J., Kar, S., & Jacotin, G. (2019). *Measuring Innovation in Education 2019: What Has Changed in the Classroom? Educational Research and Innovation*. Paris: OECD Publishing. Recuperado de https://www.oecd-ilibrary.org/docser ver/9789264311671-en.pdf ?expires=1586359992yid=idyaccname=guestychecksum=83713685B45347B501719B47ABFBEB4D

Volman, M., & Ten Dam, G. (2015). Critical thinking for educated citizenship. In M. Davies & R. Barnett (Eds.), *The Palgrave handbook of critical thinking in higher education* (pp. 593–603). Palgrave Macmillan. doi:10.1057/9781137378057_35

Wang, H., Tlili, A., Lehman, J. D., Lu, H., & Huang, R. (2021). Investigating feedback implemented by instructors to support online competency-based learning (CBL): A multiple case study. *Int J Educ Technol High Educ*, *18*(1), 5. doi:10.118641239-021-00241-6

Wang, J., Mendori, T., & Xiong, J. (2014). A language learning support system using course-centered ontology and its evaluation. *Computer Education*, *78*, 278–293. doi:10.1016/j.compedu.2014.06.009

Wang, J., Ogata, H., & Shimada, A. (2017). A meaningful discovery learning environment for e-book learners. *IEEE Global Engineering Education Conference*, 1158–1165. 10.1109/EDUCON.2017.7942995

Wang, J., Shimada, A., Oi, M., Ogata, H., & Tabata, Y. (2020). Development and evaluation of a visualization system to support meaningful e-book learning. *Interactive Learning Environments*, 1–18. Advance online publication. doi:10.1080/10494820.2020.1813178

Wardekker, W., Boersma, A., Ten Dam, G., & Volman, M. (2012). Motivation for school learning: Enhancing the meaningfulness of learning in communities of learners. In M. Hedegaard, A. Edwards, & M. Fleer (Eds.), *Motives in children's development: Cultural–historical approaches* (pp. 153–170). Cambridge University Press.

Wu, W. C. V., Hsieh, J. S. C., & Yang, J. C. (2017). Creating an online learning community in a flipped classroom to enhance EFL learners' oral proficiency. *Journal of Educational Technology & Society*, *20*(2), 142–157.

Zhan, Z., & Mei, H. (2013). Academic self-concept and social presence in face-to-face and online learning: Perceptions and effects on students' learning achievement and satisfaction across environments. *Computers & Education*, *2013*(69), 131–138. doi:10.1016/j.compedu.2013.07.002

Zhang, Y., & Mi, Y. (2010, September). Another look at the language difficulties of international students. *Journal of Studies in International Education*, *14*(4), 371–388. doi:10.1177/1028315309336031

Chapter 4
Social Media and User-Generated Content as a Teaching Innovation Tool in Universities

Alexandra Mora-Cruz
https://orcid.org/0000-0001-5157-5232
Technological Institute of Costa Rica, Costa Rica

José Ramón Saura
https://orcid.org/0000-0002-9457-7745
Rey Juan Carlos University, Spain

Pedro R. Palos-Sanchez
https://orcid.org/0000-0001-9966-0698
University of Seville, Spain

ABSTRACT

Due to the digital transformation, universities have had to renew the didactic strategies used by teachers so that they can comply with the teaching-learning process. The implementation of practices in social networks has been essential to adapt to the skills of the new generation of digital students. The main objective of this chapter is to analyze how social networks and user-generated content can be used by university teachers as tools that foster innovation. For this, a review of the literature and different sources is carried out that allows for laying the foundations of the research. In addition, the chapter provides information on the main platforms used in the different educational experiences. With the data obtained, it is possible to understand how these social interaction tools can contribute to teaching innovation and, therefore, to the significant improvement of the learning results of higher education students.

DOI: 10.4018/978-1-6684-4441-2.ch004

Copyright © 2022, IGI Global. Copying or distributing in print or electronic forms without written permission of IGI Global is prohibited.

INTRODUCTION

In recent years, the Internet connection has become indispensable in the day for a large number of people. According to the Global Report on the Digital Environment (2022), more than 424 million people are active users of social networks, which is equivalent to more than 58% of the total population of the world.

Social networks have become an essential element in the work of individuals in all areas, such as economy, communication, education and politics (López-Carril et al, 2022). The acceleration in digital transformation has meant that the different sectors must respond more efficiently to new challenges.

The new generation of digital learners has developed new ways of understanding, learning and processing information. In this disruptive environment, teachers are looking for new ways that allow them to boost their professional profile. Digitization has come to provide new tools that can be used in the academy to improve and develop knowledge and skills, transforming the educational space into a more innovative environment. In this scenario, individuals see a window of opportunity between the teaching-learning process and the Internet, not only consuming content but also creating it (Gómez-Martínez & Romero-Rodríguez, 2021).

The increasing use of social networks and other Web 2.0 technologies have evolved the way students communicate, collaborate, and learn (Tess, 2013). In this sense, Higher Education Institutions face various circumstances that force them to prepare and learn about new trends in an increasingly demanding market (Palos-Sanchez et la., 2019).

The health crisis caused by COVID-19 imposed many restrictions on university education. Therefore, the academy has been forced to innovate by providing solutions that add value and quality to education in disruptive environments. Teachers have adapted their strategies to acquire and share resources in an evolved digital world, taking advantage of the use of computers, the Internet, mobile devices, and Web 2.0 tools (García-Peñalvo et al., 2012; Saura et al., 2021).

This means that universities must enhance the proper use of these technologies, implementing a significant change in the teaching-learning process that can translate into teaching innovation. In this sense, López-Carril et al., (2022) indicate that social networks have produced an educational revolution by incorporating online or hybrid learning environments, allowing greater flexibility in terms of physical spaces and schedules. Another benefit that this incorporation into the process brings is the continuous contact between teachers and students, which largely allows the creation of new environments, different from the traditional ones, promoting the professional development of the parties (Froment et al., 2022).

Social networks are increasingly used as tools to develop formal and informal learning experiences or spaces, allowing the development of knowledge and social learning (Dabbagh & Kitsantas, 2012). From this point of view, a detailed analysis of how academic staff uses social networks and user-generated content in their teaching practices will allow a broader vision to take advantage of the use of these tools and promote the development of their activities towards a more innovative environment.

The objective of this chapter is to analyze how social networks and user-generated content can be used by university teachers as tools that foster innovation in the teaching-learning process of students. Different aspects related to teaching innovation and the use of social networks are presented, which are explained and discussed.

This chapter is structured as follows: followed by the introduction, a review section of the literature is presented, the next section develops how the content developed in social networks promotes university teaching innovation, through the investigation of the main social networks worldwide (Facebook,

YouTube, WhatsApp Instagram, Twitter, Pinterest and LinkedIn) and the most used academic social networks (Orcid, ResearchGate, Google Scholar and Academia.edu).

LITERATURE REVIEW

Social Networks as a Tool for Teaching Innovation

Technological tools have been a fundamental support for teachers of all levels to more effectively developing the content of their courses. Although social networks are not a new topic, the technological transformation has made access to this type of platform promote social activities for collaboration, communications, community, and creativity (Lim et al, 2014).

According to López-Meneses et al., (2020), the current dynamism of society and students' digital skills demand a new structure in the educational system. In this sense, technological platforms have been incorporated into teaching practices to achieve educational innovation and motivate students who are active users of different social networks. It is important to emphasize that the optimal use of social networks for informative education depends on the strategic implementation of didactic planning. Misuse of these tools can trigger a misperception of the teaching-learning process (Hertzog & Swart, 2018).

Kaplan and Haenlein, (2010), define social networks as digital tools that facilitate the creation, access and exchange of user-generated content for different purposes. Although social networks have not been created for educational purposes (Manca, 2020), the current generation of teachers has been motivated to integrate them into their teaching-learning process (Habibi et al, 2021). This is due to the change in communication between the teacher and the student, allowing a more efficient connection thanks to the use of this type of platform. Mobile devices such as tablets or cell phones are essential for the parties to install applications and contribute to a more innovative teaching-learning process (Gómez-Martínez & Romero-Rodríguez, 2021).

Social networks improve communication between all participants in the educational process, facilitate peer learning, support students and improve self-confidence; build strong connections and community (Sobaih et al., 2016). Other benefits generated from the use of these digital platforms are the development of skills necessary to boost the student's profile, the promotion of creativity, collaborative work, self-learning, constructivist learning and contact with experts (López- Carril et al., 2022; Roses et al, 2013).

Therefore, these social networks can be seen as a means through which teaching-learning practices are transformed so that they are more social, open and collaboration-oriented, supporting the process of knowledge construction and social interaction (Manca & Ranieri, 2016a).

For Manca (2020), social platforms allow mixing all kinds of activities that can be agreed upon by teachers and students, in this way taking advantage of the potential such as, for example, expanding the context for learning, the combination of information, the exchange of learning resources and the hybridization of knowledge.

The use of social networks in Higher Education Institutions results in an improved learning environment in which students are more engaged in the classroom, even so, not all institutions exploit the capacity these for their benefit (Sobaih et al., 2016). The proper use of social networks and the correct implementation of strategically designed activities by teachers mean that student performance is reflected in the improvement in academic results. Martí and Vidal (2018) indicate that pedagogical principles must be followed when including these tools to innovate and improve educational practices.

User-generated Content and Use in Higher Education

The arrival of Web 2.0 has established the foundations for creating and sharing content (Sharma et al., 2016). Universities can also make effective use of social networks as a means of communication.

The participation of the different parties in social networks is of the utmost importance for the Universities. This participation can be described as the interaction of users with the content generated by the different sources, whether internal or external (Fähnrich et al., 2020).

In today's digital economy, business success is attributed to the effective use of information and communications technology. In Higher Education Institutions, the effective use of information and communication technologies is a critical success factor (Dumpit & Fernández, 2017). Therefore, the development of digital skills in the academy is essential for the success and prestige of each institution.

Digital tools have come to contribute in a practical way to the development of courses. Both students and teachers not only search for and share information on the network, but they are also content creators, which allows learning to be improved through the management of spaces, activities and connections with external peers (Dabbagh & Kitsantas, 2012). In this sense, universities should take advantage of the fact that teachers and students are intelligent, proactive technological users and active producers of knowledge (Dumpit & Fernández, 2017) in social networks. Therefore, user-generated content (UGC) for social networks plays an important role in teaching-learning processes (Orús et al., 2016; Saura et al., 2021a).

The UGC is digital academic content that is distributed through different electronic channels, uploaded to a website and can be experienced by e-books, podcasts, tutorials and others (Ryder et al, 2021). This type of content supports the different types of learning and facilitates the teaching-learning processes. The combination of UGC, didactic strategies and technology motivates students and improves their learning results (Orús et al., 2016). A relevant point is that the UGC serves to potentiate the image of the brands, which in this case would be that of the university.

For Borge et al., 2020, learning occurs through the combination of content, the interaction of individuals and cultural tools, which can change over time and due to the objectives of the communities. This content plays a very important role in the teaching-learning process. The (UGC) is described as any type of document (images, videos, texts or audio) that are created to be disseminated through different social platforms (Kaplan & Haenlein, 2010). Being a technique linked to reality, the fact that users can share their ideas and opinions makes the learning experience more natural.

The different UGC such as podcasts, wikis, blogs, tutorials and others allow users to participate by talking, sharing, and joining communities (Bahner et al., 2012). This creates a great opportunity for the university teacher to establish effective communication with the student body. In addition to this, the adoption of mobile devices drives the creation of new options taking advantage of social networks as an educational strategy (Gikas & Grant, 2013).

UGC activities such as communicating with peers, commenting on news, sharing photos or videos, participating in forums, or chatting in real-time result in an interactive social environment that is appropriate for social learning (Sobaih et al., 2016).

The learning experiences are a combination of formal and informal learning, studies indicate that the perception of students regarding the generation of content related to the courses has contributed to directing then learning, expanding the material and promoting the development of communities' informal learning methods (Dabbagh & Kitsantas, 2012).

On the other hand, when teachers post announcements or events, share work-in-progress for feedback, participate in collaborative writing activities, create and disseminate different documents, they create value, so this should be seen as excellent educational practice and academic (Manca & Ranieri, 2016b)

Taking into account the previous arguments, teachers can incorporate UGC in their educational practices in both directions, the content generated by themselves or by students, translating as a systematic and planned transformation in the educational process, or, in other words, in an innovative educational process.

RELEVANT INFORMATION ON SOCIAL NETWORKS USED FOR ACADEMIC PURPOSES

This section explores the most popular social networks by academic staff and students such as Facebook (Meta), YouTube, WhatsApp, Instagram, TikTok, Twitter, Pinterest and LinkedIn. Some statistical data of these applications are also summarized (see Table 1). Information from the academic social networks Orcid, Researchgate, Google Scholar and Academia.edu is also analyzed.

Main Social Networks

Higher education systems constantly experience changes in the teaching-learning process. Social media and other Web 2.0 technologies have created new pathways for communication and interaction between student-instructor, student-student communication, student-community communication, and the rest of the world (Sharma et al., 2016). To apply the UGC adequately, the teachers must detect which is the social network that best suits their didactic strategy and their target audience, such as demographics, which is significant from the educational point of view (Manca, 2020).

Table 1. Statistics of the social networks investigated

Social Network	Statistics
Facebook / Meta	• Users aged 35-44 make up the largest cohort of users • 56.5% of users worldwide are men and 43.5% are women 79% of monthly users are active daily
WhatsApp	• It is the most popular messaging app for all age groups • More than 100 billion messages are sent every day • 45.8% of WhatsApp users are women, while 54.2% identify as men
Youtube	• 92% of Internet users watch some type of online video content every week. • 54% of users are men and 46%, women • How-to videos, tutorial videos, and educational videos are particularly popular with Gen Z
Instagram	• Users aged 25-34 make up the largest cohort of users • It is the preferred social platform of Generation Z • Men make up 51.6% of Instagram users. Women 48.4%
TikTok	• The vast majority of TikTok users are under the age of 30 • Users spend, on average, 19.6 hours per month • 61% of TikTok's user base identifies as female
Pinterest	• The age group is between 18 and 34 years old and is more used by women • 85% of Pinners say they use Pinterest to plan new projects • The platform now has 431 million monthly active users
Twitter	• 38.5% of Twitter users are between 25 and 34 years old • It's more popular with millennials than Gen-Z • 70.4% of platform demographics are male and 29.6% female audience
LinkedIn	• It is most popular with men aged 25-35 and least popular with women over 55 • 77 job applications are submitted every second on LinkedIn • 84% of LinkedIn users connect to the platform to help grow their professional network

Source: Global Report on the Digital Environment (2022)

Facebook or Meta

Facebook is one of the most used networks worldwide. It was created by then-Harvard student Mark Zuckerberg (Tess, 2013). An important fact to mention is that as of 2021 this social network changed its name to Meta, about the metaverse, which is the next step in the evolution of social connections. The latest Global Report on the Digital Environment (2022) shows that Facebook remains the most used social platform in the world.

This social network allows its services to be used inside and outside the classroom as a learning tool, making the most of its potential to improve the educational possibilities of students.

Meta is a key tool for the teaching-learning process that allows education to be more social and is used by many universities around the world. Students invest many hours a day in this network, so universities can take advantage of this to create activities that motivate students to create content that generates value for both parties (Perifanou et al., 2021). This can be very useful to strengthen the bond between the parties and position the university thanks to interactions such as giving a "like" or sharing a publication (Fähnrich et al. 2020).

Al - Bahrani and Patel (2015) indicate some of the strategies that a teacher can implement are: to create a group (more personalized) to communicate with students about course information or share class material; or create a page (more general) to spread news, articles, videos. Teachers can use both strategies to share material they have authored or ask students to generate it.

Manca and Ranieri, (2016a) describe Meta as a promoter of a learning environment enhanced with technology, highlighting the possibility of mixing different information and learning resources, hybridizing different knowledge, and expanding the learning context.

Youtube

YouTube is an informal learning platform where students can find a large number of tutorial videos that are related to the subject matter of the courses and that allow them to solve specific problems (Perifanou et al., 2021).

The Global Report on the Digital Environment (2022), throws several interesting statistics about this network, among them: YouTube has more than 2,560 million active users and is the second most used social network, the average use is 23.7 hours per month, 19 minutes a day, with over 14 billion total views, mobile users visit twice as many pages on YouTube as desktop users.

In the educational field, this tool has great potential, since being free allows access to the content to be used by anyone. Since its inception, YouTube has become the free UGC sharing website due to the ease of creating, uploading and sharing videos (Lee & Lehto, 2013).

A resource that has become extremely important for the teaching-learning process is the video tutorial. This type of content can be created by the teacher as a support for the understanding of a specific topic or as a didactic strategy used by the teacher so that the student obtains a more enriching educational experience. As audiovisual language is present in everyday life, the content generated on this platform allows learning to be reinforced (Balderas & Tapia, 2021). For Rapp et al., 2016, the incorporation of images and words that are presented in a video facilitates learning and the conversion of cognitive information into long-term memory.

The use of YouTube in higher education has benefits such as facilitating the search for videos on any topic, fostering collaboration of the parties, supporting the learning process of its users, facilitating the sharing of content in real-time, and obtaining feedback from students in the entire channel or a specific video (Orús et al., 2016).

WhatsApp

The third most used social network is WhatsApp and it is the favorite of all age groups (Global Report on the Digital Environment, 2022). It is an instant messaging application that works on smart mobile devices and also has a web version. The communication that occurs through this platform is more personalized and closed, allowing users greater privacy. WhatsApp allows you to send text and audio messages, images, videos, and documents in different formats quickly and easily, as well as make calls or video calls to any other user who has the application.

The use of this tool can help higher-level institutions to achieve better social communication with the new generations of digital students by creating a network that allows sharing of ideas about the content of the courses (Mpungose, 2020).

WhatsApp can be used as a communication tool in the educational field since most students use this application to carry out collaborative work with their classmates, establish communication with their teachers, share resources, news, among others (Rodríguez, 2020). Among the academic benefits of this tool is greater ease in sharing learning materials, availability of teachers, and the continuation of learning beyond class hours (Manca, 2020). Like the other tools, teachers can share the material they have created and carry out activities that motivate students to create content that is shared with the rest of the group.

Instagram

Like Facebook, it is one of the preferred networks of students. It has more than 1.5 billion users, ads reach almost 30% of internet users, it is the fourth most popular social network in the world and the average user spends approximately 11.2 hours a month on Instagram (Global Report on the Environment Digital, 2022)

Because this network focuses on the visual part, it can be used for complex educational content that can be explained by a visual representation, which can generate a bond of trust between teachers and students (Perifanou et al., 2021). The ease of use of this platform allows users to take photos or videos, edit them in a simple but professional way and share them in a certain community.

The UGC for this network can be represented by uploading and sharing photos or videos with multiple photographic effects such as filters, frames, retro colors, and others through publications, stories, reels or live videos of educational activities carried out inside or outside the classroom. This type of practice encourages direct communication between students and instructors and vice versa, improves the learning experience through publications of relevant articles or videos, and promotes collaboration among students (Manca, 2020). Like other networks, Instagram is characterized by facilitating the creation of collaborative spaces for educators (Gómez-Martínez & Romero-Rodríguez, 2021).

The fact that teachers can share material made by them through a photo or a short video can encourage students to reinforce the ideas presented in class and retain information, even improve results if students are asked to create their content (Al - Bahrani & Patel, 2015).

TikTok

TikTok is a recently created social network that has grown rapidly worldwide. It was launched in the Chinese market in 2016 as Douyin and internationally in 2017 as TikTok (Fiallos et al., 2021). According to the Global Report on the Digital Environment (2022), it is the sixth most used social platform in the world. This tool allows to create and shares short videos with almost any type of content. It has more than one billion monthly active users, these users use the platform first to find fun/entertaining content, second to post or share content, and third to keep up with the news (Global Report on the Digital Environment, 2022). Being an easy-to-use application with a large number of video editing tools, it can attract the attention of many users (Escamilla-Fajardo et al., 2021).

TikTok has the LearnOnTikTok program where academics have been able to share the educational videos they have created with topics from different areas of teaching, which are linked to the hashtag #learnontiktok (Fiallos et al., 2021). A recent study by Guiñez-Cabrera and Mansilla-Obando (2022), indicates that this platform has multiple benefits for Booktokers (users who share book reviews). Therefore, this can motivate teachers to incorporate this type of educational tactic to encourage student participation in the teaching-learning process.

Twitter

Twitter is a network or microblog that delivers information in real-time. It allows to write only 140 characters per person, this content is known as tweets, which can be original tweets or retweeting information of the people, they "follow", as well as sending private messages and public messages (Bahner et al., 2012).

The content posted on this network can serve to assess trends in the field of education and encourage students to use it as a way to establish a presence on social networks in their professional world and communicate with their peers and other professionals (Camiel et al., 2014). Some of the interactions that can occur, apart from tweets, are retweets, shares by email, replies, likes, details extensions, clicks on embedded media, clicks on hashtags, follows, clicks on user profiles, clicks on links, among others (Ryder et al, 2021)

In the case of Twitter, both teachers and students can create and share educational resources, which creates opportunities and contributes to practicality in formal and informal education (García & Martínez (2021).

Short messages can be easy to send to a large audience in a short time. Some teachers use Twitter as a one-way communication tool, and some choose to reply to any student who chooses to provide feedback, the level of engagement and frequency of communication being an individual decision (Al - Bahrani & Patel, 2015).

LinkedIn

LinkedIn is the world's largest professional network. One of the advantages that universities can have by incorporating this network into their teaching strategy is to connect students with the business world. The use of LinkedIn for the generation of UGC enhances entrepreneurship, innovation and professional development of students (López-Carril et al, 2022).

According to the study carried out by Komljenovic, (2019), the use of LinkedIn by universities can generate notable benefits when the parties share the generated content, namely: students can show their experience, courses and projects to be discovered in recruiter searches, teachers can contact their former students and use them as an example to their new students, groups can be created for discussions and communications with alumni and students, both the university and teachers can create pages to promote themselves or to motivate to students, among others.

The identification of key areas within the content of the course is essential for teachers since through this they can search on this platform for discussions or workshops that allow reinforcing learning results (Cooper & Naatus, 2014). This network fosters an online educational environment that helps develop content and, in turn, the professional profile of both teachers and students (López-Carril et al, 2022).

Pinterest

Pinterest is a visual social network that allows users to create and manage, personal themed boards, collections of images or videos, interests, hobbies, and more. This network has millions of pins that can be used to inspire both teachers and students to create educational activities that contribute to the development of courses. Users can organize their content through Pins or bookmarks and save them on the boards that are the places where all the found material is kept, collected, and organized.

According to the Global Report on the Digital Environment (2022), people use Pinterest in different ways, a significant percentage of users are planners and use the platform when they are in the early stages of a project. Another important point is that Pinterest banned political ads in 2018 and this has generated a feeling of positivity among users (Global Report on the Digital Environment, 2022). One of the advantages of Pinterest is its ability to save links to resources and organize them by theme in a very easy and accessible way for users, which allows easy access to the material.

As mentioned by Manca (2020), the pedagogical value of this tool is based on the organization of digital sources or Pins that support the process of building teaching resources. In this sense, a teacher can create a virtual scrapbook to make their students aware of the content of interest in the simplest way possible.

This tool represents a space for teachers to create, find practices, connect, interact, share new resources, establish networks, promote collaboration and content exchange (Lundgren et al., 2021)

Academic Social Networks

Thanks to the Internet, many platforms have been created that have made it possible to reinforce communication about the teaching-learning process of universities. Academic social networks have been able to link the different parties involved in the research area. These types of social networks have changed academic communication schemes by providing an alternative method for discovering publications and creating spaces for academics to publish their profile, their work, and connect with others (Thelwall & Kousha, 2015). The content generated and shared by academics on these platforms greatly contributes to teachers using quality material so that students can carry out didactic activities. Furthermore, they allow informal communication that is not possible with the formal publication process (Ovadia, 2014).

ORCID

ORCID (Open Researcher and Contributor ID) is an academic social platform with more than 13.7 million iDs. ORCID provides a digital identifier and connects and exchanges data with existing profiling services. Its features include allowing researchers to manually add references, upload publication lists, and other personal or academic information (Mikki et al., 2015). This academic network allows linking digital research papers and other contributions supporting research, collaboration and evaluation (Haak et al., 2012).

ResearchGate

On ResearchGate, researchers create their profiles with academic information, share posts, participate in discussions, write messages, and vote for or against content (Mikki et al., 2015). This network allows academics to share each of their publications on their profiles, which can potentially provide an additional point of access to research (Thelwall & Kousha, 2015). Among the functionalities of are that it allows loading and classifying a wide variety of academic materials such as articles published in high-impact journals to patents, conference communications, course materials, presentations, or datasets, as well as the interaction of people and institutions interested in shared content (Orduña-Malea et al., 2016).

Google Scholar

Google Scholar is a free search engine for academic literature, the citations of associates provide the possibility of creating a unique profile that contains the list of publications authored or co-authored by the researcher, and based on this the number of citations and the number of citations is calculated h-index (Mikki et al., 2015). This web browser allows you to share different documents such as academic articles from journals or conferences, theses, books, summaries, technical reports and others, allowing the academic to take advantage of the social components of the platform (Zientek et al., 2018).

Academia.edu

In Academia.edu, the researcher creates a profile, uploads publications, follows colleagues, can participate in debates and, together with ORCID, offers a unique identifier independent of the researcher's publication record (Thelwall & Kousha, 2015). This website allows researchers to publish their articles, and discover and read articles from their peers, combining the function of social networks, such as profiles, news sources, recommendations and the ability to follow people and topics (Niyazov et al., 2016).

DISCUSSION AND CONCLUSION

The information collected in this chapter allows for establishing some conclusions related to the research question, which are discussed in this section.

Web 2.0 has achieved that Universities have transformed their teaching-learning process and can be available anywhere and at any time. Today's digital world makes it easier for people to stay connected and for communication to be more seamless and virtually borderless. Social networks are already part of everyday life, most teachers use them in their personal lives and have involved them in part of their academic life. With the crisis caused by the COVID-19 pandemic, governments decreed the closure of different institutions, including those of higher education. With the new measures, classes were allowed to resume virtually, which caused academics to start looking for new strategies to be able to teach their lessons, developing creativity and turning it into teaching innovation.

There is great value in the use of social networks for academic purposes, even so, their use should be exploited in educational activities (Sobaih et al., 2016). In this sense, the university authorities must consider that for adequate incorporation of social networks and related didactic strategies to take place, they must know what the previous experiences of teachers are with information and communication technologies in education, their attitudes towards digital media, and their expectations, their pedagogical beliefs and current practices (Manca & Ranieri, 2016a).

One of the key points in the success of the implementation of social networks and the generation of content by teachers and students is to have clear rules. Spending time explaining how to use social networks for class purposes and content generation activities can benefit the parties in feeling comfortable and satisfied in the process and in the result that can be obtained (Al - Bahrani & Patel, 2015). The use of social networks can complement learning management systems and combine traditional learning with new technologies, taking advantage of the benefits of each platform to develop pedagogical activities that contribute to teaching innovation and that are perceived by students positively.

It is important to emphasize that academic social networks also bring many benefits that teachers can take advantage of to promote their teaching strategies. An objective of the universities is to carry out research and its due publication. The creation of this type of content positions and gives prestige to Higher Education Institutions. These networks allow academics to upload and share their work, and also protect their copyright (Ovadia, 2014).

Theoretical Implications

From a theoretical point of view, other researchers can take this research as an exploratory starting point for the development of research focused on understanding how to boost the digital presence and reputation of teachers in academic social networks. In this way, future theoretical models focused on identifying the influence of social networks on the academic results of teachers could be carried out. Furthermore, from a theoretical point of view, this study proposes the use of UGC databases as a valid means for the development of academic studies.

Practical Implications

Universities should encourage teachers to be active creators of content and to incorporate educational activities into their teaching strategies that encourage the generation of valuable content for the Institution's social networks. The UGC allows for strengthening trust between Higher Education Institutions and the parties involved in the teaching-learning process.

Universities and academic staff must take into account that the current technological transformation brings with it a new way of interacting with the new digital generations. The creation of creative and innovative content is fundamental, if it is analyzed from the point of view that it is produced with high-quality standards, it will have repercussions on the positioning of institutions at a local and international level.

However, it cannot be ignored that there is a digital divide. These disparities are reflected in the material, content, cultural and academic divisions (Habibi et al, 2021). Social media can be an effective tool for the teaching-learning process and can help bridge the digital divide between institutions and their new generation of digital native students (Sobaih et al., 2016).

Through this research, it can be concluded that social networks and UGC contribute significantly to teaching innovation if used correctly. With clear didactic objectives and creative practical activities, teachers can promote and motivate student learning, seeing their effort reflected in better results.

Limitations and Future Research

Finally, other studies on this topic could address the limitations regarding the methodology used and complement the descriptive methods. Future research may focus on analyzing how social networking sites are changing scholarly communication in different parts of the world.

REFERENCES

Al-Bahrani, A., & Patel, D. (2015). Incorporating Twitter, Instagram, and Facebook in economics classrooms. *The Journal of Economic Education*, *46*(1), 56–67. doi:10.1080/00220485.2014.978922

Bahner, D. P., Adkins, E., Patel, N., Donley, C., Nagel, R., & Kman, N. E. (2012). How we use social media to supplement a novel curriculum in medical education. *Medical Teacher*, *34*(6), 439–444. doi:10.3109/0142159X.2012.668245 PMID:22449268

Balderas, S. V., & Tapia, J. M. (2021). Learning experiences on YouTube, an analysis during the COVID-19 pandemic. *IE Journal of Educational Research of the REDIECH*, (12), 18.

Borge, M., Ong, Y. S., & Goggins, S. (2020). A sociocultural approach to using social networking sites as learning tools. *Educational Technology Research and Development*, *68*(3), 1089–1120. doi:10.100711423-019-09721-z

Camiel, L. D., Goldman-Levine, J. D., Kostka-Rokosz, M. D., & McCloskey, W. W. (2014). Twitter as a medium for pharmacy students' personal learning network development. *Currents in Pharmacy Teaching & Learning*, *6*(4), 463–470. doi:10.1016/j.cptl.2014.04.008

Cooper, B., & Naatus, M. K. (2014). LinkedIn as a learning tool in business education. *American Journal of Business Education*, *7*(4), 299–306. doi:10.19030/ajbe.v7i4.8815

Dabbagh, N., & Kitsantas, A. (2012). Personal Learning Environments, social media, and self-regulated learning: A natural formula for connecting formal and informal learning. *The Internet and higher education*, *15*(1), 3–8. doi:10.1016/j.iheduc.2011.06.002

Dumpit, D. Z., & Fernandez, C. J. (2017). Analysis of the use of social media in Higher Education Institutions (HEIs) using the Technology Acceptance Model. *International Journal of Educational Technology in Higher Education*, *14*(1), 1–16. doi:10.118641239-017-0045-2

Escamilla-Fajardo, P., Sheriff, M., & López-Carril, S. (2021). Incorporating TikTok in higher education: Pedagogical perspectives from a corporal expression sport sciences course. *Journal of Hospitality, Leisure, Sport and Tourism Education*, *28*, 100302. doi:10.1016/j.jhlste.2021.100302

Fähnrich, B., Vogelgesang, J., & Scharkow, M. (2020). Evaluating universities' strategic online communication: How do Shanghai Ranking's top 50 universities grow stakeholder engagement with Facebook posts? *Journal of Communication Management (London)*, *3*(24), 265–283. doi:10.1108/JCOM-06-2019-0090

Fiallos, A., Fiallos, C., & Figueroa, S. (2021, July). Tiktok and Education: Discovering Knowledge through Learning Videos. *2021 Eighth International Conference on eDemocracy & eGovernment (ICEDEG)*, 172-176 10.1109/ICEDEG52154.2021.9530988

Froment, F., García-González, A. J., & Cabero-Almenara, J. (2022). The relationship of Twitter with teacher credibility and motivation in university students. *Communicate (High Wycombe)*, *30*(71), 131–142. doi:10.3916/C71-2022-10

García-Peñalvo, F. J., Johnson, M., Alves, G. R., Minović, M., & Conde-González, M. Á. (2014). Informal learning recognition through a cloud ecosystem. *Future Generation Computer Systems*, *32*, 282–294. doi:10.1016/j.future.2013.08.004

Gikas, J., & Grant, M. M. (2013). Mobile computing devices in higher education: Student perspectives on learning with cellphones, smartphones & social media. *The Internet and Higher Education*, *19*, 18–26. doi:10.1016/j.iheduc.2013.06.002

Global Report on the Digital Environment 2022. (2022). *Hootsuite*. https://hootsuite.com/en/resources/digital-trends-2021

Gómez-Martínez, R., & Romero-Rodriguez, L. M. (2021). Coworking spaces and virtual learning communities in Social Networks: Case Study of# ElClaustroDeIG on Instagram. *Open Classroom*, *50*(1), 453–464. doi:10.17811/rifie.50.1.2021.453-464

Guiñez-Cabrera, N., & Mansilla-Obando, K. (2022). Booktokers: Generate and share content about books through TikTok. *Communicate: Scientific Journal of Communication and Education*, *30*(71).

Haak, L. L., Fenner, M., Paglione, L., Pentz, E., & Ratner, H. (2012). ORCID: A system to uniquely identify researchers. *Learned Publishing*, *25*(4), 259–264. doi:10.1087/20120404

Habibi, A., Yaakob, M. F. M., Mukminin, A., Muhaimin, M., Prasojo, L. D., Yusop, F. D., & Muzakkir, M. (2021). Teachers' digital technology access to motivation, skills and use: A structural equation modeling study. *Aslib Journal of Information Management*, *4*(73), 543–559. doi:10.1108/AJIM-11-2020-0382

Hertzog, P. E., & Swart, A. J. (2018, April). The use of WhatsApp in design-based modules. In *2018 IEEE Global Engineering Education Conference (EDUCON)* (pp. 445-450). IEEE. 10.1109/EDUCON.2018.8363264

Kaplan, A. M., & Haenlein, M. (2010). Users of the world, unite! The challenges and opportunities of Social Media. *Business Horizons*, *53*(1), 59–68. doi:10.1016/j.bushor.2009.09.003

Komljenovic, J. (2019). Linkedin, platforming labour, and the new employability mandate for universities. *Globalisation, Societies and Education*, *17*(1), 28–43. doi:10.1080/14767724.2018.1500275

Lee, D. Y., & Lehto, M. R. (2013). User acceptance of YouTube for procedural learning: An extension of the Technology Acceptance Model. *Computers & Education*, *61*, 193–208. doi:10.1016/j.compedu.2012.10.001

Lim, J. S. Y., Agostinho, S., Harper, B., & Chicharo, J. (2014). The engagement of social media technologies by undergraduate informatics students for academic purpose in Malaysia. *Journal of Information. Communication and Ethics in Society*, *3*(12), 177–194.

López-Carril, S., Sheriff, M., & Anagnostopoulos, C. (2022). LinkedIn in sport management education: Developing the students' professional profile boosting the teaching-learning process. *International Journal of Management Education*, *20*(1), 100611.

López-Meneses, E., Sirignano, F. M., Vázquez-Cano, E., & Ramírez-Hurtado, J. M. (2020). University students' digital competence in three areas of the DigCom 2.1 model: A comparative study at three European universities. *Australasian Journal of Educational Technology*, *36*(3), 69–88.

Lundgren, L., Curcio, R., & Schroeder, S. E. (2021). Are you a team player or a personal pinner? situating pinterest as part of teachers' online and offline professional learning networks. *Innovación Educativa (México, D.F.)*, *3*(1), 1–13.

Manca, S. (2020). Snapping, pinning, liking or texting: Investigating social media in higher education beyond Facebook. *The Internet and Higher Education*, *44*, 100707.

Manca, S., & Ranieri, M. (2016). Yes for sharing, not for teaching!": Social Media in academic practices. *The Internet and Higher Education*, *29*, 63–74.

Manca, S., & Ranieri, M. (2016). Facebook and the others. Potentials and obstacles of social media for teaching in higher education. *Computers & Education*, *95*, 216–230.

Marcelo Garcia, C., & Marcelo Martinez, P. (2021). Educational influencers on Twitter: Hashtag analysis and relational structure. *Comunicar: Ibero-American Scientific Journal of Communication and Education, 29*(68), 73-83.

Mikki, S., Zygmuntowska, M., Gjesdal, Ø. L., & Al Ruwehy, H. A. (2015). Digital presence of Norwegian scholars on academic network sites—Where and who are they? *PLoS One*, *10*(11), e0142709.

Mpungose, C. B. (2020). Is Moodle or WhatsApp the preferred e-learning platform at a South African university? First-year students' experiences. *Education and Information Technologies*, *25*(2), 927–941.

Niyazov, Y., Vogel, C., Price, R., Lund, B., Judd, D., Akil, A., & Shron, M. (2016). Open access meets discoverability: Citations to articles posted to Academia. edu. *Plos One, 11*(2), e0148257.

Orduña-Malea, E., Martín-Martín, A., & Delgado-López-Cózar, E. (2016). ResearchGate as a source of scientific evaluation: Revealing its bibliometric applications. *Information Professional*, *25*(2), 303–310.

Ovadia, S. (2014). ResearchGate and Academia. edu: Academic social networks. *Behavioral & Social Sciences Librarian*, *33*(3), 165–169.

Palos-Sanchez, P., Saura, J. R., & Martin-Velicia, F. (2019). A study of the effects of programmatic advertising on users' concerns about privacy overtime. *Journal of Business Research*, *96*, 61–72. https://doi.org/10.1016/j.jbusres.2018.10.059

Perifanou, M., Tzafilkou, K., & Economides, A. A. (2021). The Role of Instagram, Facebook, and YouTube Frequency of Use in University Students' Digital Skills Components. *Education in Science*, *11*(12), 766.

Rapp, A. K., Healy, M. G., Charlton, M. E., Keith, J. N., Rosenbaum, M. E., & Kapadia, M. R. (2016). YouTube is the most frequently used educational video source for surgical preparation. *Journal of Surgical Education*, *73*(6), 1072–1076.

Rodriguez Valerio, D. (2020). Beyond instant messaging: WhatsApp as a mediation and support tool in the teaching of Library Science. *Información, Cultura y Sociedad*, (42), 107–126.

Roses, S., Aguilar, M.G., & Farias, P. (2013). the academic use of social networks: a comparative analysis between Science students and social science students / Academic use of social networks: comparative analysis between science and literature students. *History and Social Communication*, 667-679.

Ryder, B., Zhang, T., & Hua, N. (2021). The Social Media "Magic": Virtually Engaging Visitors during COVID-19 Temporary Closures. *Administrative Sciences*, *11*(2), 53.

Saura, J. R., Ribeiro-Soriano, D., & Palacios-Marqués, D. (2021). Setting privacy "by default" in social IoT: Theorizing the challenges and directions in Big Data Research. *Big Data Research*, *25*. doi:10.1016/j.bdr.2021.100245

Saura, J. R., Ribeiro-Soriano, D., & Palacios-Marqués, D. (2021a). Using data mining techniques to explore security issues in smart living environments in Twitter. *Computer Communications*, *179*, 285–295. https://doi.org/10.1016/j.comcom.2021.08.021

Sharma, S. K., Joshi, A., & Sharma, H. (2016). A multi-analytical approach to predict the Facebook usage in higher education. *Computers in Human Behavior*, *55*, 340–353.

Sobaih, A. E. E., Moustafa, M. A., Ghandforoush, P., & Khan, M. (2016). To use or not to use? Social media in higher education in developing countries. *Computers in Human Behavior*, *58*, 296–305.

Tess, P. A. (2013). The role of social media in higher education classes (real and virtual)–A literature review. *Computers in Human Behavior*, *29*(5), A60–A68.

Thelwall, M., & Kousha, K. (2015). ResearchGate: Disseminating, communicating, and measuring Scholarship? *Journal of the Association for Information Science and Technology*, *66*(5), 876–889.

Zientek, L. R., Werner, J. M., Campuzano, M. V., & Nimon, K. (2018). The use of Google Scholar for research and research dissemination. *New Horizons in Adult Education and Human Resource Development*, *30*(1), 39–46.

KEY TERMS AND DEFINITIONS

Academic Content: A set of knowledge, skills and abilities that are embodied in a study plan.

Social Networks: Social networks are structures formed on the Internet by people or organizations that connect based on common interests or values.

Teaching Innovation: Systematic and planned incorporation of practices that transform and improve teaching-learning processes.

Teaching Strategies: Procedures and resources used by the teacher to promote meaningful learning efficiently and effectively.

Teaching-Learning Process: A relationship that exists between the teacher and the student by which it is intended to transmit knowledge in a certain area.

User-Generated Content: Images, videos, text, or audio files, which are posted online on social networks.

Web 2.0: Websites that facilitate information sharing, interoperability, user-centered design, and collaboration.

Section 2

Section 2 compiles the main case studies that analyze the implementation of teaching innovation practices in universities. Likewise, it presents in-depth case studies of teaching innovation in different subjects and academic themes.

Chapter 5
Shifting the Ownership of Learning From Instructor to Students Through Student-Led Instructor-Facilitated Guided-Inquiry Learning

Tanya Gupta
https://orcid.org/0000-0003-2246-9611
University of Oregon, USA

K. A. Burke
Iowa State University, USA

Thomas J. Greenbowe
University of Oregon, USA

ABSTRACT

This chapter presents an overview of the development and implementation of a student-centered teaching approach, namely the Student-Led Instructor Facilitated Guided-Inquiry Learning (SLIFGIL), in an undergraduate chemistry laboratory course. SLIFGIL is a hybrid approach to teaching and is based on the science writing heuristic (SWH) approach used in the laboratory settings. The SWH approach has been used for two decades in school and college science classrooms. Prior studies have reported the effectiveness of the SWH approach in improving student academic performance and conceptual understanding. Though the SWH approach has its strengths, student participation in collaborative group work and continued reliance on the instructor to step in to guide the flow of laboratory activities and facilitate student learning was observed to be a challenge by the first author. To address these challenges, SLIFGIL approach was developed to shift the ownership of learning to the students. In this chapter, an overview of the SLIFGIL approach and results on its effectiveness are presented.

DOI: 10.4018/978-1-6684-4441-2.ch005

Copyright © 2022, IGI Global. Copying or distributing in print or electronic forms without written permission of IGI Global is prohibited.

INTRODUCTION

Laboratory instruction is important to engage students in scientific investigations and to provide them a firsthand experience of conducting an authentic scientific study. Laboratory instruction should enable students to support or refute a hypothesis through experimentation and build their scientific understanding and laboratory skills during the laboratory work. Despite repeated calls for incorporating student-centered practices in college chemistry laboratory courses and engaging students in active-learning inquiry-based experiences there has been little success in achieving the goal of fostering an appreciation and liking for scientific inquiry among students through laboratory experimentation. Two major issues have impacted laboratory instruction. First, the student perceptions of scientific inquiry and their interactions in the laboratory are often neglected by instructors. Secondly, across the nation most laboratory instructors engage in traditional verification laboratory practices (Hofstein & Lunetta, 1982; Johnson & Johnson, 1985). The problem with the traditional verification laboratory instruction is that the students already know the outcome of the laboratory experiment which limits any opportunities for the students to engage in the process of scientific inquiry through experimentation. These issues have remained unaddressed despite proven research on the use of extended, reflective inquiry-based investigations for a meaningful learning of science.

The present study addresses these challenges in the context of chemistry laboratory teaching by highlighting the development and implementation of the Student Led Instructor Facilitated Guided Inquiry Learning (SLIFGIL) approach. This study fills an important gap in the literature on active learning in science teaching laboratories specifically on the use of guided inquiry teaching wherein it is feasible to gradually train students to be actively involved in the learning process. The study shows that laboratories could be transformative for student learning with carefully and systematically designed pedagogical approaches that focus on the role of instructor as a facilitator and students as peer-leaders.

BACKGROUND

Prior Research on the SWH Approach

Prior studies on the SWH approach have highlighted the merits of using the SWH approach in laboratory teaching and provided evidence of the impact of the SWH approach on student critical thinking skills (Gupta et al., 2014), conceptual understanding and student beliefs and attitudes toward chemistry (Putti, 2011; Poock et al., 2007; Rudd et al., 2001; Stephenson & McKnight, 2016). These studies have compared the SWH approach to traditional laboratory teaching. Table 1 highlights the differences between the SWH approach and the traditional laboratory instruction.

Table 1. Difference between traditional and SWH approach to laboratory instruction

Segment of Laboratory	Traditional Laboratory Instruction	The SWH Approach
Pre-laboratory session	a. Instructor centered: Teaching Assistant (TA) or the instructor gives explicit directions and asks questions that require students to regurgitate the procedure as described in the experimental write-up (laboratory manual). b. Instructor leads the pre-laboratory session and asks students to follow the procedure and the safety guidelines.	a. Student-centered: students come prepared with beginning questions, safety and procedure outline based on an experimental write-up that requires students to have an input in procedure based on the information provided about equipment, and reagents. The procedure is not explicit. b. Students discuss their individual beginning questions in small groups and share their group questions on the board. c. The instructor leads discussion of class beginning questions and the class narrows down the question that can be answered by experimentation. d. Students discuss the safety and procedure and the data that needs to be collected to answer the beginning questions. A template of data table is made on the white board and the excel spreadsheet in computer. e. Instructor demonstrates the equipment and techniques. During demonstration the instructor asks questions to scaffold student understanding.
During Laboratory: Students perform the experimental work	a. Students follow the procedure outlined in the laboratory manual and as instructed. b. Students remain at their bench for laboratory work and perhaps interact with their peer when working on experiment in pairs. c. Students may receive some directions from the instructor if they have incorrect set-up.	a. Students perform laboratory experiment to answer the beginning questions. b. Students talk to other group members and with different groups to compare and discuss their findings.
Data collection	Students check with one another on correctness of data, and completion of experiment and when they collect the data and observations, they leave the laboratory.	a. Each group enters the data in the class data table on the whiteboard and in the excel spreadsheet. b. Groups that finish their experimental part and data collection, moved around the laboratory to check with other groups and help their peers with completing their tasks and with performing calculations. c. Instructor usually facilitates students collaborative group work and thought processes by asking questions and guiding the flow of activities.
Discussion	Students may ask questions from their peer (lab-partner) or from the instructor and then leave the laboratory. There is no structured discussion.	a. When more than half (about 75% students) have entered the class data, students are encouraged to seek trends to answer the class beginning questions. If data are inconsistent with the trend, or if there are errors, then students are expected to do more trials. b. Students work together with their peers and the instructor to negotiate the meaning, construct their conceptual understanding and answer BQs as a large group. c. Students write and discuss claims to answer their BQs and provide supporting evidence for their claims. d. The laboratory ends with a post-laboratory discussion among all students. Discussion is facilitated by the instructor and is focused on the overall experimental investigation, pattens and anomalies in data and findings, and errors that may have led to the anomalies. At this point the applications of the concepts relevant to the subject and some real-world examples are also discussed among the students or presented by the instructor.

Since the scientific argument and writing to learn science are the key emphasis of the SWH approach, the SWH approach involves an emphasis on the student-written laboratory report in a format that differs from the traditionally written student-laboratory reports. These differences in the laboratory report formats are summarized in Table 2.

Table 2. A comparison of traditional and SWH report format

Traditional Lab Report	SWH Lab Report
Title, purpose: Students write the title and purpose of the experiment as provided in laboratory manual	**Beginning Question (BQ)**: What are some questions that I can investigate in the laboratory?
Safety: Safety precautions are listed based on the description of procedure	**Safety Concerns and Waste Disposal**: How will I stay safe? How will I address the waste generated in laboratory?
Outline and procedure: detailed step-by-step procedure is provided to students, and they provide outline of the detailed procedure	**Procedure and Tests**: How can I answer my question? What experiments will I perform?
Data and observations: Students collect data based on procedure. They know what to expect and observe.	**Observations**: What do I see? What is my data and what calculations I need to do?
Balanced equations, calculations, and graphs: Balanced equations and descriptions, sample calculations and graphs are provided for students. They provide information from experiment based on these examples from the laboratory manual once the findings have been verified to be according to the details of the experiment provided in the laboratory manual.	**Claim**: What can I claim? Claim answers Beginning questions and is specific to the questions that students decide during the laboratory as a group.
Discussions and conclusion: Students discuss their results and make conclusions verifying that their results were consistent with experimental description and why their findings are closer to or different from the expected results.	**Evidence**: How do I know, what I know (claim). How do the data and observations support my claim?
	Reading and Reflection: What are some sources of errors? What will I do to address these errors in future investigations? How do my ideas compare with other's ideas in class through reading of literature and other scientific resources? How have my ideas changed? What is the application of the concepts discovered through investigation? Based on the experiments, what are some new questions worth investigating?

The effectiveness of guided-inquiry based teaching approaches such as the SWH depends on the training and preparation of instructors and graduate teaching assistants (who usually teach laboratory courses at the college-level) and their experience with student-centered practices in laboratory. In case of the SWH approach, the quality of implementation and the subsequent student success depends on the appropriate use of four pedagogical foci identified by Hand (2008). These include dialogical interaction, focus of learning, connection to the big ideas, and scientific argument. Implementation of the SWH approach and student buy-in of the SWH approach is not an automatic process. A high-quality implementation of the SWH approach while using each of the four foci depends on the prior knowledge and experience of the instructor regarding learning theories, and experience with guided inquiry as an instructional approach. Some researchers who have studied the SWH approach have provided evidence of the high quality of implementation of the SWH approach and its impact on student academic performance.

Despite these success stories, the SWH approach has limitations that hold it from operating at a high level of student participation and engagement in scientific practices in the first and second semester of general chemistry courses. These limitations arise from the a) TA resistance to using an unfamiliar teaching approach, b) student understanding of the SWH laboratory instruction, c) the time it takes for the students to understand and adapt to the SWH based laboratories and writing laboratory reports in the SWH format, and d) Lack of student motivation to complete the pre-laboratory write-up requirement to participate and contribute to the active learning during the SWH-based laboratory experiments. Each of these limitations is explored in detail followed by overview of the SLIGIL approach, its implementation and the study comparing the SLFGIL approach, and the instructor facilitated SWH approach.

The Limitations of the SWH Approach

As mentioned in the prior section, the SWH approach is most beneficial when its implementation is of the highest quality and focused on dialogic interaction, student-learning, connection of the content to the big-ideas in science, and is argument driven. In essence, students in the SWH based laboratory experience collaborative work wherein they contribute and share their questions, refine procedure, collect data and observations, make and debate claim and evidence, and reflect on the big ideas and the applications of concepts. Students also individually write laboratory reports which involves using the SWH format (Table 2). In these laboratory reports students attempt to make sense of their collaborative experience to coherently construct the knowledge of the scientific concepts and principles that they discover and unravel while conducting the laboratory investigation and engaging in a dialogical interaction with the peers and the instructor. Several factors limit the SWH approach from being implemented at the highest level for student collaboration and engagement. Some of these factors are:

1. **Instructor resistance to using an unfamiliar teaching approach:** In the first authors institution laboratory instruction is mainly conducted by the graduate teaching assistants (GTAs). All first-year graduate students serve as GTAs during the first semester and over time they may continue to have teaching duties depending on the departmental needs. All GTAs are provided sufficient training for guided inquiry based SWH approach. However, a vast majority of GTAs who have experienced traditional instruction as students try to adapt a similar approach as a teacher and resist implementing student-centered teaching approaches. These GTAs have experienced their teachers providing them all the relevant information they need to perform the experiment following stepwise directions and verifying a result that is expected for a given experiment. The GTAs that have experienced traditional instruction as a student find the SWH approach to imply a lack of control in their teaching of laboratories and requiring more teaching and grading time as compared to the traditional approach of laboratory instruction. Usually after a semester of teaching general chemistry using the SWH approach the GTAs show a preference for teaching a laboratory course that involves traditional instruction. The GTA resistance to the SWH approach is not helpful in having a quality implementation of this teaching approach. This negatively impacts the learning of students who do not experience the benefits of engaging in SWH-based learning.
2. **Student understanding of the guided-inquiry instruction:** The challenge of the student understanding of the SWH approach arises from student prior experience in high school science courses. Students usually have little exposure to conducting laboratory experiments and writing laboratory reports. Like the GTAs most freshmen students who have experienced traditional laboratory teaching as students struggle to understand and adapt to the SWH approach that requires them to develop questions for investigation, create an outline of procedure, and consider safety aspects for the experiments. Students who come from instructor-controlled environments struggle with the idea of having a discussion with their peers. When asked to work collaboratively students either struggle with the topic of discussion or go off-topic being unsure of the expectations. Some students remain silent and chose not to contribute to discussions.

3. **Longer time for the students to understand and adapt to the guided-inquiry laboratories and writing laboratory reports in a specific format:** Scientific communication is an important skill, and the prior experience of students shapes how they perceive laboratory report writing. Lack of exposure to student centered learning and prior limited experiences with writing full laboratory reports slows student engagement during SWH laboratory. It takes persistent effort and substantial time for students to participate in the SWH based approach to learning in the laboratory. Further, instructor must provide detailed feedback to student on the structure of laboratory report and how to communicate science effectively based on weekly laboratory investigations.
4. **Lack of student motivation to participate and contribute to active learning during the SWH-based laboratory experiments:** The lack of student motivation and active participation in student-centered approaches such as SWH stems from student prior experiences, but this also relates to the level of training and implementation of student-centered approaches by the instructor. While some students display a proactive approach to learning, a fairly large number of students believe that it is the responsibility of their teaching assistants or instructor to give direct instruction on data collection and observations. Students sometimes end up rejecting the newer teaching method and block their minds to any expectations their instructor outlines for preparation of laboratory. This lowers student participation in the activity. While students may show resistance to participation by not answering questions or coming unprepared to do the laboratory, an instructor with limited experience with SWH instruction may not be able to use effective strategies and resources that foster student engagement and participation during an SWH based laboratory.
5. **Student performance in standardized tests and laboratory practical exams:** Student performance may become a deterrent for a high-quality implementation of SWH approach by the instructor. This could happen when students struggle to connect their understanding of the laboratory experiments or the macroscopic observations in the laboratory to similar problems presented in the hands-on the laboratory exams, and in the standardized assessments that cover the same chemistry concepts. Guided inquiry-based instruction through SWH requires a high level of training and use of student-centered strategies to help students make connections between the macroscopic observations in the laboratory, the symbolic conceptual and numerical problems presented in chemistry, and the real-world applications of the concepts discovered in the laboratory. Coupled with other factors of instructor resistance, student adaptation to SWH approach, time to comprehend SWH based learning and laboratory report write-up, lack of student motivation, the student performance in exams and standardized tests makes it difficult to fully utilize the benefits of the SWH approach to laboratory instruction.

The SLIFGIL Approach: An Overview

Effectiveness of the SWH depends on the preparation and training that the instructors or GTAs receive and the acceptance by the students for the approach (Rudd et al., 2001; Burke et al., 2005; Poock et al., 2007). An expert instructor is aware of strategies to enable students to share their thinking, challenges student misconceptions by carefully designing learning activities, and scaffolds students' understanding by asking guiding questions (Clough, 2002). Undergraduate chemistry laboratories are taught by GTA's in most institutions. The GTAs receive cursory training at the beginning of their TA career and may have a limited exposure to active learning during the training sessions. Students' perceptions and their interactions with one another are neglected aspects of laboratory instruction (Hofstein & Lunnetta,

1982). Studies have shown that a greater degree of participation of students in the laboratory may lead to a more positive attitude of students towards the laboratory. Cooperation should be the dominant interaction pattern in science classrooms and laboratories. In a situation where teachers perceive widely different interaction patterns among students, the approach to instruction must be modified to meet student needs. Teachers' guidance of student's interactions influences the way students learn, and the attitudes they form about the subject (Johnson & Johnson, 1985).

In this study the limitations of the SWH approach were addressed by shifting the ownership of learning to students by implementing student roles for learning in a chemistry laboratory. Students were assigned roles that are consistent with the laboratory format for the SWH approach such as Beginning Question expert, Safety expert, Data Table expert, Claims and Evidence expert. Student role assignment was done to determine if this modification in SWH approach implementation would enable (a) students own their learning; (b) come prepared with ideas and questions for the experiments and, (c) respect each other as members of collaborative learning groups. The modified SWH approach is referred to as SLIFGIL.

Modification of SWH Leading Towards the Ownership of Student Learning Through the Student-led Instructor Facilitated Guided-Inquiry Learning (SLIFGIL)

The SWH approach to teaching applies the principles of guided-inquiry and a learning cycle approach to teaching. The SWH based laboratories differ from the traditional verification/cookbook laboratories fundamentally in the laboratory environment and laboratory report format. As opposed to traditional laboratories in which the students work individually and follow a step-by-step procedure for verification of concepts/principles, SWH laboratories require students to propose a question for investigation (on topics from their lab manual), design a procedure with guidance to answer their question, and establish the safety measures required for the activity. Refer to Table 1 for the differences between the SWH and traditional laboratory approach.

In this study, the SWH approach was modified to understand the effects of assigning students the responsibility of leading laboratory discussion about targeted topics and assisting the instructor to conduct the laboratory effectively. This method was implemented in two lab sections of the first semester of a general chemistry course at a midwestern institution (N=32). The carry-over effects of implementing student roles in a SWH based laboratory were studied for students who continued with the second semester of the general chemistry sequence.

Students in these student-led instructor facilitated guided-inquiry learning based laboratories were assigned to groups designated by letters of the alphabet (A, B, C, D and E) with five students per group. Students wore their nametags in the laboratory with their group alphabet designation. Each laboratory session opened with the students of each group leading different laboratory components. Roles were assigned to students at beginning of the lab period. Students were given their role assignment each week when they met in the laboratory and were not provided any advanced information about which group would lead the laboratory on a given week. The roles were changed for students on a weekly basis.

The roles consist of Beginning Question expert, Safety expert, Procedure expert, Data Table expert, and Claims and Evidence expert. For example, at beginning of the laboratory session the instructor called all the students in group A. The students of the selected group were then provided with the role-cards to choose their role (for example, who wants to be the Beginning Question expert from the selected group). Once students selected their roles, they were referred to as the experts for that component of the

SWH format. The Beginning question expert's role was to help all the students in the class to get in their groups and discuss the beginning question that individual students had in their pre-laboratory write-up. The Beginning question expert thus facilitated all students in class students to discuss the beginning questions and write their beginning questions as a pair on the chalkboard. The experts also discuss their own questions while they lead the class within the group of experts. Each group of students in the class is encouraged to contribute at least one beginning question. The Beginning question expert then engages the entire class to select one class beginning question and identify the variables to be explored. Here the instructor assists the Beginning Question expert to prompt class to think about which questions can be answered by experimentation alone. The instructor asks questions to the BQ expert to help them facilitate the entire class discussion. The groups thus discuss with each other and propose the question they believe is worthy of answering by experimentation. The students decide the variables such as the mass range or the reagents they will be using from a list of chemicals available in their laboratory manual and on the reagent bench and divide the work among the group members.

Safety expert discusses issues of safety and waste disposal for the laboratory and oversees all safety matters for the day. The Procedure expert draws students' attention to the steps that will help them complete their group investigations by asking questions. Instead of outlining the procedure for the students, the procedure expert is encouraged to ask questions from the groups to get them to draft a procedure. The instructor facilitates the discussion in between if something needs to be added and asks questions from the procedure expert that they could further use to interact with the overall class. The experts (who are the peers of students and are drawn from lab each week) lead the lab and they are responsible along with the instructor to assist students for all student queries related to their assigned roles.

The Data Table expert discusses calculations and the data table layout with the students and makes sure that every group enters the data on the chalkboard and in the Excel spreadsheet. The Claims and Evidence expert leads the post-lab discussion along with the instructor by asking student groups to make claims supporting it with the evidence from their data, observations, and class data. The instructor mainly facilitates the end of lab discussion on reflection for the activity and connecting the concepts and encourages the student leaders to account for their observations and their experience with leading the laboratory. Different groups lead each laboratory activity and when the groups get a chance to lead the laboratory again, the roles are assigned to different students to ascertain that the same role is not repeated with the same individual in a certain group.

Research Questions

The following research questions were investigated for determining the effectiveness of SLIFGIL over SWH approach that was instructor facilitated:

1. Do the students in SLIFGIL based labs perform better on exams than the students in instructor facilitated SWH based labs?
2. What are the differences in the interaction patterns between SWH and SLIFGIL students?

Study Design

Class Assignment for the Study

Mixed methods research design was used to answer the two research questions (Figure 1). The study involved students enrolled during the fall term in a first semester of a general chemistry sequence for science and engineering majors at a midwestern university. Six laboratory sections were selected for the study and four teaching assistants were assigned to instruct these six laboratory sections.

Two teaching assistants in the study were each assigned to a laboratory section in which the students received the standard instructor facilitated SWH approach instruction and another section in which student roles were implemented (SLIFGIL). Two different TAs were assigned to teach two separate honors (chemistry majors) laboratory sections using standard instructor facilitated SWH instruction. Thus, there were three groups in the study: one group is the students who are science and engineering majors and are instructed using the SWH based instruction, the second group is chemistry majors (honors students) receiving SWH (or SWH-H), and the third group is science and engineering majors receiving SLIFGIL based instruction (student roles). Table 3 provides an overview of the study participants and implementation of SWH and SLIFGIL in a general chemistry laboratory course

Table 3. Study participants and implementation of SWH and SLIFGIL in a general chemistry laboratory course

TA	Section 1	Section 2	Section 3	Section 4	Section 5	Section 6
1	SLIFGIL*					
1		SWH*				
2			SLIFGIL*			
2				SWH*		
3					SWH – H[u]	
4						SWH - H[u]

4 TAs taught six labs; SLIFGIL = Lab with student roles; SWH = Lab with no roles; SWH – H = Honors student lab with no roles; [u] Honors student = chemistry majors; * First year general chemistry for science and engineering majors

Data Collection

To answer the two research questions data collection was done in phases according to the concurrent triangulation strategy for the mixed-methods research design (Figure-1). At the participating mid-western university where the study was implemented, these lecture and laboratory courses are co-requisites.

Figure 1. Outline of research study design

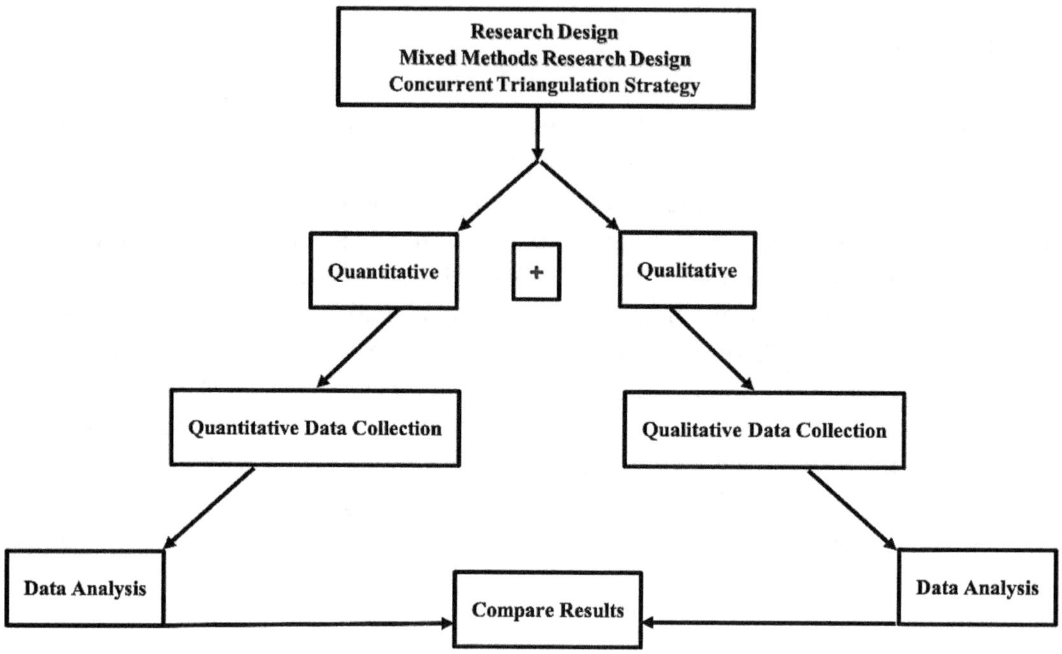

The baseline quantitative data involved administering and scoring the American Chemical Society's California Diagnostic Test during the first week of the term to ensure the equivalence of the three groups at the beginning of the study. ACS-California Diagnostic test is a standardized exam and the questions in these tests corresponded to the experiments and concepts that were taught in the guided-inquiry based laboratory course.

Students enrolled in the general chemistry laboratory course also take the co-requisite lecture course that covers the same content as the laboratory experiments. To ensure that there was no instructor effect, the lecture courses were taught by the same instructor. The description for the instruction and implementation of SLIFGIL and SWH approach in the laboratory course sections by the GTAs is provided in Table 3. The assessments of student academic performance in SWH, SLIFGIL and SWH-honors student groups was done based on student scores on the 4 mid-term exams (referred to as hour-exam during the semester) conducted in the co-requisite lecture course. Each of these mid-term exams topics corresponded with the inquiry-based experiments in the laboratory. Students were evaluated towards the end of the semester using the American Chemical Society's standardized general chemistry exam. Laboratory course also had a final laboratory practical exam that evaluated students for both conceptual knowledge and laboratory skills. Student scores on the laboratory practical tests were used to compare the academic performance of the SWH, SWH-Honors and SLIFGIL groups.

For qualitative data collection, the laboratory sessions were videotaped. Students from both the SWH-based laboratories and SLIFGIL-based laboratories were videotaped on a three-hour activity for a stoichiometry-based laboratory. The videography was done for student groups in the laboratories by a videographer instructed to capture student discussions within groups and with the instructor. The camcorder was equipped with remote sensing microphone and there were two camcorders operating per session.

For data analysis the video recordings were completely transcribed in Microsoft Word and transferred to the ATLAS.ti program for analyses. Qualitative data was used to characterize the interaction dynamics of a SLIFGIL-based laboratory and comparing SLIFGIL laboratory session to SWH-based laboratory in which the instructor was the sole facilitator. The entire video recordings for the three-hour laboratory session were coded for the interaction patterns and comparison of SWH and SLIFGIL laboratories.

The students from both the SWH-and SLIGIL-based laboratories were invited to be interviewed during an announcement to the laboratory sections participating only in the study, but only the students in the SLIFGIL based laboratory signed up for the interviews. Five students were interviewed from SLIFGIL-based laboratories. The interviews were structured and intended to derive information on the implementation of group roles and student opinion on the impact of group roles on student engagement and learning in laboratory.

Data Analysis

The students in the SLIFGIL laboratories were compared to students in the SWH based laboratories that were solely facilitated by the instructor. Assessment of the prior chemistry knowledge of students in the treatment and control laboratory groups was done for a baseline comparison using their scores on the American Chemical Society, California Diagnostic Test. The California Diagnostic Test instrument was developed to assess the knowledge, skills and ability students need for a general chemistry course and it provides an assessment of students' knowledge of high school chemistry as well as basic math skills (Russell, 1994). Results for the quantitative portion of the study were analyzed using a t-test (at α=0.05) for the difference of means between the two groups and the Analysis of Variance (ANOVA) for the three independent groups (SLIFGIL, SWH and SWH-Honors).

The purpose of the qualitative data analysis was to compare the number of student-student and student-instructor interactions in SLIFGIL laboratory and SWH laboratories. Qualitative video data was analyzed for the interaction patterns between the students, students and the teaching assistant and student-groups and teaching assistant interaction. In addition, the qualitative data was also analyzed for differences between the conduct of SWH and SLFGIL based laboratories. The findings from qualitative analysis were integrated with the quantitative data to generate conclusions for the study. Students who participated in the study during the first semester general chemistry course were tracked for their performance in the second semester general chemistry sequence.

RESULTS AND DISCUSSION

Quantitative Data

In this study two research questions were addressed. To answer the first research question about comparison of academic performance it was important to know whether there was any difference in the groups under study. For baseline comparison of students' prior knowledge, the students were given the ACS California Diagnostic Test. Table 4 shows a comparison of student scores on the ACS California Diagnostic Test for students in three groups: the students in the SWH-group; the SWH-instructed honors students, and the SLIFGIL group.

Table 4. ACS-California Diagnostic pre-test for first semester general chemistry means and standard deviations

	SWH	SWH-Honors	SLIFGIL
N	32	32	34
Mean (Std.dev.)	22.68 (3.92)	23.09 (6.32)	23.67 (5.24)
Major	Science and Engineering	Chemistry	Science and Engineering

The means and standard deviations for the ACS-California Diagnostic Test are given in Table 4 followed by one-way ANOVA comparisons for the three groups in Table 5.

Table 5. Summary of one-way ANOVA for ACS California-Diagnostic (pre-test)

Source	SS	DF	MS	F	Prob>F
Groups	73.45	2	36.72	1.33	0.26
Error	2623.09	95	27.61		
Total	2696.48	97			

Based on the mean values and one-way ANOVA test there were no significant differences among the three groups at the beginning of the first semester general chemistry course. The mean, $\overline{x}$ and the standard deviation, s (or the variances s^2), are descriptive measures that together provide useful information about the distribution of an observed set of values. The sample variance s, for n observed values with the mean $\overline{x}$, though not presented in the tables are simply the sum of the squared standard deviation divided by (n-1). For a normal bell-shaped distribution, the interval follows an empirical rule such that:

1. The interval ($\overline{x} \pm s$) contains approximately 68% of the observations.
2. The interval $\overline{x} \pm 2s$ contains 95% of the observations
3. The interval $\overline{x} \pm 3s$ contains all the observations.

In each of the intervals mentioned above, the mean explains the location and the standard-deviation indicates the dispersion of the given part of the data. Thus, for n=32 for SWH group, the $\overline{x}$=22.68 and standard deviation is 3.92. Thus a) $\overline{x}$ ±s, for SWH group 22.68±3.92, indicates the interval 18.76 to 26.6 and thus should include (0.68)(32)=21.76 observations; for the SWH-Honors students group $\overline{x}$ =23.09 ±6.32 gives the range 16.77 to 29.41and (0.68)(32)=21.76 observations; for the SLIFGIL group $\overline{x}$=23.67 ±5.24 gives the range 18.43-28.91 and (0.68)(34)= 23.12 observations. With respect to the calculations for the $\overline{x}$ ±2s the range for the SWH group is 14.84-30.52 with (0.95) (32) =30.4 observations; for the SWH-Honors group the range is 10.45-35.73, which indicates (0.95) (32) =35.73 observations; the range for the SLIFGIL group is 13.19-34.17 and includes 32.3 observations. In case of $\overline{x}$ ±3s the interval range for the SWH group is 10.92-34.44 and includes all the observations; the SWH-Honors group has an interval range of 4.13-42.05; and the SLIFGIL group has an interval range of 7.95-39.59 and includes all the observations as well.

The mean values of the three groups were found to be close. Since 95% of the observations for SWH, SWH-Honors and SLIFGIL groups were within two standard deviations of the mean in either direction; the range of the data for each group was close to four standard deviations enabling estimation of the standard deviation by computing the range for the student scores on the ACS California Diagnostic Test. The estimated standard deviation for SWH group was found to be 4.0 which is close to 3.92 ((30-14) 4=4); the SLIFGIL group had an estimated standard deviation 5.25 ((36-15)/4=5.25) and the SWH-Honors group had an estimated standard deviation of 6.25 ((36-11)/4=6.25). This indicates that the distribution is normal in each of the groups as the intervals computed for each group follow the empirical rules outlined above.

A one-way ANOVA was done to find the differences among the means of the California-Diagnostic Test for the three groups in the study (Table 5). It is important to understand whether the groups started out differently or they had a similar set of chemistry and math skills at the beginning of the semester. The one-way ANOVA procedure is used to determine whether there are significant differences among the means when there are more than two groups. In an ANOVA, the test-statistic computed is called the F-ratio or F-test or Fischer's test. Thus, a one-way ANOVA is simply another form of t-test for independent samples and is used to compare two or more means simultaneously (Ravid, 2011). The statistics for the ACS-California Diagnostic Test is displayed in Table -5 for one-way ANOVA.

The F-ratio is not significant at $p<0.05$ level. A post-hoc comparison of the means was done to do pairwise comparisons of the means for the three groups using Tukey's method for multiple comparisons (also known as honestly significant difference HSD). By pair wise analysis it was found that the SWH, SWH-Honors and SLIFGIL groups have no statistical difference with p-value being 0.26 at ($\alpha=0.05$).

Student participants in the first semester of general chemistry were given four hour-exams worth 100 points each and an end of semester final exam. The final exam was the American Chemical Society's one-semester general chemistry test with 70 questions worth 150 points. As seen from Table 6, students in the SLIFGIL group had higher means as compared to the students who are in the Honors group and the SWH group. One-way ANOVA tests establish significant differences between the groups on ACS General Chemistry Test with an F-ratio=4.11and Prob.>F=0.0194. Similarly for the final laboratory practical examination, students in the SLIFGIL groups performed statistically significantly better than the students in the SWH and the SWH-Honors group with F-ratio=3.92 and Prob>F=0.023.

Table 6. Student performance in First Semester of general chemistry

	SWH (N=32)		SWH HONORS (N=32)		SLIFGIL (N=34)	
	Mean	SD	Mean	SD	Mean	SD
Hour Exam 1	78.68	13.05	77.90	13.86	82.79	11.26
Hour Exam 2	78.65	12.96	77.75	18.20	82.5	15.50
Hour Exam 3	71.68	16.02	67.96	14.80	76.26	10.20
Hour Exam 4	79.12	11.51	77.18	13.25	81.85	11.85
ACS Final Exam (150 points)	100.23 (66.8%)	21.75	102.93 (68.6%)	23.37	114.37* (76.2%)	18.81
Laboratory Practical Exam (71 points)	50.40 (71%)	13.71	50.3 (70.8%)	13.8	58.00** (81.7%)	10.65

*F-ratio=4.11; Prob.>F=0.0194 ** F-ratio=3.92; Prob>F=0.023

The carry-over effect of SLIFGIL student role implementation was studied further in the second semester of general chemistry. Students who participated in SLIFGIL laboratories were monitored for their progress in the second semester of general course (CHEM-178/178L). Not all the students from general chemistry I enrolled in general chemistry II the following semester. During the second semester, students received laboratory instruction using the instructor facilitated SWH approach and no SLIFGIL (SWH with student roles) was implemented.

Assessment of student performance in the SWH approach laboratory activities and the carry over effect of SLIFGIL was done based on total points for hour exams, score on an ACS Final General Chemistry Exam and score on laboratory practical test. Students who continued in the second semester of general chemistry had the same lecturer, same textbook, same HW problems, same lab procedure (SWH/guided inquiry). The students tracked in this study were students from General Chemistry I who took General Chemistry II in next semester. The study thus had:

1. SWH students from General Chemistry I from the SWH group who continued in the SWH approach laboratories in the second semester.
2. SLIFGIL students who were now in SWH approach laboratories in the second semester.
3. TAs who taught using the SWH approach (SWH group roles were not implemented).

Table 7 displays a summary of student performance in the second semester of general chemistry. The SLIFGIL students (n=29) had higher means on hour exams during the second semester of general chemistry, but the means are not significant as compared to the students in the SWH group. A similar trend is observed for the ACS general chemistry exam with SLIFGIL students having a higher mean as compared to SWH students (112.73 vs 108.67; $p|t|=0.49$). For laboratory practical exams, an independent samples t-test indicated that the scores were statistically significantly higher for students in SLIFGIL group ($M=21.10$, $SD=2.24$) than for SWH students ($M=19.55$; $SD=3.02$), $t(55.21)=2.27$, $p=.02$, $d=0.58$.

Table 7. Carry-over effect of SLIFGIL implementation on student performance in second semester of general chemistry

	SWH (N=31)		SLIFGIL (N=29)		Statistical Analysis	
	Mean	SD	Mean	SD	t-Ratio	Prob>|t|
Exam 1	69.09	14.76	75.4	14.6	1.66	0.1
Exam 2	71.22	12.9	72.0	16	0.23	0.8
Exam 3	71.38	2.71	74.72	2.80	0.85	0.39
ACS Final Exam (150 points)	108.67	26.08	112.73	19.51	0.68	0.49
Lab Exam (24 points)	19.55	3.02	21.10	2.24	2.27	0.02*

Qualitative Video Data to Study Student Interaction Patterns in SWH and SLIFGIL Laboratories

The qualitative data was used to find evidence of differences in the interaction patterns of students during a laboratory activity when using the SLIFGIL approach and SWH approach. The quantitative findings show that students receiving SLFIGIL instruction have a better academic performance. Does the implementation of student roles lead to changes in interaction patterns among students in SLIFGIL based and SWH based laboratories? The qualitative video data was thus used to further highlight the differences between the SWH laboratory instruction and the SLIFGIL approach.

Interaction Patterns in SWH and SLIFGIL Based Laboratory

Interactions play a major role in laboratory learning. In traditional laboratory settings, the instructor plays a lead role and is the only person talking and giving directions for most of the three hours that students spend in the laboratory. Students have a procedure that outlines step by step directions and instructions on what to expect for each step that occurs during the experiment. The interactions that occur in such a directive environment may be exemplified as follows:

Student: *Am I doing this right?*

Student: *Can you please look over my experiment and tell me if I have set up everything correctly?*

Student: *Can you check my calculations and see if they are as shown in the procedure?*

Student: *I am done with my experiment. Can I leave now?*

The instructor's response in such a situation is either an affirmative yes or a no and the role dims down to checking the set-up, looking at calculations and confirming whether the steps undertaken by the students are consistent with what is being directed by the laboratory manual. If one assumes that each laboratory is safe for students, the laboratory is equipped with correct materials and equipment needed, and that the laboratory manual is written perfectly, then the instructor's role is minimal in a scenario where the goal is technical set-up.

As compared, for students in inquiry-based laboratories (which may be open-ended or guided-inquiry like the SWH approach), a lot of decision-making is required. It is a two-way process in which the instructor knows the learning outcomes of an activity and gently guides students in the direction of these outcomes; students are actively engaged in their learning process. The purpose of such an instruction is not verification of explicit outcomes but it is learner-centered and demands preparation and input on the part of the students. Students cannot leave the laboratory after completing with their part of the activity as it is collaborative, interdependent group work and requires student contribution to class data and discussions. Traditional settings are thus minimally constructive as students barely talk to each other, then in inquiry mode when working as peers, the purpose of the joint work is data collection and making/sharing observations besides joint experimental set-up and sharing of equipment.

In SLIFGIL-based laboratories, where students lead the laboratory in the expert role, the student leaders had to think through various aspects of their laboratory activity ahead of time. But since they were not yet aware how everyone was involved in the entire class as one large group, and how the experts as a sub-group would contribute to shaping questions, a lot of decision-making happened in the laboratory with peers as experts and collaborators in a group and the instructor as facilitator. This was a key difference between a SWH laboratory and a SLIFGIL group. As evidenced by the video observations, in a SWH-based laboratory, the interaction was mainly happening between students and the instructor whereas in SLIFGIL-based laboratories, student-student interactions happened most.

Teaching assistant and student interactions were next. While in SWH laboratories some students contribute very little to the overall class discussion, in SLIFGIL-based laboratories there are few students being left out as everyone must contribute to the class discussions due to student-expert with student interactions in addition to teaching assistant with student interactions and teaching assistant with student group interactions. Table 8 displays the frequencies of student-student interactions and TA-student interactions in SWH- and SLFIGIL-based laboratories followed by some excerpts from the video-recordings of both formats exemplifying these interactions.

Table 8. Interaction frequencies in SWH and SLIGIL based laboratories

	SWH Laboratories	SLIFGIL Laboratories
Total interaction frequencies	557	453
Student-Student interactions	59 (10.59%)	111 (24.50%)
TA-Student interactions	282 (50.63%)	103 (22.73%)
TA-Student group interactions	216 (38.78%)	239 (52.76%)

For finding the frequencies of interactions, all the instances from transcripts of the three-hour video for SWH and SLIFGIL laboratories were counted and classified as student-student interactions where two students are interacting with each other, and their conversations were captured distinctly on the video. Similarly, the interactions of the TA with individual students or with a group of students were counted and classified as TA-student interactions and TA student group interactions. Later the percentage of interactions was calculated for each kind of interaction based on the total number of interactions transcribed from the video clips per laboratory. As is evident from the Table 8, the interactions in the SLIFGIL-based laboratories as well as SWH-based laboratories are high. The difference between the two laboratory approaches lies in the patterns of these interactions. Though SWH-based laboratories had a higher number of interactions for the same length of time compared to SLIFGIL-based laboratories, it was relatively difficult to code all the interactions due to lack of audio or video clarity on some spots. Examples of the three types of interactions for SWH based and a SLIFGIL laboratory are as follows.

SWH Based Laboratory

1. **Student-Student interactions**

Rick: *my stuff is changing to dark color, what does your look like? I guess I might be doing something wrong.*

JK: *I just started, don't know you might want to check with the TA.*

2. **Student-TA interactions**

TA: *What are you doing here??*

Nolan: *heating my stuff, the point [flame] is not quite underneath the copper dish.*

TA: *So are you gonna [going to] do anything differently*

Nolan: *I don't know, like I see its getting hot here.*

TA: *What are you looking for, why are you heating this red powder?*

Nolan: *Looking for some kind of change you mean?*

TA: *like what?*

Nolan: *color change, I guess.*

3. **Student group-TA interactions**

TA: *what are you all doing here?*

Sam: *we did, I think this will be our third time heating.*

Joe: *the mass went up when we did it two times so we are just waiting to see what will happen to this one.*

TA: *So, what do you all say about it? Why do you think mass is going up?*

Karen: *its adding stuff.*

TA: *adding what?*

Max: *Oxygen its gaining oxygen from air.*

Sam: *I thought it will break apart. When I was heating but seems like it is what Max is saying. Gaining that thing. Oxygen.*

TA: *Ok we will discuss that as a class. Did you start entering your data yet.*

Max: *we will, after finishing up our heating. We are gonna [going to] work out calculations together.*

TA: *Ok!*

SLIFGIL Based Laboratory

1. **Student-Student interactions**

Eric: *all right guys so what is the big idea? Do we even have that on the chalkboard?*

Courtney: *Yes, we do, look at the mole ratio one [reaction]. It is just not worded correctly. That question should be about empirical formula. After all that's what you get when you know the mole ratio.*

Eric: *why do you need to know mole ratio?*

Courtney: *Because you really don't know what your initial stuff is. You know that it can be copper or some compound of copper, but it does not tell which of the either.*

2. **Student-TA interactions**

TA: *So, what are you doing here?*

Mike: *I am heating my dish?*

TA: *Why do you need to heat the dish? What did you understand from Kyle on that part?*

Mike: *that we need to constant the dish.*

TA: *Ok, so what will you be doing after getting your dish constant.*

Mike: *I guess I will add the red thing to this dish. Hey Sonya (TA) can I ask you a question regarding the data.*

TA: *Is it something that would you seek Step's advice on first, and if you still don't have a solution sure we can look at it together.*

Mike: *Ok, where is Steph. Oh, she is there.*

3. **Student group-TA interactions**

TA: *What do you think it is we talked about that. Read your experiment and I will come back again and would like to know what you have found. Did your red powder gain mass or lose mass after heating?*

Jared (Steph, lab partner): *It added mass.*

TA: *What was your initial thought?*

Steph: *I thought it will lose.*

TA: *Lose what.*

Jared: *Mass of course.*

TA: *So, what is happening here can you provide a possible explanation of what is happening on heating red powder. Is this just your groups observation? [Katie interrupts]*

Katie: *No, we have other groups who have also similar things.*

TA: *like?*

Steph: *add mass.*

TA: *so, what did you add?*

Jared: *what do you mean?*

TA: *what could have led to gain of mass?*

Katie: *May be something from air got in.*

TA: *What from air?*

Steph: *oxygen.*

Jared: *but if our compound is Copper oxide how can it add oxygen?*

TA: *are you sure it is Copper oxide?*

Katie: *No, we are trying to figure out than. It could be copper becoming copper oxide.*

TA: *how can you confirm it is copper oxide what is your evidence?*

Steph: *we gained mass so it could be copper going to copper oxide.*

TA: *Which oxide of copper? What is your product going to be?*

Katie: *black*

TA: *Yup.*

Step: *wait didn't we say that it would be copper II oxide.*

TA: *what is the formula can you write that in your journals.*

Katie: *yes, like this [writes Cu_2O].*

TA: *so, what is the charge on oxygen?*

Jared: *negative 2.*

TA: *so, what should be the charge for copper which Katie is showing [Points to students notebook].*

Steph: *wait the copper is +1 here, so this cannot be copper II oxide.*

TA: *so, what would be copper II oxide?*

Jared: *you mean just CuO.*

In both the laboratory approaches, the TA-student interaction/ TA student group-interactions revealed that by correctly questioning students about their observations, students had an idea that they needed to apply the concept of a limiting reagent to understand the experiment and be attentive to the observable changes during the activity (find the original red compound is completely converted to coarse black solid). The student-student interactions and TA-student group interactions were found to be higher in SLIFGIL-based laboratories whereas the TA-individual student interactions were found to be higher in SWH-based laboratories.

A plausible explanation for this difference could be due to the implementation of group roles in SLIFGIL-based laboratories. Students in courses using the SLIFGIL approach lead the laboratory as experts and are required to communicate with their peers, while in SWH-based sections the pre-laboratory and post-laboratory discussion was solely facilitated by the instructor. This explains why the TA-student interactions were higher in SWH-based laboratories. Similarly, the TA-student group interactions were higher in SLIFGIL-based laboratories because the student experts communicate with the instructor as a group and the instructor further interacts with each of the student groups as they work on the SWH approach, since the students work in pairs (another form of group) students rely more on their TAs as compared to relying on their peers from other groups for activity-based queries.

As found from the analysis of video transcripts, in SLIFGIL-based laboratories, students were asking questions to one another, and the TA was asking questions to students individually or in groups. In SWH-based laboratories, the questions were mainly asked by the TA and were directed to individual students or student groups. The pre-laboratory phase is the point where students contribute their questions to the class and discuss class beginning questions but after that the student questioning decreases in the SWH-based laboratory.

In the SLIFGIL-based laboratory, students lead the laboratory as a group of experts and were asking questions of the class as a group or involving the TA in questioning and even seeking help to frame good questions. Students are encouraged to share their ideas with each other by asking questions from each other instead of giving a direct answer to their peers. The questions being asked in the SWH-based laboratories are more directed toward seeking help or affirmation from the instructor about the procedure or confirming the calculations. When the instructor was asking questions, they were phrased to derive input from the students and were directed to the individual student or student groups for example - "What are we doing here?" or "What is your prediction?" "How do you know it is copper?" In the SLIFGIL-based laboratory, the questioning involves frequent use of how, what why, and when kind of questions, but these were used by TA as well as students (example of script above).

In both the SWH- and SLIFGIL-based laboratory students talk about the experimental setup to their peers or the TA. Students are mainly concerned about (a) their set-up and the flame configuration for the copper oxide activity and (b) in finding out when their reaction get over or (c) signs that they are done with heating. For example:

Student 1: *For how long do I need to cook this stuff?*

Student 2: *When does this (reaction) get over?*

Findings From Interview Data

The interview questions were focused on the following aspects of the laboratory each of which is discussed in further detail:

- Student background in chemistry laboratory
- Student view of implementation of group roles
- Student view of the extent of engagement with the activity
- Student view of the laboratory report format
- Student suggestions for improvements that can be made in the laboratory instruction

Student Background in Chemistry Laboratory

Students interviewed were either freshmen or sophomores in chemistry. All the students interviewed had general chemistry as their first laboratory experience. Students had experienced laboratory during the high school chemistry, which was, in general a 45-minute to 1-hour laboratory session. Students interviewed mentioned that the laboratories related to the class, and they did an activity once a week or once a month depending on the instructor. (Pseudonyms are used for student names; I = Interviewer).

Brad: *my junior year (in high school), I had a chemistry lab, but it was really like sort of timed like we had an hour to do everything.*

I: *One hour to do everything?*

Brad: *Maybe forty-five minutes so everything was rushed and a lot of times you wouldn't even get your stuff done so.*

I: *So, and this was your first chemistry lab 177L?*

Cam: Yes!

I: *And have you ever had chemistry in your school time or something?*

Cam: *In high school I took just general chemistry.*

I: *General chemistry okay so, uh, how do you compare your high school chemistry class or lab with your first year here?*

Cam: *Um, in my high school chemistry lab, we just had like worksheets that we would fill out when we did a lab.*

Student View of Implementation of Group Roles

During the interviews, students stated that the implementation of group roles kept them involved in the laboratory and improved their communication skills. Group role implementation had its own challenges, requiring students to be prepared ahead of time. Students benefited from this laboratory instruction format. Students also mentioned that they learned chemistry better when involved in the laboratory in this way as compared to their high school chemistry laboratory experience and were able to connect with the concepts taught in the lecture by applying what they learned in the lecture to laboratory or what they learned in the laboratory to connect with what was covered in the lecture. In addition, when asked about the role of the instructor, students mentioned that even though the students did most of the work in the laboratory as a team, their instructor was very much involved with them and would guide them through when they got stuck on any aspect of laboratory and were clueless of the next step.

Brad: *Um, yes, I did like it, it everything was good. I didn't, I obviously didn't like chemistry, I came in and like uh I dreaded to come in the three-hour lab or whatever, but then after I got to understand everything and know what I was doing I like it. Now that its all done, I am glad that I got all the knowledge, and I know a lot more and its taught me so. I am happy with it. It was good teaching and good ways of doing it. I like, I like how she kind of told us what we had to do but then we had the kids coming and helping us do it so there is kind of two different ways of learning out there and they were kind of good for me anyway.*

Evan: *I have been in charge of beginning questions which is, like, you know, getting, uh, getting the whole class to be working on the same experiment and make sure that they are going after the same goal. I have been in charge of safety, um, and making sure everybody disposes all the chemicals in same place, making sure that if there is any broken glass, we take care of it accordingly and making sure everybody is well-equipped for the lab. Um, I, oh, I was also in charge of the procedure making sure everybody was following the right procedure during the lab, um, and oh, and there was data table, um, which was making sure we got all the data neatly organized. I was never in charge of the claims, though.*

Josh: *Yeah, she did even though like the group leaders were, you know, like the leaders of the, like the lab like, you know, we had, like, questions as leaders or as regular groups. Our TA would always help us out and stuff. And she always knew what she was doing better than any of us so, like, she was always there for help to guide us through and ask us questions.*

Evan: *she was just kind of like a facilitator, like, you know, it really kind of like, you know, when we do everything on our own a little bit and then, um, she would like kind of give us feedback as to know if she thought we were headed in the right direction or if she thought maybe we were headed in the wrong direction. She would kind of steer us to what we probably should be doing. So, she was just, she just kind of like provided guidance to help us stay on track.*

Student View of Involvement With the Laboratory Activity

Students felt that they were very much involved in the laboratory which led to a better and richer learning experience. Students expressed that they liked the way in which their laboratory was structured, and their peers were the facilitators *along with* the instructor which helped them to focus, learn from the laboratory activity, and make connections between lecture and laboratory instruction.

Brad: *The high school, not the high school but the college one helps me learn a lot better. Because they are actually pushing you and you are working hard at it. Yeah, you understand it, [high school laboratory] you just don't kind of see it and it just goes right, whoosh, out in one ear and out through the next and you are, like, oh, ok. So you understand what you are doing when you are done. Yes, I connected some [concepts with lecture], there was a lot I still didn't understand but I knew a lot more when I was done than when I started, so I felt like that helped me a lot. Some of the things that were in my lab class, yeah, with the just chem. 177. Yeah, it connected together well. Like when we do experiments and whatever you would, uh, do your titrations whatever we were going to do, and you do the formulas, and then when you have your questions in chemistry, they have the same idea and then they talk about the things you did in lab. And they, it kind of connect with it, and then you understand, oh, yes, that's what I did in lab and it's how I got to do it with this equation. I can get it right, so.. Um, I just like said pretty much I liked just how the class, like, we got involved in it, and pretty much did it ourselves. Which is the best, teach yourself pretty much learned from yourself and learned from what you do. And there wasn't really anything that I didn't like. It gets kind of long, three hours, but you almost need it, standing up there for three hours the first day. I get in there I was, like, wow there is no chairs. I got to stand here for three hours, and this is morning and I got to starve in for noon to come so that you could go to lunch, but it turns out that everything is good. Yeah, that's pretty much it I guess.*

Cam: *Um, here it was kind of more independent learning like we got to apply the things we learned in class in the lab and sort of it has helped me learn it better because you know I could see a way to apply it and yeah.*

Josh: *Um, like my involvement like, I got to be a leader probably like, three or four times. And, uh, so I was involved in that way. And then, just, you know, when I wasn't leader, like it was very, like uh, I don't like the whole group participating. Like if you know if we all tried to decide the beginning questions and then you know, we all went through the procedure and, like, what we were doing. And all the* *safety stuff like, you are very involved the whole time there was not a lot of, like, just standing quietly, so which is good, I think.*

Student View of Laboratory Format

Students were asked to compare the format they had used in the high school and how it was different from what they did in Chemistry 177 laboratory. All the five students mentioned that they were required to write a lot in the SLIFGIL-based laboratory and explain their observations and data. Students indicated that their prior chemistry laboratory report format was more fill-in-the-blank format. In their report writing, students felt they had to think and explain (a) what they did and why they did it, (b) errors, (c) applications and (d) how their laboratory connects to what they did in lecture. As compared to their high school laboratory report writing experience, all students who were interviewed felt that the format in their college chemistry course was more in-depth, laid out, and very specific which helped them learn better from the laboratory.

Brad: *We didn't really have a lab [high school], I was like, I guess, it was that you just saw, he'd like to give you a worksheet and you just write down what you think. It was really what you put, you would have not, like, a thing you said, like, calculations or anything. It was totally different. Here it was specific. It pretty much said what you need to do and not as much, I know, everyone that you could pretty much write anything down and turn that in. Uh, it would be like, kind of fill-in-the-blank, like you would have figured it out. And now that you fill that blank in there and like write what you just thought about it but it wasn't, like, it was totally different than from here. Because here you had to go in detail and then you had to actually do it. But high school, you just kind of whatever you just wrote it, we did not take it serious at all. Here it is more a lot more serious. Well obviously, college [format is better], because it's not a joke. You actually do it. It's like your own job, seems like that's, like, the way I take it. So, you got to do it, and you got to do good at it otherwise you fail so.*

Cam: *I think here [format is better]. Because it's more than just, uh, more than just filling out a worksheet about it. Like you actually have to think, okay, how does this happen, how does this reaction, how is this reaction happening? Why does this happen? What causes this and like why is this important? kind of thing.*

Evan: *Well, I really liked the lab format here because, um, we got, we got more experience in working with groups and we had to actually figure out what we were doing before we did it so instead of simply just answering a question, we were able to figure out why we had to answer that question and how to answer that question. I definitely liked the way 177 was set up with the lab reports because, um, it made you do enough before the lab that you fully understood it, but it didn't make you go do a ton of work before you did the lab because, after the lab, then you had to do the discussion of reading or reflection so that you learned more about what you did, so that you can understand it better. But I am glad we didn't have to do it before so it may have been confusing or given us answers to our lab that we didn't know yet um, but, yeah, I think it was set up very well.*

Josh: *Um, I just think it (the format) was conducive for learning. I think just, um, it helped me just you know understand what was going on and everything and yeah! It just kind of helped me like, specially* *like the evidence and analysis section, um, that really helped me just kind of think about like, it, you know, like, you know, like what we really did that will help support the claim that we made. And you, like, the claim answers the beginning questions, so you know all this kind of tied it all together. And, uh, so the evidence was really what I thought was good, because it helped me just think about it and think about what was actually happening.*

Student Opinion on Improvements That Can Be Made in the Laboratory Instruction

Students were overall satisfied with the laboratory experiments that they had in the syllabus. One student out of five who were interviewed wanted to type in the laboratory reports, but the other students suggested including activities that were more visual, included a description of the equipment to be used and lay out more expectations in the syllabus so that they understood beforehand the level of involvement they would have in the laboratory with the activities.

Dan: *Yeah, like more on certain techniques, like when you are up there doing in front of students the set-up like a burette or a flask, like, you know, that and can do it well in your roles. So, yeah, some more time with techniques would be better we did that, but it could have been done better if I had just gone through it myself. But I believe the way it was structured, we did it with our peers, and it helped.*

Evan: *One thing I was thinking about is you could include an equipment section in the lab report, probably in the pre-lab, where you have to do the beginning questions, safety and then I was thinking an equipment section where to know what equipment you are going to be using in the lab and what it is usually used for because you can use certain things to perform certain labs.*

CONCLUSION

The findings from the quantitative and qualitative data indicate that students are more engaged in SLIFGIL-based laboratories when assigned group roles and they perform better on hour exams, the ACS final exam and laboratory practical exam assessments. Findings from the qualitative data indicate differences in between the SLIFGIL and SWH based laboratory especially the pre-laboratory and post-laboratory session with respect to students leading the laboratory in facilitation with the instructor as compared to SWH based laboratory in which the instructor is the sole facilitator. In addition, student-student interaction is higher in SLIFGIL based laboratory as compared to student-student interactions in SWH based laboratories.

Challenges With Implementation of Student Roles

At the beginning, implementation of group roles was a challenge as it faced TA resistance. Out of six teaching assistants signed up for the study, only two teaching assistants continued with the study for the entire semester. Not all students accepted signing up for the study to undertake group roles. Although they participated in the roles, their data is not included in the study. At times the pre-laboratory session lasted much longer, frustrating the teaching assistants but they mentioned it was all worth it. As the semester progressed students became more organized and were more communicative in the laboratory.

Theoretical and Practical Implications of the Study

Student engagement and meaningful learning in science laboratory courses has remained a challenge. The study on the SLIFGIL based laboratories addresses this important concern on student learning in science laboratories. The findings have several theoretical and practical implications for STEM (Science Technology, Engineering and Mathematics) courses that involve laboratory courses as either co- or prerequisites. The study shows that by shifting the ownership of learning by a systematic design and implementation of collaborative learning teams improves student academic performance and fosters scientific communication among students through small group and class discussions.

This study fills an important gap in literature on the guided inquiry-based learning and shows that it is possible to gradually involve students in active learning in the laboratory. There are several possible avenues that can be explored for the theoretical and practical considerations based on this study. For example, new survey tools and instruments could be developed to study-student-student, and student-instructor interaction in the inquiry-based laboratories. While American Chemical Society's (ACS) exams have been used to measure student performance for this study, educators in STEM areas could develop and tailor assessments that are more representative of inquiry-based collaborative learning in the laboratory and classroom settings for courses that have an integrated curriculum for lecture and the laboratory.

Recently due to COVID there has been a major shift towards remote and hybrid learning approaches. It is feasible to implement SLIFGIL in the remote or hybrid format with online-learning teams following the same format in the remote setting. Students in remote setting could lead their peers through zoom breakout rooms for conducting an online version of the similar laboratory activity as used in SLIFGIL. In studies involving the remote laboratory teaching, the sentiment analysis of the User Generated Content for laboratory discussions via chat function of zoom could be used (Saura et. al., 2022). Further studies are also required on a larger scale to study the impact of implementing SLIFGIL. In addition, student attitudes and instructor attitudes need to be studied pre- and post-study to see whether the implementation of student roles brings about a significant change in student and instructor attitudes on laboratory instruction. Corresponding data on student perspectives on the use of SLIFGIL approach and its effectiveness could also be gathered through Twitter microblogs and analyzed via social media data mining techniques as described by Saura et. al (2022).

REFERENCES

Adams, D. L. (1998). What works in the non-major's science laboratory: Some practical advice on building a workable and meaningful introductory science laboratory? *Journal of College Science Teaching*, 103–108.

Aksan, N., Kisac, B., Aydin, M., & Demirbuken, S. (2009). Symbolic Interaction Theory. *Procedia: Social and Behavioral Sciences*, *1*(1), 902–904. doi:10.1016/j.sbspro.2009.01.160

Aronson, E. (Ed.). (1978). *The Jigsaw Classroom*. Sage Publications.

Barbosa, R., Jófili, Z., & Watts, M. (2004). Cooperating in constructing knowledge: Case studies and citizenship. *International Journal of Science Education*, *26*(8), 935–949. doi:10.1080/0950069032000138842

Blosser, P. E. (1993). Using Cooperative learning in Science Education. Clearinghouse for Science, Mathematics, Environmental Science Education. ERIC ED351207.

Blumer, H. (1969). The methodological position of symbolic interactionism. In *Symbolic interactionism: Perspective and Method* (pp. 1–60). Prentice-Hall.

Bodner, G. M. (1986). Constructivism: A theory of knowledge. *Journal of Chemical Education, 63*(10), 873–878. doi:10.1021/ed063p873

Bodner, G. M., Klobuchar, M., & Geelan, D. (2001). The many forms of constructivism. *Journal of Chemical Education, 78*(8), 1107. doi:10.1021/ed078p1107.4

Brown, S. B., Collins, A., & Duguid, P. (1989). Situated Cognition and the Culture of Learning. *Educational Researcher, 18*(1), 32–42. doi:10.3102/0013189X018001032

Brown, T. E., LeMay, E. H., Bursten, B. E., Murphy, C., & Woodward, P. (2008). *Chemistry: The Central Science*. Pearson Education Inc.

Burke, K. A., Greenbowe, T. J., & Hand, B. M. (2006). Implementing the Science Writing Heuristic in the chemistry laboratory. *Journal of Chemical Education, 83*(7), 1032–1038. doi:10.1021/ed083p1032

Burke, K. A., Hand, B. M., Poock, J. R., & Greenbowe, T. J. (2005). Using the Science Writing Heuristic: Training chemistry teaching assistants. *Journal of College Science Teaching, 35*, 36–41.

Carter, G., & Jones, M. G. (1994). Verbal and nonverbal behavior of ability-grouped dyads. *Journal of Research in Science Teaching, 31*(6), 603–619. doi:10.1002/tea.3660310604

Choi, A. (2008). *Dissertation: A Study of Student Written Argument Using the Science Writing Heuristic Approach in Inquiry-Based Freshman General Chemistry Laboratory Classes* [Dissertation].

Clough, M. P. (2003). Using the laboratory to enhance student learning. In R. W. Bybee (Ed.), *Learning science and the essence of learning, 2002 NSTA yearbook*. National Science Teachers' Association.

Cooper, M. (1995). Cooperative learning: An approach for large enrollment courses. *Journal of Chemical Education, 72*(2), 162–164. doi:10.1021/ed072p162

Corder, G. W., & Foreman, D. I. (2009). *Nonparametric Statistics for non-statisticians: A step-by-step approach*. John-Wiley & Sons Inc. doi:10.1002/9781118165881

Crotty, M. (1998). *The foundations of social research: Meaning and perspectives in the research process*. Sage Publications.

Denzin, N. K., & Lincoln, Y. S. (1998). *Collecting and interpreting qualitative materials*. Sage Publications.

Domin, S. D. (1999). A review of Laboratory instruction styles. *Journal of Chemical Education, 76*(4), 543–547. doi:10.1021/ed076p543

Erceg-Hurn, D. M., & Mirosevich, V. M. (2008). Modern Robust Statistical Methods: An easy way to maximize the accuracy and power of your research. *The American Psychologist, 63*(7), 591–601. doi:10.1037/0003-066X.63.7.591 PMID:18855490

Forman, E., & Cazen, C. (1985). Exploring Vygotskian perspectives in education: the cognitive value of peer interaction. In Culture, Communication, and Cognition: Vygotskian Perspectives. Cambridge, UK: Cambridge University Press.

Freund, R. J., Wilson, W. J., & Mohr, D. L. (2010). *Statistical Methods*. Academic Press, Elsevier Inc.

Greenbowe, T. J., & Hand, B. M. (2005). Introduction to Science Writing Heuristic. In N. J. Peinta, M. Cooper, & T. J. Greenbowe (Eds.), *Chemists Guide to Effective Teaching* (Vol. 140). Prentice Hall.

Gupta, T., Burke, K. A., Mehta, A., & Greenbowe, T. J. (2014). Impact of Guided-Inquiry-Based Instruction with a Writing and Reflection Emphasis on Chemistry Students' Critical Thinking Abilities. *Journal of Chemical Education*, *92*(1), 32–38. doi:10.1021/ed500059r

Gurney, B. (1989). Constructivism and Professional Development: A stereoscopic view. *ERIC Document ED*, *305*(259), 1–28.

Hofstein, A. (2004). The laboratory in Chemistry Education: Thirty years of experience with developments, implementation, and research. *Chemistry Education Research and Practice*, *5*, 247–264.

Hofstein, A., & Lunetta, V. N. (1982). The role of the laboratory in science teaching: Neglected Aspects of Research. *Review of Educational Research*, *52*, 201–217.

Hollander, M., & Wolfe, D. A. (1973). *Nonparametric Statistical Methods*. John Wiley & Sons.

Johnson, D. W. (1984). *Circles of Learning: Cooperation in the Classroom*. Association for Supervision and Curriculum Development.

Johnson, R. T., & Johnson, D. W. (1985). Student-Student Interaction: Ignored but Powerful. *Journal of Teacher Education*, *36*, 22–26.

Jones, M. G., Rua, M. J., & Carter, G. (1998). Science Teachers' Conceptual Growth within Vygotsky's Zone of Proximal Development. *Journal of Research in Science Teaching*, *35*, 967–985.

Kagan, S. (1989). The structural approach to cooperative learning. *Educational Leadership*, *47*, 12–15.

Kuhn, M. H. (1964). Major Trends in Symbolic Interaction Theory in the past Twenty-Five years. *The Sociological Quarterly*, *5*, 61–84.

Lazarowitz, R., & Tamir, P. (1997). Research on using laboratory instruction in science. In Handbook of Research on Science Teaching. Routledge Publishers.

Leech, N. L., & Onwuegbuzie, A. J. (2002). *A Call for Greater Use on Non-Parametric Statistics* (ERIC Document Reproduction Service No. ED 471346). Paper Presented at the annual meeting of the Mid-South Educational Research Association, Chattanooga, TN.

Lunetta, V. N., Hofstein, A., & Clough, M. P. (2007). Learning and Teaching in the School Science Laboratory: An analysis of Research, Theory & Practice. In Handbook of Research in Science Education. Routledge Publishers.

Maines, D. R. (1997). Interactionism and Practice. *Applied Behavioral Science Review*, *5*, 1–18.

McSeeney, M., & Katz, B. M. (1978). Nonparametric Statistics: Use and nonuse. *Perceptual and Motor Skills*, *4*, 1023–1032.

Mead, G. H. (1962) Mind, self, and society from the standpoint of a social behaviorist. Chicago, IL: University of Chicago Press.

Moses, L. A. (1952). Non-Parametric Statistics for Psychological Research. *Psychological Bulletin*, *49*, 122–143.

Newmann, F. M., and Thomson, J. A. (1987). *Effects of cooperative learning on achievement in secondary schools: A summary of research.* ERIC Document Reproduction Service No. ED 288 853.

Okebukola, P. A. (1986). An investigation of some factors affecting students' attitudes towards laboratory chemistry. *Journal of Chemical Education*, *63*, 531–532.

Poock, J. R., Burke, K. A., Greenbowe, T. J., & Hand, B. M. (2007). Using the Science Writing Heuristic in the general chemistry laboratory to improve student's academic performance. *Journal of Chemical Education*, *84*, 1371–1379.

Resnick, L. B. (1988). Learning in School and out. *Educational Researcher*, *16*, 13–20.

Rudd, J. A. II, Greenbowe, T. J., & Hand, B. M. (2001). Recrafting the general chemistry lab report. *Journal of College Science Teaching*, *31*, 230–234.

Russell, A. A. (1994). A rationally designed General Chemistry Diagnostic Test. *Journal of Chemical Education*, *71*, 314–317.

Saura, J. R., Palacios-Marqués, D., & Ribeiro-Soriano, D. (2022). *Exploring the boundaries of Open Innovation: Evidence from social media mining*. Technovation. doi:10.1016/j.technovation.2021.102447

Saura, J. R., Ribeiro-Soriano, D., & Iturricha-Fernández, A. (2022). Exploring the challenges of remote work on Twitter users' sentiments: From digital technology development to a post-pandemic era. *Journal of Business Research*, *142*(March), 242–254. https://doi.org/10.1016/j.jbusres.2021.12.052

Schroeder, J. D. (2007). The lab-lecture correlation: From the science writing heuristic to the traditional organic chemistry laboratory. In B. M. Hand (Ed.), *Science Inquiry, Argument and Language: A case for the Science Writing Heuristic*. Sense Publishers.

Sharan, Y., & Sharan, S. (1989). Training teachers for cooperative learning. *Educational Leadership*, *45*, 20–25.

Siegel, S. (1956). *Nonparametric Statistics for the behavioral Sciences*. Mc Graw-Hill.

Slavin, R. E. (1988). Cooperative learning and student achievement. *Educational Leadership*, *46*, 31–33.

Slavin, R. E. (1988). *Student team learning: An overview and practical guide*. National Education Association.

Traux, D. D. (2007). Restructuring the undergraduate laboratory process. *Journal of Professional Issues in Engineering Education and Practice*, 192–198.

Von Glaserfeld, E. (1984). *The Invented Reality: How do we know what we believe we know?* (P. Waltzlawick, Ed.). W. W. Norton & Co Inc.

KEY TERMS AND DEFINITIONS

Active Learning: Engaging in learning process through note taking, participating in hands-on activities virtually or in a classroom room setting either individually or in learning teams.

Collaborative Learning: Learning in small groups or teams facilitated by an expert or an instructor.

Guided Inquiry: A structured approach to teaching science through carefully designed activities to guide student through exploration and discovery.

Hybrid Instruction: The use of remote or online learning activities such as videos and podcasts with a face-to-face component.

Laboratory Teaching: Instruction with experimental component specifically hands-on investigations of scientific concepts and principles accompanied with laboratory related skills and techniques.

Peer Learning: A format of learning where peers lead instruction in a laboratory or classroom setting.

Science Writing Heuristic: A guided inquiry-based approach that involves writing to learn science.

Chapter 6
Introducing an Interdisciplinary Course Into General Higher Education:
Information Theory

Liguo Yu
Indiana University, South Bend, USA

ABSTRACT

This chapter describes a new interdisciplinary course introduced at Indiana University South Bend. The course is designed for students of any majors to meet their general education requirement on 'the natural world' subject. The course topics are divided into three parts. First, using 'information' as the main thread, this course connects physical information, chemical information, biological information, and social information. Second, using basic computing model and information entropy, this course generalizes information and information theory. Third, information is correlated to cutting-edge computing topics such as quantum computing, complexity, and uncertainty. The main objective of this course is to provide an outline of information theory to students using an interdisciplinary approach.

INTRODUCTION

Indiana University South Bend is a public university located in South Bend, Indiana. It is the third largest campus of Indiana University. Its campus-wide general education curriculum provides students with knowledge and skills of a variety of academic disciplines, including writing, critical thinking, oral communication, quantitative reasoning, visual literacy, health, finance, contemporary social values, art, human and society, and the natural world (Cordell, 2013). The general education curriculum at Indiana University South Bend is designed to complement the major programs and ensure the graduates will have the breadth of knowledge and experience enabling them to think critically, act intelligently, and behave professionally in their future career and personal life. The ultimate goal of general education curriculum at IU South Bend is to educate students as valued citizens and life-long learners.

DOI: 10.4018/978-1-6684-4441-2.ch006

Copyright © 2022, IGI Global. Copying or distributing in print or electronic forms without written permission of IGI Global is prohibited.

Among the aforementioned general education disciplines, *the nature world* is a common core subject. Based on the university policy, the common core courses should provide disciplinary content with interdisciplinary components that allow students to view the course as a cross-discipline topic. Before 2018, *the natural world* courses included the disciplines of astronomy, biology, chemistry, geology, physics, and mathematics.

Because nowadays, computer technology is widely used in business and our daily life and computer science is becoming part of the fundamental knowledge for a regular citizen, in 2017 Computer Science Department of IU South Bend decided to propose a new course CSCI-N390 (Information Theory) to enrich the contents and disciplines of *the natural world* common core subject.

The objective of this course (CSCI-N390: Information Theory) is to provide an outline of information theory to students using an interdisciplinary approach. Through taking this course, students are expected to appreciate information as a fundamental component of the physical world and understand how information relates to the functioning of our complex society.

This chapter describes the rationale of offering this course, course contents, scheduling, assessment, and sample case studies. The objective of this chapter is to present the higher education community an interdisciplinary course example that covers the most important knowledge of this era–information theory, which is the key element to acutely understanding the functioning of the physical world and the human society.

To our knowledge, this is the first report that information theory is introduced in college general education curriculum. Given the importance of information and computer technology, this topic could make considerable impact on students' college study and their future career development and life experience. The significance of the study presented in this chapter can be summarized as the following. First, this course can serve as a pilot study to investigating the feasibility of introducing cutting-edge knowledge and technologies into college general education. Second, this study can be used to demonstrate how general education can shape college students' practical knowledge base, affect their worldview, and improve their decision-making. Third, theoretically, this study enriches the literature of higher-education innovation through presenting a case study that is both pragmatic and essential in the era of education revolution.

The remaining of the chapter is organized as follows. We first review the background work in general education. Then, we provide the course description, including topics, rationale for course offering, learning methods, schedule, assignment, and assessment. Next, we discuss implications and limitations of the study and present future work. Finally, we conclude the chapter.

BACKGROUND

We live in an era that is rapidly changing. Knowledge explosion and technology revolution have transformed the business models of many fields, such as retail, finance, healthcare, law enforcement, sports, and entertainment. Education is not an exception, especially higher education. For example, both the management and teaching models of higher-education institutions have dramatically changed in the past years (Fidalgo-Blanco et al. 2014). One such change is the wide adoption of remote education due to the advancement of information technology (Saura, et al., 2022a; Saura, et al., 2022b). It is fair to say that now days, majority of teaching innovations in universities are technology-oriented, which means new courses or new teaching models are based on new information technologies, such as social media, mobile computing, cloud-resource sharing, etc. Instead, this study focusses on a different aspect of teaching innovation: the introduction of new modules (courses) in colleges. Specifically, a new course which differs from traditional offerings is presented to satisfy the learning objectives and improve the learning outcome of general education.

Nationally and internationally, general education is part of an undergraduate study, besides the area of major classes that define the degree. In other words, general education is the foundation of an undergraduate degree across programs (Hanushek et al., 2017). General education emerged in the early of the 19th century to satisfy the requirement of liberal education (Westmeyer, 1985; O'Banion, 2016; Warner & Koeppel, 2009). Nowadays, general education is commonly accepted in higher education across states and across countries (Krueger & Kumar, 2004).

Why should students take general education courses? It may seem more reasonable that higher education should be only about major courses. However, the reality is that our modern society requires the higher education graduates are not only specialists, but are also knowledgeable citizens. Here are some basic skills a knowledgeable citizen should have: communication, critical thinking, quantitative analysis, problem solving, and understanding of the arts, humanities, and the sciences. In addition, general education could empower graduates to tackle their professional work in a complex business and social environment. More importantly, general education promotes the training of responsible, reasonable, and intelligent citizens, which are critical to the functioning of our democratic world (Aloi et al., 2003; Bourke et al., 2009; Brint et al., 2009; Glynn et al., 2005).

Intense work has been done to promote general education in the areas of communication (Mazer et al., 2008), critical thinking (Rowe et al., 2015), art (Miraglia, 2008), and science, including computer science (Stegink etal., 1999). For example, in a survey conducted by Ratcliff et al. (2001), people found out that general education has gained its importance in the past years, and it remains a high priority item on the majority of campuses in the United States.

However, little work has been reported that the cross-disciplinary concept "*information*" has been taught as a standard alone general education course. Certainly, the concept of "*information*" could be included in science courses, such as physics and biology, library courses, and computer science courses. Unfortunately, to the best of our knowledge there has been no general education course about "*information*" and "*information theory*" offered in colleges as an inter-disciplinary concept. In addition, research (Ratcliff et al., 2001) found out that we have not made advances in developing shared educational values that could be embedded in students' lives after their graduation.

Accordingly, there is a need to develop a course that can relates to students' daily life over a long time, which can enable students to understand the complex world, adapt to the dynamic business environment, and handle unpredictable life challenges. We believe a course about "*information*" and "*information theory*" can partially serve this need.

COURSE DESCRIPTION

If you are a college instructor, you might be approached by students and asked this question: What is love? Your answer could vary depending on your area of expertise.

- If you are a physicist, you might consider love an electromagnetic interaction.
- If you are a chemist, you might consider love a chemical reaction.

- If you are a biologist, you might consider love part of the process for passing genetic code to next generations.
- If you are a sociologist, you might interpret love as a self-organization process that increases the order of society.

No matter what answer you give, you will for sure consider love an information exchanging process between two entities, specifically here, two human beings. Our students start to appreciate the world after they are born, usually haphazardly and experimentally. In k-12, they understand the world systematically through science and social study educations. Therefore, we expect any high school graduate be able to explain a natural phenomenon and have an opinion about a social issue. These explanations and opinions are usually reflecting their knowledge and view of a specific discipline.

As for higher education, we expect our graduates be able to look at any natural phenomenon and any social issue from multiple viewpoints based on multiple disciplines, which will help them avoid biased decisions so that they can better get integrated into the complex and diverse world. The course described in this chapter is intended to serve this objective.

Course Topics

Information is the key knowledge of the 21st century and is an interdisciplinary concept. From artificial intelligence, quantum computing, to genetic engineering, information and information technology play unique roles in revolutionizing our society. It is important for our students to have this knowledge and the holistic view about information to meet the new challenges in their careers and in their lives.
The various topics covered in this course (CSCI-N390: Information Theory) is listed below.

- **Physical information**: big bang theory, fundamental interactions (forces), and evolution of the universe
- **Chemical information**: chemical bond, chemical reaction, and earth revolution
- **Biological information**: chromosome, DNA, genetic code, and evolution of life on earth
- **Cognitive information**: human evolution, cognitive revolution, and human language
- **Social information**: education, trade, war, social orders and organizations
- **Computer information**: binary language, turing machine, and information encoding
- **Quantum information**: quantum mechanics, string theory, and quantum computing
- **Evolution of complexity**: physical entropy and information entropy
- **Predictability and uncertainty**: chaos theory and black swan theory
- **The future**: black hole and event horizon

It can be seen that the topics covered in this course are all related to information in certain context. Moreover, information can be viewed as the medium or force that drives the evolution of the physical world and human society.

Rationale for Course Offering

Students might have learned and have a basic understanding about the concept of information in different fields, such as physics, biology, and sociology. However, it is important to connect the isolated knowledge about information together and to have a broader view to understand how information and information technology plays its role in the physical world and in the human society.

As mentioned before, information is an interdisciplinary concept. Although it has been studied in different areas and in different contexts, only after the revolution of computer technology, *information theory* emerged as a new model intended to generalize the information concepts in all these fields. In this course, computer and information technology are embedded and described in all the aforementioned topics.

To summarize, this course (CSCI-N390: Information Theory) presents interdisciplinary concepts, where "*information*" as the backbone subject, connects knowledge in physics (fundamental interactions, entropy, quantum computing), biology (chromosome, DNA, and genetic code), computer science (turing machine, binary language), sociology (social information), and other disciplines.

This course (CSCI-N390: Information Theory) is designed to be offered to sophomore, junior, and senior students who have at least one year of college experience. Because of the diverse topics covered in this course, there is no ready-to-use textbooks. The instructor provides handout, reference books, and online resources to students.

Learning Methods

The following learning methods are utilized in this course.

- **Lectures**: Instructors give lectures on every topic. Online resources are intensively used in lectures, including documentaries and magazines.
- **Discussions**: During the lectures, students are engaged to participate discussions. Students are encouraged to ask and answer questions based on their knowledge and life experience.
- **Presentations**: Students are asked to write a final report on their selected topics, and they are asked to give individual or team presentations on their report.
- **Case studies presented by the instructor**: On some topics, during the lecture, the instructor will use a case study to describe the subject and illustrate the theories.
- **Case studies by students**: On some topics, students are asked to conduct a case study to investigate some real-world findings or real-world issues using their acquired knowledge on that topic.

The key to the successful application of these teaching methods is to engage students in classroom discussions and encourage them to use analogical reasoning to examine problems.

Course Schedule

This 3-credit hour course is designed to be offered in a regular semester of 16 weeks with two lectures per week. The detailed course schedule, prior (background) knowledge, topics description, and references are described below.

- **Week 01 (Day 1)**
    - **Topic**: Introduction to information theory
    - **Prior knowledge**: No
    - **Description**: Introduce the concept of information, its appearance and its role in the physical world and human society.

    - **Reference**: Roederer, 2006
- **Week 01 (Day 2)**
    - **Prior knowledge introduction (review)**: prepare students for next topic "Physical Information"
- **Week 02 (Day 1 and Day 2)**
    - **Topic**: Physical information
    - **Prior knowledge**: Atom, structure of atom, gravity, light, electricity. Some of these concepts are covered in high school Physics I and Chemistry I. However, high school Physics I and Chemistry I are elective in some schools. Therefore, the prior knowledge is introduced in Day 2 of Week 01 to better prepare students for understanding physical information.
    - **Description**: Describe how the physical world functions through information exchanging. Four fundamental interactions (strong interaction, weak interaction, gravitational interaction, and electromagnetic interaction) are discussed.
    - **Reference**: Seife, 2007
- **Week 03 (Day 1)**
    - **Prior knowledge introduction (review)**: prepare students for next topic "Chemical Information"
- **Week 03 (Day 2)**
    - **Topic**: Chemical information
    - **Prior knowledge**: Atom, element, compound, and molecule. Although these concepts are covered in high school Chemistry I, considering that some students might not have taken that course, the prior knowledge is given in Day 1 of Week 03.
    - **Description**: Describe chemical bond and chemical reactions as molecule-level information and information exchange. Introduce the concept of entropy.
    - **Reference:** Gleick, 2012
- **Week 04 (Day 1 and Day 2)**
    - **Topic**: Biological information
    - **Prior knowledge**: Organism, evolution, and cell. These concepts are covered in high school Biology I. They will be reviewed if needed.
    - **Description**: Describe chromosome, DNA, and genetic code as the biological information.
    - **Reference**: Raff, 2012
- **Week 05 (Day 1)**
    - **Topic**: Intelligence and cognitive information
    - **Prior knowledge**: High school level knowledge of social studies.
    - **Description**: Describe human evolution as the result of cognitive revolution. Specific topics include knowledge, belief, and human language.
    - **Reference book:** Harari, 2014
- **Week 05 (Day 2)**
    - **Topic**: Science and scientific revolution
    - **Prior knowledge**: High school level knowledge of social studies
    - **Description**: Describe the scientific method and the scientific revolution that occurred in the past 500 years. Understand how science has broaden our knowledge (information) and widen our horizons.
    - **Reference**: Shapin, 2018

- **Week 06 (Day 1 and Day 2)**
    - **Topic**: Social information
    - **Prior knowledge**: High school level knowledge of social studies.
    - **Description**: Describe human interactions and social activities as information sharing and information dissemination. Specific topics include education, trade, social orders and organizations, etc.
    - **Reference**: Baase, 2012
- **Week 07 (Day 1 and Day 2)**
    - **Topic**: Binary language
    - **Prior knowledge**: No
    - **Description**: Describe the universal communication language used by human-invented computers.
    - **Reference**: Petzold, 2000
- **Week 08 (Day 1 and Day 2)**
    - **Topic**: Turing machine and modern computer
    - **Prior knowledge**: High school level of mathematics.
    - **Description**: Review the fundamentals of computing and information technology. Discuss the difference of how computers and human beings process information.
    - **Reference**: Copeland et al., 2013
- **Week 09 (Day 1 and Day 2)**
    - **Topic**: Information entropy
    - **Prior knowledge**: logarithm (covered in high school Algebra II)
    - **Description**: Describe information storage measurement.
    - **Reference**: Stone, 2015
- **Week 10 (Day 1 and Day 2)**
    - **Topic**: Information encoding
    - **Prior knowledge**: prime numbers, factorization (covered in elementary school or middle school)
    - **Description**: Describe information encryption, protection, and transformation.
    - **Reference**: Paar & Pelzl, 2009
- **Week 11 (Day 1)**
    - **Prior knowledge introduction (review)**: prepare students for next topic "Quantum Information and Quantum Computing".
- **Week 11 (Day 2)**
    - **Topic**: Quantum information and quantum computing
    - **Prior knowledge**: Structure of atom and fundamental particles and their properties, covered in Day 1 of Week 11.
    - **Description**: Describe quantum computing—the possible future of computing technology.
    - **Reference**: Katwala, 2021
- **Week 12 (Day 1 and Day 2)**
    - **Topic**: Evolution of complexity
    - **Prior knowledge**: No.
    - **Description**: Use entropy (introduced in Week 03) and information entropy (introduced in Week 09) to discuss hierarchical structure of the physical world and social world.

- **Reference**: Gribbin, 2005
- **Week 13 (Day 1 and Day 2)**
    - **Topic**: Predictability and uncertainty
    - **Prior knowledge**: investment, demand, supply, and price (covered in high school Economics I)
    - **Description**: Introduce chaos theory and black swan theory. Describe information and predictability, and the uncertainty nature of the physical world and human society.
    - **Reference**: Fromm, 2004
- **Week 14 (Day 1 and Day 2)**
    - **Topic**: Technology revolution
    - **Prior knowledge**: No.
    - **Description**: Discuss how technology revolution and information explosion have affected and will affect human society and human evolution.
    - **Reference**: Georgios, 2016
- **Week 15 (Day 1 and Day 2)**
    - **Topic**: The unknown
    - **Prior knowledge**: No.
    - **Description**: Explore the frontier of our understanding of information, such as event horizon, and its relation to the ultimate fate of the physical world.
    - **Reference**: Hawking, 2009
- **Week 16 (final week)**
    - Students presentations

Learning Assessment

The following assessment methods are utilized in this course.

- Homework assignments are given to students to solve clearly specified problems. Mathematics skills and quantitative analysis skills are needed to work on these assignments.
- Case study assignments are designed for students to study a physical phenomenon, a social issue or read an article on a specific topic. Students are then required to identify, analyze, characterize, and interpret the key information. Finally, students should write a short report to describe their findings and understandings.
- Exams (Quizzes) are given to students to assess their understanding of the basic concepts in "*information theory*", the roles played by "*information*", and the applications.
- Final presentation and report are used to evaluate students' comprehensive knowledge of this course and their capability of applying the knowledge to interpret real world issues and solve real world problems.

The detailed learning objectives and assessment methods are described in Table 1.

Table 1. Assessment of learning objectives

Topics	Learning Objectives	Assessment of Learning Outcomes*
Introduction	Recognize that information is everywhere in our lives.	Open discussions in class.
Physical information	Be able to categorize fundamental interactions in real world.	Read an article or investigate a physical phenomenon and write a report to describe the fundamental interaction.
Chemical information	(1) Justify chemical reaction is the fundamental of any activities of all organisms. (2) Be able to compute entropy.	(1) Open discussions in class. (2) Work on assignment to calculate entropy.
Biological information	Explain chromosome, DNA, and genetic code.	Read an article and write a report about a latest development in gene technology.
Intelligence and Cognitive information	Recognize cognition is a key difference between human beings and other organisms.	Open discussions in class.
Scientific revolution	Describe science and scientific method.	Open discussions in class.
Social information	Be able to analyze social institutions and social events using information theory.	Write a report to describe a social institution or a social event using information theory.
Binary language	(1) Justify why binary language is a universal communication language. (2) Be able to interpret binary numbers.	(1) Open discussions in class. (2) Work on assignment about number conversions.
Turing machine	Describe the operations of modern computers and their strength and weakness.	Open discussions in class.
Information entropy	Be able to compute information uncertainty.	Work on an assignment to measure information entropy.
Information encoding	(1) Be able to apply some computer encoding and encryption techniques. (2) Be able to distinguish the biological information replication processes.	(1) Work on an assignment to encode computer data. (2) Open discussions in class.
Quantum information	Be able to explain the underlying principles of quantum computing.	Open discussions in class.
Evolution of complexity	Be able to identify and describe emergence and self-organization process of complex systems.	Read an article or investigate a complex system and write a report to describe it.
Predictability and uncertainty	Be able to explain some social events and natural events with chaos theory and black swan theory.	Open discussions in class.
Technology revolution	Be able to assess the social impact, business impact, and ethical impact of emerging technologies.	Investigate a new technology and write a report to describe its possible social impact, business impact, and ethical impact.
The unknown	Describe the theory of black hole, expanding universe, and event horizon.	Open discussions in class.
Comprehensive **knowledge**	Be able to apply the comprehensive knowledge learned in this class to have a deep understanding of real-world issues and problems.	Write a final report and give a final presentation to describe their deep understanding of a physical phenomenon or a social issue.

*Note: Some of these learning outcomes are assessed with exams.

Lecture Case Studies

This course uses case studies to explain how 'information' is correlated with the complex world we are living in. Here we describe several of these case studies discussed in lectures.

- The big bang theory. In week 2, we describe the big bang theory and relate it to the four fundamental interactions (strong interaction, weak interaction, gravity, electromagnetism) of nature.
- Heat death of the universe. In Week 3, we describe the hypothesis of heat death of the universe using the theory of entropy.
- Timeline of life on earth. In Week 4, we talk about the emergence and extinction of various of lives on earth.
- Gossip. Gossip is a kind of social skill, and it plays an important role in human evolution. In Week 5, we use this case study to illustrate how Sapiens individuals could form groups and develop into complex societies.
- Six degree of separation. Six degree of separation is the idea that people in the world is six or fewer steps away from each other so that a chain of "a friend of a friend" can be established to connect any two people in a maximum of six steps. In Week 6, we use this case study to describe the exchange of social information.
- Alien message. In 1974, an interstellar radio message carrying basic information about humanity and Earth was sent to globular star cluster M13 in the hope that extraterrestrial intelligence might receive and decipher it. In Week 7 (binary language), we talk about this message. The interesting fact about this message is that it is written in binary language (computer language), which is used to represent our decimal system, nucleotides, planets, human body, and the telescope sending the message. Through this case study, we want to stress the significance of binary languages: if there are intelligent aliens who could communicate with us, most likely, a binary language will be used. Accordingly, we believe binary language is the universal intelligent language.
- Bitcoin and blockchain. In Week 11, we use bitcoin and blockchain technology to describe the usage of different encryption technologies in modern society and business transactions.
- 2016 presidential election. The 2016 presidential election of the United States is remembered both politically and academically because both the main media and the major polls failed to correctly predict the winner. This election is discussed and analyzed in Week 13 (predictability and uncertainty). In fact, we have well established theories (chaos theory, black swan theory) that can explain this election. The uncertainty view of the world represents the most significant thinking revolution of human beings in the past century.
- Human-machine marriage. Same-sex marriage has become widely accepted and legalized in many countries. What if you unfortunately cannot find a human partner, can you marry a highly intelligent robot who can deeply understand you and support you? In Week 14, we talk about the evolution of technology, especially artificial intelligence and its impact on our values, culture, and society.
- Black hole. Black hole is a dense place in space where gravity has become so extreme that it attracts everything nearby and not even light can escape from it. In Week 15 (the unknown), we will talk about black hole, which includes topics on event horizon, entropy and information inside the black hole. We will also explain why black hole can continually absorb everything it attracts while not explodes using Hawking's radiation theory. Through this case study, we want to demonstrate the significant role played by "*information*" in determining the destination of the universe.

IMPLICATIONS, LIMITATIONS, AND FUTURE WORK

This study has implications on higher education both theoretically and practically. Theoretically, this study proves that it is possible to combine topics from multiple disciplines into one course seamlessly. Practically, this study demonstrates that the knowledge gap between diverse subjects can be closed by carefully selecting a theme of the course, which covers various domains.

As with any study, the research presented in this chapter has some limitations. First, this course requires students to have some mathematics and science background; it might not be feasible for students majoring in Arts, Liberal Arts, or other fields without necessary background knowledge. Second, this course demands the instructor to have cross-discipline knowledge, which makes it a challenging task to prepare and teach the course.

Our future research is planned to focus on three directions. First, we will promote this course to other Indiana University campuses. Our university has total nine campuses across Indiana. We will seek opportunities to present our research to our colleagues so that multiple sessions of this course could be offered on different campuses. Second, with more offerings in the foreseeable future, we will collect more data about the teaching and learning of this course. Third, in the long run, we will conduct surveys to our graduates to evaluate the impact of this courses on their academic study, professional development, and life journey.

CONCLUSION

This chapter describes an interdisciplinary course proposed at Indiana University South Bend to fulfill the general education requirement on *the natural world* subject. The course talks about a cross-major topic, *information*, which covers interdisciplinary knowledge, including physics, chemistry, biology, computer science, anthropology, sociology, history, and more. Through taking this course, students will be able to (1) identify and interpret 'information' as a fundamental component of the physical world; (2) recognize and generalize how information relates to the functioning of our complex society; and (3) use information theory to understand and deal with real-world issues and real-world problems.

This interdisciplinary course is currently designed to be taught by a computer science instructor whose bachelor's degree, master's degree, and PhD degree are in three different fields. For other instructors to teach this course, it might be challenging because of the diverse topics covered in this course. In the future course coffering, we might invite instructors from different programs to give guest lectures on different topics. Scheduling could be an issue for this teaching model. However, it is worth of trying different teaching strategies so that we can collect data to evaluate and compare the outcomes of different teaching methods.

We are living in an era with exploding knowledge, changing technologies, and emerging ideas. It is essential to equip college students the key skills they need to comprehend and deal with the complex world and society. This study intends to present an approach in college general education to fulfill this goal. The central aspect of this study is to interpret "*information*" comprehensively, which could have a far-reaching impact on our students. We do not expect to educate our students mature enough by a single course of *information theory*. However, combing other general education subjects, such as critical thinking, quantitative reasoning, verbal and non-verbal communications, we believe we can educate our students as responsible, wised, and valued citizens and life-long learners.

REFERENCES

Aloi, S. L., Gardner, W. S., & Lusher, A. L. (2003). A framework for assessing general education outcomes within the majors. *The Journal of General Education, 52*(4), 237–252. doi:10.1353/jge.2004.0009

Baase, S. (2012). *A gift of fire*. Pearson Education Limited.

Bourke, B., Bray, N. J., & Horton, C. C. (2009). Approaches to the core curriculum: An exploratory analysis of top liberal arts and doctoral-granting institutions. *The Journal of General Education, 58*(4), 219–240. doi:10.2307/25702445

Brint, S., Proctor, K., Murphy, S. P., Turk-Bicakci, L., & Hanneman, R. A. (2009). General education models: Continuity and change in the US undergraduate curriculum, 1975–2000. *The Journal of Higher Education, 80*(6), 605–642. doi:10.1080/00221546.2009.11779037

Copeland, B. J., Posy, C. J., & Shagrir, O. (Eds.). (2013). *Computability: Turing, gödel, church, and beyond*. Mit Press. doi:10.7551/mitpress/8009.001.0001

Cordell, R. M. (2013). Indiana University South Bend. In Library Reference Services and Information Literacy: Models for Academic Institutions (pp. 153–170). IGI Global. doi:10.4018/978-1-4666-4241-6.ch011

Fidalgo-Blanco, Á., Sein-Echaluce, M. L., & García-Peñalvo, F. J. (2014). Knowledge spirals in higher education teaching innovation. *International Journal of Knowledge Management, 10*(4), 16–37. doi:10.4018/ijkm.2014100102

Fromm, J. (2004). The emergence of complexity. Kassel University Press.

Georgios, Z. (2016). *In our own image: Savior or destroyer? The history and future of artificial intelligence*. Pegasus Books.

Gleick, J. (2012). *The information: A history, a theory, a flood*. Vintage.

Glynn, S. M., Aultman, L. P., & Owens, A. M. (2005). Motivation to learn in general education programs. *The Journal of General Education, 54*(2), 150–170. doi:10.2307/27798014

Gribbin, J. (2005). *Deep simplicity: Chaos, complexity and the emergence of life*. Penguin UK.

Hanushek, E. A., Schwerdt, G., Woessmann, L., & Zhang, L. (2017). General education, vocational education, and labor-market outcomes over the lifecycle. *The Journal of Human Resources, 52*(1), 48–87. doi:10.3368/jhr.52.1.0415-7074R

Harari, Y. N. (2014). *Sapiens: A brief history of humankind*. Random House.

Hawking, S. (2009). *A brief history of time: From big bang to black holes*. Random House.

Katwala, A. (2021). *Quantum computing: How it works and how it could change the world*. Random House.

Krueger, D., & Kumar, K. B. (2004). Skill-specific rather than general education: A reason for US–Europe growth differences. *Journal of Economic Growth*, *9*(2), 167–207. doi:10.1023/B:JOEG.0000031426.09886.bd

Mazer, J. P., Hunt, S. K., & Kuznekoff, J. H. (2008). Revising general education: Assessing a critical thinking instructional model in the basic communication course. *The Journal of General Education*, *56*(3-4), 173–199. doi:10.2307/27798079

Miraglia, K. M. (2008). Attitudes of preservice general education teachers toward art. *Visual Arts Research*, 53–62.

O'Banion, T. (2016). A brief history of general education. *Community College Journal of Research and Practice*, *40*(4), 327–334. doi:10.1080/10668926.2015.1117996

Paar, C., & Pelzl, J. (2009). *Understanding cryptography: A textbook for students and practitioners*. Springer Science & Business Media.

Petzold, C. (2000). *Code: The hidden language of computer hardware and software*. Microsoft Press.

Raff, R. A. (2012). *The shape of life: Genes, development, and the evolution of animal form*. University of Chicago Press.

Ratcliff, J. L., Johnson, D. K., La Nasa, S. M., & Gaff, J. G. (2001). *The status of general education in the year 2000: Summary of a national survey*. Association of American Colleges & Universities.

Roederer, J. G. (2006). *Information and its role in nature*. Springer Science & Business Media.

Rowe, M. P., Gillespie, B. M., Harris, K. R., Koether, S. D., Shannon, L. J. Y., & Rose, L. A. (2015). Redesigning a general education science course to promote critical thinking. *CBE Life Sciences Education*, *14*(3), ar30. doi:10.1187/cbe.15-02-0032 PMID:26231561

Saura, J. R., Palacios-Marqués, D., & Ribeiro-Soriano, D. (2022b). Exploring the boundaries of Open Innovation: Evidence from social media mining. *Technovation*, 102447. doi:10.1016/j.technovation.2021.102447

Saura, J. R., Ribeiro-Soriano, D., & Saldaña, P. Z. (2022a). Exploring the challenges of remote work on Twitter users' sentiments: From digital technology development to a post-pandemic era. *Journal of Business Research*, *142*, 242–254. doi:10.1016/j.jbusres.2021.12.052

Seife, C. (2007). *Decoding the universe: How the new science of information is explaining everything in the cosmos, from our brains to black holes*. Penguin.

Shapin, S. (2018). *The scientific revolution*. University of Chicago Press.

Stegink, G., Pater, J., & Vroon, D. (n.d.). Computer science and general education: Java, graphics, and the web. In *Proceedings of the 13th SIGCSE Technical Symposium on Computer Science Education* (pp. 146–149). Academic Press.

Stone, J. V. (2015). *Information theory: A tutorial introduction*. Sebtel Press.

Warner, D. B., & Koeppel, K. (2009). General education requirements: A comparative analysis. *The Journal of General Education*, *58*(4), 241–258. doi:10.2307/25702446

Westmeyer, P. (1985). *A History of American Higher Education*. Charles C. Thomas, Publisher.

KEY TERMS AND DEFINITIONS

Biological Information: The chromosome, DNA, and genetic code of lives on earth.

Chemical Information: The chemical bond, which is the driving force of chemical reaction.

Cognitive Information: The information used in human communication, such as language, literature, arts, which is the driving force of human evolution.

Computer Information: Information used in man-made computers, such as binary language, encrypted data.

General Education: Part of an undergraduate study besides the area of major classes that define the degree.

Information Theory: The scientific study of information representation, storage, and communication at different levels and in different domains.

Interdisciplinary Course: A course that covers topics of various fields.

Physical Information: The fundamental particle interactions in the physical world.

Quantum Information: Information represented at the quantum mechanic's level.

Social Information: The components and their interactions of social entities that govern the functioning of our society.

Chapter 7

Practice-Integrated Teaching at Universities of Applied Sciences: Models and Good Practices

Matthias Lederer
Technical University of Applied Sciences Amberg-Weiden, Germany

Silke Finken
ISM International School of Management, Munich, Germany

ABSTRACT

What is special about the German-speaking education system is that there are two types of higher education institutions. While classical universities do academic teaching, so-called universities of applied sciences (UAS) focus more on practical training for the labour market. This chapter presents the experiences of two professors with practice-integrated teaching at two UAS that ensure employability to a large extent. The common setting of the four courses presented is that students work on real business cases, practical challenges, and real fields of innovation. Methodologically, design think and SCRUM are used. It is described for these cases how the design of the course contributes to students developing innovative and digital approaches for real companies. The chapter concludes with a compilation of good practices that emerged from experiences. These can serve as input for other teachers to design their own practice-integrated courses.

INTRODUCTION AND BACKGROUND

In contrast to many other countries, the German higher education system recognizes two main forms of university organizations. On the one hand, classical "universities" focus on top-level scientific education, which is mainly theoretical and sometimes also partly application-oriented. So-called "universities of applied sciences" (UAS), on the other hand, aim at practice-oriented broad-based education and have become an increasingly popular alternative to in-company training since the European Bologna reforms. Both types of institution educate students in bachelor's and master's degree programs at the same level

DOI: 10.4018/978-1-6684-4441-2.ch007

Copyright © 2022, IGI Global. Copying or distributing in print or electronic forms without written permission of IGI Global is prohibited.

and often offer a variety of degree programs with specializations. Typically, the difference between a UAS and a classical university is strikingly described by the fact that the former are practice/application-oriented and the latter have a strong theoretical teaching and scientific research focus (Denert, 2005; Horcher, 1998; Hüther & Krücken, 2018).

Nevertheless, the relationship between these two types in the tertiary education sector is the subject of ongoing discussions that include both alignments and demarcations. If, according to the fundamental orientation described in the first paragraph, one would expect universities to teach only a very low number of students in small groups to prepare them for careers in research or for doctoral studies and, in contrast, UAS to offer a large number of practice-oriented exercises, the status is strangely the other way around (Denert, 2005; Horcher, 1998; Hüther & Krücken, 2018). Universities often offer courses for a huge number of students and graduates usually do not work in research after graduation, but more often have the chance to work for big corporations. UAS, on the other hand, generally train students in small groups, are comparatively structured in their curriculum, and support students in obtaining internships at companies and organizing exchanges with international partner universities. Professors here usually have a teaching load that is twice as high as at universities, have no research assistants and very little equipment for research work, as well as no right to award doctorates (Denert, 2005). This makes practical training possible but is also demanding given the workload and conditions. However, students at UAS typically appreciate these structures because instructors are more approachable and administration units (e.g., advising, scheduling, etc.) are very service-oriented. Instead of the research-based learning at classical universities, UAS prepare their students for entry into companies through cooperation with companies, case studies, practical work and the training of social skills (Denert, 2005; Horcher, 1998).

Some professors have noticed in recent years that the distinction between these two types of universities is shifting. In general, the academic content of UAS has become comparable or nearly identical to that of universities. However, the configurations of the UAS are explicitly geared towards application-oriented teaching: For example, professors must demonstrate a minimum of practical activities in companies and students have to complete an internship in the course of their studies (Hüther & Krücken, 2018).

The two authors of this article come from two UAS in Germany from the disciplines of business administration and information systems and have been in constructive dialog for years about how practice-oriented teaching at UAS can be taken seriously and implemented sensibly within the given conditions. They consider an academic and theoretically founded education to be very good and important, but above all they want to particularly promote the core of the UAS through modern concepts. In accordance with the mission of this type of university, they go beyond the known practice-oriented teaching and do not just work on case studies or invite external speakers for lectures. Rather, they organize practice-integrated teaching that is intensively supporting the knowledge and technology transfer. In this approach, practical questions from companies do not become a supplement, but rather the essential starting point for the teaching units. The professors take advantage of the small group sizes and work on the problems and real practical cases live in the course. Communication, feedback rounds and the presentation of their results within the company environment ensure not only a high learning outcome for the students, but also a massive employability and also great satisfaction in the courses.

How to implement such a practice-oriented or application-oriented teaching in higher education is, of course, already the subject of much research (Abykanova et al., 2017) and practical guidelines (e.g., Fidalgo-Blanco et al., 2022). This is true on an international as well as on a national level. Internationally, it is of course a permanent question how business practice can be brought into universities. The guidelines and studies often focus on very specific advice on technical tools (e.g., Maltseva et al.,

2020; Redondo et al., 2020) or on the exact content to be taught (e.g., Smirnova et al., 2018) as well as on specific methods (e.g., Pavlova et al, 2020). Likewise, we find recommendations on how to design the context of practice-oriented teaching. For example, publications outline how to establish a general relationship with companies or how to create an entrepreneurial-friendly ecosystem (e.g., Prosalova & Nikolaeva, 2020). What is exciting when looking at related work is that solutions are often country- (e.g., Zautorova & Bodrova, 2021) or very domain-specific (e.g., Korchinskaya et al., 2019; Dyganoca & Yavgildina, 2020) education are often addressed.

For the specifics of the German university landscape with its UAS, such publications can be found mainly in German and less in international publications. Many of the discussions conducted in German address predominantly formal issues (e.g., Anlauf, 2018) or are limited in their consideration to classically German topics (e.g., Stewart, 2006). Yet it is precisely the German characteristic of deliberately practical training at UAS that opens up a basis for international attention and communication of experience. This paper aims to close this gap by not limiting the developed approaches for practice-integrated teaching to the partial questions or small topics described above. Rather, the authors demonstrate approaches that have proven themselves across universities of different UAS, across different degree programs (business and technical focus), and also across different channels (virtual and face-to-face as well as combinations). In addition to operational hints from teaching experience, the approaches presented in this contribution should give the readers the idea of a new mindset of corporate questions as starting point for any teaching initiative.

This contribution presents the particular form of *practice-integrated teaching* based on different course settings that can serve as inspiration for other teachers. The forms were tested in various modules in business and technical subjects at both bachelor's and master's level. Of course, the describing professors from the UAS have teaching experience, relevant certificates for university didactics and work experience in corporate practice. However, the compilation in this contribution is intended to cover less mundane issues of teaching or practice orientation. The possible settings (section 2) as well as the success factors that follow as recommendation (section 3) are rather intended as a guide for all teachers and interested parties who want to go a fundamental step further in the application orientation of their teaching - precisely from an orientation of teaching to business practice to business practice as an integral part of teaching, as the special form of the UAS demands.

COURSE SETTINGS

In this second section, we present four basic types of practice-integrated teaching with which the authors have had particularly good experiences. The basis of the assessment for this includes:

- **Perspective of the teachers:** Subjective assessment of competence acquisition (professional and personal) as well as objective assessment of acquired skills (e.g. excellent exam results),
- **Business perspective:** Suitability of the developed concepts or artifacts for direct use (e.g., transferring ideas to development, implementing the models into the company's existing information systems),
- **Student perspective:** Qualitative satisfaction during the course and positive qualitative evaluation results at the end of the semester.

As a rule, the practice-integrated courses have some form of company problem as the initial situation, which must be solved by the students based on specialist knowledge and the application of suitable methods. Due to the novelty of the introduced artifacts (e.g. ideas for the solution, new strategies, new IT models) and the demand for implementation in business practice, many projects fulfil the core definition for *innovation*. All projects carried out by the authors in this style lead to interesting and applicable innovations for the companies involved (van den Ende, 2021).

Figure 1 describes these practice-integrated ideal approaches according to their temporal and functional-technical orientation. Conceptual-visionary questions are characterized by a rather long-term time horizon of the solution, while operational questions tend to aim at a direct and short-term implementation at the business partner's side. Technical questions aim to create IT artifacts such as code, models, or procedures, while management orientation stands for focus on innovations in the form of concepts, business models, or strategies.

Figure 1. Overview of practice-integrated course settings
(own illustration)

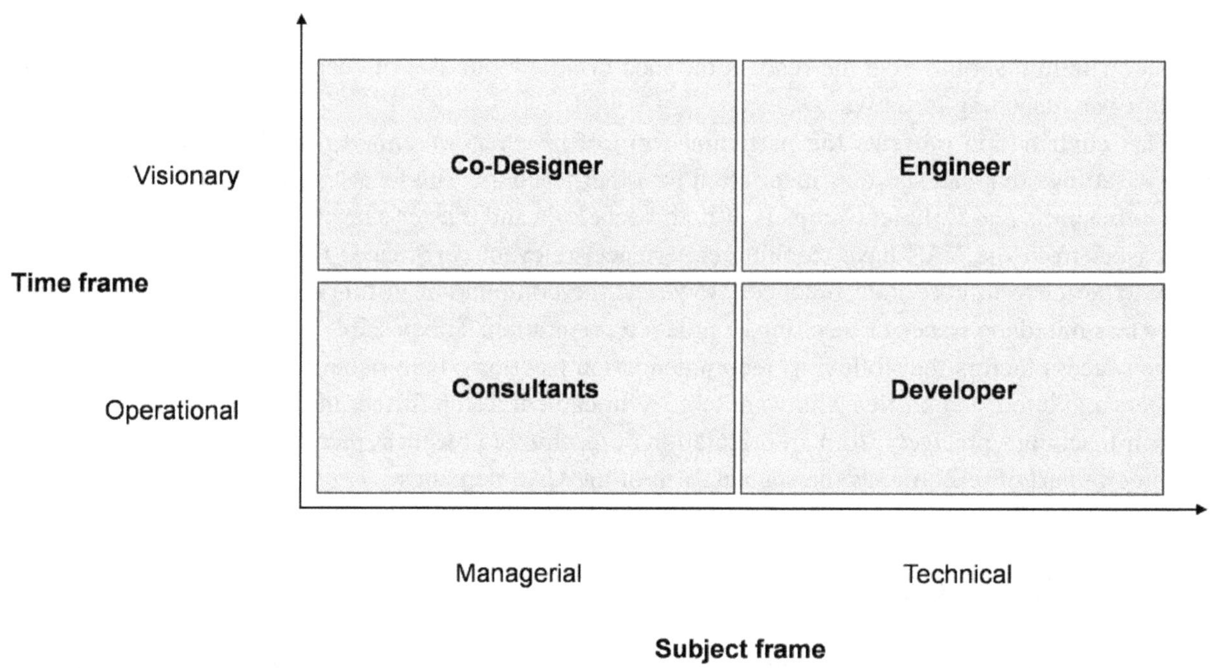

The following subsections describe each ideal type with its recommended process, roles, outcomes, and constraints.

Approach 1: Students as Designers

In a design thinking class, students are taught the methodologies and tools of design thinking and apply them in a real-world challenge. In general, design thinking is a current and popular approach in innovation management that follows a clearly defined process while combining analytical as well as highly creative steps. The key element of design thinking is to truly and thoroughly understand the latent and emerging needs and wants as well as unsolved problems of a particular user group in regard to a specific product, service or situation (Brown, 2021). Initially developed in Stanford (Auernhammer & Roth, 2021), it has its theoretical roots in a number of theories on creativity, the analysis of human needs and visual thinking (Von Thienen et al., 2017; Von Thienen et al., 2019; Von Thienen et al.,2021) and has been adopted by many corporations across a wide range of industries. It can be applied to solve a variety of challenges, though in the context of the lecture the development of a new product, service or strategy for a given user group is the most practical.

The design thinking process consists of five steps (see Figure 2): It starts with the "emphasize" step in which the students identify the needs and problems of the users through direct interaction with the users, e.g., in the form of interviews, observation of the users, and immersion, e.g., by duplicating the experiences the user goes through in specific settings. The second step called "define" consists of the analysis and clustering of the feedback from the emphasize phase and the precise definition of the "job to be done" which the product or service should provide for the user. In the third step called "ideate", creativity methods are employed to derive a variety of possible solutions which are then prioritized. In the fourth step, a prototype is built which is then tested in the fifth and final step.

Figure 2. Design thinking process for practice-integrated teaching
(own illustration based on the Stanford School Design Thinking Process)

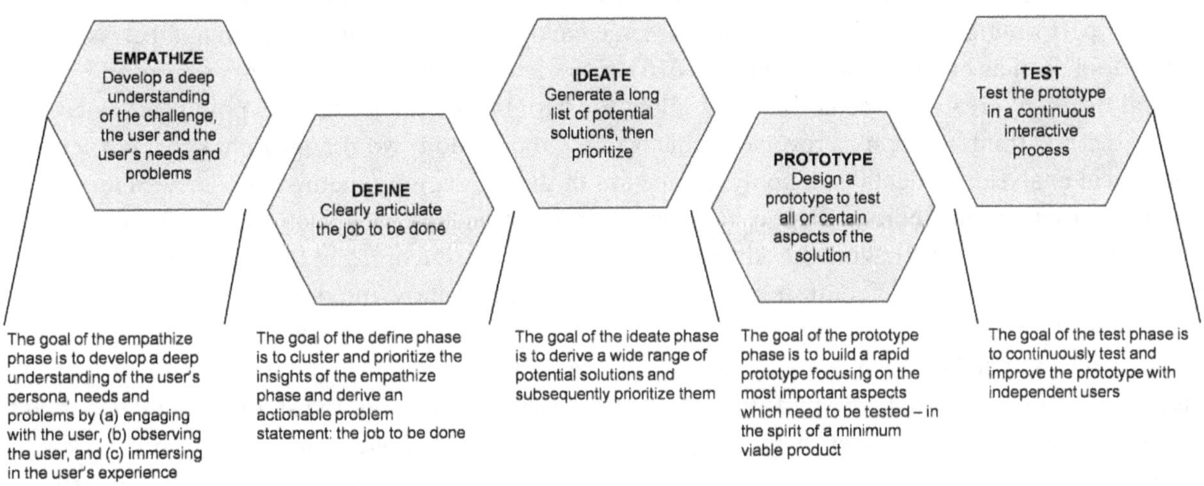

In the beginning of the class, the students form groups of five to seven members and choose a challenge presented by the instructor (professor or business partner/external client). The specific details for this case are discussed in the next setting (see next sub-section). Ideally, the challenge (a) concerns either the development of a new product or service for a hypothetical company in each industry or an idea for a new venture for a particular user group or (b) alternatively emerges out of a specific need or unsolved problem that a certain user group has. Individual roles within the teams do not need to be assigned, though the instructor should assume the role of a design thinking coach during the in-class exercises to ensure that methodologies and tools are applied correctly. Generally, the course follows a sequential structure of in class lectures and exercises as well as field assignments.

Students receive an in-classroom introduction to the overall design thinking process and the specific tools and approaches of the first two steps are explained. A high degree of interactivity (e.g. using short exercises and role-play) is used to illustrate how the methods are to be applied in practice. The students then begin with the interaction, the observation and if possible, the immersion to characterize typical users in more detail and identify their needs and problems. A minimum of five to ten interviews per team member is advisable. To increase practicability and tangibility, students are also required to describe two to four personas representing the users employing tools such as mood boards and empathy maps (Nielsen, 2011). Depending on the setting of the challenge, also future personas can be constructed (Fergani, 2019).

The second step contains the analysis and clustering of the insights of the first step as well as the definition of the specific "job to be done" (Christensen et al., 2016). A space allowing for variable settings and a large wall or screen for displaying the individual insights from the interviews is the ideal setup for this phase. Students typically record the insights on post-its – either in tangible paper format or in a digital equivalent – and identify clusters and patterns of needs and problems in a group discussion. The beginning of the analysis and the formulation of the "job to be done" is either conducted in class with the instructor serving as facilitator or the results of the group work conducted outside the classroom are presented in class to receive feedback by the instructor as especially a precise formulation of the "job to be done" is critical for the success of the ideation phase. An important element during the analysis of the feedback from the emphasize phase is also an extensive documentation, ideally also in the form of photographic documentary.

For the third step, a variety of creativity methods is initially presented and exercised in class. Ground rules for performing creativity sessions are explained and demonstrated in the setting of a classical creativity tool such as brainstorming (Kelley, 2016). Experience shows that results are improved by using several different creativity methods which allow for various positions and viewpoints and encourage out of the box thinking such as reverse brainstorming, the random word approach, synectics, or morphological analysis. Students then apply a selection of these creativity methods to derive a long list of potential solutions for their challenge. For their prioritization, methods such as "De Bonos thinking hats" can also be applied, having the advantage that students are encouraged to adapt different roles and mindsets outside their usual comfort zone (Kivunja, 2015). Similarly, the theoretical concept and tools for the fourth and fifth step are explained in class while the actual prototyping and testing with real users is then conducted independently by the students. Again, at least five to ten tests would be advisable and should be documented e.g., by filming the tests. During the testing, the students are compelled to reflect on the desirability as well as feasibility of the solution they created and to make necessary adaptions. This step also allows them to critically reflect their application of the theoretical knowledge of the design thinking process to real world situations in the previous steps and to derive valuable lesons learned for future projects.

The examination ideally takes the form of a final presentation (about 60 minutes) followed by a Question-and-Answer session (about 30 minutes) in which the teams present the key steps of the design thinking challenge and their resulting idea in the form of the tested prototype. Intermediate results such as (i) the patterns and key insights on the users' needs and problems, (ii) the description of the personas, the corresponding mood boards, and other artefacts, (iii) the final "job to be done", (iv) the short list of prioritized ideas, (v) the prototype and (vi) the test feedback should also be included in the presentation for grading.

If for some reasons a written examination such as a term paper is stipulated, the grading should take on the form of a written documentation of the challenge with identical contents as would be required in the presentation and an extensive photo documentation of the various steps. The prototype may be included in an appendix. If the challenge is issued by a third party such as a business partner, the challenge needs to include various touchpoints and regular interaction with the client as described in the setup of a consulting project (see next sub-chapter).

Approach 2: Students as Consultants

Another example of practice-integrative teaching are consulting projects in which the students work on a task assigned by an business partner (external client). While these projects typically can be applied to a variety of problem definitions, in the context of innovation management, design thinking projects are popular with clients and students as they do not require the students to have confidential in-depth information about the clients' processes and strategy and also tap the creativity of both the students as well as the client to a substantial extend. Ideally, the project succeeds a project management and a design thinking class as described above, allowing the students to become familiar with the tools and methodologies of the design thinking process before formally working on the project for the client (see Figure 3).

Figure 3. Project structure in the integrative approach "Students as Consultants"
(own illustration)

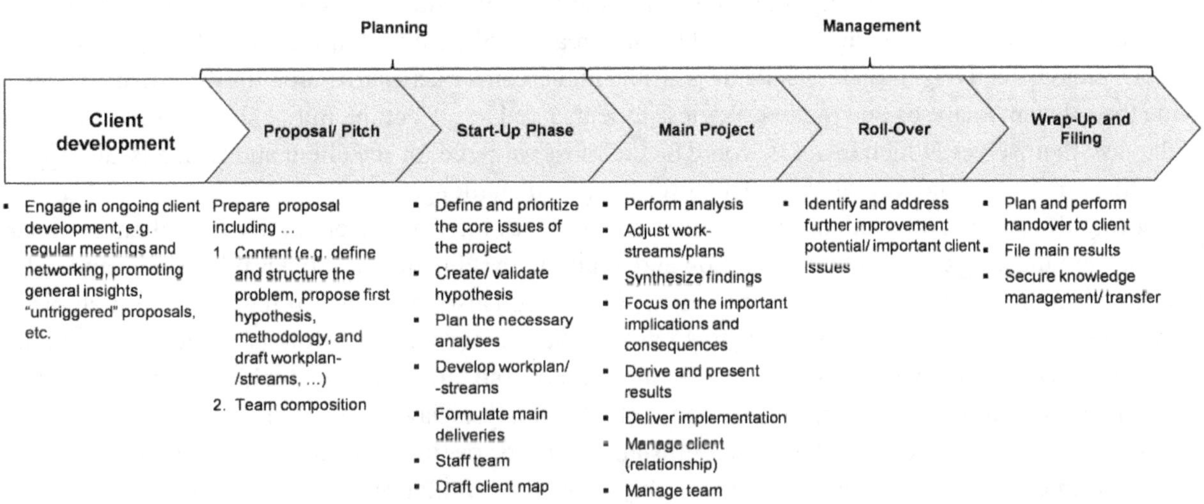

Before the start of the project, the instructor agrees on the specific challenge with the corporate client and the client, or the instructor prepare an initial briefing for the students in the form of a kick-off meeting. Prior to the kick-off meeting, a non-disclosure-agreement should be signed by all participating students. If time allows, the students can also first receive a formal call for proposal for which they will then have to pitch. Before the initial launch of the project, the lecturer introduces or revises the fundamentals of project management with the students depending on whether a general project management class was part of the curriculum before the start of the actual project. Emphasis is placed on the specifics of consulting projects with external clients such as agreeing early on the project deliverables with the client, continuously managing the expectation of the relevant client contacts to avoid spending time on non-value adding activities and delivering concise and appealing presentations of the project results to the client (Appelbaum & Steed, 2005; McKenna, 2006; Wickham & Wilcock, 2012).

After the kick-off in which the client briefs the students on the specific assignment for the project, e.g., the description of the design thinking challenge as well as the expectation which the client has regarding the project outcome, the students decide on an appropriate team structure to accommodate the scope and the necessary work streams and organize themselves internally in an appropriate project structure. While there are usually benefits of having one clearly assigned project leader, in a university setting in which the projects typically run parallel to other lectures during the semester, there are benefits to having two co-leaders for a project, especially when students simultaneously work on term papers or as working students. Occasionally, elements of shared or collective leaderships can also prove to be beneficial (Zhu, 2018). The remaining project structure including the number of workstreams depends on the specific assignment. Experience shows though that the size of sub-teams ideally ranges between three and six members depending on the specific topic. To ensure sufficient and frequent inter-team communication and regular team meetings, dedicated time slots should already be integrated by the instructor beforehand in the class schedule.

Ensuing the briefing respectively kick-of meeting, students describe their initial hypotheses, intended analyses and methodologies they are planning to use as well as the proposed work plan and deliverables for the project and obtain the clients approval. Agreeing very early on the expected results and output formats of the project is very important to ensure that the time and effort spend on the actual analysis, derivation of insights and solutions as well as the creation of potential artefacts such as prototypes is performed as effectively and efficiently as possible and creates maximum value for the client. To determine the relevant analyses and methodologies students need to reflect the initial status quo of the client and to ask themselves, which insights would be the most valuable for the client and which issues appear to be the core issues and key success factors for the given challenge.

During the project, the students give at least one in-depth interim presentation to the client to ensure that they are meeting the client's expectation and to allow for adjustment of the project scope and deliverables depending on initial results. The interim presentation also serves as a milestone for the students' reflection of the generated insights generated within the project scope as well as of the efficiency and effectiveness of the project management and team formation so far. As students critically reassess, which of the theoretical concepts and approaches chosen for the analysis have proven to be successful and which may have to be adapted to the practical circumstances of the specific project setting, they become more proficient in evaluating the practical applicability as well as limitations of the specific frameworks as well. This also applies for various instruments of leadership skills as well as team management tools.

Ideally, students interact on a regular basis with the client to inform the client contacts of the progress and current status of the project and to discuss preliminary results that may require the input of the client. This can be in the form of status updates via e-mail or regular physical or remote jour fixes. For larger projects and multiple client contact points, a client map is beneficial in avoiding unstructured and potentially redundant communication between various team members and the client. Especially in a design thinking project, actively including the client at various stages can be highly beneficial to install a higher degree of buy-in. The "job to be done" should be agreed upon with the client and involving the client in the creativity session as well as the testing of the prototype can also increase acceptance of the final ideas.

The examination takes place in the form of the presentations of the project results to the client. The main emphasis is usually placed on the final presentation, though also the interim presentations influence the final grade. To encourage all students to fully contribute to the project, the grading needs to be at least partially based on individual performance as well. One way to ensure this is to assign grades to individual parts and deliverables of the project and for the students to hand in activity reports or reflection papers stating how much of their time they spend on the individual tasks. Additionally, individual students should present status updates and preliminary results at the regular team meetings which the instructor attends.

Following the final presentation, a feedback session is conducted in which the students reflect on their experiences during the individual steps of the project. This allows the students to derive valuable lessons learned for future projects they are conducting on the individual as well as the group level. Additionally, the feedback of the students is taken into consideration for future consulting projects with new students. Over the course of several years, this has led to various organizational measures such as the upfront integration of team meetings into the class schedule by the lecturer as well as designing the content and scope of the project in a way to minimize the dependence on internal and confidential client data for the project success.

Approach 3: Students as Developers

In this third approach, students work on technical artifacts in the classic SCRUM approach. Many authors have already described how SCRUM is used as an approach in teaching; with Mahnic (2015), there is even already a meta-study on this. In contrast to the fourth and the second approach, in which more visionary issues are worked on over an entire semester, the operational development task is completed in about one week.

Since it is often important for technical tasks to clarify methodological basics (e.g., Unified Modeling Language [UML] standards) and frameworks (e.g., software to be used), some modules for self-study are to be worked on before the block week. For this purpose, the students are provided with video lectures and accompanying documents in a virtual course room. These are conducted individually and independent of time and location. While the technical content varies depending on the company's issues, a unit on SCRUM methodology ("Project Managemet" in Figure 4) must always be completed. Here, the agile process model with its roles, artifacts, events and rules is outlined in detail (e.g. according to scrum.org standards), so that all students have the same understanding of the actual project process (e.g. the company provides stories as product owner and participates in planning and review) and also the underlying SCRUM principles (e.g. self-organization in the team, agile and incremental development, immediate testing of results, ongoing integration) during the following block week (Schwab, 2014; Damian et al., 2012)

Figure 4. Two-stage structure of the course
(own illustration)

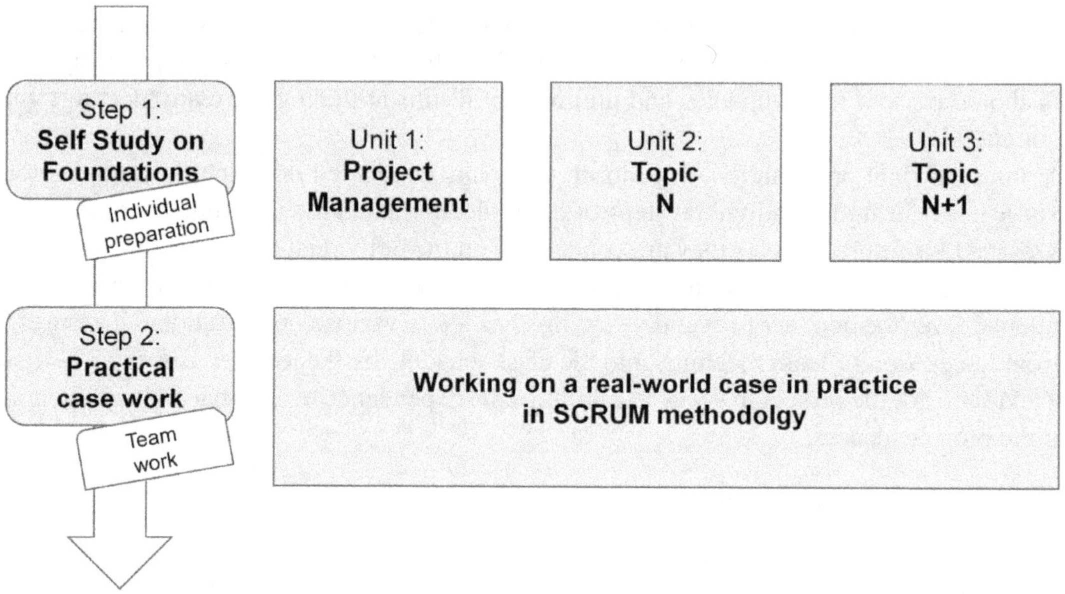

Within one week, usually only two sprints are realistic with real companies. On the one hand, this is due to the availability of the product owners from industry. On the other hand, this double sprint is enough for the students to have the chance to understand and experience the *SCRUM* methodology. Figure 5 summarizes the schedule during the week with naming of the standard events according to Schwab (2014) and Umer (2020).

Figure 5. Weekly schedule with SCRUM events
(own illustration)

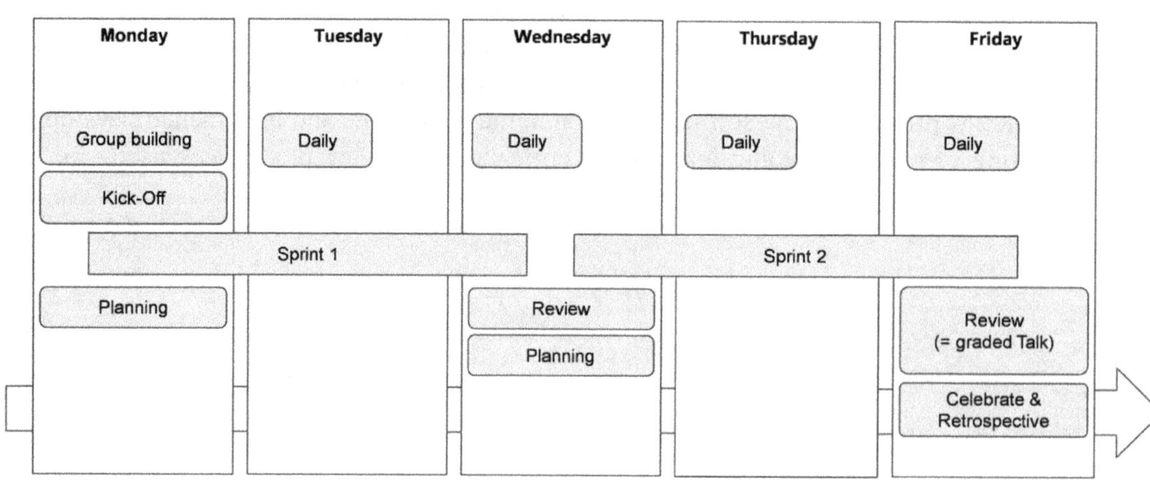

First, the students form groups (maximum eight people) and clarify their roles. For this, the students' wishes for further development (e.g., want to experience the tasks of a SCRUM Master), but also specific previous knowledge (e.g., good programmers may become developers) must be considered. A guideline supports the students in clarifying their roles as well as in all further events (Schwab, 2014; Umer, 2020).

After that, the company representatives come into the groups and present their question/their development project. The main thing to clarify is which technical or technology-related artifacts are expected at the end. The authors have already had positive experiences with many different goals (e.g., landing pages, advertisements, software, process models, maturity levels, etc.). While the kick-off involves describing the issues in their overall context (e.g., importance to the company, project background, etc.), the planning event requires systematizing the company's desires using stories. As the week progresses, the focus is only on maximizing artifacts and quickly achieving a Minimum Viable Product. This orientation is similar to the "job to be done" idea of the first setting described (see above). The students work exactly according to the SCRUM methodology at the beginning of the first sprint, so it is clarified which features will be considered in which iteration. The ongoing results are discussed daily at the stand-up (Daily SCRUM) and visualized on a Kanban board. The review of the results together with the company are scheduled in the middle of the week and are also organized strictly according to SCRUM principles (e.g., weaknesses of the previous solution go into the new planning as a new story and compete for the other ideas for further development). The second review is also used as a graded presentation. This requires openness from the supervising professor in the form of delivery (e.g., walkthrough instead of presentation) but has the great advantage for students that the practical work becomes a real integral part of the course and assessment. Students act in all events like professional developers and thus have the feeling of a real industry projects. This includes an invitation with an agenda, adherence to SCRUM rules in the process, and application of recognized voting methods (e.g., planning poker in planning, integration in development, and perspective appraisal in review). After each sprint, not only external feedback rounds are planned, but also an internal retrospective. This can be combined with a social event at the end of the week, where the company can express its appreciation (e.g., inviting the students for dinner) and further approaches for practice integration can arise (e.g., job placement) (Schwab, 2014; Jurado-Navas & Munoz-Luna, 2017; May et al., 2016; Matthies, 2018).

During the week, the teams work in a self-organized manner, which gives the participants a lot of freedom. The supervising professor must therefore ensure right from the start (including in the self-study units) that students understand that the responsibility for incremental processing passes to the team. Master's students often meet this requirement, and they often make very good use of the degrees of freedom (e.g., balancing different time zones in international study programs). In any case, this setting of practice-integrated teaching demands a high level of motivation from the participants and good preparation for the process model but rewards them with quick successes and the experience of a particularly practically relevant project management methodology.

Approach 4: Students as Engineers

The fourth approach differs from the third in that students no longer just take the role of a developer in a recognized process model, but have a view of the overall context of the technical problem. The designation of "engineer" is meant to illustrate that the business case is not only solved quickly and operationally (e.g., through development and integration of software) but that long-term visionary areas of the problem are also addressed. In order to integrate business practice into the project-based teaching, the lecturer first selects a suitable phase model (e.g., from business administration, IT management, software engineering or IT process management) (Boss, 2015).

Ideally, this model can be taken from the subject to be taught itself (e.g., life cycle model of an information system for the subject of software engineering). It takes at least four phases of engineering, which are named differently depending on the concrete subject discipline and are of varying intensity (Brunsell, 2012):

- **Learn:** Students learn about the company's challenge, for example at a kick-off, and research the background. In addition, they describe essential alternatives to the solution (e.g. make or buy) with a rough evaluation (e.g.t, Proof of Concept). Requirement engineering methods can be used.
- **Design:** Students capture in models (e.g., UML) what a technical solution to the problem might look like. The level of detail as well as the number of views to be specified (e.g. functions, context, behaviour, etc.) is determined by the necessary information during implementation.
- **Build:** In this phase, the specified model is implemented. This can happen either in an environment of the university that is then given to the company via interface (e.g., Export via Extensible Markup Language or Representational State Transfer). However, true integration of practice is achieved when students have the chance to work directly on the company's systems. Projects whose implementation takes place in the cloud environment are ideal for this.
- **Testing:** Depending on the focus in the project, testing can be based on a prototype (e.g., wireframes or running instance) or on measuring the effect (e.g., efficiency increase in the productive system). In any case, verification and validation methods are used here.

Figure 6. Example phase model of practice-integrated engineering
(own illustration)

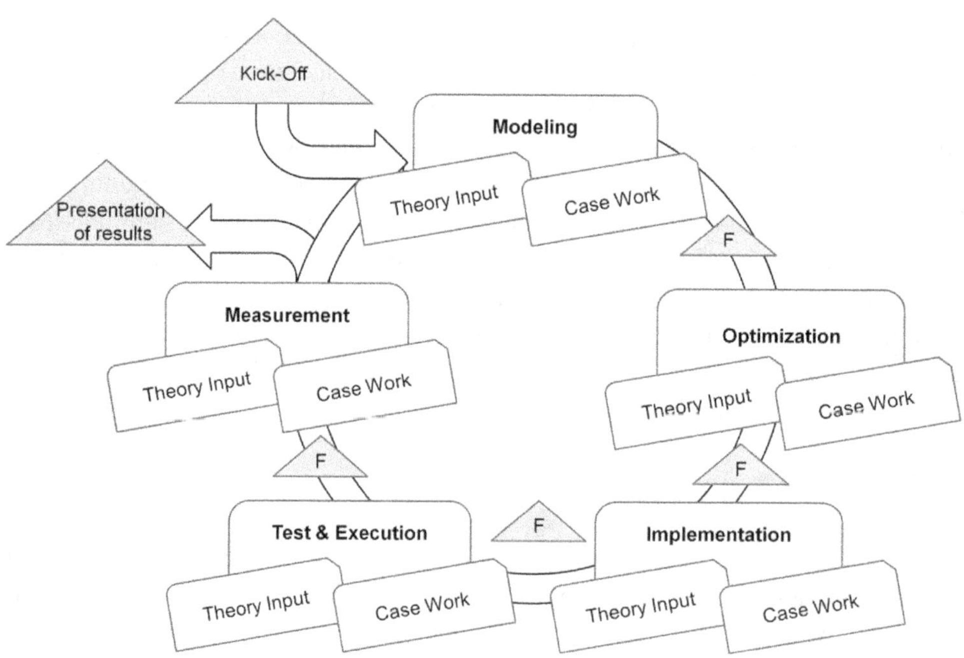

While in the previous approach ("Developer") incremental work is used for the rapid implementation of operational artifacts, this approach follows classical engineering (e.g., according to the waterfall model). The phases of a basic model of the discipline are passed through gradually without iterations but with gates. Figure 6 shows how these phases were used as an example in a technical discipline for business process management (Lederer & Schott, 2020). After the as-is modeling of the processes, they were optimized qualitatively and quantitatively by simulation and mining techniques in the BPMN diagrams. The concept for implementation provides for the actual migration of the models as well as accompanying notes for organizational measures. If the processes are executed in an engine and key figures (e.g., time and cost improvement through automation in the process) can be collected, the goals from the kick-off can be compared with the achieved values at the end of the seminar (Larmer et al., 2015; Boss, 2015).

The real transfer between theory and practice is solved during the semester in such a way that in each phase, students first receive theoretical instruction. There, they learn the methods and techniques of the phase. The students then select the appropriate procedure for the company's case and apply it to the case. After each phase, feedback is provided (see Figure 6; triangles symbolize meetings, F stands for feedback), which can take place with or without the client from practice, depending on the availability of the company. Of course, we can speak of a real practice integration when a real review with the company is organized. This quality gate between the phases can also be used by the lecturer for grading. In the experience of the authors, depending on the scope of the subject, (i) only the results of the practical case, (ii) a theoretical (written exam is also conceivable) and the practical work, and (iii) only the theoretical acquisition of competencies can be examined at the gate. The first and second alternatives represent true practice-integrated teaching. Experience shows that a shift of these variants in the course of the project is possible (e.g., at the beginning there is still theoretical learning and practical work, towards the end further steps are only explained theoretically), if it is explained and justified to the students in advance (Larmer et al., 2015).

Due to the simple phased processing and the intensive supervision by professors and the practice partner, this approach is suitable for both Bachelor and Master level.

SUCCESS FACTORS AND RECOMMENDATIONS

After the description of the individual four approaches (see section before), with which the authors have had very good experiences in practice-integrated teaching, success factors for this will now be described. This is not about technical issues (e.g., integration into formalities such as module handbooks, grading criteria, etc.), because these are to be designed according to the university and according to the professor's assessment.

Figure 7. Overview of success factors for practice-integrated teaching
(own illustration)

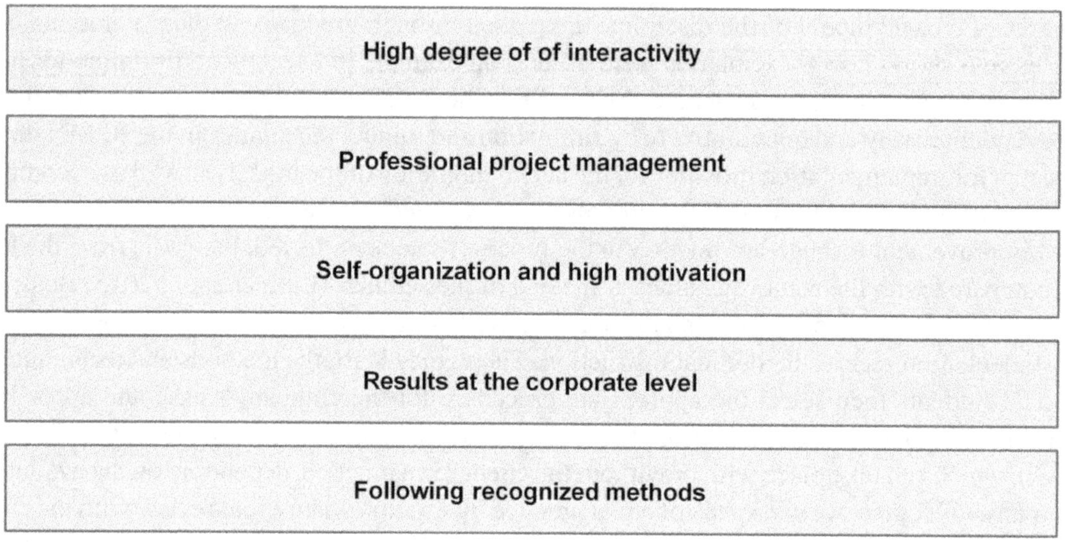

Rather, the goal of the compiled factors (see Figure 7) is to provide a guidance on the process within the settings that maximizes the practical transfer for all four approaches and also the outcomes for all parties involved (students: gaining competences; business partners: innovative and usable concepts/ artifacts; professors: teaching task and sustainability of courses).

An important success factor for all of the above outlined classes and projects is the *high degree of interactivity* especially at the beginning of the class, which forces students to identify critical questions and identify suitable approaches and methodologies designed to deliver appropriate and high-quality results. Student need to independently scrutinize different possible approaches to understand which would be suitable for the specific case setting. To avoid (i) ineffectiveness by choosing wrong approaches and (ii) inefficiencies by not applying the approaches correctly, timely feedback by the instructor (internal by professors or [even better] external by the business partner) is necessary. The instructor should always take on the role of a coach or sparring partner. In this way, the students become more confident and self-sufficient in planning and executing the task or project. At every new stage of the process, this degree of interactivity becomes relevant again. As the projects progress and the students become more proficient with regards to the methodologies and the general management of the project, the instructor increasingly takes over the role of a sounding board and quality insurance.

Especially in the context of a project for an independent third external client (business partner), an *introduction to the planning and management* of a consulting project before the launch of the project is also an important success factor. This includes

- typical roles within a project,
- an overview as well as the most important tasks of typical project phases such as planning, pitch, set-up, ongoing management as well as project wrap-up including documentation,
- important skills such as hypothesis development and work-planning, and

- important aspects of delivering impactful presentations such as audience analysis, slide design, and structure of the presentation.

Experience shows that written descriptions of the projects are beneficial, prepared cooperatively by professors and the business partners to combine both perspectives on the joint seminar. At a minimum, the following content should be described, which can be distributed as a one pager even before the course, so that students have the chance to prepare missing knowledge: (i) initial business situation and challenge (e.g. due to internal or external changes), (ii) explicit questions to be answered, (iii) expected artifacts, and (iv) constraints not to be discussed (e.g., resources, schedule, strategic decisions, given technical platforms).

As the students are ultimately responsible for the project success, they must efficiently organize themselves at the beginning of the project (*self-organized teams*). As mentioned above, in a university setting in which additional coursework runs parallel to the project, a leadership team of two project leaders typically is beneficial. One of the challenges for these project leaders is to continuously motivate the other team members to fully engage in the project and deliver the agreed upon results. Especially if a large proportion of the grade depend on the team effort, a proportion of students may try to free-ride on the effort of their classmates. Contrary to a hierarchical structure in a company, the project or work stream leaders have no true sanctioning mechanisms to appropriately punish slacking students, hence have to resort to mechanism common to lateral leadership (Koromzay, 2021) and provide opportunities for individual team members to routinely present to the entire group, the instructor and potentially also the client. Overall, all the approaches described require a high level of *motivation and willingness* on the part of everyone involved. Students must have genuine interest in the topics, in addition to technical competence, which goes beyond the goal of the course grade. Business partners must clearly commit to the methodological plan (e.g., not only to deadlines for feedback, but also to rules such as planning and peer review).

As the described approaches to practice-integrated teaching should generate the type and level of *results also expected in a corporate environment*, an appropriate degree of applicability and relevance of the derived solutions and created artefacts are required. An important element is the continuous scrutiny of the practical implications and consequences of the process and the results of the analysis as well as of the derived results and solutions. This is also integral part of the initial training sessions of leading global strategy consulting companies. The focus on the most important insights and consequences helps students to prioritize their analysis and to focus on the areas which generate the highest value add for the client. Derived results and recommendations become more actionable and implementable for the corporate client which in turn increases the impact which the students have with their projects.

Moreover, once *soundly chosen methods* (e.g., SCRUM, Design Thinking) must be strictly followed to in all cases and in their essential rules. This creates planning security for all participants in the project as well as for everyday university life. If recognized methods are used, this also has the advantage that students not only learn the method itself, but also have already used its application once in a protected environment (university) and gained experience as preparation for their career (job). Furthermore, the agreement and seminar work with external business partners is more efficiently because the method as such does not have to be discussed.

FUTURE RESEARCH DIRECTIONS

All described approaches have been performed several times by the authors and have been iteratively improved. Nevertheless, further practical challenges and open research questions arise, also because the context of practice-integrated teaching (e.g., companies' topics, technical possibilities) is constantly changing.

Future research directions include the systematic evaluation of the long-term impact and benefits of practice-integrated teaching as proposed in the form of the above-described approaches. This could include meta-studies on student satisfaction with the practicability of the described approaches as well as the relevance in the context of their careers. A different form of verification of the added value of practice-integrated teaching in form of the above presented course settings would be to empirically test the relevance of the specific experience on the employability of students e.g., in the form of surveys addressed to typical employers of students from German UAS.

A second avenue for future research would be to explore possibilities to expand the codification of generated knowledge from the proposed approaches within the active management of educational innovation as for example presented by Fidalgo-Blanco et al. (2014). As the authors argue, innovation as well as the sharing and exchange of best practices fosters the continuous improvement of the quality of education, and hence its institutionalized codification and management benefits individual students and teachers as well as the universities on an organizational level as well. As the individual set-up and scope of the projects differ depending on the specific challenge, it is important to generalize the used approaches and generated learnings to fit a set of meaningful ontologies such as for example proposed in Fidalgo-Blanco et al. (2014).

As the organizational forms of education also continue to become more differentiated with the emergence of hybrid and online-only study programs as well as extra-occupational and part-time programs, a third direction for future research would be to examine various models to transfer the described approaches involving practice-integrated teaching also in hybrid and remote as well as part-time settings. This may include the integration of social media (Saura et al., 2022a) or web-based forms of open innovation (Saura et al., 2022b).

SUMMARY AND CONCLUSION

To summarize, the above-described approaches to practice-integrated teaching ensure a high degree of applicability and relevance for the corporate domain while at the same time contributing to the theoretical and academic literature on practice-integrated teaching respectively experience-based teaching. Various authors such as Kolb (1984), Boud et al. (1993), Hornyak et al. (2007) affirm the relevance of practical experience in learning. Beyond the practical experience, guided reflection and analysis also constitute important elements of insuring sustainable success of the learning experience (e.g., Hornyak et al., 2007). According to Kolb's (1984) cycle of learning the experimental learning process consists of the key four elements of Abstract Conceptualization, Active Experimentation, Concrete Experience, and Reflective Observation which basically cover the formation and sharing of knowledge in the form of concepts, facts, and information, the activity in the form of application of the knowledge to real world problems and the reflection in the form of the analysis and the derivation of new insights. The present paper describes four replicable case studies for class settings in the context of practice-integrated teaching that provide not only practical experience as a stand-alone experience but also the guided reflection and analysis in the form of interaction within the project team and with the lecturer in his role as active coach and sparring partner in the spirit of the literature on experience-based teaching similar to Schaupp & Vitullo (2020). The presented approaches specifically allow students to immerse in the practical application of theoretical concepts and approaches to real world problems as well as active experimentation in the form of evaluating, choosing, and applying specific approaches to these practical situations. They also include milestones for reflective observation and critical assessment of the appropriateness and limitations of the chosen methodologies in the specific practical setting. Additionally the described approaches have been refined based on the practical experience from the instructors as well as the feedback from students over the course of several years and have proven themselves across universities of different UAS, across different degree programs such as business and technical programs, and have also been conducted across different channels such as hybrid and online-only.

Beyond contributing to the description of specific case studies for practice-integrated teaching, the present paper also provides a range of practical implications by providing a hands-on guideline for lecturers on how to prepare, set-up and execute the described classes and projects including specific success factors. In combination with an in-depth academic and theoretically foundation regarding the applied models and methodologies, these described approaches ensure that students are subsequently able to bridge the gap between the predominately academic knowledge obtained in various traditional classes and the specific requirements and challenges governing real-live corporate projects and settings. This also ensures a higher degree of employability compared to a purely academic education. Students typically benefit highly from the feedback of the corporate clients and become more proficient in regard to project- and time management as well as other soft skills such as self- and team management and giving high impact presentations as an added benefit. Working effectively in a team setting and resolving emerging conflicts largely by themselves also enhances their ability to integrate themselves more quickly and seamlessly into existing team structures at the start of their employment. Additionally, the competencies they achieve regarding the applied models and methodologies are strengthened by their practical application as students more fully understand the strength but also the challenges and limitations of these models and methodologies. Often, they start to view the various approaches and models as part of a larger tool set of which they are comfortable to choose appropriate elements depending on the specific situation or project setting.

Nevertheless, the proposed approaches to practice integrated teaching also contain certain limitations of which the lecturers need to be aware. Lecturers need to possess theoretical knowledge and practical experience regarding the specific methodologies used as well as project management experience to successfully guide students through the learning experience. As Wrenn & Wrenn (2009) point out, the teaching experience is enhanced if instructors for example convey a higher credibility due to the maintenance of active client contacts, keep practice skills current, serve as positive role models due to their experience, effectively relate theory to practice, and adapt course materials and project set-ups continuously based on their current practical experience. Additionally, professors who want to follow the idea of practice-integrated teaching have to show a certain degree of flexibility, composure and trust. After all, the corporate practice is not completely fixed and plannable, and thus neither is practice-integrated teaching – certainly also an important learning effect for the students.

REFERENCES

Abykanova, B., Idrissov, S., Saltanova, G., Shazhdekeyeva, N., & Syrbayeva, S. (2017). The problem of practice-oriented instruction in higher education. *Revista, 38*(56), 2–5.

Anlauf, R. (2016). Aspekte anwendungsorientierter Hochschullehre in Deutschland. In J. Cai & H. Lackner (Eds.), *Jahrbuch Angewandte Hochschulbildung* (pp. 201–213). Springer.

Appelbaum, S., & Steed, A. (2005). The critical success factors in the client-consulting relationship. *Journal of Management Development, 24*(1), 68–93. doi:10.1108/02621710510572362

Auernhammer, J., & Roth, B. (2021). The Origin and Evolution of Stanford University's Design Thinking: From Product Design to Design Thinking in Innovation Management. *Journal of Product Innovation Management, 38*(6), 623–644. doi:10.1111/jpim.12594

Boss, S. (2015). *Implementing Project-Based Learning*. Solution Tree.

Boud, D., Cohen, R., & Walker, D. (1993). Introduction: Understanding learning from experience. In D. Boud, R. Cohen, & D. Walker (Eds.), *Using experience for learning* (pp. 1–17). Lehmanns.

Brunsell, E. (2012). *Integrating Engineering and Science in Your Classroom*. National Science Teachers Association.

Christensen, C., Hall, T., Dillon, K., & Duncan, D. (2016). Know Your Customers' Jobs to Be Done. *Harvard Business Review, 2016*(9), 54–62.

Damian, D., Lassenius, C., & Paasivaar, M. (2012). Teaching a globally distributed project course using Scrum practices. In *Proceedings of the Second International Workshop on Collaborative Teaching of Globally Distributed Software Development*. IEEE. 10.1109/CTGDSD.2012.6226947

Denert, E. (2005). Zum Verschwinden des Diploms und zum Verhältnis Fachhochschule/Universität. *Informatik Spektrum, 23*(2), 45–47. doi:10.100700287-004-0464-z

Dyganoca, E. A., & Yavgildina, Z. M. (2020). Development of Student Musician's Methodological Competence in Practice-Oriented University Environment. *Utopía y Praxis Latinoamericana, 25*(5), 113–124.

Fergani, A. (2019). The future persona: A futures method to let your scenarios come to life. *Foresight, 21*(4), 445–466. doi:10.1108/FS-10-2018-0086

Fidalgo-Blanco, A., Sein-Echaluce, M. L., & García-Peñalvo, F. J. (2014). Knowledge Spirals in Higher Education Teaching Innovation. *International Journal of Knowledge Management, 10*(4), 16–37. doi:10.4018/ijkm.2014100102

Grossman, P., Dean, C. G. P., Herrmann, Z., & Schneider Kavanaght, S. (2021). *Core Practices for Project-Based Learning*. Harvard Education Press.

Horcher, R. (1998). Fachhochschule oder Universität? In H. W. Stahl & W. W. Stahl (Eds.), *Effizient Studieren: Wirtschaftswissenschaften an Fachhochschulen* (pp. 115–120). Gabler. doi:10.1007/978-3-322-84594-8_8

Hornyak, M., Green, S. G., & Heppard, K. A. (2007). Implementing experiential learning. In M. Reynolds & R. Vince (Eds.), *The handbook of experiential learning and management education* (pp. 137–152). Oxford University Press.

Hüther, O., & Krücken, G. (2018). *Higher education in Germany - Recent developments in an international perspective*. Springer. doi:10.1007/978-3-319-61479-3

Jurado-Navas, A., & Munoz-Luna, R. (2017). Scrum Methodology in Higher Education: Innovation in Teaching, Learning and Assessment. *International Journal of Higher Education*, *6*(6), 1–18. doi:10.5430/ijhe.v6n6p1

Kelley, T. (2016). *The art of innovation: Lessons in creativity from IDEO, America's leading design firm*. Profile.

Kivunja, C. (2015). Using De Bono's Six Thinking Hats Model to Teach Critical Thinking and Problem Solving Skills Essential for Success in the 21st Century Economy. *Creative Education*, *2015*(6), 380–391. doi:10.4236/ce.2015.63037

Kolb, D. A. (1984). *Experiential learning: Experience as the source of learning and development*. Prentice-Hall.

Korchinskaya, O., Ivanova, I., Shchukina, N., & Mendziv, M. (2019). Business Games as a Teaching Strategy for Delivering a Practice-Oriented Course in Mathematics at Agricultural University. In *Proceedings of the International Scientific Conference The Fifth Technological Order - Prospects for the Development and Modernization of the Russian Agro-Industrial Sector*. Atlantis Press.

Koromzay, T. (2021). *Integrative Leadership*. Springer. doi:10.1007/978-3-662-62973-4

Larmer, J., Mergendoller, J., & Boss, S. (2015). *Setting the Standard for Project Based Learning*. ASCD.

Lederer, M., & Schott, P. (2020). Business Process Management. In M. Khosrow-Pour (Ed.), *Encyclopedia of Organizational Knowledge, Administration, and Technologies* (pp. 2287–2302). IGI Global.

Mahnic, V. (2015). Scrum in software engineering courses: An outline of the literature. *Global Journal of Engineering Education*, *17*(2), 77–83.

Maltseva, O. A., Khovanskaya, E. A., Martynova, N. A., & Karpova, I. V. (2020). The Digitalization of Education in Higher Education: Methodological and Practice-Oriented Aspects. In *Proceedings of the International Scientific Conference Digitalization of Education - History, Trends and Prospects*. Atlantis Press. 10.2991/assehr.k.200509.152

Matthies, C. (2018). Scrum2Kanban: Integrating Kanban and Scrum in a University Software Engineering Capstone Course. In *Proceedings of the International Workshop on Software Engineering Education for Millennials*. IEEE/ACM. 10.1145/3194779.3194784

May, J., York, J., & Lending, D. (2016). Teaching Tip Play Ball: Bringing Scrum into the Classroom. *Journal of Information Systems Education*, *27*(2), 87–92.

McKenny, C. (2006). *The World's Newest Profession. Management Consulting in the Twentieth Century*. Cambridge University Press. doi:10.1017/CBO9780511511622

Nielsen, L. (2011). *Personas - User Focused Design*. Springer.

Pavlova, O., Chirkova, N., & Burlakova, I. (2020). Building a practice-oriented model of preservice teacher education. In *Proceedings of the SHS Web of Conferences*. EDP Sciences.

Prosalova, V. S., & Nikolaeva, A. A. (2020). Implementation of Practice-Oriented Training as the Basis of University Competitiveness. In *Proceedings of the International Scientific Conference Far East Con*. Atlantis Press. 10.2991/aebmr.k.200312.054

Redondo, R. D. R., Ktena, A., Kunicina, N., Zabasta, A., Patlins, A., & Mele, D. E. (2020). Advanced practices: micro learning, practice oriented teaching and gamified learning. In *Proceedings of the International Scientific Conference on Power and Electrical Engineering of Riga Technical University*. IEEE. 10.1109/RTUCON51174.2020.9316555

Rush, D. E., & Connolly, A. J. (2020). An Agile Framework for Teaching with Scrum in the IT Project Management Classroom. *Journal of Information Systems Education*, *31*(3), 196–207.

Saura, J. R., Palacios-Marqués, D., & Ribeiro-Soriano, D. (2022b). Exploring the boundaries of Open Innovation: Evidence from social media mining. *Technovation*, 102447. doi:10.1016/j.technovation.2021.102447

Saura, J. R., Ribeiro-Soriano, D., & Iturricha-Fernández, A. (2022a). Exploring the challenges of remote work on Twitter users' sentiments: From digital technology development to a post-pandemic era. *Journal of Business Research*, *142*, 242–254. doi:10.1016/j.jbusres.2021.12.052

Schaupp, L., & Vitullo, E. (2020). Implementing experiential action learning in the MBA: Use of an international consulting experience. *International Journal of Educational Management*, *34*(3), 505–517. doi:10.1108/IJEM-04-2019-0154

Schwaber, K. (2004). *Agile Project Management with Scrum*. Microsoft Press.

Smirnova, Z. V., Vaganova, O. I., Loshkareva, D. A., Konyaeva, E. A., & Gladkova, M. N. (2018). Practice-oriented approach implementation in vocational education. In *Proceedings of the Materials Science and Engineering Conference*. IOP.

Stewart, G. (2006). Praxisbezug als profilbildendes Element in Bachelorstudiengängen an bayerischen Fachhochschulen. *Beiträge zur Hochschulforschung*, *2*(28), 90–114.

Umer, W. (2020). *Agile Scrum Crash Course*. Amazon Digital Services.

Van den Ende, J. (2021). *Innovation Management*. Macmillan Education.

Von Thienen, J., Clancey, W., Corazza, G., & Meinel, C. (2017). Theoretical foundations of design thinking. Part I: John E. Arnold's creative thinking theories. In H. Plattner, C. Meinel, & L. Leifer (Eds.), *Design thinking research. Making distinctions: Collaboration versus cooperation* (pp. 13–40). Springer.

Von Thienen, J., Clancey, W., & Meinel, V. (2019). Theoretical Foundations of Design Thinking. Part II: Robert H. McKim's Need-Based Design Theory. In C. Meinel & L. Leifer (Eds.), *Design thinking research. Looking Further: Design Thinking Beyond Solution-Fixation* (pp. 13–40). Springer. doi:10.1007/978-3-319-97082-0_2

Von Thienen, J., Clancey, W., & Meinel, V. (2021). Theoretical Foundations of Design Thinking. Part III: Robert H. McKim's Visual Thinking Theories. In C. Meinel & L. Leifer (Eds.), *Design thinking research. Interrogating the Doing* (pp. 9–23). Springer. doi:10.1007/978-3-030-62037-0_2

Wickham, L., & Wilcock, J. (2012). *Management Consulting. Delivering an effective project*. Pearson.

Wrenn, J., & Wrenn, B. (2009). Enhancing Learning by Integrating, Theory and Practice. *International Journal on Teaching and Learning in Higher Education*, *21*(2), 258–265.

Zautorova, E.V., & Bodrova, E.V. (2021). Practice-Oriented Training in Higher Education Institutions of the Federal Penitentiary Service of Russia. *Penitentiary science, 15*(55), 575–584.

Zhu, J., Liao, Z., Yam, K., & Johnson, R. (2018). Shared leadership: A state-of-the-art review and future research agenda. *Journal of Organizational Behavior*, *39*(7), 834–852. doi:10.1002/job.2296

ADDITIONAL READING

Jurado-Navas, A., & Munoz-Luna, R. (2017). Scrum Methodology in Higher Education: Innovation in Teaching, Learning and Assessment. *International Journal of Higher Education*, *6*(6), 1–18. doi:10.5430/ijhe.v6n6p1

Lederer, M., & Schott, P. (2020). Business Process Management. In M. Khosrow-Pour (Ed.), *Encyclopedia of Organizational Knowledge, Administration, and Technologies* (pp. 2287–2302). IGI Global.

Lor, R. (2017). Design Thinking in Education: A Critical Review of Literature. In *Proceedings of the Asian Conference on Education & Psychology*. IACSSM.

Malmqvist, J., Young, P. Y., Hallström, S., Kuttenkeuler, J., & Svensson, T. (2004). Lessons learned from design-build-test-based project courses. In *Proceedings of DESIGN 2004*. ICED.

Meinel, C. (2022). *Design Thinking in Education: Innovation Can Be Learned*. Springer. doi:10.1007/978-3-030-89113-8

Parsons, D., & MacCallum, K. (2018). *Agile and Lean Concepts for Teaching and Learning - Bringing Methodologies from Industry to the Classroom*. Springer.

Verheyen, G. (2013). *Scrum – A Pocket Guide*. Van Haren.

Wickham, L., & Wilcock, J. (2012). *Management Consulting - Delivering an effective project*. Pearson.

KEY TERMS AND DEFINITIONS

Design Thinking: An approach that is intended to lead to the finding and development of solutions by focusing in a special way on the user's view of the problem.

Developer: A role in SCRUM that is responsible for the development and testing of solutions/artifacts.

Employability: An ability of a person to participate in the labor market and an important goal of education at technical colleges to enable entry into working and professional life.

Iteration: The repeated execution of steps to solve a problem or implement a requirement by successively improving the existing solution.

Practice-Integrated Teaching: A special form of teaching in which practical topics are not only a component, but the essential starting and design point of all education efforts.

SCRUM: An agile process model that originated in software development and is now used in many areas (e.g., product development) when the project environment may change in the course of time.

University of Applied Sciences: A type of university in the German-speaking world at which particularly application-oriented courses of study are offered.

Chapter 8
Reflection on Teaching Practice for Agile Methodology Based Product Development Management

Kamalendu Pal
https://orcid.org/0000-0001-7158-6481
City, University of London, UK

ABSTRACT

This chapter reflects on teaching practice in an undergraduate induction session introducing agile methodology-based product (e.g., software, paper-aircraft) development and project management. The induction session took place in a paper-aircraft design and development workshop at the City, University of London. The central theme of the teaching practice is step-by-step exercise-oriented (i.e., constructivism) product development activities and the contextual relationship with the distributed software production business processes. Students worked in development teams to understand and appreciate how to capture requirements, design, and build products following agile methodology. Initially, the workshop instructor introduced the different software development process models, activities, and comparative challenges to the students. In addition, students track their progress within the team structure and collaborate with classroom-based teaching and learning activities. Finally, a set of questionaries helped get students' feedback on the appropriateness of agile methodology in product development activities through classroom-based exercises.

INTRODUCTION

In recent decades constructivism has motivated both computer science and software engineering educators because of its usefulness for enhancing teaching and learning practice (Ben-Ari, 1998). Instructors require a generic pedagogical working method to effectively link constructivist principles to apply constructivism to software engineering and computer science education. Constructivism is a dominant

DOI: 10.4018/978-1-6684-4441-2.ch008

Copyright © 2022, IGI Global. Copying or distributing in print or electronic forms without written permission of IGI Global is prohibited.

theory of learning in which students construct knowledge rather than solely receive and store knowledge passed on by the teaching instructor (e.g., academic, teaching assistant) and learn if they build knowledge and understanding from their experiences. This learning theory also encourages teaching instructors to encompass and develop real-life class dynamics that tie the subject (e.g., project management) teaching activities to a central narrative. It also draws more attention and engages students in project-based engineering education, relying on constructivism.

For example, a paper aircraft design framework can engage students and enhance their understanding of product development activities, roles involved, and project management-related skills. This design framework provides a narrative including diverse activities using the strength and peculiarity related to each without memorization skills, as is often the case of *agile software development* activities and management in constraint mitigation. The attention is on expanding complex ideas and how concepts can merge to create an answer to a challenge. Students enhance their idea and experiment with different contextual examples related to the problem to gather all the specific pieces and skills needed for reaching an adequate understanding. Also, an individual student may grasp the necessary comprehension at different times but in an individualistic manner. This way, the higher education community can create good teaching practices (Roffe, 1989) to continually improve the quality of teaching and learning-related services (Garcia-Perialvo, 2011).

Moreover, in the teaching improvement process transferring ideas and knowledge from experts to novice learners (Hinds et al., 2001), communicating the most relevant information, and using resources more appropriately are essential objectives (Davenport & Prusak, 1998). In this way, open innovation in teaching practice is a part of regular planning (Child, 1972) (Whitworth, 2012) that provide an opportunity to learn a subject by doing a step-by-step activity and reviewing the success or failure in every step (Saura et al., 2022a) (Saura et al., 2022b). In addition, one or more instructors or mentors often supervise the learning processes to provide feedback and explanation when pursuing the final goal. Besides, teaching activity management mechanisms are essential, such as space where innovative practices (e.g., laboratory to do some experiment, tutorial room where prototype need to develop) (Gunn, 2010), replicated and used in students learning process.

Consequently, finding and using the knowledge created in different teaching practices has significant advantages in enhancing performance (Hansen, 2022) (Boh, 2014) (Fidalgo-Blanco et al., 2014) in teaching-related services. Knowledge management plays an essential part in modern teaching and learning practices. Knowledge management is based on collecting, organizing, distributing, sharing, and using the intellectual assets of an organization (persons, knowledge resources and relationships) and should benefit its members (Tseng and Kuo, 2014). In this way, an activity centred on knowledge implies the exchange of knowledge between organization members (Bartol and Srivastava, 2002; Koulikov, 2011) and this exchange can contribute to the application of knowledge and innovation (Sheng and Noe, 2010). Innovation in organizations is closely linked to knowledge management (Nonaka 1991; Nonaka and Takeuchi, 1995; Davila et al., 2006) and improve competitiveness (Al-Husseini and Elbeltagi, 2015). On the other hand, higher education is also in a competitive context (students and funding) (Roffe, 1998), so it incorporates knowledge management to improve the quality of its services (Weatherly, 2003) (Fidalgo-Blanco et al., 2014).

For the agile paper aircraft design scenario, the instructor exercises agile methodology skills to improve student understanding until they accomplish their goals. Thus, introducing an agile product development participation deal with paper aircraft design in ways that allow a direct and real-life connection. Students will frequently ask about the topic's usefulness and mentally check out the concepts undergoing discussions while building essential skills. This new paradigm makes subjects like agile product (e.g., software, engineering artefacts) development more appealing.

As the paper aircraft design session evolves, students understand agile product development concepts and their applications because their projects' triumph is contingent on acquiring specific concepts and skills. Students cannot cheat by going to another group and copying their results due to the isolation of the working group space. The correctness of the designs comes as a final project result or working behaviour, using both physical design investigations and quality assurance results. If the quality assurance result does not align with expected results, learners need to assess their rationale to discover the problem and define how to fix the project.

More research will help study where the simulated classroom-based exercises (i.e., paper aircraft design) diverge from traditional approaches in both the classroom and communication ecosystems. A critical issue is to stitch together all the different class narrative pieces, with strategic placement of threads to maximize subject immersion and an essential experience of project management and its related issues. For example, most engineering projects (including software engineering) involve optimizing a set of variables given some constraints. Unfortunately, students are not aware that they will solve such problems professionally. Therefore, the optimization concept must be introduced as early as possible since it appears throughout the induction session in several ways. These simple concepts help consolidate even the material from the simple arithmetic calculation.

Development processes are used in agile product development activity, which can help students understand the problem structure and establish a good foundation for professional software engineers. For example, paper aircraft design is not only a technical but also an organizational challenge. Significantly, integrating unconventional components into novel system architectures requires fast design interactions, including revising requirements and intelligent progress of changes across various disciplines to minimize project risk. Therefore, unlike standard aircraft conceptual design tasks, the determination of appropriate top-level requirements is needed to be part of the iterative design procedure, a multi-disciplinary collaboration. Accordingly, the scope of the research on current methodologies was broadened to other industry sectors developing hugely complex systems. Eventually, the decision was taken to include a process model from the family of *'Agile Methods'*, known as *Scrum*, which is commonly applied in the software industry.

The engineering industry has moved its production management from traditional software development practice to agile methodologies to mitigate the ever-increasing software complexity and globalization of software design and development (Pal, 2019) (Pal, 2020) (Pal & Karakostas, 2021) (Pal, 2021) (Pal & Williams, 2021). Agile methodologies are a reaction to traditional ways of developing software and acknowledge the requirement for an alternative to a document-driven, heavyweight software development process (Beck & Fowler, 2001). The primary purpose of these methodologies is to keep close customer collaboration, provide business value as quickly as possible in an incremental way, and respond promptly to changing customer requirements (Cockburn & Williams, 2003).

The agile product development methodology was introduced in the 1990s by Kent Beck when working on a Chrysler project (although its beginning stretches back to Smalltalk (a programming language) projects that he and Ward Cunningham worked on at Tektronix in the mid-1980s). The agile methodology emphasizes document-centric processes into practices that enable people (Beck, 2000) and represents one of the fastest-growing movements in engineering product development.

Agile methodology is a software design and development methodology based on simplicity, communication, and business processes development-related feedback. The agile methodology works by bringing the whole team together in simple practices, with sufficient feedback to enable the team to assess where they are and tune the practices to their unique situation. This methodology recognizes that a development project's end goal is to produce a quality, appropriate business solution to develop and maintain the ultimate product.

To function appropriately in changing business requirements, agile methodology emphasizes practices that enable people (Beck, 2000). One of the critical roles within the agile methodology-based product development team is the customer role. Researchers (Beck & Fowler, 2001) describe the right customer with some qualities:

- The customer understands the domain well by working in it and understanding how it works.
- With development's help, customers can understand how software can provide business value in the domain.
- Customers can decide on what is needed now and what is needed later.

The usefulness of the characteristics mentioned above is reviewed by academics and practitioners (Deursen, 2001) (Cohn & Paul, 2001) to real-world implementation-related issues. The agile method initiative's founding members have clarified this vital role in the agile team, but they (Beck & Fowler, 2001) acknowledge the risk associated with this role.

In this way, many questions remain unanswered regarding agile scrum development methodology. This chapter introduces a set of class activities connected to paper aircraft design using the agile scrum method. The research questions this chapter will answer is whether adopting the Scrum methodology to the specific organizational context proved effective in tackling the specific challenges of the conceptual design task. Specifically, Scrum-specific time restriction and meeting culture led to high situational awareness among team members and product stakeholders.

The rest of the chapter is as follows. Section 2 introduces the Agile software development practice-related issues. Section 3 presents a review of related research work. Section 4 outlines the agile method, concentrating on practice-oriented teaching and learning. Section 5 highlights the characteristics of teaching agile methodology through simulation games. Section 6 identifies the implications of the study and the future research plan. Finally, Section 7 provides brief concluding remarks.

BACKGROUND AND RELATED RESEARCH

In the early part of 2001, a group of academics and practitioners (Cockburn, 2006) (Highsmith, 2002) (Fowler, 2002) met in Utah, United States of America, for a workshop to present the growing idea that was referred to, at the time, *lightweight* or *light methods*. The workshop's result was the new term, *Agile*, to refer to four fundamental principles as enumerated in a tabular representation (Table 1) and the *Agile Manifesto* (Beck et al., 2001).

Table 1. Four fundamental principles

Number	Item	Value
1	Individual	Interactions over processes and tools
2	Working	Software over comprehensive documentation
3	Customer	Collaboration over contract negotiation
4	Responding	Change over following a plan

Today, agile methodologies promising rapid delivery and time to market have started to dominate the software industry, removing traditional methodologies such as Waterfall from the mainstream (Schwaber & Beedle, 2002). In this way, the agile manifesto creators uncovered better software development methods. For example, the above tabular representation presents the value of the items on the right; the creators (or the manifesto's authors) want to value the items on the left.

The above concepts do not directly fit the conventional software development lifecycle, including deriving the specification, design, evaluation, and evolution. As a result, several methodologies have evolved from the Agile concept's basic principles, with Scrum, eXtreme Programming, Lean, and Kanban the prominent examples.

Also, academics and practitioners have provided a detailed description of the manifesto (Highsmith, 2002), (Fowler, 2002) (Cockburn, 2006). The Agile Manifesto also includes some basic principles that provide additional guidance:

1. the main priority is customer satisfaction using early and continuous delivery of valuable software.
2. ready to accept changing requirements, agile processes harness change for the customer's competitive advantage even late in development.
3. deliver intermediate prototype software frequently, with a shorter timescale preference, from a couple of weeks to a couple of months.
4. requirement engineers, clients, and software implementers need to exchange views and ideas regularly. Finally,
5. a most effective and efficient method of conveying information to and within a development team is face-to-face conversation.
6. the team regularly reflects on becoming more effective, then tunes and adjusts its behaviour accordingly (Beck & Fowler, 2001). The agile manifesto's values and principles provide standard foundations for agile methodologies. The agile methodology works towards providing iterative and recurrent software releases all along the project life cycle. Finally, the agile methodology considers a software development related activity as a system of four control *variables*. These variables are – Cost, Time, Quality, and Scope. A brief description of these variables is presented in Table 2.

A simple diagrammatic representation of these variables and their dependencies is shown in Figure 1. Time is the central variable in agile methodology. Enhancing the software system's quality can increase the time needed to improve software processes and the related testing for assurance. Sometimes increasing the financial resources can reduce the length of time to complete the software development project. The increase in financial resources is attributed to hiring more software development personnel and procuring better equipment. However, increasing the number of software developers can increase the time overhead of communication. Also, decreasing financial resources can increase the project duration dramatically.

Table 2. Four fundamental variables in agile methodology

Variable	Description
Cost	The cost variable relates to the number of financial resources to be spent.
Time	The time variable indicates when the software system (or a particular release) should be completed.
Quality	The quality variable defines the correctness related measures of the software system, as defined by the client or customer. It also describes the quality assurance related software testing criteria and measurement procedures.
Scope	The scope variable describes the software system's functionality. It includes what and how much will be done.

The dependable relations among these variables also highlight other properties of the agile methodology. For example, increasing scope means extra time is required because more software development-related activities are required to complete. At the same time, decreasing scope reduces the software development time. In this way, if, for example, business project management and customer increases scope (e.g., additional characteristics of the proposed software) and holds onto cost (using the same resources) and quality, project completion time must be increased.

The agile design provides a value-added methodology. The values are based on four distinct attributes – Simplicity, Communication, Feedback, and Courage. The essential characteristics of these attributes are summarized below:

Simplicity Encouraged

Agile methodology strives for a simple software system. In this way, agile methodology tries to deliver the most straightforward functionality that matches the business requirements. This means that the system should be as simple as possible; simultaneously, the system must work. It includes designing the most straightforward software that supports the required functionality. It also encourages building software systems for today and not for tomorrow. Agile also encourages the minimum number of artefacts to an absolute minimum – the user requirements (or stories), plans (Planning Game) and the software product (i.e., code). Software coding style needs to be easy to read, understand, maintain, and modify. The agile practices and techniques can be learned in a short duration (however, mastering them, of course, takes enough time). The primary purpose for simplicity is that AGILE tries to manage changes and other related risks.

Figure 1. The relationship between the variables

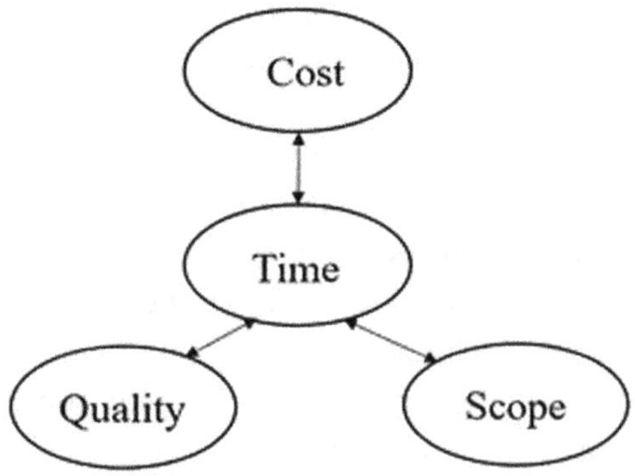

Accomplish Communication

Different problems can be realized to the breakdown of communication (e.g., the software engineer forgot to ask the customer an essential question). The agile methodology encourages keeping communication flowing in a variety of ways. For example, it can be accomplished by – (i) collaborative workspaces, (ii) co-location of customer business space and software development, (iii) software development by paired staff, (iv) alternating paired staff frequently, (v) changing the software development tasks frequently, (vi) brief staff meetings for review the progress, and (vii) unit tests, prototype demonstrations, verbal communication is not documented.

Value of Feedback

Agile methodology-based software development is heavily dependent on feedback. It is helpful for feedback at all scales (e.g., customer feedback, manager comments, developer review provision). Feedback is encouraged in – (i) incremental releases, (ii) automated unit tests, and (iii) automated software functional tests. The earlier and more frequently the software development team get feedback, the better. This way, problems are usually more minor, and hence, amendments are more accessible and cheaper.

Importance of Courage

Courage is an essential element in agile-based software development. Courage is required because a considerable part of this development practices extreme in the way that goes against the traditional software product development knowledge. Besides, agile-based software development differs in the role of the customer in the process. For this to work, courage is needed from both the developers and the customer.

Agile based software design and development follows an iterative and incremental process.

The Process Agile

Agile based software design and development project consists of a smaller increment of implementation, known as release. A release version of the software system describes a sub-system of the proposed software. All the functionalities of the release need to be developed thoroughly. Customer requirements are captured in natural language; informal '*user story*' cards are like use cases (Cockburn, 2000). In real applications, software developers estimate each card's times, and customers prioritize each card. In the "Planning Game", the customer selects the user stories that comprise the essential part for a short and deliverable regular interval (e.g., one month). Also, every small incremental implementation is accepted and tried by the client (or customer). The rest of the user stories are re-assessed for requirements and priority changes, and the project is executed for the following software incremental implementation.

In this way, the releases incrementally create the solicited functionality (assuming the software system grows over time). Releases are negotiated in the Planning Games. The customer provides what should be part of the release, and the developers determine how much time it will take to implement the software release, or the customer decides the strategic plan. In addition, the software developers assess the amount of development work that can be done within the available time. The individual release cycle is made of a few iterations. The iteration is a software development facility that is used to ease the required project planning. A simple diagrammatic representation of the agile software development process structure is shown in Figure 2.

Planning Game

The Planning Game consists of three phases: (i) agile location, (ii) planning, and (iii) steering. The customer describes the system requirements in the agile location phase, and software developers estimate the complete implementation duration. In the planning phase, both the customers and developers negotiate which desired features can be completed within the given resources (time and other resources).

The steering phase negotiate plan is changed whenever needed in response to what is learned in development while putting the plan in effect.

Customer Tests

The planning activities are event-oriented, and they produce excellent information and excellent steering control in the customer's hands. The agile customer defines the desired feature of a software product, and they also describe automated product acceptance tests. The software development team crafts these tests and uses them to justify that the property is implemented appropriately for themselves and customers. Automation is essential because manual tests are avoided due to time shortages.

Figure 2. Simple process structure

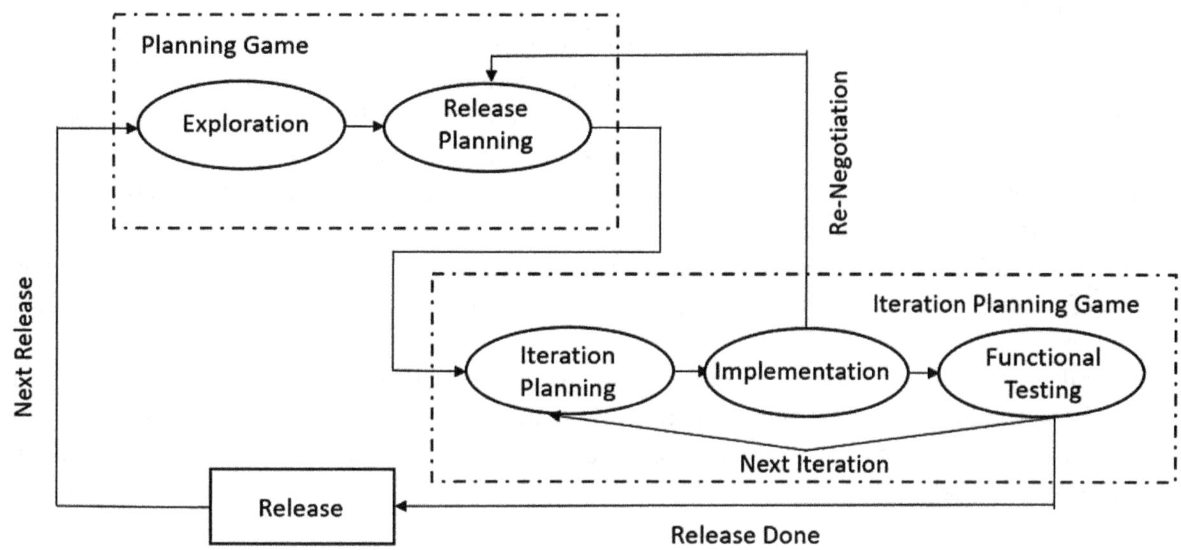

Designing an agile-based software system is neither a one-time activity nor an up-front thing, but it is an all-the-time thing. The development team follows specific design steps. These design steps are release planning and iteration planning, and development teams engage in quick design sessions and design revision through refactoring in the project's entire lifecycle. Besides, agile software project design is based on sound design principles.

Continuous Integration

Agile methodology is driven by the idea that a team of developers delivers benefits to the customer (or client) by its ability to react even to late change efficiently. In that context, changes can be extrinsic, like changes in requirements or prioritization by the customer, but also intrinsic, like changes in the required effort for achieving development goals or technological requirements for a chosen system design.

Direct interactions between individuals contribute to the project's success more than processes and software development tools (e.g., project management tool, process development tool). For example, maintaining an integrated working product has a higher priority than providing consistent documentation. Establishing a productive and close relationship with the customer is more important than negotiating a contract. The capability to efficiently react to late changes is valued higher than the organizational ability to follow a plan.

In agile methodology, projects are planned to use the planning game. Agile projects are decomposed into minor public software releases and iterations within each release. Releases are minor, typically two to three months. Iterations are typically one to two weeks. The planning game is run at both levels at different granularities. The planning game typically occurs as a '*face-to-face*' meeting, where:

- The customer prioritizes the user stories in business value order.

- The programmers sign up to estimate the user stories they will develop. Then, they estimate the time needed to develop the story by breaking it into tasks.
- The customer confirms the final scope of the iteration or release. This step can include manipulating the stories, including breaking a story into parts, to ensure business value is delivered.
- Once the scope is determined, the programmers can enter the coding phase. This phase primarily consists of discussing the story with the customer, implementing the story, and ensuring the story passes all the customer's acceptance tests. In addition, an acceptance test proves the function works as required by the customer.
- Agile uses quick releases to maximize feedback from end-users and other business stakeholders. Therefore, regular releases are encouraged, as often as every day, but more typically every couple of months.
- Several agile practices support the coding phase, including metaphor, simple design, test-first coding, Refactoring, pair programming, collective ownership, continuous integration, coding standards and the 40-hour week. Beck and fellow researchers (Beck et al., 2001) provide an excellent overview of these practices.

Advantages of user involvement in the projects have many benefits: improved product quality through a better understanding of the user requirements, improved knowledge of clients' organization, minimized risk of making unacceptable functionality, improved ability to negotiate agile expectations among users, improved ability to resolve conflicts regarding the design of the system, increased feeling of ownership among users, reduction in the natural resistance towards change in work practices, remedies lack decision capability in management, improved project performance and an increased willingness to agile experiment and improvise in search for solutions (Hanssen & Faegri, 2006). User involvement in system development success concluded that user productivity was increased, whereas training costs and user support calls were decreased with a practical user-involvement approach (Salihoglu, 2001).

RELATED RESEARCH

Effective collaboration, communication, and coordination are the main contributing factors to success in agile methods. Communication is defined as imparting or interchanging thoughts, opinions, or information by speech, writing, or signs. Collaboration is defined as working together to accomplish a task and discussing to solve complex problems. The effective collaboration includes both individually focused duties and interactive group work. Coordination is defined as the harmonious adjustment or interaction of different people or things to achieve a goal or effect. Learning is impossible without communication as communication is a prime factor. Communication can be nonverbal or verbal through media like books, white papers, pictures, or observations. Employees cannot learn from other engineers without information exchange, and knowledge acquisition and sharing would be inhibited. Duncan and Moriarty (1998) describe communication as the human activity that links people together and creates relationships.

Cockburn (Cockburn, 2000) also supports this view. According to a group of researchers (Cao & Ramesh, 2007), agile development involves intensive teamwork and high task interdependence. As task interdependence increases, the requirement for coordination becomes greater (Cao & Ramesh, 2007). The physical design of the workspace also plays a vital role in effective communication and collaboration. If people working on the same team are close to each other physically, it may be easier for them to communicate when required to eliminate ambiguity.

Software development is considered a cooperative game of communication, implying that a project's appreciation of progress is related to how long it takes information to get from one person's head to the head (Cockburn, 2000). Media Richness Theory suggests that the wealthiest communication channel enables instant feedback, can transmit multiple cues, has a high language variety, and can transmit emotional content. A face-to-face meeting is the richest form of communication because it can transmit multiple cues (e.g., voice inflexion, body language) and facilitate shared meaning with rapid mutual feedback and personal focus, feelings, and emotions infusing the conversation. From a functional perspective, informal face-to-face interactions aid understanding and problem-solving due to the enriched context, including facial expressions, gestures, posture, appearance, and other people's reactions (Kendon, 1995). Face-to-face interaction is also more flexible and can respond better to ambiguity and uncertainty (Allen & Cohen, 1969). It is further supported by Cockburn (2000) that the most effective form of communication (for transmitting ideas) is interactive and face-to-face.

PRACTICE-ORIENTED TEACHING AND LEARNING

There has been widespread acceptance of agile methodology for application development in the industry during recent decades. It has motivated the higher education sector to reexamine software design and development concepts in the computer science curriculum. The agile methodology (Cunningham, 2001) consists of business operation principles that guide the staff, process, and work practices to design, develop, and deliver software applications. However, it differs from the traditional software process model (e.g., Waterfall), which depends on sequentially collecting user requirements, designing, developing, testing, and deploying activities. In addition, the agile methodology uses a cross-functional group of development staff to design application systems by rapid iteration methods.

Both Waterfall and agile software development process models try to bring the right resources to the software project at the individual phase of design and deployment activities. The waterfall process model is organizationally agnostic and siloed work in software development practice, while agile methodology provides cross-functional teams in the individual deployment phase.

The main objective of the simulation game is to introduce both models and aircraft-related design activities. Students work in development teams to analyze, design, build, and test paper aircraft following agile design principles to understand the advantages of the roles, processes, and challenges. In addition, students track their group's progress throughout the activity to conclude the benefits and challenges of each approach. Survey results indicate that students learned and appreciated the different roles and agile process as a system design principle through this classroom practice.

Figure 3. The waterfall software process model

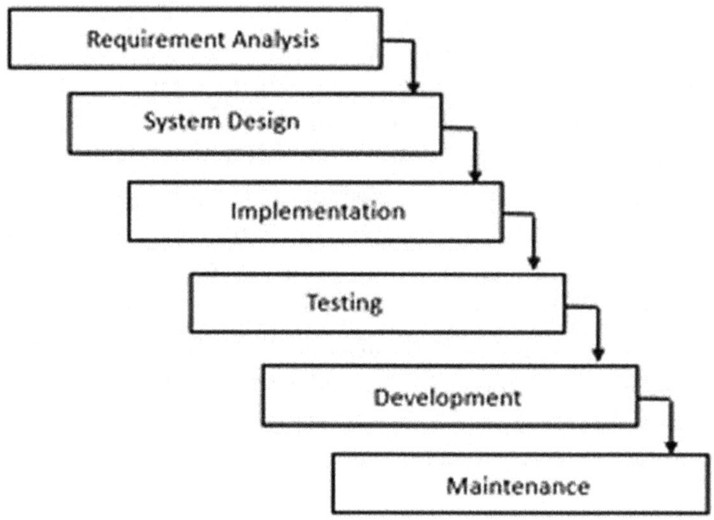

The given design task was executed in the instruction-based tutorial environment. It includes project planning aspects, forming task-oriented teams within the project, the organization of roles and responsibilities within these teams, and way of working procedures. Four groups of students performed the collaborative work. An overview of both Waterfall and Agile methodologies were introduced to the students. Also, the participants' roles according to the agile methodology are discussed. The team's role-playing game contributed to designing and developing a complete artefact (i.e., paper aircraft) with appropriate quality guidance for production processes. Finally, the workshop's instructor has simplified the names and descriptions of the roles to introduce the participants, as shown in Table 3. Figure 3 provides the step-by-step approach of the waterfall model (Royce, 1970) for a sequential way product design practice.

Business communities are adopting agile development methods because of their aim of delivering value and their catalytic effect on innovation. Implementing diffident industrial sectors projects using the agile method needs a customer to whom an agile development team will deliver a product (e.g., aircraft, software, hardware). Agile methodology guides the development team's activities and events to create the product to deliver value to the customer. Therefore, delivering value to the customer, however, defined, becomes the central aim of the team.

Agile product development teams are organized to provide maximum value to the business in as little time as possible. Development teams rely on teamwork, focus, and collaboration. Having an agile team focus on and produce value for a customer is an essential mechanism.

The roles implemented in agile development activities and this methodology's vocabulary are shown in Table 3 and Table 4, respectively.

Table 3. Agile methodology roles and descriptions

Role Name	Role Description
Business Analyst	A business analyst is an individual responsible for gathering user requirements, analyzing the requirements, making design documents, making a project management plan, and delivering value to the customer.
Product Owner	Accommodates and adjusts stakeholders' requirements to constitute user stories and ensure the product's quality assurance.
Scrum Master	Scrum masters are responsible for their team's agile development processes, delivering user stories for the current iteration, and guiding the team.
Developer	Developers focus on delivering components of the product needed in the present iteration.

Table 4. Agile methodology vocabulary and concepts

Concept	Definition
User Stories	Describe the '*why*, *what* and *who*' of desired application value for different types of product backlog elements, particularly characteristics.
Product Backlog	Prearrange a list of the elements – characteristics and other capabilities – needed to design and develop an excellent item of interest.
Standup	Prepare daily meetings in which team members explain what they did the day before, what they will do that day, and where they require help.
Sprint	Iteration of product delivery has four activities: planning, execution, review, and recollective.

TEACHING AGILE METHODOLOGY THROUGH SIMULATION GAMES

The main aim is to plan, build, and 'test as many paper aircraft as possible in 5 minutes, following the agile development methodology. The author of this chapter acted as the instructor to create a simulation game for first-year computer science students. The learning objectives of the simulation game were:

- Understand Waterfall and agile development process models.
- Explain tasks, concepts, and roles in traditional and agile software development processes.
- Create product requirements in user stories, including roles, actions, outcomes, and motivation.
- Perform roles of agile development team members to experience the advantages of each method; and
- Apply agile development principles to personal and work tasks.

The instructor began the session by asking participants, '*what would you need to do if you were going to build an application*?'. The participant responded, '*have an idea*', '*find someone to program it*', '*test it*' and '*complete it*'. Also, participants said these tasks should happen one after the other, in this order. Finally, the instructor pointed out the connections between the students' responses and the waterfall methodology shown in Figure 3. Next, the facilitators explained that they would experience the waterfall methodology by building paper aircraft instead of developing software applications.

Figure 4. Students form a scrum group for paper aircraft design

The instructor first briefed the students on three critical components of the exercise: the objective, the role, and the restrictions.

Objective

The intension of the waterfall model simulation is to build as many papers' aircrafts as conceivable in 15 minutes that will fly well over a specified distance of seven feet when tested. The simulation assesses a team's performance by measuring volume (number of aircraft built) and quality (percentage of aircraft that flew the required distance). These metrics reflect the value (efficiency and quality) delivered to a customer in a aircraft development project.

Roles

Students self-organized into groups of five or six and, when their groups, identified the role that each participant would play, as shown in Figure 4. One student took on the role of analyst, who would write the specifications for constructing the paper aircraft; one student took on the role of tester, who would test the paper aircraft constructed; and the remaining participants acted as the development team responsible for building the paper aircraft.

Each analyst wrote the requirements and design specifications for the team's aircraft during the planning and design phase and could not communicate with other team members, nor could the analyst assist in building a prototype. For example, the development team could begin work only during the build phase and was restricted from asking the analyst any questions or clarification on the design specifications provided to them and from testing any aircraft built. However, each tester could not begin testing until the test phase and could not modify the aircrafts the development team built. The instructor tracked time for each phase and recorded for each team the number of paper aircraft built during the build phase and the number that flew seven feet successfully.

The instructor debriefed the participants about what worked well and what did not to end the exercise simulating an agile approach. The debrief discussion ensured that participants met the learning objectives of the traditional waterfall development approach by observing and discussing the key challenges organizations experience when it comes to delivering custom applications.

Through their participation in the simulation, participants recognized several application developments challenges organizations may experience in the agile development approach:

- Defining requirements upfront is very difficult because business requirements change.
- A lack of discussion and communication between developers and the customer may have an unfavorable influence on the final product; and
- Delivering the application often takes a long time, and often the resulting product does not meet a business' expectations in the end.

Students had ample time in the agile simulation activity and split into three sprints: one minute for planning and design, two minutes to build, and one minute to test their aircraft. At the end of each sprint, they could share their results with the team, whose members would offer the builders suggestions for improving the design prior to the next testing phase. Throughout each sprint, the facilitators recorded the number of aircraft built and the number successfully flown for each group. At the end of the three sprints, the facilitator's engaged participants in a similar debrief discussion. They reflected on the results of the agile version of the activity, compared how their experience differed between the traditional water methodology and agile and compared the results of agile methodology based on the individual groups' predicted output and actual outcome in each sprint.

Figure 5. Average success rates

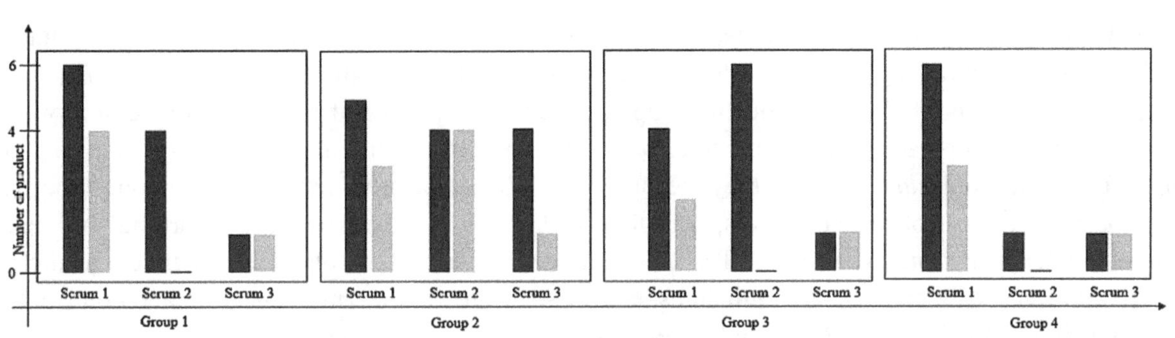

The instructor tracked the number of aircraft built and flown successfully using agile methodology. Figure 5 shows the success rates for an individual group of participants using agile methodology. During the agile activity, participants commented on their roles. For example, business analysts recalled, 'I had to find a model for the paper plane to be built. I have repeated the exercise four times to conclude'. Tester said, "I had to test the paper aircraft to see which ones flew 7 feet and which ones did not", and "my job was to throw the paper aircraft at the best distance possible".

Many students noted that agile methods are a good model for improved collaboration and group work. Increasing communication multiple times in a product's production cycle will improve the final product. Students were engaged in the exercise and comprehended the basic ideas of both methodologies (i.e., waterfall, agile scrum).

FUTURE WORK

The most important lesson learned from the classroom-based exercise is structuring the product development project timeline in '*Sprints*' as iterations delivering a finished product increment was advantageous in many ways. Firstly, the changing target problem intrinsic to the presented design work was stabilized at discussion points between team-members. Secondly, the fixed-time characteristics of the sprints provided the conformity of task completion with the overall project plan. Moreover, frequent, and appropriate meeting arrangements and encouraging direct communication helped share knowledge, solve problems, mitigate risks better, and create situation awareness within the team.

The retrospective suggests many enhancements in future agile projects, particularly regarding observation practice, method adoption, and fluctuation of team member performance. Product owners and scrum masters are required to be aligned, so that team members are aware of the basic functionalities of these team members. Therefore, handling spiral knowledge is essential for keeping up the focus and spirit of a team and maintaining design effectiveness. Furthermore, the applicability of Agile methods to the full development of large-scale critical systems such as distributed software development, and complex engineering product development, remains an essential research question in real-world applications development in computer science.

CONCLUSION

This chapter presents a reflection on teaching practice in an undergraduate induction session that introduces agile methodology-based product (e.g., software, paper-aircraft) design project management. There were two central objectives of this chapter. The first objective of the induction session was to '*learn-by-doing*' approach allows youth to experience something with minimal guidance from an adult. Instead of being told '*the answers*', they are presented with a question, problem, situation, or activity they must make sense of for themselves. Learning by doing is called "experiential learning" because it is based on learning from experiences. The secondary objectives were to introduce a suitable methodology to address social, cultural, and human aspects of software engineering education and contribution to rich insights into software design and development in a group environment.

In addition, the effective management of inter-disciplinary collaboration and fast design iteration cycles are critical for the success of a conceptual design project, particularly when progressive ideas and solutions are pursued. Finally, this chapter describes on agile (i.e., scrum-based) method of working and observation during the project, complemented with a post-project evaluation of project-related artefacts and a survey among team members of the induction session.

Based on the observation, it can be highlighted that agile methods are well applicable to conceptual aircraft design. Therefore, it is adopting the scrum methodology to the specific organizational context, effectively tackling the specific challenges of the conceptual design task. For example, scrum-specific time restrictions and meeting culture led to high situational awareness among team members and product stakeholders.

The result of the classroom-based teaching and learning practice and evaluation of paper aircraft design encourages exploration further of the potential of agile methods in future conceptual engineering product design (e.g., software) projects. However, it should be investigated how further adoption of scrum affects this compatibility and how agile methods can help the small team cope with personnel and resource fluctuation. Finally, new insights would be relevant for the software industry and other industries developing high-value-added engineering systems.

REFERENCES

Al-Husseini, S., & Elbeltagi, I. (2015). Knowledge Sharing Practices as a Basis of Product Innovation: A Case of Higher Education in Iraq. *International Journal of Social Science and Humanity*, *5*(2), 182–185. doi:10.7763/IJSSH.2015.V5.449

Allen, T. J., & Cohen, D. J. (1969). Information flow in research and development laboratories. *Administrative Science Quarterly*, *14*(1), 12–20. doi:10.2307/2391357

Bartol, K., & Srivastava, A. (2002). Encouraging knowledge sharing: The role of organizational reward systems. *Journal of Leadership & Organizational Studies*, *9*(1), 64–76. doi:10.1177/107179190200900105

Bartol, M. K., & Srivastava, A. (2002). Motivation and Barriers to Participation in Virtual Knowledge-Sharing Communities of Practice. *Journal of Leadership & Organizational Studies*, *9*(1), 64–75. doi:10.1177/107179190200900105

Baskervill, R. L., & Stage, J. (1996). Controlling Prototype Development Through Risk Analysis. *Management Information Systems Quarterly*, *20*(4), 481–502. doi:10.2307/249565

Beck, K. (2004). eXtreme Programming Eagilelained: Embrace change (2nd ed.). Addison-Wesley.

Beck, K., Cockburn, A., Jeffries, R., & Highsmith, J. (2001). *Agile manifesto*. http://www.agilemanifesto.org

Ben-Ari, M. (1998). Constructivism in Computer Science. *Proceedings of the 29th SIGCSE Technical Symposium on Computer Science Education*, 257-261.

Boh, W. F. (2014). Knowledge Sharing in Communities of Practice: Examining Usefulness of Knowledge from Discussion Forums versus Repositories. *The Data Base for Advances in Information Systems*, *45*(2), 8–31. doi:10.1145/2621906.2621908

Boh, W. F. (2014). Knowledge Sharing in Communities of Practice: Examining Usefulness of Knowledge from Discussion Forums versus Repositories. *The Data Base for Advances in Information Systems*, *45*(2), 8–31. doi:10.1145/2621906.2621908

Bostrom, R. P., & Thomas, B. D. (1983). Achieving Excellence in Communications: A Key to Developing Complete, Accurate and Shared Information Requirements. *Twentieth Annual Computer Personnel on Research Conference*.

Cao, L., & Ramesh, B. (2007). Agile Software Development: Ad Hoc Practices or Sound Principles? *IT Professional*, *9*(2), 41–47. doi:10.1109/MITP.2007.27

Child, J. (1972). Organisation structure, environment, and performance: The role of strategic choice. *Sociology*, *6*(1), 1–22. doi:10.1177/003803857200600101

Chin, G. (2006). *Agile Project Management*. AEW Services.

Cockburn, A. (2000). *Writing Effective Use Cases*. Addison-Wesley.

Cockburn, A. (2006). *Agile Software Development: The Cooperative Game*. Addison-Wesley.

Cockburn, A. & Williams, L. (2003). Agile software development: It's about feedback and change *IEEE Computer, 36*(6), 39–43.

Cohn, T., & Paul, R. (2001). A Comparison of Requirements Engineering in Extreme Programming (AGILE) and Conventional Software Development Methodologies. *Seventh Americas Conference on Information Systems*.

Coram, M., & Bohner, S. (2005). The Impact of Agile Methods on Software Project Management. *Proceedings of the 12th IEEE International Conference and Workshops on the Engineering of Computer-Based Systems (ECBS'05)*, 363-370. 10.1109/ECBS.2005.68

Cunningham, W. (2001). *Agile Manifesto*. http://www.agilemanifesto.org

Damodaran, L., & Olphert, W. (2000). Barriers and facilitators to the use of knowledge management systems. *Behaviour & Information Technology, 19*(6), 405–413. doi:10.1080/014492900750052660

Davenport, T. H., & Prusak, L. (1998). *Working knowledge: How organizations manage what they know, MA*. Harvard Business School Press.

Davila, T., Epstein, M. J., & Shelton, R. (2006). *Making Innovation Work: How to Manage it, Measure it, and Profit from it*. Pearson Education.

Duncan, T., & Sandra, E. M. (1998). A Communication Based Marketing Model for Managing Relationships. *Journal of Marketing, 62*(April), 1–12. doi:10.1177/002224299806200201

Fidalgo-Blanco. Saura, J. R, Palacios-Marqués, D., & Ribeiro-Soriano, D. (2022). Exploring the boundaries of Open Innovation: Evidence from social media mining. *Technovation*. Advance online publication. doi:10.1016/j.technovation.2021.102447

Fidalgo-Blanco, A., Sein-Echaluce, M. L., & García-Peñalvo, F. J. (2014). Knowledge spirals in higher education teaching innovation. *International Journal of Knowledge Management, 10*(4), 16–37. doi:10.4018/ijkm.2014100102

Fowler, M. (2002). *AGILE Customer Quotes*. WikiWikiWeb. https://martinfowler.com/articles/agileStory.html

García-Peñalvo, F. J. (2011). La Universidad de la próxima década: La Universidad Digital. In C. SuárezGuerrero & F. J. García-Peñalvo (Eds.), Universidad y Desarrollo Social de la Web (pp. 181-197). Editandum.

Gilby, T. (1988). Principle of Software Engineering Management. Addison-Wesley.

Gittins, R., Hope, S., & Williams, L. (2002). Qualitative Studies of AGILE in a medium-sized Business. In M. Marchesi, G. Succi, D. Wells, & L. Williams (Eds.), *Extreme Programming Perspectives*. Addison-Wesley.

Gunn, C. (2010). Sustainability factors for e-learning initiatives. *ALT-J Research in Learning Technology, 18*(2), 89–103. doi:10.1080/09687769.2010.492848

Hansen, M. T. (2002). Knowledge networks: Explaining effective knowledge sharing in multiunit companies. *Organization Science, 13*(3), 232–248. doi:10.1287/orsc.13.3.232.2771

Hanssen, G. K., & Fægri, T. E. (2006). Agile Customer Engagement: A Longitudinal Qualitative Case Study. In *ISESE'06* (pp. 164–173). ACM Press. doi:10.1145/1159733.1159759

Highsmith, J. (2001). The Great Methodologies Debate, Part I: Opening Statement. *Cutter IT Journal, 14*, 2–4.

Hinds, P. J., Patterson, M., & Pfeffer, J. (2001). Bothered by abstraction: The effect of expertise on knowledge transfer and subsequent novice performance. *The Journal of Applied Psychology, 86*(6), 1232–1243. doi:10.1037/0021-9010.86.6.1232 PMID:11768064

Kendon, A. (1995). Gestures as illocutionary and discourse structure markers in Southern Italian conversation. *Journal of Pragmatics, 23*(3), 1–31. doi:10.1016/0378-2166(94)00037-F

Koulikov, M. (2011). Emerging Problems in Knowledge Sharing and the Three New Ethics of Knowledge Transfer. *Knowledge Management & E-Learning. International Journal, 3*(2), 237–250.

Kujala, S. (2007). Effective user involvement in product development by improving the analysis of user needs. *Behaviour & Information Technology, Taylor & Francis, 2007*, 1–16.

Nicoleta, C. (2005). Agile Software Project Management Methodologies. *Economy Informatics*, 1-4.

Nonaka, I. (1991). The knowledge-creating company. *Harvard Business Review, 69*(6), 96–104.

Nonaka, I., & Takeuchi, H. (1995). *The Knowledge-Creating Company*. Oxford University Press.

Pal, K. (2019). Markov Decision Theory Based Crowdsourcing Software Process Model. In Crowdsourcing and Probabilistic Decision-Making in Software Engineering: Emerging Research and Opportunities. IGI Global.

Pal, K. (2020). Framework for Reusable Test Case Generation in Software Systems Testing. In Software Engineering for Agile Application Development. IGI Global

Pal, K. (2021). A Case Study of Knowledge Management and Organizational Culture in an Undergraduate Software Development Team Project. In Contemporary Challenges for Agile Project Management. IGI Global.

Pal, K., & Karakostas, B. (2021). Software Testing Under Agile, Scrum, and DevOps. In Agile Scrum Implementation and its Long-Term Impact on Organization. IGI Global.

Pal, K., & Williams, I. (2021). Global Software Development Knowledge Management Using Semantic Web Technology. IGI Global.

Roffe, I. M. (1998). Conceptual problems of continuous quality improvement and innovation in higher education. *Quality Assurance in Education, 6*(2), 74–82. doi:10.1108/09684889810205723

Royce, W. W. (1970). Managing the Development of Large Software Systems. *Proceedings of IEEE WESCON*, *26*(August), 1–9.

Salihoğlu, Y. (2001). *User Involvement in Software Project Development: A Review of Models*. Software Project Management Research Paper.

Salihoğlu, Y. (2001). *User Involvement in Software Project Development: A Review of Models*. Software Project Management Research Paper.

Saura, J. R., Ribeiro-Soriano, D., & Iturricha-Fernández, A. (2022). Exploring the challenges of remote work on Twitter users' sentiments: From digital technology development to a post-pandemic era. *Journal of Business Research*, *142*, 242–254. doi:10.1016/j.jbusres.2021.12.052

Schwaber, K., & Beedle, M. (2001). *Agile Software Development with Scrum*. Prentice-Hall.

Sheng, W., & Noe, R. A. (2010). Knowledge sharing: A review and directions for future research. *Human Resource Management Review*, *20*(2), 115–131. doi:10.1016/j.hrmr.2009.10.001

Tseng, F.-C., & Kuo, F.-Y. (2014). A study of social participation and knowledge sharing in the teachers' online professional community of practice. *Computers & Education*, *72*, 37–47. doi:10.1016/j.compedu.2013.10.005

Van Deursen, A. (2001a). *Customer Involvement Experiences in a Software Product Line*. XP2001 workshop on customer involvement, Italy. Available online at https://homepages.cwi.nl/~arie/wci2001/vandeursen.pdf

Van Deursen, A. (2001b). Customer Involvement in Extreme Programming, XP2001 Workshop Report. *XP2001 Workshop on Customer Involvement*, 70-73.

VersionOne. (2011). *State of Agile Survey 2011 - The State of Agile Development*. Author.

Wastell, D. (1999). Learning Dysfunctions in Information Systems Development: Overcoming the Social Defences with Transitional Objects. *Management Information Systems Quarterly*, *23*(4), 581–600. doi:10.2307/249490

Weatherly, L. A. (2003). The value of people: The challenges and opportunities of human capital measurement and reporting. *Research Quarterly*, *123*, 1–11.

Whitworth, A. (2012). Invisible success: Problems with the grand technological innovation in higher education. *Computers & Education*, *59*(1), 145–155. doi:10.1016/j.compedu.2011.09.023

Xiao-Li, L., Wei, G., Xin-Li, C., & Ke-Gang, H. (2006). Designing a test case library system of supporting sharing and reusing. *Journal of Computational Science*, *33*, 290–291.

KEY TERMS AND DEFINITIONS

Agile Methodology: Agile development represents a new approach to planning and managing projects. It emphasizes up-front plans and strict control and relies more on information collaboration, coordination, and learning. In other words, it is an evolutionary and iterative approach to development that focuses on adaption to changes.

Agile Project Management: Agile project can be seen as a collection of activities that create an identifiable value outcome. Project management consists of planning, executing, and monitoring these activities in their simplest form. Description of the work (tasks) and the resources (e.g., time, people, materials) needed to accomplish goals and objectives. The plan's task corresponds to the selected process model.

Customer: The person, or persons, who pay for the software product and other services (e.g., installation, amendments, user training).

Scrum: An agile process framework for managing knowledge work, emphasizing software development.

Software Engineering: Development of software based on theoretical foundations and practical disciplines traditional to engineering.

User: The person, or persons, who uses (or operates, interacts) directly with the software product. The user(s) and the customer(s) are often not the same people (s).

Waterfall Model: A sequential design used in software development processes that progress steadily towards the end (like Waterfall flows top to down) through the phases of Requirements, Specifications, Coding, Testing, and Release.

Chapter 9
Applying Active Methodologies in Complex Subjects at University:
A Combination of PBL, ICT, and Analysis of Real Cases

Alba Gómez-Ortega
Rey Juan Carlos University, Spain

Almudena Macías-Guillén
Rey Juan Carlos University, Spain

ABSTRACT

This study describes an experience carried out at a university that combines problem-based learning and the use of information and communication technologies (ICT). The activity pursues to deepen the learning of a subject with complex and singular content, taking as a reference the study of real cases. Specifically, the aim is to develop knowledge about the different sectoral accounting standards that are applied in the preparation of companies' financial information. The student checks for himself the usefulness of accounting knowledge to understand the financial situation of real companies. The results show a generalized improvement in student motivation and in results obtained in the subject. It demonstrates how in complex subjects that are less attractive to students active methodologies can be used to connect with them. They learn to take advantage of the resources offered by ICT to access information of great relevance in the business world.

INTRODUCTION

The adoption of the philosophy of the European Higher Education Area implied changes in the traditional way of doing things for many teachers and students. This suggests that students will have to acquire

DOI: 10.4018/978-1-6684-4441-2.ch009

Copyright © 2022, IGI Global. Copying or distributing in print or electronic forms without written permission of IGI Global is prohibited.

learning that encompasses not only the specific knowledge of their degree, but also a wide range of skills and competences (Saura et al., 2022). The effective acquisition of the many competences that define each degree requires students to "learn by doing". This triggers a profound process towards innovation at all levels (Benito & Cruz, 2005). Recent studies have found that a process of innovation is also essential in education (Ellis & Childs, 2019; Giordano et al., 2020; Lašáková et al., 2017; Phi & Clausen, 2020). This situation is causing teachers to look for new ways to better prepare their students, as the educational goals are not for students to memorise a significant amount of data, but for students to gain the foundations necessary to achieve lifelong learning (Hunt et al., 2019; Kanuru & Priyaadharshini, 2020).

It is essential that learners develop their own autonomy during problem solving. Doing so would increase their innovative capacity to improve their participation in future business challenges. It has also been shown that introducing innovations within any field enables the participants therein to improve their ability to generate ideas and solutions and enables them to negotiate and work in teams, among other multiple advantages (González, 2018). Yet, it should be noted that educational innovations, however valuable they may be, do not necessarily have the same positive effects on all learners. Therefore, teachers are obliged to identify those activities that are truly appropriate for the learner in each context. However, although the objective is very clear, achieving it is a very complex challenge, as it is not only necessary to create new educational techniques to maximise student performance, but it is also important to analyse teaching methodologies to determine which educational techniques are the most efficient (Cruz, 2019; Macías et al., 2018).

In view of this, it is essential for teachers to make sure that they identify the real concerns of their students to ensure their success in the labour market that they will have to face a few years later (Valerio & Rodríguez, 2017; Toding & Venesaar, 2018). It could be said that in contemporary education contexts it is necessary to open up new pedagogical paths that allow students to participate more actively pursuant of ensuring that they acquire all the necessary knowledge to ensure their professional success in the future (Silva & Maturana, 2017; Saura et al., 2022a). On the other hand, building and sharing have become transversal objectives that give meaning to the use of Information and Communication Technologies (ICT) in curriculum development and student training (García-Valcárcel et al., 2014). Nowadays ICT allow us, with minimal effort, to configure teaching that is truly adapted to the personal characteristics of students, to their learning style needs, and to their preferences regarding the symbolic systems with which they wish to interact with information. All this has been materialised in the creation of new basic competences linked, logically, to ICT and the notion of lifelong learning; competences that are now in force and have replaced the old objectives as assessment indicators (Blanco & Amigo, 2016). These competences are necessary so that, once students enter the labour market, the new technologies adoption can have a positive impact on their learning (Saura et al., 2022b).

The aim of this article is to analyse the application of an active methodology in complex subject at the university, which combines Problem Based Learning (PBL) and the use of ICT. With this objective in mind, this work sets out to answer the following research questions: RQ1. Is the study of a subject about the real world perceived as useful by students? RQ2. Can active methodologies such as PBL improve the satisfaction of university students with complex subjects of study?

The results show a great majority of the students found this experience very useful and motivating. The students also expressed a special interest in analysis and approach to the professional and real world of the company. Finally, the research demonstrates a significant improvement in the results obtained in the subject.

The originality of this study lies in its contribution to a change in the approach to teaching accounting-related subjects. In general, these are complex subjects, full of regulations and can be excessively tedious for students, being perceived by them as less dynamic and creative subjects. The main academic implication is that this study demonstrates how the application of active learning methodologies can help to increase the motivation and interest of students in this kind of subjects, through the study of the more theoretical concepts taught in the classroom applied to real cases and companies. In this way, their practical usefulness and applicability in the business world is demonstrated. From the practical point of view, through the problem posed in the classroom, students will be able to see for themselves the need to understand financial reporting standards and sectorial accounting in order to be able to evaluate the activity of a real company and understand its situation. The project allows students to transfer knowledge from the classroom to a professional and practical application in real companies, simulating a reality very close to the one they will experience at the end of their university studies.

The paper can contribute to the growing literature on active learning methodologies, about Problem Based Learning, through a study of real cases (as is the case of the analysis of financial information in the training of future business managers), as it provides clear arguments for an experience that is not only motivating, but also useful for students by contributing to the improvement of their competences in this area.

BACKGROUND

The Importance of Active Learning Methodologies

In the context of today's world, it could be said that self-directed learning contributes greatly to students' motivation and learning, enhancing skills such as selection, analysis and evaluation of information. Students become responsible for their own knowledge. A suitable change in teaching practices will allow us to offer society creative, reflective professionals, with a solid base of technical and technological knowledge, capable of lifelong learning and with essential communication skills to move in contemporary workplaces (Benito & Cruz, 2005; Saura et al., 2022c).

The adaptation of both content and teaching methodologies has become a necessary, and even urgent, challenge in a constantly changing social context, in which young people, surrounded by screens from birth, have acquired traits that are different from those of any previous generation (Blanco & Amigo, 2016). These traits allow them to accept technology as part of the world in which they live and they do so naturally, defending the possibilities it offers them. However, in an environment where information is available at the click of a button on the web, rote learning basically serves as training for the student and they are exposed to problems such as over-information and infoxication. It is important that the new methodologies tend to strengthen the study of the fundamentals of subjects, providing the student with sufficient tools to be able to locate, select and use the information that he/she finds useful, considers reliable and allows him/her to create arguments (Herrero-Diz et al., 2021).

According to Bonilla del Río et al. (2018), in today's world, communicative processes take place in an environment where digital resources acquire great relevance at all levels, including the professional one, so educational institutions must not remain oblivious to this context. In the words of Romero-Rodríguez et al. (2018), "at a time when values, which could rather be considered counter-values, prevail, the curricular integration of media education in the classroom and the development of critical awareness in society in general are essential". For all these reasons, it is important for students to learn what are the official sources of information, taking into account the discipline they are dealing with, the reality under study and the line of argument they wish to follow. In this experience, the teaching staff encourage students to consult primary sources concerning companies´ financial information and the official bodies that issue this information.

Problem Based Learning (PBL)

This methodology is based on a strategy in which the learning process allows students to acquire key skills and knowledge through the development of activities that respond to real problems. And that is precisely its main characteristic: students work actively and evaluate problems that have real-world applications beyond the classroom. Likewise, PBL is based on research and reflection by the student, generally carried out autonomously, to find a solution to a problem posed by the teacher (Fernández-Jiménez et al., 2014; Gil-Galván et al., 2021).

In turn, solving the problem will entail the development and acquisition of certain competences useful for their future employment (Hincapié et al., 2018). The more involved students are in the process, the more they will retain and take responsibility for their own learning. The role of the teacher is to be a guide, focusing on facilitating the student to find the best solution to the problem. In the practice of PBL, the student represents the cornerstone of the learning process, where they have the possibility of developing their skills and abilities, thus turning reflection into a habit that would give them professional and human criteria to face the vicissitudes they will encounter in later life, not least in workplaces (Fach Gómez, 2012). Therefore, this methodology plays an important role in the new conception of university curricula and may have benefits for new generation universities (Korkmaz & Kalayci, 2019). According to Parrado-Martínez and Sánchez-Andújar (2020), in higher education, the implementation of this teaching-learning strategy is generally associated with engineering (Arias et al., 2018; Uziak & Kommula, 2019) or medicine (Alrahlah, 2016; Collard et al., 2016). In the specific field of finance, the literature on the application of PBL is not as extensive. However, in view of the works cited, it could be said that this methodology provides significant benefits for the development of skills such as group work, leadership and the use of information technologies. Therefore, the authors consider that it is applicable to the area of accounting and finance, and this paper is an example of the result of this application, in line with the work carried out by Parrado-Martínez and Sánchez-Andújar (2020), Yang (2017) and Young and Legister (2018).

However, this learning model initially poses difficulties of adaptation for both teachers and learners, as it changes traditional roles. Among them, it may produce insecurity when learners are faced with the choice of sources for the search for information, although it may be more beneficial for certain types of personalities (the less introverted). Moreover, the tutor's own personality and teaching style may influence perceptions of the practice to be carried out (Sepúlveda et al., 2021). Resistance to change may even be provoked in a certain profile of students who support the traditional model, as this involves facing a new approach that will require additional effort on their part, an adaptation to a different way of teaching or collaboration with other students for teamwork purposes. In addition, this type of methodology will involve a relatively high workload, which may thus lead to lower acceptance by students (González-Hernando et al., 2013). All of the above implies the need to anticipate these limitations in order to try to approach the activity in the best possible way so that these problems can be minimised.

As a proposal, in this teaching experience, the authors consider that the best way to contact this methodology is to associate it with an activity that does not generate excessive pressure for the student in terms of the repercussion on their final grade. The project consists of a voluntary activity that does not involve a final mark for the subject. In this way, students feel freer and less apprehensive when carrying it out and, above all, they can enjoy the learning experience.

Learner Satisfaction in the Evaluation of Teaching Innovations

Student feedback is always an important part of knowing the student's condition and development in the classroom, of knowing the teacher's performance and, above all, of improving teaching methods. The evaluation of an innovative teaching practise, through surveys completed by the students themselves, allows us to know first-hand their level of satisfaction with the experience, as well as to contrast their opinions with those of the teachers who prepared and facilitated the activity (Torío et al., 2010). According to Tacca et al. (2019), student satisfaction responds to a set of experiences lived inside and outside the classroom. It is a multidimensional process that has several edges to be analysed. These edges, or aspects, referred to by the authors can lead to greater or lesser success of the teaching innovation and it is important to know what factors condition them (Saura et al., 2021).

Numerous authors have evaluated teaching experiences by measuring student satisfaction (Abella et al., 2018; Espada et al., 2020; Fernández et al., 2020). In this paper the authors conducted a satisfaction survey to elicit students' perceptions and to evaluate the experience for future courses and applications in other disciplines, where complex content and real-world analysis are the main focus.

STUDY DESIGN AND METHOD

Target

The main objective of this educational research is to explore the perceptions of students undertaking bachelor's degrees in accounting and finance when faced with the challenge of carrying out a real diagnosis of different companies, studying the key items of their financial statements and audit reports (Saura et al., 2021a). This approach to the study of real companies, from the point of view of accounting, is approached from a new perspective, opening up the horizon of analysis to different sectors of activity, financial casuistry and very different balance sheet and profit and loss account structures, depending on the business carried out by the company being analysed, which are not usually studied in common accounting subjects. The study of these companies with "multidisciplinary" activities, such as banking, investment or financial intermediation activities, attracts and interests students from the very beginning of the experience, capturing and maintaining their attention.

Participants

The sample of undergraduates who participated in this experience was constituted by 115 students, from different Accounting and Finance degrees, and all of them were undertaking the common module of "Financial Diagnosis", which is taught in the second year. In all cases, the students had already taken a basic financial accounting module. However, this module had not addressed the multisectoral study of annual accounts and the perspective of the diversity of accounting regulations.

This experience was of a voluntary nature, forming part of the classroom lessons for three weeks. According to Camacho and Del Campo (2015), it could be said that all those tasks proposed by the teacher on a voluntary basis would form part of the student's intrinsic motivation, as there is no direct 'reward' but rather the student's desire to learn. In addition, they point out that students will be more motivated to study subjects related to accounting, as it is a "summative" subject, i.e. the previous foundations build future knowledge. In our case, it is precisely the premise of the project to carry out this activity at the beginning of the module in order to subsequently facilitate a follow-up of the concepts to be taught in class and which will also be useful for students in other degree modules, such as economic analysis, financial auditing or the preparation of their Final Degree Project. Despite the fact that the experience did not represent a percentage of the final mark for the module, a participation rate of 82.14% was achieved, specifically 115 students out of the 140 who were enrolled.

Instrument

To set up the activity, a digital dossier was prepared specifying the basic instructions for carrying out the analysis. It was made available to students in the Virtual Classroom of the subject. However, despite giving some basic guidelines, much emphasis was placed on freedom and autonomy when carrying out the analysis, to allow each group to choose an approach which they felt was optimal to transmit the financial information they were obtaining from the company. Likewise, the students had to obtain financial information concerning the companies through the official records of the National Securities Market Commission, learning about the telematic and digital tools that the information issuing bodies make available to the public and the market. To illustrate the content of the dossier provided to students, Figure 1 shows four screenshots as examples from the file that was uploaded to the module's Virtual Classroom.

Figure 1. Screenshots from the dossier "An approach to the analysis and interpretation of annual accounts from different sectors"
Source: own elaboration

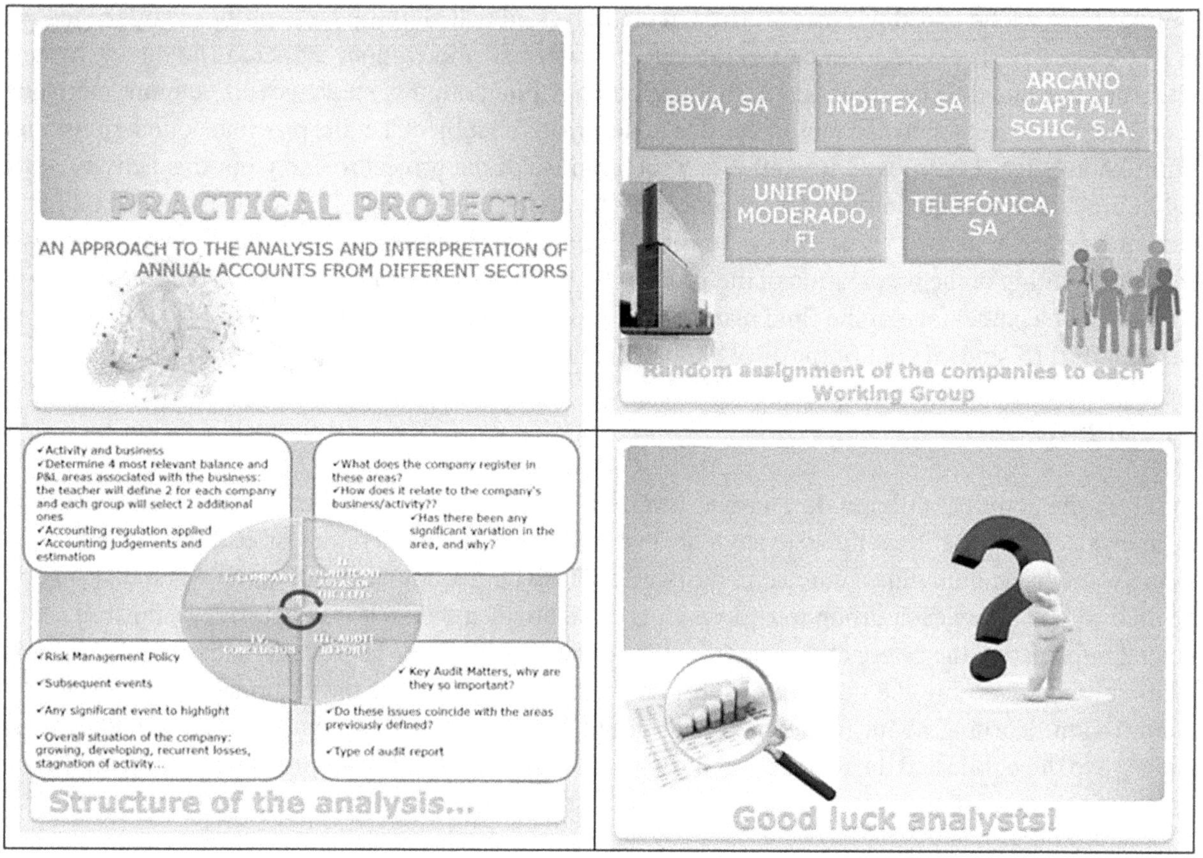

During the classes devoted to the activity, the teacher addressed questions and doubts about the interpretation of the information they were analysing, always from an objective point of view, trying not to modify students' perceptions of their analysis. Although this activity did not generate additional marks for the module, an evaluation was carried out to provide feedback to the students about their work and dedication, for which an evaluation rubric was used. Many authors support the use of these rubrics in university education (Manzanares & Arreba, 2014; Martiañez et al., 2015). The evaluation rubric used for this activity includes the assessment of three different sections (Figure 2): (1) quality of the process of obtaining annual accounts; (2) resolution; (3) delivery and presentation of results.

Figure 2. Activity evaluation rubric
Source: own elaboration

QUALITY OF THE PROCESS OF OBTAINING ANNUAL ACCOUNTS

- Fluency in locating information
- Variety in searching through different sources of information
- Distinction between audited annual financial information and other reporting

Rating 1 (lowest) to 5 (highest)

RESOLUTION

- Degree of identification of the most significant accounting areas related to the sector and of the accounting standard applied in the formulation of the annual accounts
- Level of justification of the identified areas described above.
- Degree of understanding of the company's financial risks and their management
- Degree of understanding of the audit report
- Conclusion on the overall situation of the company

Rating 1 (lowest) to 5 (highest)

DELIVERY AND PRESENTATION OF RESULTS

- Compliance with the deadline stipulated for the resolution of the activity
- Content of the exhibition
- Synthesis of main ideas and fluency in communicating them
- Expression and degree of participation in the group
- Resolution of questions posed by the teacher on the presentation given

Rating 1 (lowest) to 5 (highest)

To answer the research questions and consolidate the objective of this work, a student satisfaction survey was carried out, which will be analysed in the Results section. The survey was carried out using the Socrative tool. This application allows tests, evaluations and activities to be carried out and the data to be managed by the teacher. The questions that were asked, as well as their coding, are detailed in Figure 3. They included dichotomous questions, whose answer could be affirmative or negative; questions with a Likert scale from 1 to 5, with 1 being the most negative rating possible and 5 the most positive rating; and, at the end of the survey, an open question was included so that students could briefly evaluate the experience.

Figure 3. Activity satisfaction survey
Source: Own elaboration based on Macías et al. (2018)

1. If you were asked again if you would be interested in participating in this activity, what would your answer be? [REPEAT_PARTICIPATION]
2. Indicate the degree to which you LIKE the experience carried out in relation to the project "multisectoral accounting analysis". [LIKED_EXPERIENCE]
3. Rate the improvement obtained in your LEARNING in the area of ANNUAL ACCOUNT ANALYSIS in different sectors of activity. [LEARNING_IMPROVEMENT]
4. Indicate your DEGREE OF MOTIVATION and INTEREST in the process of this experience. [MOTIVATION+INTEREST]
5. Do you consider it interesting to implement new learning methodologies for a better understanding and use of subjects in the accounting domain? [INTEREST_NEW_METHODOLOGIES]
6. Rate the USEFULNESS of the activity as a STARTING POINT and ILLUSTRATIVE EXAMPLE for the FOLLOW-UP TO the financial diagnostics module. [USEFULNESS_FOLLOW-UP SUBJECT]
7. Indicate to what extent making a brief EXPOSITION of the results obtained by your team CONTRIBUTES to further learning, through the exchange of ideas about the same and different sectors with the other teams. [EXPO_CONTRIBUTION]
8. Bearing in mind that in this experience we tried to analyse different sectorial accounting standards (something that is not the norm in other accounting modules), indicate to what extent the activity DEVELOPS the GENERAL COMPETENCES on "autonomous learning" and on "ability to adapt to changing environments". [DEVELOP_GENERAL COMPETENCES]
9. Indicate the extent to which the activity DEVELOPS the SPECIFIC COMPETENCE on "analysis of balance sheets, profit and loss accounts and cash flow to detect possible financial and accounting problems and propose solutions to them". [DEVELOP_SPECIFIC COMPETENCES]
10. In a simple sentence, please provide any comments on the experience in relation to the project activity "multisectoral accounting analysis".

The SPSS software package was then used to quantify Cronbach's alpha (Table 1). This test allows us to gauge the validity of our questionnaire quantitatively based on the dispersion in the responses to the questions, or lack thereof; the obvious exception being the non-numerical answers to Question 10. Acceptable alpha values range from 0.70 to 0.95 (Hair et al., 2019), which would indicate a low dispersion in the responses recorded and a certain homogeneity or trend. The overall alpha value of 0.804 indicates an acceptable level of reliability.

Table 1. Reliability statistics: Cronbach's alpha

Cronbach's Alpha	Cronbach's Alpha Based on Standardised Items	No. of Elements
0.804	0.805	9

Survey Variable	Cronbach's Alpha if the Item Has Been Removed
REPEAT_PARTICIPATION	0.790
LIKED_EXPERIENCE	0.758
LEARNING_IMPROVEMENT	0.785
MOTIVATION + INTEREST	0.782
INTEREST_NEW_METHODOLOGY	0.811
USEFULNESS_FOLLOW-UP SUBJECT	0.786
EXPO_CONTRIBUTION	0.791
DEVELOP_GENERAL COMPETENCES	0.755
DEVELOP_ESPECIFIC COMPETENCES	0.789

Source: own elaboration

Procedure

This experience occurred at the beginning of the course, to deepen students' knowledge about real financial statements from different sectors and the diversity of Spanish accounting regulations. Prior to the activity, guidelines were given on how to search for annual financial information issued by companies. Theoretical concepts about annual accounts, accounting regulations and their interpretation were also explained.

In teams of approximately six people, each of the five companies previously selected by the teacher was randomly assigned using Excel's "random.between" function. The companies belong to different business sectors and are shown in Table 2. Each company was analysed by two different groups, with the aim of contrasting the evaluation obtained by the two different teams on the basis of the same accounting information issued by the company, and thus enriching the knowledge acquired. The individual annual accounts for the last available audited financial year were analysed. The closing date for all the companies is 31 December, except in the case of Inditex, S.A., where the closing date is 31 January.

The analysis carried out by the students took place during the lectures over a period of three weeks. When the class began, the students organised themselves into teams and the teacher only participated to resolve specific doubts. Based on these doubts, the teacher also complemented the theoretical knowledge of the subject and gave short explanations for the whole group. The process required more guidance from the teacher at the beginning of the activity, which gradually decreased until the students reached almost complete autonomy by the end of the project.

The structure of the analysis to be carried out was previously defined by the teacher, delineated as follows:

1. **Company:**

    a. Activity and business analysis.

b. Selection of four financial statements' areas that can be considered representative of the business and justify why they are considered relevant. The teacher predefined two of them (Table 2), leaving the teams to choose two additional areas.

Table 2. Target companies by sector of activity, accounting standards and significant areas determined by teacher

Company	Sector and Accounting Standards	Relevant Area
BBVA, S.A.	Credit institutions. Bank of Spain Circular.	• Loans and receivables. • Interest income.
Inditex, S.A.	Industrial, textiles. General Accounting Plan.	• Stocks. • Supplies.
Arcano capital, SGIIC, S.A.	Management companies of collective investment institutions. CNMV Circular.	• Commissions received. • Credit to financial intermediaries.
Unifond moderado, F.I.	Collective investment institutions, investment funds. CNMV Circular.	• Financial investment portfolio. • Creditors.
Telefónica, S.A.	Holdings companies. General Accounting Plan.	• Net turnover. • Long-term investments in group companies.

Source: own elaboration

c. Analyse the applied accounting standard in the formulation of annual accounts in the sector in question and considering the particularities that it may regulate.
d. Obtain information about the significant accounting judgements and estimates made by the entity's directors in the preparation of the financial statements and the impact this may have on the interpretation of the financial information.

2. **The most significant areas:**
    a. Analyse the company records in these areas and how it relates to a particular characteristic of the business.
    b. Identify significant variations during the last financial year and possible explanations for them.
3. **Audit report**
    a. Identify the key audit matters expressed in the report.
    b. Search the relation between these key issues and the areas selected for analysis.
    c. Type of audit report: favourable or modified.
4. **Conclusions**
    a. Analysis of the company's financial risks and its management policy.
    b. Identification of significant post-balance sheet events.
    c. Explain any significant highlight that have caught your attention.
    d. Conclusion on the overall situation of the company.
5. **Exposition, evaluation by the teacher and questions:** for fifteen minutes per team, using a presentation in digital format.

RESULTS

Satisfaction Survey

This section is focused on the results of the anonymous satisfaction survey carried out among the students participating in the experience. The results obtained were as follows:

Table 3. Descriptive statistics for Likert scale questions

	Min.	Max.	Mean	Std. Dev.
LIKED_EXPERIENCE	2.00	5.00	4.0714	0.70857
LEARNING_IMPROVEMENT	2.00	5.00	4.0857	0.73707
MOTIVATION + INTEREST	2.00	5.00	3.9714	0.77966
USEFULNESS_FOLLOW-UP SUBJECT	2.00	5.00	4.3571	0.70270
EXPO_CONTRIBUTION	2.00	5.00	4.1594	0.77882
DEVELOP_GENERAL COMPETENCES	2.00	5.00	4.1739	0.78509
DEVELOP_ESPECIFIC COMPETENCES	3.00	5.00	4.3043	0.71341

Source: own elaboration

The first question asked about the possibility of participating in this activity again, reaching 89% of affirmative responses, 10% suggesting indifference, with only one response showing a refusal. As shown in Table 3, in the Likert-scale questions, the minimum rating given was 2. Only one student specified this score – the one who refused to take part in the activity again and who, in the open question, alluded to problems related to the team. Taking this situation into account, it could be said that, with this exception, none of the students rated any aspects of the activity negatively, registering a minimum of 3 on all the items. By contrast, numerous responses were recorded at the maximum level of the scale, i.e. 5.

Regarding their opinion on the degree of satisfaction with the experience, 26% of the students answered that they liked it very much, 59% liked it quite a lot, 13% were indifferent and 3% of the students did not like it very much. In relation to the contribution to learning of annual accounts analysis, 54% of the students stated that it contributed quite a lot, 29% considered that it contributed a lot, 14% were indifferent and 3% considered that they had learned little. About the motivation and interest in the experience, 26% were very motivated, 49% were quite motivated, 23% were indifferent and 3% were not very motivated. Regarding the degree of usefulness of this teaching-learning methodology, 97% considered it useful and 3% were indifferent.

The usefulness of this experience as a starting point and illustrative example for following the subject, was evaluated by 47% of the students as very useful, 43% considered it quite useful, 9% were indifferent and 1% considered it not very useful. Regarding the contribution of the oral presentation to learning and knowledge exchange among students, 38% of the students considered that it contributed a lot, 41% considered that it contributed quite a lot, 19% were indifferent and 1% considered that it contributed little.

The students were asked about the level of development of two of the general subject competences through experience. 38% of the students considered that the activity developed these competences a lot, 45% considered that it developed them quite a lot, 14% considered that they were indifferent and

3% considered that it developed them a little. In relation to the subject specific competence, 45% of the students considered that they developed it a lot, 41% that they developed it quite a lot and the remaining 14% were indifferent.

Table 4 shows the t-test that allows us to determine whether the means were significantly different from 3.

Table 4. One-sample t test results

	Mean	St. Dev	[95% Conf. Interval]		t	p-value	
						Mean < 3	Mean ≥ 3
LIKED_EXPERIENCE	4.0714	0.70857	3.90247	4.24038	12.6511	1.0000	0.0000
LEARNING_IMPROVEMENT	4.0857	0.73707	3.90996	4.26146	12.3241	1.0000	0.0000
MOTIVATION + INTEREST	3.9714	0.77966	3.78553	4.15733	10.4245	1.0000	0.0000
USEFULNESS_FOLLOW-UP SUBJECT	4.3571	0.70270	4.18959	4.52470	16.1586	1.0000	0.0000
EXPO_CONTRIBUTION	4.1594	0.77882	3.97233	4.34651	12.3659	1.0000	0.0000
DEVELOP_GENERAL COMPETENCES	4.1739	0.78509	3.98531	4.36251	12.4205	1.0000	0.0000
DEVELOP_ESPECIFIC COMPETENCES	4.3043	0.71341	4.13297	4.47573	15.1873	1.0000	0.0000

Source: own elaboration

The p-value result is significant for means equal or greater than 3 for all variables. In addition, the confidence interval shows a range very close to 4. Therefore, there is sufficient statistical evidence to state that in all cases the tendency is a very positive assessment of the variables, considering a Likert scale between 1 and 5 for the satisfaction survey.

Finally, the students surveyed gave their opinion in a short sentence through an open question, in relation to their experience in analysing the annual accounts of different sectors of activity. In order to display the responses, a common denominator was identified for all of them, and they were typified as shown in Figure 4.

Figure 4. Typified responses about the students' opinion of the experience
Source: Own elaboration

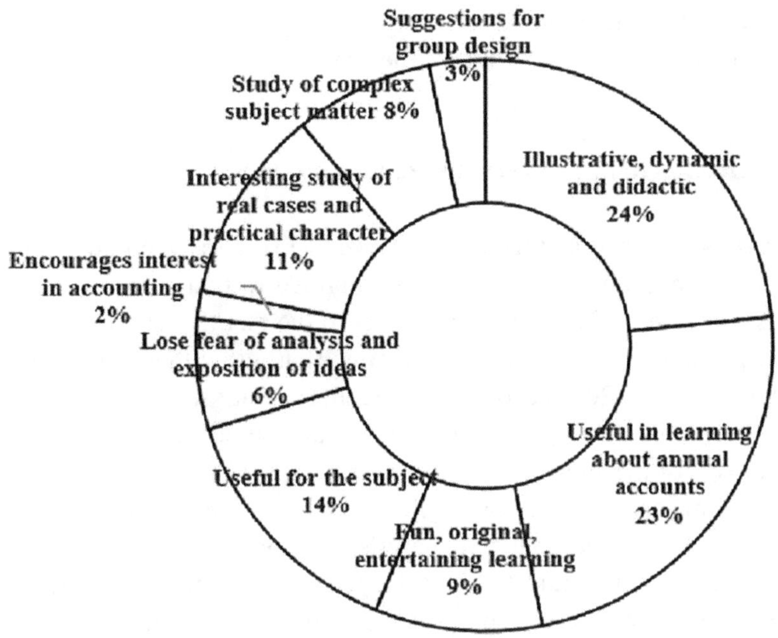

All the responses recorded are aimed at supporting this type of learning methodology, highlighting its practical usefulness for acquiring new knowledge in accounting and its practical contribution to future professional development. 24% of the students highlighted the illustrative and didactic nature of the experience. 23% and 14% highlighted its usefulness in learning about annual accounts and for the subject, respectively. 11% highlighted the interest in the study of real cases and the practical nature of the activity.

Results in Student Grades

In order to investigate the impact of this activity on student learning, from a more objective point of view and outside the students' perception, the results obtained in the subject are analysed. These results are shown in Table 5, differentiating whether the student had participated or not in the PBL experience on real cases.

Table 5. Students' obtained grades

Grades	Participated (%)	Not Participated (%)
Not present	1%	31%
Fail	3%	0%
Pass	32%	35%
Very good	52%	35%
Excellent	10%	0%
Honour degree	2%	0%

Source: own elaboration

Table 5 shows a considerable improvement in the results obtained for those students who participated compared to those who did not. In addition, it could be said that there is an increase in the motivation of the student who did participate in the experience, as those who did not participate have a higher percentage of "not present" grade, who did not take the exam.

DISCUSSION, CONCLUSION, AND IMPLICATIONS

In the light of the results obtained and trying to answer the first research question raised in the study, the authors could affirm that the study of a subject, applied to real companies, allows the student to better understand its usefulness. This usefulness refers to the fact that students see for themselves how the theoretical concepts studied have a real application, that allow them to learn about and analyse a given company (Saura et al., 2022d). It shows that students acquire skills that will be useful in the future companies in which they will work. The students also considered this experience useful as a starting point for the subject (47% of the students considered it to be very useful, 43% considered it to be quite useful). Specifically, in this case, the authors could say this experience has could improve the image of accounting and its usefulness in the financial analysis of a company, helping to deepen understanding and learning (23% of the students indicated, in the open question, the useful in learning about annual accounts and 2% indicated the encourages interest in accounting). Additionally, from an objective point of view and outside of student's perception, the obtained results in subject shows that there is a higher grade on students who participated than on students who did not do.

This statement supports the idea of Camacho et al. (2016) that students are more interested in activities related to the real world of business. It is also in line with authors such as Rué et al. (2011), who stated that working with the PBL model encourages students to value learning activities linked to the subject.

Regarding the second research question, the authors can affirm that students positively value the application of active methodologies, such as Problem-Based Learning, considering its implementation interesting for a better understanding and use of complex subjects, as is the case of sectorial accounting and its analysis. These results align with Macías et al. (2018), in which the participating students considered that the implementation of Digital Innovation Techniques (Saura et al., 2021b) for a better understanding and use of the subject was excellent and very good, respectively. This highlights the need to use ICT to facilitate these active methodologies. Specifically, and as Gil-Galván et al. (2021) state, Problem-Based Learning contributes to and favours the acquisition of technical, methodological, participative and personal competences.

Theoretical Implications

The authors can conclude that this experience is an important support tool for university teaching. As in other specialities, teachers in accounting and finance area are encouraged to modify certain teaching habits in order to increase the motivation of our students. Teachers are an essential part of the teaching-learning binomial and, therefore, they are obliged to promote an active environment for our students through motivational strategies and encouraging the use of ICT. Such has been the involvement in this innovative teaching project and the interest aroused by the students in the study of sectorial accounting, that it has led to the publication of a teaching manual for the analysis of the annual accounts of different sectors of activity (Gómez, 2021).

Likewise, the authors hope this work to motivate who teach complex subjects in universities to carry out activities on real business cases, through the application of active methodologies such as PBL, taking advantage of the accessibility to information provided by ICT. This work has demonstrated the significant value of activities that promote intrinsic motivation in content. So much so that the academic results of students who participate in these activities clearly improve over those who do not. Also, the authors encourage to carry out these experiences even in branches of knowledge where it is not common, it will be precisely there where the differentiating factor in the subjects lies.

The approach to the problem and the focus with which it is developed, allows us to achieve the indicators of success that Fidalgo-Blanco et al. (2014) propose for an educational innovation, such as the ability to be reproduced in other subjects, achieving fully active participation by the student, generating a proven increase in their motivation and the ability to adapt to the available resources, in this case the financial information that companies submit to the CNMV and which can be accessed telematically. This study reinforces the usefulness of the indicators proposed by the aforementioned authors in the construction of innovative teaching practices.

Likewise, the main ingredients of this study are the creation of collaborative ideas through the application of a creative project with an entrepreneurial orientation for the student, the encouragement of teamwork and motivation and the use of technological resources for accessing financial information on companies, through the study of real cases. With this, the study is able to collect 5 of the 8 topics that, according to Saura et al. (2022b), provide a glimpse of the limitations of open innovation were identified, demonstrating the value of the approach applied in this study, in the current context.

Practical Implications

Through the problem posed in the classroom, students will be able to see for themselves the need to understand financial reporting standards and sectorial accounting in order to be able to evaluate the activity of a real company and understand its situation. Thanks to this project, which will form part of the subject's teaching approach for the future courses, the university-business connection is improved, and the existing gap is reduced (Méndez et al., 2016). The project allows students to transfer knowledge from the classroom to a professional and practical application in real companies, simulating a reality very close to the one they will experience at the end of their university studies. Higher education institutions must contribute as a mechanism to make this possible, this is where change processes in universities become relevant to motivate innovation and creative solutions to bring knowledge and learning closer to the real world. As teachers we must serve as agents of change, assuming the role of connectors with the environment.

This study helps to demonstrate the importance of linking university teaching to the needs of business and the real world and, above all, that students are able to see the connection between theory and practice, which is often called into question.

LIMITATIONS AND FUTURE RESEARCH

The present work is not free of limitations. The moderate sized sample of students used in this study could usefully be increased and longitudinal research designs would offer significant benefits in terms of gauging temporalities in preferences and opinions. In addition, the study does not consider the role of the teacher as a moderator in the greater or lesser motivation generated in the student. In a continuation of this study, it is planned to implement it with different groups of students with different teachers acting as guides in the process, in order to try to assess the teacher's skills that may have the greatest impact on their motivation and learning. On the other hand, the project is expected to include team building through a methodology that analyses the formation of its components to maximise their performance, as would be the case of applying Belbin's roles as proposed by Aranzabal et al. (2022), which will allow further analysis of the results.

REFERENCES

Abella, V., Delgado, V., Ausín, V., & Hortigüela, D. (2018). Satisfacción de los estudiantes en una experiencia de ABP mediado por tecnologías [Student satisfaction in a technology-mediated PBL experience]. *Investigación y práctica en la educación superior*, 421-426.

Alrahlah, A. (2016). How effective the problem-based learning (PBL) in dental education. A critical review. *The Saudi Dental Journal*, *28*(4), 155–161. doi:10.1016/j.sdentj.2016.08.003 PMID:27872545

Aranzabal, A., Epelde, E., & Artetxe, M. (2022). Team formation on the basis of Belbin's roles to enhance students' performance in project based learning. *Education for Chemical Engineers*, *38*, 22–37. doi:10.1016/j.ece.2021.09.001

Arias, E., Barba-Sánchez, V., Carrión, C., & Casado, R. (2018). Enhancing Entrepreneurship Education in a Master's Degree in Computer Engineering: A Project-Based Learning Approach. *Administrative Sciences*, *8*(4), 58. doi:10.3390/admsci8040058

Benito, Á., & Cruz, A. (2005). *Nuevas claves para la docencia universitaria en el Espacio Europeo de Educación Superior* [New keys to university teaching in the European Higher Education Area]. Narcea Ediciones.

Blanco, A. V., & Amigo, J. C. (2016). El rol del docente en la era digital [The role of the teacher in the digital age]. *Revista interuniversitaria de formación del profesorado, 30*(2), 103-114.

Bonilla del Río, M., Diego Mantecón, J. M., & Lena Acebo, F. J. (2018). Estudiantes Universitarios: Prosumidores de recursos digitales y mediáticos en la era de internet [University students: prosumers of digital and media resources in the internet age]. *Aula Abierta*, *47*(3), 319–326. doi:10.17811/rifie.47.3.2018.319-326

Camacho, M. D. M., & Del Campo, C. (2015). Impacto de la motivación intrínseca en el rendimiento académico a través de trabajos voluntarios: Un análisis empírico [Impact of intrinsic motivation on academic performance through voluntary work: An empirical analysis]. *Revista Complutense de Educación*, *26*(1), 67–80. doi:10.5209/rev_RCED.2015.v26.n1.42581

Camacho, M. D. M., Urquía, E., Pascual, D., & Rivero Menéndez, M. (2016). Recursos multimedia para el aprendizaje de Contabilidad Financiera en los grados bilingües [Multimedia resources for learning Financial Accounting in bilingual grades]. *Educación XX1, 19*(1), 63-89. doi:10.5944/educxx1.15578

Collard, A., Brédart, S., & Bourguignon, J. P. (2016). Context impact of clinical scenario on knowledge transfer and reasoning capacity in a medical problem-based learning curriculum. *Higher Education Research & Development, 35*(2), 242–253. doi:10.1080/07294360.2015.1087383

Ellis, V., & Childs, A. (2019). Innovation in teacher education: Collective creativity in the development of a teacher education internship. *Teaching and Teacher Education, 77*, 277–286. doi:10.1016/j.tate.2018.10.020

Espada, M., Rocu, P., Navia, J. A., & Gómez-López, M. (2020). Rendimiento académico y satisfacción de los estudiantes universitarios hacia el método flipped classroom [Academic performance and university students' satisfaction with the flipped classroom method]. *Profesorado. Revista de Currículum y Formación del Profesorado, 24*(1), 116–135. doi:10.30827/profesorado.v24i1.8710

Fach Gómez, K. (2012). Ventajas del Problem Based Learning (PBL) como método de aprendizaje del Derecho internacional [Advantages of Problem Based Learning (PBL) as a method of learning international law]. *Bordón. Revista de Pedagogía., 64*(1), 59–73.

Fernández, A., García, B., Verde, Z., & Fernández, D. (2020). Satisfacción, motivación y aprendizaje de los estudiantes de enfermería en prácticas farmacológicas con metodología flipped classroom [Satisfaction, motivation and learning of nursing students in pharmacological internships with flipped classroom methodology]. *La docencia en la Enseñanza Superior: Nuevas aportaciones desde la investigación e innovación educativas,* 1202-1213.

Fernández-Jiménez, C., López-Justicia, M.D., Fernández, M., & Polo, M.T. (2014). Aplicación del aprendizaje basado en problemas para la formación del alumnado de Educación en la atención a la discapacidad [Application of problem-based learning for the training of education students in disability care]. *Revista de Currículum y formación del profesorado, 18*(2), 334-352.

Fidalgo-Blanco, Á., Sein-Echaluce, M. L., & García-Peñalvo, F. J. (2014). Espirales de conocimiento en la innovación docente en la educación superior [Spirals of knowledge in teaching innovation in higher Education]. *International Journal of Knowledge Management, 10*(4), 16–37. doi:10.4018/ijkm.2014100102

García-Valcárcel, A., Basilotta, V., & López, C. (2014). Las TIC en el aprendizaje colaborativo en el aula de Primaria y Secundaria [ICT in collaborative learning in primary and secondary classrooms]. *Comunicar, 21*(42), 65–74.

Gil-Galván, R., Martín-Espinosa, I., & Gil-Galvan, F. J. (2021). Percepciones de los estudiantes universitarios sobre las competencias adquiridas mediante el aprendizaje basado en problemas [University students' perceptions of competencies acquired through problem-based Learning]. *Educación XX1, 24*(1), 271-295. doi:10.5944/educxx1.26800

Giordano, N. A., Compton, P., Joseph, P. V., Romano, C. A., Piano, M. R., & Naylor, M. D. (2020). Opportunities and challenges presented by recent pedagogical innovations in doctoral nursing education. *Journal of Professional Nursing*. Advance online publication. doi:10.1016/j.profnurs.2020.09.003 PMID:33674100

Gómez, A. (Coord.). (2021). Análisis multisectorial de cuentas anuales y sus informes de auditoría [Multisectoral analysis of annual accounts and their audit reports]. Ediciones Pirámide.

González, J. (2018). *Uso de la Tecnología en la Educación* [Use of Technology in Education]. México, UNID editorial digital 31. Available at https://bit.ly/2SPRxQw

González-Hernando, C., Martín-Villamor, P., Carbonero-Martín, M. Á., & Lara-Ortega, F. (2013). Evaluación por competencias de los estudiantes de Enfermería a través de Aprendizaje Basado en Problemas [Competency-based assessment of nursing students through Problem-Based Learning]. *Enfermería Universitaria, 10*(4), 120–124. doi:10.1016/S1665-7063(13)72640-X

Hair, J. F., Risher, J. J., Sarstedt, M., & Ringle, C. M. (2018). When to use and how to report the results of PLS-SEM. *European Business Review*. Advance online publication. doi:10.1108/EBR-11-2018-0203

Herrero-Diz, P., Conde-Jiménez, J., & Reyes-de-Cózar, S. (2021). Spanish adolescents and fake news: Level of awareness and credibility of information. *Culture and Education, 33*(1), 1–27. doi:10.1080/11356405.2020.1859739

Hincapié, D., Ramos, A., & Chirino, V. (2018). Aprendizaje Basado en Problemas como estrategia de Aprendizaje Activo y su incidencia en el rendimiento académico y pensamiento crítico de estudiantes de Medicina de Segundo Semestre [Problem Based Learning as an Active Learning strategy and its impact on the academic performance and critical thinking of second semester medical students]. *Revista Complutense de Educación, 29*(3), 665–681. doi:10.5209/RCED.53581

Hunt, J., Brannan, E., & Sexson, S. (2019). Lifelong Learning for Professional Development in Psychiatry: Pedagogy, Innovations, and Maintenance of Certification. *Psychiatria Clinica, 42*(3), 425–437. doi:10.1016/j.psc.2019.05.014 PMID:31358122

Kanuru, S. L., & Priyaadharshini, M. (2020). Lifelong Learning in higher education using Learning Analytics. *Procedia Computer Science, 172*, 848–852. doi:10.1016/j.procs.2020.05.122

Korkmaz, G., & Kalayci, N. (2019). Theoretical foundations of project based curricula in higher education. *Çukurova University. Faculty of Education Journal, 48*(1), 236–274. doi:10.14812/cufej.479322

Lašáková, A., Bajzíková, Ľ., & Dedze, I. (2017). Barriers and drivers of innovation in higher education: Case study-based evidence across ten European universities. *International Journal of Educational Development, 55*, 69–79. doi:10.1016/j.ijedudev.2017.06.002

Macías, A., Sánchez, M. A., & Prado, M. (2018). Evaluación de la implantación de aprendizaje basado en proyectos como herramienta para el estudio de la economía de la empresa [Evaluation of the implementation of project-based learning as a tool for the study of business Economics]. *Journal of Management and Business Education, 1*(3), 190–209. doi:10.35564/jmbe.2018.0014

Manzanares, M. C. S., & Arreba, A. B. (2014). Aprendizaje basado en la evaluación mediante rúbricas en educación superior [Learning based on evaluation through rubrics in higher Education]. *Suma Psicologica, 21*(1), 28–35. doi:10.1016/S0121-4381(14)70004-9

Martiañez, N. L., Rubio, M., Terrón, M. J., & Gallego, T. (2015). Diseño de una rúbrica para evaluar las competencias del Prácticum del Grado en Fisioterapia. Percepción de su utilidad por los estudiantes [Design of a rubric to assess the competences of the Practicum of the Degree in Physiotherapy. Students' perception of its usefulness]. *Fisioterapia, 37*(2), 83–95. doi:10.1016/j.ft.2014.06.005

Méndez Peón, C. Á., Herrera Avilés, M., Toriz Palacios, A., & González Pérez, M. (2016). Estudio de la brecha Empresario-Investigador. La Percepción del Investigador [Study of the Entrepreneur-Researcher Gap. The Researcher's Perception]. *European Scientific Journal, ESJ*, *12*(28), 28. doi:10.19044/esj.2016.v12n28p109

Parrado-Martínez, P., & Sánchez-Andújar, S. (2020). Development of competences in postgraduate studies of finance: A project-based learning (PBL) case study. *International Review of Economics Education*, *35*, 100192. doi:10.1016/j.iree.2020.100192

Phi, G. T., & Clausen, H. B. (2020). Fostering innovation competencies in tourism higher education via design-based and value-based learning. *Journal of Hospitality, Leisure, Sport and Tourism Education*, *100298*. Advance online publication. doi:10.1016/j.jhlste.2020.100298

Romero-Rodríguez, L. M., De-Casas-Moreno, P., & Caldeiro-Pedreira, M. C. (2018). Desinformación e infoxicación en las cuartas pantallas [Disinformation and infoxication on the fourth screens]. In I. Aguaded & L.M. Romero-Rodríguez (Coord.), Competencias mediáticas en medios digitales emergentes (pp. 73-90). Comunicación Social Ediciones y Publicaciones.

Rué, J., Font, A., & Cebrian, G. (2011). El ABP, un enfoque estratégico para la formación en Educación Superior. Aportaciones de un análisis de la formación en Derecho [PBL, a strategic approach to training in Higher Education. Contributions from an analysis of training in law]. *Revista de Docencia Universitaria*, *9*(1), 25–44. doi:10.4995/redu.2011.6178

Saura, J. R., Dwivedi, Y. K., & Palacios-Marqués, D. (2022d). Online User Behavior and User-Generated Content. *Frontiers in Psychology*, *13*, 895467. Advance online publication. doi:10.3389/fpsyg.2022.895467 PMID:35548513

Saura, J. R., Palacios-Marqués, D., & Ribeiro-Soriano, D. (2021). How SMEs use data sciences in their online marketing performance: A systematic literature review of the state-of-the-art. *Journal of Small Business Management*, 1–36. doi:10.1080/00472778.2021.1955127

Saura, J. R., Palacios-Marqués, D., & Ribeiro-Soriano, D. (2022a). Exploring the boundaries of Open Innovation: Evidence from social media mining. *Technovation*, 102447. Advance online publication. doi:10.1016/j.technovation.2021.102447

Saura, J. R., Ribeiro-Soriano, D., & Palacios-Marqués, D. (2021a, July 15). Setting privacy "by default" in social IoT: Theorizing the challenges and directions in Big Data Research. *Big Data Research*, *25*, 100245. doi:10.1016/j.bdr.2021.100245

Saura, J. R., Ribeiro-Soriano, D., & Palacios-Marqués, D. (2021b). Using data mining techniques to explore security issues in smart living environments in Twitter. *Computer Communications*, *179*, 285–295. doi:10.1016/j.comcom.2021.08.021

Saura, J. R., Ribeiro-Soriano, D., & Palacios-Marqués, D. (2022b). Assessing behavioral data science privacy issues in government artificial intelligence deployment. *Government Information Quarterly*, *101679*, 101679. Advance online publication. doi:10.1016/j.giq.2022.101679

Saura, J. R., Ribeiro-Soriano, D., & Palacios-Marqués, D. (2022c). Adopting digital reservation systems to enable circular economy in entrepreneurship. *Management Decision*. doi:10.1108/MD-02-2022-0190

Saura, J. R., Ribeiro-Soriano, D., & Saldaña, P. Z. (2022). Exploring the challenges of remote work on Twitter users' sentiments: From digital technology development to a post-pandemic era. *Journal of Business Research, 142*, 242–254. doi:10.1016/j.jbusres.2021.12.052

Sepúlveda, P., Cabezas, M., García, J., & Fonseca-Salamanca, F. (2019). *Aprendizaje basado en problemas: percepción del proceso enseñanza aprendizaje de las ciencias preclínicas por estudiantes de Kinesiología* [Problem-based learning: Kinesiology students' perception of the teaching-learning process in pre-clinical sciences]. Educación Médica., doi:10.1016/j.edumed.2019.01.004

Silva, J., & Maturana, D. (2017). Una propuesta de modelo para introducir metodologías activas en educación superior [A proposed model for introducing active methodologies in higher Education]. *Revista Innovación Educativa, 17*(73), 117–131.

Tacca, D. R., Tacca, A. L., & Alva, M. A. (2019). Estrategias neurodidácticas, satisfacción y rendimiento académico en estudiantes universitarios [Neurodidactic strategies, satisfaction and academic performance in university students]. *Cuaderno de Investigacion en la Educacion: Serie Especial de Temas Especiales. University of Puerto Rico. Recinto de Rio Piedras. Centro de Investigaciones Educativas, 10*(2), 15–32. doi:10.18861/cied.2019.10.2.2905

Toding, M., & Venesaar, U. (2018). Discovering and developing conceptual understanding of teaching and learning in entrepreneurship lecturers. *Education + Training, 60*(7/8), 696–718. doi:10.1108/ET-07-2017-0101

Torío López, S., Peña Calvo, J. V., & Fernández García, C. M. (2010). Evaluación de una experiencia de innovación docente para el aprendizaje significativo en pedagogía: Un marco para la reflexión a partir de la percepción de los estudiantes [Evaluation of a teaching innovation experience for meaningful learning in pedagogy: a framework for reflection based on student perceptions]. *ESE. Estudios sobre Educación, 18*, 229–254.

Uziak, J., & Kommula, V. P. (2019). Application of problem based learning in mechanics of machines course. *International Journal of Engineering Pedagogy., 9*(1), 68–83. doi:10.3991/ijep.v9i1.9673

Valerio Ureña, G., & Rodríguez Martínez, M. C. (2017). Perfil del profesor universitario desde la perspectiva del estudiante [Profile of the university lecturer from the student's perspective]. *Revista Innovación Educativa, 17*(74), 109–124.

KEY TERMS AND DEFINITIONS

Active Learning: A teaching approach in which students participate in the learning process by developing knowledge and understanding. It is about learning by doing.

Annual Report: A document containing the financial statements and additional information that companies are required to submit each year to provide an official record of their financial position.

Financial Analysis: Techniques and procedures that allow the analysis of the company's accounting information to obtain an objective view of its current situation and how it is expected to evolve in the future.

Problem-Based Learning: A problem statement where the analysis and/or solution of the problem is the central focus of the experience, and where the teacher deliberately promotes the process of enquiry and resolution of the problem in question.

Real Cases Study: Teaching methodology that confronts students with real-life 'circumstances' applied to the subjects of each educational level and which they have to solve through analysis, critical thinking and collaborative work.

Sectoral Accounting: Accounting applied to the recording, processing and control of financial operations and transactions carried out in entities of different sectors, regulating their specific characteristics.

Student Motivation: Student involvement in educational tasks that has an impact on the achievement of their academic goals and performance.

University-Business Connection: Bringing together the business and university worlds, which generates knowledge in both directions.

Chapter 10
Teaching Innovation Through the Use of Hashtag in Social Networks for the Educational Development of University Students of Accounting and Finance:
A Case Study

María Fernández-Fernández
Rey Juan Carlos University, Spain

Juan Gabriel Martínez-Navalón
Rey Juan Carlos University, Spain

ABSTRACT

This research will focus on a specific case of teaching innovation involving the use of the "hashtag" phenomenon on the digital platform Twitter by students as a measure of educational improvement. The objective, therefore, is to analyze how this system acts a teaching innovation measure in the educational development of university students. This experience puts into practice the use of social networks as platforms for publication and analysis of relevant news in university students. The sample analyzed is composed of accounting and finance students enrolled in the subjects of Financial Management and Working Capital Management at the Universidad Rey Juan Carlos in three different campuses, where the teaching innovation system was only applied in two of the campus, and results were compared. The purpose, therefore, is to observe and analyze how this innovation system affects the group and what results are obtained in comparison with the group that did not apply it.

DOI: 10.4018/978-1-6684-4441-2.ch010

Copyright © 2022, IGI Global. Copying or distributing in print or electronic forms without written permission of IGI Global is prohibited.

INTRODUCTION

The advance and implementation of new technologies in recent years has boosted innovation in teaching to the point of making it a crucial basis for education (Hamdan, Ashour, & Daher, 2021; Lachman, Glasgow, & Donnelly, 2009). This is why education, and more specifically, higher education and the university world, have become one of the most relevant areas of study in teaching innovation. In academia, teaching innovation is the process that, through the application of creativity by using digital platforms and technologies, optimizes teaching and learning models to drive the improvement of educational methodologies (Borges, Dias, & Santos, 2020).

This research will focus on a specific case of teaching innovation that encompasses the use of the "hashtag" phenomenon on the digital platform "Twitter" by students as a measure of educational improvement. Therefore, the main objective of this study is to analyze how this system affects a teaching innovation measure in the educational development of university students (Laserna & Miguel, 2018). This experience implemented the use of social networks as a platform for publication, and analysis of relevant news in university students (Saura et al., 2022; Saura et al., 2022a).

As mentioned above, the general goal of the introduction of this teaching innovation case is to promote dialogue, provide information and encourage student participation as a learning tool (Lin & Han, 2017; Torres-Barzabal et al., 2020). The purpose, specifically, of this case study is to study how the use of the social network Twitter affects students as a complementary tool to face-to-face classes in different university subjects; so as to encourage communication and favour the exchange of knowledge from the professor to the students (Bai, 2017). The specific objectives proposed to be achieved with the application of this case study are the following:

- To increase and optimize the participation and interrelation between university students, professor and society, through services via Twitter.
- Increase the level of involvement of students with the subject, and encourage their interest in a more practical and active type of teaching.
- Encourage reflection on current teaching systems and investigate the contents that can be complemented with innovative teaching methods such as the present one through social networks or other systems.

The sample of this research is composed by Accounting and Finance students, enrolled in the subject of Financial Management and Working Capital Management at the Rey Juan Carlos University during 2019-2020 academic year from three different campus: Fuenlabrada, Móstoles and Madrid-Vicálvaro. In this case, the teaching innovation system was applied at both the Fuenlabrada and Móstoles campuses, while at the Madrid-Vicálvaro campus, the initiative was not carried out, and later, results were compared. The purpose was therefore to observe and analyze how this innovation system affected the groups and what results were obtained in comparison with the group that did not apply it.

The methodology carried out in this case study was based on a series of analysis and observation techniques, followed by data collection, analysis and interpretation of the information, and the drawing of conclusions (Torres-Barzabal et al., 2020). The results suggest a high degree of student satisfaction with the experience, a significant improvement in their academic grades and an increased understanding of financial current affairs, which allows students to have greater financial knowledge and insight

(Hu & McGrath, 2011). In addition, this type of teaching innovation allows them to have not only better academic results, but also cultivates positive attitudes towards saving and life-cycle planning.

Financial education and topicality allows them to gain greater knowledge and understanding of financial concepts and risks, and to acquire skills, motivation and confidence to apply that knowledge and understanding (Laserna & Miguel, 2018). This will enable effective decision-making in different financial contexts, which improves the financial well-being of individuals and society, and enables their participation in economic life.

To carry out this case study, a bibliographic summary of the literature on the most important concepts that are part of this project will be presented. Terms such as teaching innovation and the use of Information and Communication Technologies (ICT), social networks and the Twitter platform will be detailed, and the objectives of the case study will be presented. Next, the methodology used will be described, and the results obtained in the project will be analysed. Finally, the conclusions and implications of the research will be presented.

TEACHING INNOVATION

In the context of traditional education, the use of expository systems mainly supported by the professor's performance is still common in Higher Education (Perez, Omar, & Velazquez, 2019). This system is fundamentally based on the unidirectional communication of the professor with the student. It is the professor who teaches, exposing in the classroom the contents that students must learn, so that they learn them through attention, listening and note-taking. However, the advocacy of an innovative learner-centered educational system has been gaining ground in order to foster more effective and deeper learning resulting from the action and active intervention of the student (Grillon et al., 2020).

In line with the support of a new teaching model, educational policies for Higher Education have been carrying out the attempt to produce a pedagogical change in relation to the teaching model, betting more and more on a system focused on student involvement and participation. At the European level, the Bologna Process was concerned with increasing advocacy and support for a change in the educational model from a system based on teaching to a model focused on learning (Borges et al., 2020; Cored, Liesa, Vázquez, Latorre, & Anzano, 2021; Wei, Wang, & Liu, 2016).

The changes and transformations in higher education suggest positioning universities in an international context, in which the preferences are to foster high-level research, and to ensure the quality of the teaching system that is committed to learning (Hodges, Moore, Lockee, Trust, & Bond, 2020). Today, teaching is still at a great distance from these objectives, since professors and researchers are increasingly bound by bureaucratic commitments and management positions, which implies a reduction of their independence, self-determination and autonomy.

On the other hand, the evolution of technologies, digitization and the advancement of their implementation has brought with it the introduction of ICT (Saura et al., 2022b) to also become a crucial aspect in education (Fernández & Gelashvili, 2019; Zempoalteca, González, Barragán, & Guzmán, 2018). The introduction of ICT as a consequence of technological advancement has brought benefits, such as speed in the development of study material and advancement of communication in teaching staff and students, which has transformed them into a new aspect of competitive advantage for teaching, highly related to most teaching innovation proposals developed today.

Thus, with the introduction of ICT in university teaching, in the online teaching and learning process, there are several roles for the teaching staff. The professor must be able to structure the content to favour learning in an efficient way, being skilled in the use of different ICT-based techniques, as well as incorporating problem-based learning (Borges et al., 2020; Rowntree, 1994).

The new teaching modality, whether through the use of ICT or some system of teaching innovation, should involve students in time issues, through the imposition of tasks in a time frame, since efficient training and instruction involves effort and dedication through the practice of an activity or task. Students require guidance when performing a task, since the professor's role is to direct and guide them to the sources of information needed to carry out the activity. In this way, students stimulate and encourage their self-learning, reaching an infinitely higher level of complexity (Laurillard, 2002).

Admitting the assumption that teaching innovation should focus mainly on what students need means, undoubtedly, that they should carry out a program of application or use of ICT based on the practice of efficient professors. That is why it seems appropriate to retain or sustain the debate in a stable manner about the effectiveness of this learning system (Sadiq, Rasa, Shami, Seemadaud, & Bhatti, 2018).

In some aspects or contexts, the activity of teaching personnel is not necessarily linked to scientific demonstration. Despite the fact that today's institutional criteria are committed to the progress of research about education and teaching, there has been a frequent and general preference for maintaining the debate instead of perfecting, improving or seeking solutions to the problems of teaching (Remesal, Colomina, Mauri, & Rochera, 2017). Therefore, a cultural transformation is needed in which all parties involved assume the importance of having scientific demonstration that supports teaching practices that are effective and beneficial for student learning, through the exchange of scientific notions and discoveries within the world of teaching (Alonso, Valles, & Muñoz de Luna, 2016).

This debate or controversy gains scope and importance in the present scope of the European Higher Education Area (EHEA), in which universities are established as places for the attainment of professional competencies. The implementation of ICT and new models of teaching innovation, have allowed the emergence of a new teaching modality, blended learning or hybrid learning, which is described as a pedagogical perspective that incorporates face-to-face teaching with online teaching or teaching established through a computer (Owston, York, & Malhotra, 2019). The concepts "blended learning" and "hybrid learning" are used synonymously in today's research. Professors agree in affirming that this perspective has the property of granting personalized teaching through the use of certain resources of student control over the path they are following, the pace of work and the time they are spending, although, it is also important to keep in mind that hybrid learning can be implemented in very different ways (O'Byrne & Pytash, 2015).

In the specific case of Spain, it should be noted that this pedagogical perspective has been successfully established in the Spanish university environment, where more than 78% of professors use some type of virtual platform to assist their teaching methodology. In order to see in a little more depth the advantages of the use of ICT as a teaching innovation (Ukut & Krairit, 2019) in the new teaching modality between professors and students, we will delve into the teaching practice of hybrid education in the Spanish public university through the approach of the use of ICT (Lin, 2020).

As we have mentioned, blended teaching is reaching a fundamental weight nowadays, in a world in which face-to-face teaching is supported by an online learning model as a complementary tool that makes the teaching experience and, therefore, the training also moves out of the classroom" (Salmerón-Pérez, Rodríguez-Fernández, & Gutiérrez-Braojos, 2010). In this way, the professor becomes a designer of steps and levels, leading students in the direction of the proposed objective and facilitating creativity on the part of both (Groen, Ghani, Germain-Rutherford, & Taylor, 2020).

In this case, digital platforms such as the virtual classroom is one of the best-known tools in the blended learning context. This open-source software has been gaining fame for the ease of building and inventing online learning systems for both online and face-to-face classes. Some researchers recently talk about the use of virtual campus in blended learning environments where they point out that there is relevant correlation between possessing a high degree of professor support and increased student performance (Ifinedo, Pyke, & Anwar, 2018; Lamia, Ashouri, & Sarra, 2017; Mwalumbwe & Mtebe, 2017).

There are many studies that delve through variables the levels of student achievement and work with the use of digital platforms in teaching (Islam, 2013, 2016). These articles show how various methods have been put in place to collect evidence of this in this sector and case studies (Herbert, Velan, Pryor, & Kumar, 2017; Kumar et al., 2021; Lal et al., 2020). Some of the benefits of using digital platforms are the traceability of student work traffic and immediate feedback (Martín-Blas & Serrano-Fernández, 2009).

Researchers have also studied the effectiveness of using virtual campus and digital platforms as an additional tool for student self-assessment (Charitopoulos, Vassiliadis, Rangoussi, & Koulouriotis, 2017). In addition, literature research points out that much of the studies on digital platforms in teaching have focused on measuring how satisfied students are. In this sense, Ibero-American studies also indicate that the degree of satisfaction among professors and students was very high. In addition, students who value their learning in environments that combine face-to-face teaching with the use of digital platforms describe their experience as useful, mechanical and active, and the feedback with the professor as personalized and effective (Mayo-Cubero, 2021).

SOCIAL NETWORKS IN TEACHING INNOVATION

As mentioned above, the integration of information and communication technologies in teaching has had a great reception in recent years, both to address theoretical aspects in the development and implementation of teaching innovations and to evaluate them. There are many studies that can be found about innovations (Kounenou, Roussos, Yotsidi, & Tountopoulou, 2015). However there is still a long journey to be studied for their consolidation in the pedagogical literature of higher education systems. As detailed in their research Torres-Barzabal et al. (2020), it is not only about including technological tools and training faculty, but there are also internal and external causes that benefit or not the inclusion of ICT as an essential support for teaching; such as, for example, attitudes, perceptions and interests of professors towards the use of digital platforms (Gil-Flores, Santero, & Torres-Gordillo, 2017; Kounenou et al., 2015).

On the other hand, an increase in the participation of university students in social networks can be perceived; figures obtained thanks to organizations such as Interactive Advertising Bureau IAB Spain (IAB, 2018) where annual data on social networks are collected. These reports indicate how the incorporation of social networks in Spanish society continues to increase. The report found that 85% of people between the ages of 16 and 65 use social networks, which was part of a pool of more than 25.5 million people in our country.

The use of social networks has recently become a daily and habitual activity for a large part of the university population. These increasingly specialized social places make possible the connection between individuals who share the same interests (Almenara & Díaz, 2014). On the other hand, the technological revolution of the last decades, have shown how the way of communicating and interrelating among society has changed, basically due to the acquisition of the use of smartphones and mobile devices (Laserna & Miguel, 2018; Saura et al., 2022c).

In this sense, the constant use of social networks among university students promotes the possibility for professors to use these tools to achieve the premises marked in the European Higher Education Area (EHEA), since "social media, in general, and social networks, in particular, provide various ways to face the challenges of higher education, both from a technical and pedagogical point of view", forming citizens who must face the challenging social and global problems of the 21st century (Cejas, Navio, & Barroso, 2016).

In addition to what has been commented above, it should be taken into account that using social networks for teaching has the objective of understanding that educational systems must get as close as possible to the reality in which students live and not stay away from all the social changes that are occurring (Saura et al., 2022d). The appropriate use of social networks as a complementary teaching method creates novel communication channels and opens up training possibilities that also provide a different dynamic to day-to-day teaching (Torres-Barzabal et al., 2020).

The new socio-environmental state and teaching innovations, require the progress of competences in the field of sustainability in university students in their training plans to facilitate their possible development and projection in the different areas of their future professional activities (Gómez-Aguilar, Roses-Campos, & Farias-Batlle, 2012; Saura et al., 2021). Education is seen as a fundamental factor for societal change towards sustainable development. In the development of these new concepts (Antolí, Jarauta, & Campos, 2012), which are intended to help the orientation of teaching staff, aims to make students inquire, search and form themselves by maintaining connections in this new model of society that is more technological and more concerned about sustainability. Faced with the inadequacies shown by this teaching modality, it will be important to establish a different system of methodology (Abuzant, Ghanem, Abd-Rabo, & Daher, 2021; Kumar et al., 2021).

In this sense, it is important to take into account the theory called connectivism (Tello & Ruiz, 2016); a doctrine that orients towards basically interactive and dynamic learning systems that offer solutions to today's problems of teaching in the digital world. Corbett and Spinello (2020) define the theory of connectivism as "a proposition of teaching innovation that responds to the current way of generating new knowledge, where students learn with the set of tools that technology and connectivity put at their disposal. It is the duty of today's professors to take responsibility for acquiring the knowledge of these new teaching alternatives in order to be up to date with technology and provide their students with innovative and appropriate teaching" (Schwarz & Asterhan, 2011).

Understanding that this innovative teaching modality is a new need implies changing and transforming the role of professors, students, as well as classrooms, spaces, and considering different ways of understanding ICT (Saura et al., 2021a). In this sense, they should not be used to do the same things that have been used without these computer systems or to present information, but to do different things and establish future communicative environments (Machado, Sepúlveda, & Montoya, 2016). The TPACK (technology, pedagogy and content knowledge) model shows an exciting way for professors to incorporate technology, pedagogy and disciplinary knowledge in their teaching activities (Torres-Barzabal et al., 2020).

TWITTER IN TEACHING INNOVATION

To this end, and taking into account that there are numerous benefits and opportunities that social networks can contribute to teaching, it has been considered interesting to study in a practical and real case, how it affects students and their performance achieved during the course using the social networks as a complementary method of teaching (Luo, Shah, & Cromptom, 2019; Pele, 2012). In this case, Twitter is discussed as a highly beneficial tool for the enhancement of academic and professional skills fostered in the European approach procedure. Twitter is, therefore, a very simple computer platform for communication as it is characterized by having a microblogging nature (Saura et al., 2021b). Microblogging is a mode of communication corresponding to a post delivery system (Twitter currently allows 280 characters), whose information stands out for its ease, simplicity, thus becoming a simple and effective way to reach students (Hsu & Ching, 2012; Liebana-Cabanillas, Martinez-Fiestas, & Rejon-Guardia, 2012; Xie & Zhang, 2013).

Thus, the use of the network in educational settings is extensive, to this is added its ease of publication: with mobile, computer or devices with instant messaging software (Rodriguez, 2017; Tur, Marín-Juarros, & Carpenter, 2017). The application of Twitter as a new complementary teaching methodology in higher education helps to increase the level of engagement in educational activities, both students and professors and is a perfect tool system to boost this learning system (Bryer & Chen, 2010). For all these reasons, it can be concluded by stating that, in the university educational system, Twitter enables immediate feedback (Gupta & Katarya, 2020), facilitates the exchange of information and favours reflection on specific concepts, with the aim of arguing the current teaching concept based on the interactive, reflective and critical modality.

The annexation of social networks in university teaching makes possible novel communication channels and enables different training options, which also contributes to the promotion of communication initiatives linked to sustainability and social responsibility (Fernández-Fernández, Martínez-Navalón, & Gelashvili, 2021). In this way, the proposal for teaching innovation with university students highlights that the success of these technologies will vary depending on the degree of knowledge that students possess about the use of these digital platforms and their attitude (positive or negative) towards them (Hu & McGrath, 2011). The use of social networks and technological tools would mean bringing information and education closer to the place where students relate to the so that they approach them in a natural and unbiased way. This relationship system not only allows the extension of the classroom to other contexts outside the classroom (Prince, Tenorio, & Ramirez, 2016), but also favours the incorporation of new contents that would have a difficult place in the development of the subject in face-to-face modality.

METHODOLOGY

As mentioned above, Twitter was used as an instrument to promote communicative actions between the professor and the students. The idea put forward in this case study was to search for news related to the subject "Financial Management and Working Capital Management" with the idea of sharing them with the students and encouraging student interaction with the subject and the world of financial news. In order to group and monitor the activity, it was decided to create a hashtag called #DIRECTIVOSURJC2020. In this way, students had to search for the financial news and share it by adding that hashtag, which later made it possible to find all the tweets that students had posted quickly and easily. This system also made it easier for the professor to monitor which students were doing the activity, while at the same time allowing students to learn and read the rest of their classmates' posts.

Thanks to this, the students obtained a much more complete, effective and real source of information on the subject through current news closely related to it. In this way, moreover, information, knowledge, ideas and relevant points of view are exchanged, which fosters a very interesting environment for debate and discussion, and stimulates a real-world interactive community that is often difficult to foster in a course based on a traditional learning management model.

To carry out this case study, the professor of the course presented the proposal to the students and led the class to concretize with the students the basis of the project. To do this, the professor of the course explained how the Twitter platform worked, which most of the students already knew, and showed them how to create a new Twitter user account for the subject, as well as how to publish tweets and follow the instructions that the professor had given in class for this specific case. The professor, in order to provide help during the whole procedure and to be clearer and more visual, used several YouTube videos, in order to offer an explanation as explicit and concrete as possible (Wakefield, Warren, & Alsobrook, 2011).

The professor asked the students to tweet once a week, i.e., they should look for news related to the subject of Financial Management and Working Capital Management, and retweet them under the hashtag #DIRECTIVOSURJC2020 every week. In this way, in the next class the professor would show the tweets in class quickly and easily, and comment on them so that, in this way, the exchange of information would be even greater. This is because, although students could see their classmates' tweets on Twitter, by commenting on them in class, the content of the news was doubly studied.

In addition, the proposal of this case study with students aimed to solve the following series of problems (Laserna & Miguel, 2018): on the one hand, it was intended to increase the active participation of students in groups that had a large number of students enrolled in class. In these situations, for reasons of embarrassment, fear of error or ridicule, student participation in class is much smaller and scarce and, in many cases, classes with little student involvement are reduced to theoretical classes in which only the professor is a participant. In this sense, digital platforms and, above all, social networks, with which most students feel comfortable, can serve as a complementary and additional means in which the relationship between professor and students is closer, and develops in a more fluid way.

On the other hand, the benefits for professors that are expected to be achieved with the implementation of this case study are the following: firstly, progress and development of communication between professors and students, and even among the students themselves, is expected. In face-to-face and traditional classes, this relationship is limited due to the number of students enrolled and the large number of groups in some of the subjects. Through the use of social networks and these cases of teaching innovation, the relationship between the professor and the students is brought closer and their communication is improved.

Secondly, the independent and autonomous work of the students is enhanced, their reading, written and critical comprehension is developed and increased, the search for information on the platform is encouraged, as well as their development, comprehension and news selection process. This is an important aspect for later writing tweets, which also serves as a starting point for them to search for related news.

In addition, the motivation of the students would be increased, since they would have the necessary resources and materials to be able to extend their knowledge on aspects that are interesting to them. Browsing, researching and searching for information in the social networks they are used to working with will be an important source of information for them, which can also be shared with both the professor and the rest of their classmates.

Finally, going beyond the benefits that students can obtain, these profiles and hashtags that students have had to create on social networks can serve as a doorway to the outside of the subject to become a loudspeaker for the dissemination of content and news on current financial events, from which users of the social platform can also be enriched. It should be noted that the information shared by the students would be filtered and reviewed beforehand by the professors, who would be responsible for the project, thus ensuring the quality of the research.

As mentioned above, the case study of this project plans to compare the results and carry out the experiment with students only on two campuses, in Fuenlabrada and Móstoles, but not in Madrid-Vicálvaro, with the aim of comparing results and observing whether the teaching innovation proposal is efficient or not. To this end, a comparative study will be made of the students' grades at the end of the course, without taking into account those who did not show up, and it will be observed whether there are differences in grades between the courses that carried out the teaching innovation case and those that did not.

A noteworthy fact in the study is that the three groups analysed from the different campuses of the Universidad Rey Juan Carlos had the same professor, the same teaching material and the same evaluation criteria. This means that there is no bias due to the knowledge of the professor or the evolution criteria. This allows for an effective comparison without bias in the sample.

RESULTS AND DISCUSSION

Once the execution of this case study with the students of the Financial Management and Working Capital Management course of the Accounting and Finance Degree was completed, the final grades obtained by the students of the Fuenlabrada, Madrid-Vicálvaro and Móstoles campuses were analysed. The results are shown in Table 1.

Table 1. Results of the case study on students

Campus	Fuenlabrada	Móstoles	Vicálvaro
Average grade	5,73	6,29	5,03
Use of the hashtag	Sí	Sí	No

Table prepared by the authors based on the data collected.

As can be seen in the table above, the average grade on the Fuenlabrada campus is 5.73, on the Móstoles campus it is 6.29 and, on the Madrid-Vicálvaro campus it is 5.03. With these results we can conclude that the campuses where the teaching innovation method was applied through the use of the hashtag on the social network Twitter, obtained better grades and better results than the students where it was not applied. More specifically, the Fuenlabrada campus obtained 13.72% better results than the Madrid-Vicálvaro campus, and on the Móstoles campus, the results were even more striking, where the grades were 25% higher than those of Madrid-Vicálvaro.

The results collected by the final grades of the students of the three campuses show, therefore, that the case study conducted with the students during the 2019/2020 academic year was managed by the students in a very efficient way. The publications made by the students were active and regular; and are consequently revealed as a very useful tool towards communication and exchange of information, news and content relevant to the subject. In this way, it was possible to generate debate and talk about topics and aspects of current affairs that would not have been possible to develop in class, that were not included in the program or that simply would not have arisen had it not been for having established this system of information search with social networks.

Thanks to this, the students broadened their knowledge, disseminated contents that could be useful for their future professional life and, from the professor's point of view, it can serve to expand or modify the program by increasing topics to talk about with the students, exchange real experiences or specific cases on applied topics and, therefore, increase the motivation and interest of the students in the contents of the subject.

If we compare with other studies that have also used social networks as a method of teaching innovation, we can see that the results are also similar (Hsu & Ching, 2012; Laserna & Miguel, 2018; Torres-Barzabal et al., 2020; Xie & Zhang, 2013). It is concluded, therefore, that the results obtained with the implementation of this proposal were very positive. On the one hand, the follow up by the students has been very high, since almost all the students of the Móstoles campus and also most of the students of the Fuenlabrada campus followed the activity without any problem, and posted tweets periodically once a week throughout the months in which the project was carried out.

In addition, the feedback received from the students was very good, who were very participative, interacting among themselves and with the professor, and they valued the proposed activity very positively and showed special attention to the news shared by their classmates on social networks. They also showed a positive valuation and relationship of the activity with the contents and the study program planned for the subject, which motivated the students as they could see the professional opportunities offered by learning the content of the subject and what the theoretical concepts they were studying were for.

On the other hand, although this is a complementary purpose, the tour of the publications made by the students on Twitter showed that these activities were beneficial for the scientific expansion in this sector reaching a greater number of profiles and groups of people or interested parties. With the support and guarantee of having been verified and supervised by the professor in this case, expert in the field concerned.

Thanks to the implementation of the Twitter social network, students were motivated to allocate more hours to subject activities, improve discussion among students, support better learning and provide students with the feeling that they are part of a community of learners. As a consequence, also, to the normative and strategic support provided by the professor in the development of information sharing and communication actions in the use of Twitter with students.

CONCLUSION

In conclusion and summary, it can be stated that a very positive trend was found on the part of the students to consider Twitter as a key tool to help increase and enhance the understanding of the content of the Financial Management and Working Capital Management course. This was supported by the interactive environment and the very comprehensive and prompt feedback received from the students. On the other hand, the overall impression of this computer platform used in the teaching innovation process and its use to enhance learning shows us that it is a very beneficial tool to implement in the classroom for future occasions and that it also stimulates effective, fruitful and continuous communication among the participating students and with the professor, thus promoting teaching.

Thanks to this case study or this experience, and the literature found and research already existing and also collected in this research, it can be considered that learning and teaching through interactive actions and teaching innovation with the application of technology and digital platforms is a very beneficial and effective field for the 21st century. This is because it drives students, stimulating learning through the interrelationships of social networks that most students use in their private lives to relate to other people, by making them participants in social discussions that enables the creation of content, its exchange and the expression of personal identity.

In general, the results of this case study show that digital social networking platforms such as Twitter allow students' academic experiences to be enhanced through an increase in the interactivity of the proposed activities, which transform traditional learning methods. In addition, it has been possible to witness those students have perceived the use of digital tools and technology through the use of Twitter and the hashtag as a system to interrelate and get to know each other, enhancing the presence and improving the relationships between them, creating a sense of community among them much more intense. This arises as a consequence of the students' participation not only in the search for their news and the realization of their activity, but also towards the understanding of the content exchanged with their peers. This allows the creation of interdependence among students as a consequence of the natural and simple dialogue among students. Finally, in relation to this, it can be observed that giving students a possible digital tool or platform in class could optimize their apprehension when using social networks as a complementary teaching modality.

During the last few years, digital platforms, more specifically social networks, have manifested themselves as one of the most effective and powerful communication tools that exist today. Moreover, it is considered that they can be of great benefit and be very beneficial in teaching innovation in higher education (Laserna & Miguel, 2018). Therefore, and as a final conclusion of this case study, it is of vital importance to keep in mind that for a research as to be successful, it is very important that the person responsible for the management of the students and the proposed activity has dedication, is well organized and reviews the work of the students periodically.

Thus, in the results of the case study presented above, the participation and involvement of the teaching staff in both the proposal and the evaluation of the contents developed by the students, as well as the management of the debates originated later in the classroom, has been essential. Thanks to all this, it is concluded that the activity has been carried out and developed efficiently, the results offered by the students have been significantly better than those of the students who did not carry out the activity and furthermore, the satisfaction of the students encourages them to put the activity into practice for future years and to be happy with the results. For all these reasons, Twitter is considered a very valuable tool for its efficiency, ease of use and for being very useful for communication and dissemination of information and content. Social networks, therefore, are considered a very valuable tool to integrate in a clear way in the new teaching methods as a new model of teaching innovation (Laserna & Miguel, 2018).

LIMITATIONS, IMPLICATIONS AND FUTURE RESEARCH DIRECTIONS

This study shows and offers as original, a comparison of the application of this tool, comparing in the same year courses in different campuses of the Universidad Rey Juan Carlos de Madrid in which compares and analyses the differences in its application. Besides, this case study offers a door to the application or use of combining interactive and communicative activities focused on teaching through the use of social networks. Future research on this social platform, Twitter, and other social networking tools, could be implemented in a perhaps more integrated way in a more extensive subject. This is because the latest research on cases of integration of teaching innovation models in the classroom sheds light on how useful is the use of social networks in teaching. For all these reasons, the present research started from a scientific reference based on a structure in which the formative itinerary of the subject would be created counting on social networks as a basic tool to allow learning discussions to be created and knowledge to be exchanged in a dynamic and interactive way instead of being considered as a complement to other teaching activities (Wakefield et al., 2011).

As mentioned above, it is very important to establish guidelines and promote the use of social networks so that they become an indispensable tool in educational teaching. This is due to the fact that this system has great potential because it does not involve any cost and because of its ease of access by students (Torres-Barzabal et al., 2020). However, this practice also has a number of limitations. On the one hand, most students have social networks and are regular users. Nevertheless, although it is considered a very useful tool for information and communication, in general it does not imply that they use these social networks for academic purposes.

Moreover, at the same time, teachers are not always motivated or have the minimum knowledge to use them. For this reason, it is also important to take into account that in some educational centers this same system. In this sense, it should be noted that since the tool has a great teaching potential, it is important to provide good training in the use and practice of this social network beforehand in order to be able to extend it later and use it in the educational environment.

REFERENCES

Abuzant, M., Ghanem, M., Abd-Rabo, A., & Daher, W. (2021). Quality of using google classroom to support the learning processes in the automation and programming course. *International Journal of Emerging Technologies in Learning*, *16*(6), 72–87. doi:10.3991/ijet.v16i06.18847

Almenara, J. C., & Díaz, V. M. (2014). Educational possibilities of social networks and group work. University students' perceptions. *Comunicar. Media Education Research Journal*, *22*(1), 165–172.

Alonso, M. H., Valles, J. E. G., & Muñoz de Luna, A. B. (2016). Advantages and disadvantages of using electronic devices in the classroom: Perception of undergraduate students in communication sciences. *Revista de Comunicacion de la Seeci*, (41), 136–154. doi:10.15198eeci.2016.41.136-154

Antolí, N. S., Jarauta, B., & Campos, S. (2012). Active methodologies and Facebook in higher education. *International Journal of Technology and Educational Innovation*, 3134–3143.

Bai, X. L. (2017). Research on the Innovation Ability of PE Teaching under the Multi Objective Dynamic Condition. *International Conference on Economics, Management Engineering and Education Technology (ICEMEET)*, 56–61. 10.2991/icemeet-16.2017.11

Bryer, T. A., & Chen, B. (2010). *The use of social media and networks in teaching public administration. Cutting-edge Social Media Approaches to Business Education: Teaching with LinkedIn, Facebook, Twitter, Second Life, and Blogs (HC)*. Information Age Publishing.

Cejas, R., Navio, A., & Barroso, J. (2016). The university teacher's abilities from the tpack model (technological and pedagogical content knowledge). *Pixel-Bit-Revista De Medios Y Educacion, 49*, 105–119.

Charitopoulos, A., Vassiliadis, S., Rangoussi, M., & Koulouriotis, D. (2017). E-learning and blended learning in textile engineering education: A closed feedback loop approach. *IOP Conference Series. Materials Science and Engineering*, *254*(22), 222002. Advance online publication. doi:10.1088/1757-899X/254/22/222002

Corbett, F., & Spinello, E. (2020). Connectivism and leadership: Harnessing a learning theory for the digital age to redefine leadership in the twenty-first century. *Heliyon*, *6*(1), e03250. doi:10.1016/j.heliyon.2020.e03250 PMID:31993523

Cored, S., Liesa, M., Vázquez, S., Latorre, C., & Anzano, S. (2021). Digital Competence of University Teachers of Social and Legal Sciences from a Gender Perspective. *Education Sciences*, *11*(12), 806. doi:10.3390/educsci11120806

de Borges, M. I., Dias, C., & Santos, C. (2020). COVID-19 and online learning in higher education – A case study of students from the Polytechnic Institutes of Portalegre and Beja [COVID-19 y el aprendizaje en línea en la educación superior – Un estudio de caso de alumnos de los Institutos Politécnicos de Portalegre y Beja]. *IJERI: International Journal of Educational Research and Innovation*, (15), 317–325. doi:10.46661/ijeri.5253

Fernández-Fernández, M., Martínez-Navalón, J. G., & Gelashvili, V. (2021). Sustainability and online classes at the university in times of COVID-19: Has it served as a starting point for a new teaching modality? [La sostenibilidad y las clases online en la universidad en tiempos de COVID-19: ¿Nos ha servido como punto de partida para una nueva modalidad de enseñanza?]. *Espacios*, *42*(5), 127–144. doi:10.48082/espacios-a21v42n05p09

Gil-Flores, J., Santero, J. R., & Torres-Gordillo, J.-J. (2017). Factors that explain the use of ICT in secondary-education classrooms: The role of teacher characteristics and school infrastructure. *Computers in Human Behavior*, *68*, 441–449. doi:10.1016/j.chb.2016.11.057

Gómez-Aguilar, M., Roses-Campos, S., & Farias-Batlle, P. (2012). The academic use of social networks among university students. *Comunicar: Revista Científica de Comunicación y Educación*, *19*(38), 131–138. doi:10.3916/C38-2012-03-04

Grillon, C., Lago, T., Stahl, S., Beale, A., Balderston, N., & Ernst, M. (2020). Better cognitive efficiency is associated with increased experimental anxiety. *Psychophysiology*, *57*(8), 1–10. doi:10.1111/psyp.13559 PMID:32180239

Groen, J., Ghani, S., Germain-Rutherford, A., & Taylor, M. (2020). Institutional Adoption of Blended Learning: Analysis of an Initiative in Action. *The Canadian Journal for the Scholarship of Teaching and Learning*, *11*(3), 3. doi:10.5206/cjsotl-rcacea.2020.3.8288

Gupta, A., & Katarya, R. (2020). Social media based surveillance systems for healthcare using machine learning: A systematic review. *Journal of Biomedical Informatics*, *108*, 103500. doi:10.1016/j.jbi.2020.103500 PMID:32622833

Hamdan, R., Ashour, W., & Daher, W. (2021). The role of the e-learning departments in controlling the quality of electronic assessments in Palestinian universities during the COVID-19 pandemic. *Sustainability*, *13*(21), 12021. doi:10.3390u132112021

Herbert, C., Velan, G. M., Pryor, W. M., & Kumar, R. K. (2017). A model for the use of blended learning in large group teaching sessions. *BMC Medical Education*, *17*(1), 1–11. doi:10.118612909-017-1057-2 PMID:29121908

Hodges, C., Moore, S., Lockee, B., Trust, T., & Bond, A. (2020). The difference between emergency remote teaching and online learning. *EDUCAUSE Review*.

Hsu, Y. C., & Ching, Y. H. (2012). Mobile microblogging: Using Twitter and mobile devices in an online course to promote learning in authentic contexts. *International Review of Research in Open and Distributed Learning*, *13*(4), 211–227. doi:10.19173/irrodl.v13i4.1222

Hu, Z., & McGrath, I. (2011). Innovation in higher education in China: Are teachers ready to integrate ICT in English language teaching? *Technology, Pedagogy and Education*, *20*(1), 41–59. doi:10.1080/1475939X.2011.554014

Ifinedo, P., Pyke, J., & Anwar, A. (2018). Business undergraduates' perceived use outcomes of moodle in a blended learning environment: The roles of usability factors and external support. *Telematics and Informatics, 35*(1), 93–102. .10.001 doi:10.1016/j.tele.2017

Islam, A. K. M. N. (2013). Investigating e-learning system usage outcomes in the university context. *Computers and Education, 69*, 387–399. .2013.07.037 doi:10.1016/J.COMPEDU

Islam, A. K. M. N. (2016). E-learning system use and its outcomes: Moderating role of perceived compatibility. *Telematics and Informatics*, *33*(1), 48–55. doi:10.1016/j.tele.2015.06.010

Kounenou, K., Roussos, P., Yotsidi, V., & Tountopoulou, M. (2015). Trainee Teachers' Intention to Incorporating ICT Use into Teaching Practice in Relation to their Psychological Characteristics: The Case of Group-based Intervention. *Procedia: Social and Behavioral Sciences*, *190*, 120–128. doi:10.1016/j.sbspro.2015.04.925

Kumar, A., Sarkar, M., Davis, E., Morphet, J., Maloney, S., Ilic, D., & Palermo, C. (2021). Impact of the COVID-19 pandemic on teaching and learning in health professional education: A mixed methods study protocol. *BMC Medical Education*, *21*(1), 1–7. doi:10.118612909-021-02871-w PMID:34412603

Lachman, V. D., Glasgow, M. E. S., & Donnelly, G. F. (2009). Teaching innovation. *Nursing Administration Quarterly*, *33*(3), 205–211. doi:10.1097/NAQ.0b013e3181acca9a PMID:19546739

Lal, P., Kumar, A., Kumar, S., Kumari, S., Saikia, P., Dayanandan, A., Adhikari, D., & Khan, M. L. (2020). The dark cloud with a silver lining: Assessing the impact of the SARS COVID-19 pandemic on the global environment. *The Science of the Total Environment*, *732*, 139297. doi:10.1016/j.scitotenv.2020.139297 PMID:32408041

Lamia, T., Ashouri, H., & Sarra, T. (2017). Lesson via the e-learning platform MOODLE. In *2017 Joint International Conference on Information and Communication Technologies for Education and Training and International Conference on Computing in Arabic*. IEEE. . 809530410.1109/ICCA-TICET.2017

Laserna, M. S. S., & Miguel, M. C. (2018). Social media as a teaching innovation tool for the promotion of interest and motivation in higher education. *SIIE 2018 - 2018 International Symposium on Computers in Education, Proceedings*. 10.1109/SIIE.2018.8586752

Laurillard, D. (2002). *Rethinking University Teaching: a framework for the effective use of educational technology.* Academic Press.

Liebana-Cabanillas, F., Martinez-Fiestas, M., & Rejon-Guardia, F. (2012). Analysis of microblogging applications as university teaching tools. *INTED2012 Proceedings,* 6309–6314.

Lin, K. Y. (2020). Application of a blended assessment strategy to enhance student interest and effectiveness in learning: case study with information security literacy. *CIN: Computers, Informatics, Nursing, 38*(10), 508–514.

Lin, L., & Han, Y. (2017). Innovation of Teaching Method for Improvement of Higher Education Teaching Quality. *International Conference on Education, Sports, Arts and Management Engineering (ICESAME)*, 1854–1857. 10.2991/icesame-17.2017.393

Luo, T., Shah, S. J., & Cromptom, H. (2019). Using Twitter to support reflective learning in an asynchronous online course. *Australasian Journal of Educational Technology*, *35*(3). Advance online publication. doi:10.14742/ajet.4124

Machado, M. S. P., Sepúlveda, G. C. T., & Montoya, M. S. R. (2016). Educational innovation and digital competencies: The case of OER in a private Venezuelan university. *International Journal of Educational Technology in Higher Education, 13*(1), 1–10.

Martín-Blas, T., & Serrano-Fernández, A. (2009). The role of new technologies in the learning process: Moodle as a teaching tool in physics. *Computers & Education*, *52*(1), 35–44. doi:10.1016/j.compedu.2008.06.005

Mayo-Cubero, M. (2021). Teaching Innovation Experience for COVID-19 Times: A Case Study on Blended Learning of Television Journalism Courses with Moodle. *Asia Pacific Media Educator*, *31*(2), 178–194. doi:10.1177/1326365X211048619

Mwalumbwe, I., & Mtebe, J. S. (2017). Using learning analytics to predict students' performance in moodle learning management system: A case of Mbeya University of science and technology. *The Electronic Journal on Information Systems in Developing Countries*, *79*(1), 1–13. doi:10.1002/j.1681-4835.2017.tb00577.x

O'Byrne, W. I., & Pytash, K. E. (2015). Hybrid and blended learning: Modifying pedagogy across path, pace, time, and place. *Journal of Adolescent & Adult Literacy*, *59*(2), 137–140. doi:10.1002/jaal.463

Owston, R., York, D. N., & Malhotra, T. (2019). Blended learning in large enrolment courses: Student perceptions across four different instructional models. *Australasian Journal of Educational Technology*, *35*(5), 29–41. doi:10.14742/ajet.4310

Pele, A. (2012). Twitter as a teaching technique? *INTED2012: International Technology, Education and Development Conference*, 4481–4485.

Perez, A., Omar, B., & Velazquez, R. (2019). Innovación docente y empleo de las TIC en la Educación Superior. *Revista Espacios*, *40*(2), 8.

Prince, M. S., Tenorio, G. C., & Ramirez, M. S. (2016). Educational innovation and digital competencies: The case of OER in a private Venezuelan university. *International Journal of Educational Technolgy in High Education*, *13*(10), 10. Advance online publication. doi:10.118641239-016-0006-1

Remesal, A., Colomina, R. M., Mauri, T., & Rochera, M. J. (2017). *Online questionnaires use with automatic feedback for e-innovation in university students.* doi:10.3916/C51-2017-05

Rodriguez, R. (2017). A case of reflexive and critical interaction in a campaign about Twitter in the course of Legal Theory. *IJERI-International Journal of Educational Reasearch and Innovation*, (7), 186–201.

Rowntree, D. (1994). *Preparing materials for open, distance and flexible learning: an action guide for teachers and trainers.* Academic Press.

Sadiq, F., Rasa, S. I., Shami, N., Seemadaud, S., & Bhatti, S. (2018). Comparing Effectiveness of Collaborative Blended Learning and Traditional Teaching Using Students Final Test Scores. *Pakistan Journal of Medical & Health Sciences*, *12*(4), 1428–1431.

Salmerón-Pérez, H., Rodríguez-Fernández, S., & Gutiérrez-Braojos, C. (2010). Methodologies to improve communication in virtual learning environments. *Comunicar*, *17*(34), 163–171. doi:10.3916/C34-2010-03-16

Saura, J. R., Dwivedi, Y. K., & Palacios-Marqués, D. (2022d). Online User Behavior and User-Generated Content. *Frontiers in Psychology*, *13*, 895467. Advance online publication. doi:10.3389/fpsyg.2022.895467 PMID:35548513

Saura, J. R., Palacios-Marqués, D., & Ribeiro-Soriano, D. (2021). How SMEs use data sciences in their online marketing performance: A systematic literature review of the state-of-the-art. *Journal of Small Business Management*, 1–36. doi:10.1080/00472778.2021.1955127

Saura, J. R., Palacios-Marqués, D., & Ribeiro-Soriano, D. (2022a). Exploring the boundaries of Open Innovation: Evidence from social media mining. *Technovation*, 102447. Advance online publication. doi:10.1016/j.technovation.2021.102447

Saura, J. R., Ribeiro-Soriano, D., & Iturricha-Fernández, A. (2022). Exploring the challenges of remote work on Twitter users' sentiments: From digital technology development to a post-pandemic era. *Journal of Business Research*, *142*(March), 242–254. doi:10.1016/j.jbusres.2021.12.052

Saura, J. R., Ribeiro-Soriano, D., & Palacios-Marqués, D. (2021a, July 15). Setting privacy "by default" in social IoT: Theorizing the challenges and directions in Big Data Research. *Big Data Research*, *25*, 100245. doi:10.1016/j.bdr.2021.100245

Saura, J. R., Ribeiro-Soriano, D., & Palacios-Marqués, D. (2021b). Using data mining techniques to explore security issues in smart living environments in Twitter. *Computer Communications*, *179*, 285–295. doi:10.1016/j.comcom.2021.08.021

Saura, J. R., Ribeiro-Soriano, D., & Palacios-Marqués, D. (2022b). Assessing behavioral data science privacy issues in government artificial intelligence deployment. *Government Information Quarterly, 101679*. Advance online publication. doi:10.1016/j.giq.2022.101679

Saura, J. R., Ribeiro-Soriano, D., & Palacios-Marqués, D. (2022c). Adopting digital reservation systems to enable circular economy in entrepreneurship. *Management Decision*. doi:10.1108/MD-02-2022-0190

Schwarz, B. B., & Asterhan, C. S. (2011). E-Moderation of Synchronous Discussions in Educational Settings: A Nascent Practice. *Journal of the Learning Sciences*, *20*(3), 395–442. doi:10.1080/10508406.2011.553257

Spain, I. (2018). *Estudio Anual Redes Sociales*. Retrieved from https://iabspain.es/wp-content/uploads/estudio- redes-sociales-2018_vreducida.pdf

Tello, O. W., & Ruiz, D. (2016). Didactic use of Web 2.0 tools for teachers in subject of Communication. *Campus Virtuales*, *5*(1), 48–61.

Torres-Barzabal, L. M., Martínez-Gimeno, A., & Hermosilla-Rodríguez, J. M. (2020). Twitter social network in university teaching. Digital innovation strategy for social responsibility. *Sustainability (Switzerland)*, *12*(8), 3350. Advance online publication. doi:10.3390u12083350

Tur, G., Marín-Juarros, V., & Carpenter, J. (2017). Using Twitter in higher education in Spain and the USA. Comunicar. *Media Education Research Journal, 25*(1).

Ukut, I. I. T., & Krairit, D. (2019). Justifying students' performance: A comparative study of both ICT students' and instructors' perspective. *Interactive Technology and Smart Education*, *16*(1), 18–35. doi:10.1108/ITSE-05-2018-0028

Wakefield, J. S., Warren, S. J., & Alsobrook, M. (2011). Learning and teaching as communicative actions: A mixed-methods twitter study. *Knowledge Management and E-Learning*, *3*(4), 563–584. doi:10.34105/j.kmel.2011.03.038

Wei, S., Wang, X., & Liu, Z. (2016). Teaching Research on the University Practical Course Based on Taxonomy of Educational Objectives. *Management Science*, *66*, 108.

Xie, Y., & Zhang, Y. L. (2013). Research on Extracurricular Teaching System Based on Twitter Mode. In Applied Mechanics and Materials. Trans Tech Publications Ltd. doi:10.4028/www.scientific.net/AMM.409-410.1624

Zempoalteca, B., González, J., Barragán, J., & Guzmán, T. (2018). Factors influencing incorporation of Information and Communication Technologies in public universities: Approach based on teacher self-perception. *Revista de la Educación Superior*, *47*(186), 51–74. doi:10.36857/resu.2018.186.348

Chapter 11
Technology-Based Gamification in the Classroom:
An Application to Production Management Teaching

Eloísa Díaz-Garrido
Rey Juan Carlos University, Spain

María Luz Martín-Peña
https://orcid.org/0000-0002-6700-6293
Rey Juan Carlos University, Spain

Cristina García-Magro
Rey Juan Carlos University, Spain

ABSTRACT

This chapter describes the process of designing, developing, and implementing a gamification strategy in a Production Management course. The online tool Genially was used for this purpose. The strategy of using gamification as a learning method allows students not only to acquire and enhance their learning but also to develop competencies and capabilities such as problem solving, teamwork, communication, information management, and critical thinking. It also incentivizes learning self-regulation in an attractive way, thanks to the potential of games to influence the behavior and motivation of students. This chapter lists the steps required to develop and implement gamification in the classroom, describes the implementation of gamification in a specific course, and discusses the results of the experience.

INTRODUCTION

In recent years, the framework of the European Space for Higher Education (ESHE) has encouraged the application of teaching and learning methodologies that reinforce student motivation, creativity, participation, and autonomy in learning (De la Herrán-Gascón, 2005). One such technique is gamification.

DOI: 10.4018/978-1-6684-4441-2.ch011

Copyright © 2022, IGI Global. Copying or distributing in print or electronic forms without written permission of IGI Global is prohibited.

This active teaching and learning methodology is committed to changing student behavior through the mechanics of games in non-playful contexts. This approach uses a game-based scenario to make students actively involved in the learning process (González-González and Mora-Carreño, 2014).

The application of gamification techniques in higher education is an effective way to encourage intrinsic motivation by offering an attractive learning process. Games have the potential to influence student behavior and help students to achieve educational goals.

The possibilities offered by technological development have encouraged the use of online supports and tools as a resource for the implementation of gamified systems (Ocampo, 2016; Oliva, 2017; Rodríguez, 2018, among others). The technological equipment does not guarantee the desired changes in the formation of the new generations (Saura et al., 2022), thus the implementation of gamification requires the correct identification of suitable game elements because good design decisions are critical for gamification success (García-Magro et al., 2019).

Despite all this, we have not been identified papers that provide the complete development of a useful gamified experience to help students acquire generic and specific competencies. To cover this gap, the aim of this chapter is to describe the *design, development, and implementation of a gamification strategy* using Genially, a technological tool designed for this purpose. An example is described, namely the gamification of several units of a Production Management course taught in the second year of a bachelor's degree in Business Administration and Management. The chapter has the following specific aims:

- Define the steps of the gamification process (design a protocol).
- Design the gamification techniques (dynamics, mechanics, and components of the game in the form of challenges) used in the course.
- Analyze the outcomes following this experience.

Regarding the design of gamification techniques, use of the Spanish-based technological tool Genially enabled "the creation of interactive content to improve presentation, teaching, marketing and dissemination tasks" (González and Gómez 2020, p. 24). Genially offers an immense range of resources to create a dynamic, interactive environment, and it is ideal for designing the challenges involved in a gamified system.

The originality and value of the present chapter lies in the fact that, using a technological tool like Genially, we design and implement a gamification strategy in Higher Education, getting influence the behavior and motivation of students to help them achieve competences. In addition, we provide the teaching community with the complete development of a gamified experience that can be used as a reference for future teachers who wish to implement this type of experience in the classroom.

The remainder of this chapter is structured as follows. First, we present the main background. Secondly, we describe the experience design. Second, we provides the results. Finally, conclusions, theoretical and practical implications, as well as limitations of the present chapter are identified.

BACKGROUND

Subjects with a practical part consisting of exercises and problems based on applying theory and concepts have often been taught using traditional teaching methods. These traditional methods generally involve individually resolving problems by a given deadline. The result of these methods is a low level of interaction with students, and they provide little motivation.

The subject of *Production Management* studies the functional area of production in industrial firms through the major strategic and tactical decisions made in this area. It is highly practical. As part of the Production Management course considered in this chapter, students must resolve a series of exercises and problems within each unit. The traditional approach is to use an exercise book and multiple-choice questions that students must answer once they have studied the unit. In other words, the subject has traditionally been taught using teaching and learning methods based on individual student learning and lectures.

To motivate students, encourage teamwork, and develop decision-making skills, among other aims, several teachers of this course have proposed a shift toward active learning methodologies, specifically gamification, given its ability to motivate and engage students.

Gamification is "the use of game design elements in non-game contexts" (Deterding et al., 2014, 10). It is a powerful tool or strategy within education that can motivate students by helping them to enjoy activities and apply skills and capabilities more practically (Oliva, 2016). Recent studies have shown the potential of Genially as a didactic tool (e.g., Mejía-Tigre et al., 2020; Tapia-Machuca et al., 2020).

Gamification in teaching is a process aimed at engaging people, encouraging action, promoting learning, and resolving problems (Kapp, 2012). In education, gamification is acknowledged by scholars as an innovative teaching tool that utilizes the motivational context of games to attract students and ensure their active involvement in the learning process (González González and Mora Carreño, 2015; Rubio, 2014). In the specific case of higher education, there has been a notable increase in academic research showing the development and application of gamification techniques inside and outside the classroom (e.g., Caponetto et al., 2014; Moreira and González, 2015; Ocampo, 2016; Oliva, 2016; Baldeón et al., 2017; Fernández-Zamora and Arias-Aranda, 2017; Rodríguez, 2018). This research has generally focused on the impact on academic performance and motivation.

Overall, gamification can offer an effective way of helping students to acquire the skills and knowledge established within the European Space for Higher Education (ESHE) for the subject of *Production Management*.

MAIN FOCUS OF THE CHAPTER

Experience Design

Designing a gamified system is much more involved than just creating and playing a game (García-Magro, et al., 2019). It requires rigorous analysis of each of the steps of the development process. The following aspects must be defined: 1) Learning objectives; 2) Context and participant profile; 3) Experience structure; 4) Resources; 5) Gamification techniques.

Phase One: Learning Objectives

This phase is about establishing the objectives to be achieved by gamifying the course. An answer must be provided to the question of "why use gamification?" For gamification to be effective, the objectives must be defined as precisely as possible, without focusing on the means and instead focusing on the end itself. Point systems, rewards, and so on are the means to the end (Werbach and Hunter, 2012).

In the proposal presented in this chapter, one objective is for students to acquire the following generic and specific competencies defined for the Production Management course:

- **Generic competencies**
  - Analysis and synthesis
  - Organization and planning
  - Problem solving
  - Decision making
  - Critical thinking
  - Application of knowledge to practice
  - Teamwork
- **Specific competencies**
  - Use of quantitative tools for business decision making

In addition, another objective is to increase the motivation of students so that they become engaged in the practical activities of the course by using a novel method that differs from the methods used in other courses.

Phase Two: Profile and Context

It is crucial to analyze and observe the environment where gamification will be applied and to consider the target users to ensure that it has the correct scope and is optimized (Parente, 2016).

The proposal presented in this chapter was aimed at students of the Production Management course of a (semi-online learning) bachelor's degree in Business Administration in the 2020/2021 academic year. A preliminary version of the proposal was piloted in the Production Management course of a bachelor's degree in Finance and Accounting in the 2019/2020 academic year.

Phase Three: Experience Structure

This phase consists of analyzing how to structure the learning program.

The Production Management course is divided into nine units. Initially, four units (Units 2 to 5) were gamified. (Unit 1 was an introductory unit.) The selected units were Product Design (Unit 2), Production Process (Unit 3), Productive Capacity (Unit 4), and Site Location (Unit 5). These units were selected because they contained the most practical part of the content and offered students the opportunity to acquire the competencies taught in this course to the greatest degree possible. The other units, which relate to plant distribution, human resources operations, quality control, and production planning, are being added to the experience.

Phase Four: Necessary and Available Resources

The aim is to analyze what resources are available and what are necessary for gamification.

To develop this proposal, the main gamification techniques were designed using the Genially platform. The tools available in the virtual learning environment (*Aula Virtual*) were used. Genially enables the creation of interactive content to improve teaching. Among other aspects, it offers a huge range of resources to create a dynamic, interactive, and participative environment that is ideal for the design of the challenges involved in a gamified system. It also has a specific gamification section that greatly helps the process of designing and creating challenges.

Phase Five: Gamification Techniques

This phase is concerned with defining the activities and tools to implement gamification and ensure that it becomes a reality. To enhance understanding, gamification techniques define the means for achieving the goal (i.e., acquiring competencies). Specifically, the process of gamification requires three key concepts that are closely related yet conceptually distinct: game dynamics, game mechanics, and game components (Werbach and Hunter, 2012).

Game dynamics are defined as the general objective of the gamified system. In other words, they refer to the objective of the game. The mechanics describe the rules, and the components are what give the game its structure.

Table 1 shows the selected gamification techniques and gives a brief description of each one.

Table 1. Gamification techniques

Dynamics	Narrative	The story that gives meaning to the game; the mission
	Emotions	Arousing participants' interest in pursuing the proposed learning task
	Progress	The user's progress; the user's status
	Relations	Student–student and student–teacher interactions
Mechanics	Challenges	Theoretical or practical activities
	Rewards	Prize to incentivize extrinsic motivation
	Feedback	Information exchange
Components	Points	Awarded for completing challenges
	Leaderboard	Overview of achievements of each participant

Source: Authors

Development of the Experience

The learning objective of implementing the gamified system was designed to help students to acquire the competencies provided by the Production Management course by motivating them. Therefore, suitable gamification techniques were chosen to achieve this objective. Figure 1 shows how the gamified practical assignment was implemented.

Figure 1. General structure of the gamified system

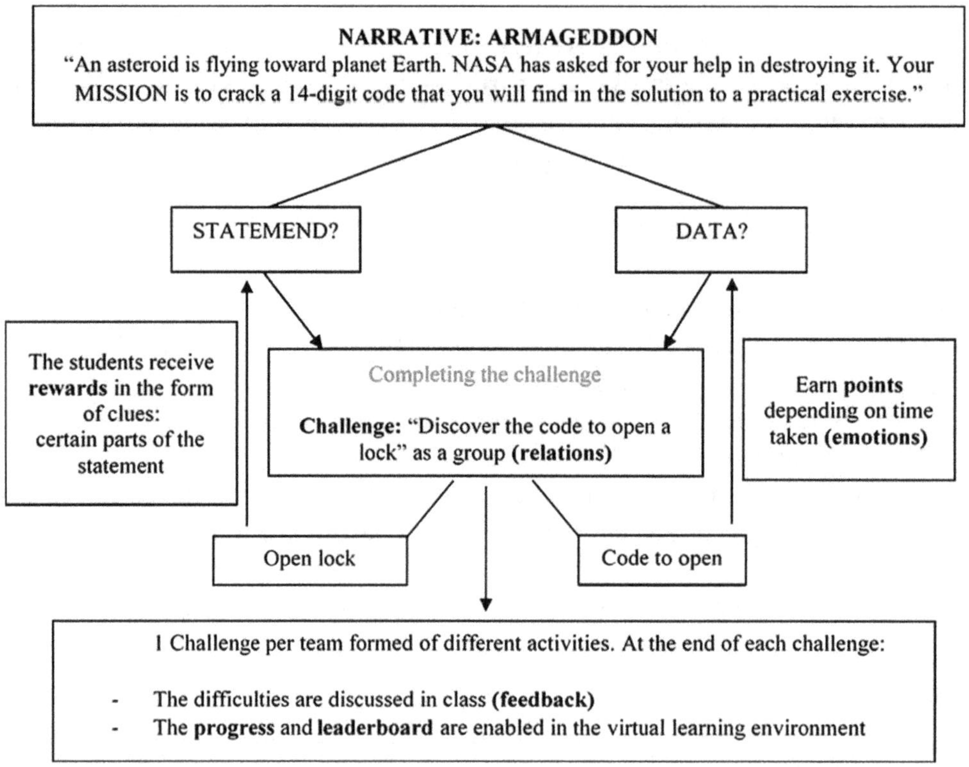

The first part of the implementation of the gamification was to show the students what is known as a narrative in gamification terms. The narrative presents the objective of the game, which, in this case, was presented in the form of a mission.

The narrative was told in a video titled "Armageddon". It explained that the participants (students) had to crack a secret code. This code would allow NASA to take control of an asteroid that was flying toward planet Earth. This 14-digit code was hidden in the solution to a practical exercise related to the course content. Each digit of the code was obtained by resolving a problem.

To crack the secret code, the students needed both exercise statement and the data for that exercise. They obtained these two elements by completing a series of challenges.

- For each part of the practical assignment, a **challenge** was designed. Each challenge consisted of various types of games (true or false, who's who, matching images, video with test, etc.). These games were created based on the course content using the tools available in Genially.

In the four challenges, the goal was the same: discover the code to open the lock. With this code, the students could solve different clues that corresponded to certain parts of the statement. They thus earned the points they needed to unlock the data required to complete the final mission.

In the virtual learning environment (*Aula Virtual*), the students had to send the code from each challenge to the instructor. The fastest to do so earned the most points. In other words, the number of points received depended on the time that the participants took to send the code to the instructor (the faster they did it, the more points they earned). This feature introduced an element of competition between the teams.

Each of the challenges consisted of four different games (activities), designed in such a way as to allow all participants to complete the challenge thanks to the constant feedback and opportunities to advance. However, the students earned more points when they received less help.

This approach was designed to help the students to acquire the generic and specific competencies associated with the course. Table 2 shows the target competencies corresponding to each of the gamification techniques.

Table 2. Gamification techniques and competencies

Gamification Technique	Element	Competency
Dynamics	Narrative	- Organization and planning - Teamwork
	Emotions	- Analysis and synthesis - Decision making - Teamwork
	Progress	- Decision making - Teamwork
	Relations	- Teamwork
Mechanics	Challenges	- Analysis and synthesis - Organization and planning - Problem solving - Decision making - Critical thinking - Application of knowledge to practice - Teamwork - Use of quantitative tools in business decision making
	Rewards	- Decision making - Teamwork
	Feedback	- Analysis and synthesis - Decision making - Critical thinking - Teamwork
Components	Points	Organization and planning - Problem solving - Decision making - Critical thinking - Application of knowledge to practice - Teamwork - Use of quantitative tools in business decision making
	Leaderboard	- Decision making - Teamwork

RESULTS: SOLUTIONS AND RECOMMENDATIONS

The results of this experience have been very positive for both students and teaching staff.

For students, this experience attracted a high level of participation, with more than 90% of students enrolled in the course participating in the activity. Throughout the activity, they displayed interest and motivation in a very positive manner by competing to be the first to send the solution to the instructor and thus earn more points. In addition, the students achieved very satisfactory academic performance, with the members of seven of the eight participating groups achieving the maximum score for the activity (100 puntos).

Before starting the activity, students were asked to complete an initial questionnaire with five questions to gather data about their expectations for the activity, the degree of initial motivation, and the type of player they considered themselves. After the activity, the students were asked to complete a second questionnaire to rate the degree to which the activity had met their expectations, as well as providing an overall rating of the experience together with the acquisition of competencies and the impact on their motivation.

The results of the first questionnaire showed that the initial motivation to learn the content of the course was very high, with a mean score of 4.2 out of 5, although the students were not keen on the activities they were usually given (problems, exercises, lectures, practical cases, etc.). Nevertheless, they seemed somewhat reluctant about gamification in terms of their initial expectation or interest (mean score of 3.3 out of 5). Regarding the type of players, 55.5% of the students who participated reported that they liked to take part in team games where they could interact and relate with each other, and 44.4% defined themselves as "ambitious" players who played to win. The initial intrinsic motivation of the students in relation to the gamified activities was very high, with all items having a mean score between 4 and 5.

The second questionnaire consisted of eight questions. The students responded to these questions on a five-point Likert scale. Specifically, some of the questions asked students to rate the course materials that had been designed for the gamification method (e.g., narrative, challenges, and rewards), and some of the questions asked students to rate the usefulness of the gamification method in terms of their perceptions of the acquisition of competencies with the gamified activities. Finally, questions were included to measure students' extrinsic and intrinsic motivation.

The data obtained from the questionnaires show that, according to the perceptions of the participating students, gamification is a useful method to acquire competencies focused on applying knowledge to practice, teamwork, analysis, and the search for information. These competencies are generic and are taught in many degree programs. The participating students rated the materials very positively, such as the narrative, challenges, and rewards designed for the application of gamification. Finally, there was a clear increase in students' extrinsic and intrinsic motivation after the application of gamification, with participants reporting that the use of gamification in different courses within their degree program was a good idea. Notably, the overall rating of the experience had a mean value of 4.65 out of 5, with 87% of students reporting that the use of gamification in all courses was a good idea.

For the teaching staff, the implementation of gamification in the classroom certainly involved a considerable effort in terms of the time needed to implement it (planning, design, implementation, and coordination). However, it undoubtedly motivated instructors. In particular, seeing the engagement of the teams of students and the competencies they developed in attempting to complete all the challenges provided extra motivation. In addition, the instructors have learnt more about the use of active methods in an online teaching environment, where there is a continuous need to capture students' attention to ensure that they follow the course methodically and on time. The instructors also learned about and applied digital tools that present many possibilities for learning design.

In sum, the instructors involved in this activity rated it very positively because the students, who are the essence of teachers' work, found the experience motivating, fun, and positive for their learning.

CONCLUSION

It can be concluded that the proposal presented here met the initial objectives.

First, the strategy of gamification for this Production Management course was implemented following a series of steps that form a protocol.

Second, a series of dynamics, mechanics, and components for the "Save humanity" game were designed. These dynamics, mechanics, and components were made available to students in the online learning environment (*Aula Virtual*). They provide the basis for open access documentation that can help other instructors to implement this method.

Third, implementing this instance of gamification and evaluating its results confirms that gamification is a highly effective teaching and learning method because it not only motivates students but also helps them to acquire the knowledge and competencies associated with a given course.

Therefore, gamification can guide students toward learning self-regulation (García-Magro and Martín-Peña, 2021), given that one of the characteristics of this type of learning is that students are able to gain a series of adaptive attitudes and beliefs that encourage their involvement and persistence in academic tasks.

Finally, this proposal has major implications, both from a theoretical and practical point of view. From a theoretical point of view, it contributes to the academic literature on gamification, since a detailed protocol has been applied to gamify a subject, covering the existing gap on the option of gamifying in the educational environment with the use of very simple technological tools, like Genially. From a practical point of view, the implications of the work are different for teachers and students. From the teacher's perspective, this proposal provides knowledge to help with the creation and preparation of gamification experiences and can be used as a reference to implement this type of experience in the classroom. From the student's perspective, gamification is expected to increase student motivation and interest in a course. Allowing students to learn through challenges can increase their intrinsic motivation and consequently their academic achievement.

Despite these implications for education, the proposal presents some limitations, mainly motivated by the fact that the study has been carried out in only one subject, which makes it difficult to generalize the results.

FUTURE RESEARCH DIRECTIONS

Given the positive results of this practice, the aim is to add the remaining units of this course, as well as to implement it with other learning formats such as fully face-to-face learning. It would be of interest to perform more detailed studies that show the efficacy of these kinds of methods in different learning environments and different student profiles. The authors also intend to make the practical assignment public so that it can help other instructors who are interested in implementing this approach.

ACKNOWLEDGMENT

This research was supported by the Teaching Innovation Group in Operations and Technology Management - Rey Juan Carlos University [GID OMTECH]; and the Educational Innovation Project, "Learning with Gamification: design and implementation of a playful tool in the classroom", financed by the Faculty of Legal and Social Sciences - Rey Juan Carlos University [Educational Innovation Projects 2020].

REFERENCES

Baldeón, J., Rodríguez, I., Puig, A., & López-Sánchez, M. (2017). Evaluación y rediseño de una experiencia de gamificación en el aula basada en estilos de aprendizaje y tipos de jugador [Evaluation and redesign of a gamification experience in the classroom based on learning styles and player types]. In R. Contreras & J. Eguia, J.(Eds.), Experiencias de gamificación en aulas [Gamification experiences in classrooms (pp. 95-111). Academic Press.

Caponetto, I., Earp, J., & Ott, M. (2014). Gamification and education: A literature review. In *European Conference on Games Based Learning* (*vol. 1*, p. 50). Academic Conferences International Limited.

Deterding, S., Dixon, D., Khaled, R., & Nacke, L. (2011). From game design elements to gamefulness: defining "gamification". In *Proceedings of the 15th international academic MindTrek conference: Envisioning future media environments* (pp. 9-15). 10.1145/2181037.2181040

Fernández-Zamora, J. C., & Arias-Aranda, D. (2017). Implementation of a gamification platform in a master degree (master in economics). *WPOM-Working Papers on Operations Management, 8*, 181-190.

García Magro, C., & Martín Peña, M. L. (2021). Aprendizaje autorregulado y gamificación en educación superior [Self-regulated learning and gamification in higher education: a proposal for an analysis model]. *Revista Española de Pedagogía, 79*(279), 341–362. doi:10.22550/REP79-2-2021-02

García Magro, C., Martín Peña, M. L., & Díaz Garrido, E. (2019). Protocol: Gamify a Subject without Advanced Technology. *WPOM-Working Papers on Operations Management, 10*(2), 20-35.

González González, C. S., & Mora Carreño, A. (2015). Técnicas de gamificación aplicadas en la docencia de Ingeniería Informática [Gamification techniques applied in the teaching of Computer Engineering]. *ReVisión, 8*(1).

Kapp, K. M. (2012). Games, gamification, and the quest for learner engagement. *T+D, 66*(6), 64-68.

Moreira, M. A., & González, C. S. G. (2015). De la enseñanza con libros de texto al aprendizaje en espacios online gamificados [From Teaching with Textbooks to Learning on Online Gamified Spaces]. *Educatio Siglo XXI, 33*(3), 15–38. doi:10.6018/j/240791

Ocampo, R. D. L. S. (2016). Aplicación de juegos digitales en educación superior [Application of digital games in higher education]. *Revista San Gregorio, 11*, 82–91.

Oliva, H. A. (2016). La gamificación como estrategia metodológica en el contexto educativo universitario [The gamification as a methodological strategy in the university educational context]. *Realidad y Reflexión, 16*(44), 108–118.

Parente, D. (2016). Gamificacion en la educación. *Gamificación en aulas universitarias*, 11.

Rodríguez, C. A. C. (2018). Gamificación en educación superior: experiencia innovadora para motivar estudiantes y dinamizar contenidos en el aula [Gamification in higher education: innovative experience to motivate students and stimulate content in the classroom]. *Edutec. Revista Electrónica de Tecnología Educativa*, *63*, 29–41.

Rubio, E. P. (2014). Juegos como elemento docente en un entorno TIC [Games as an educational element in an ICT environment]. *Revista Aequitas: Estudios sobre historia, derecho e instituciones, 4,* 407-416.

Saura, J. R., Palacios-Marqués, D., & Ribeiro-Soriano, D. (2022). Exploring the boundaries of Open Innovation: Evidence from social media mining. *Technovation*, 102447. Advance online publication. doi:10.1016/j.technovation.2021.102447

Saura, J. R., Ribeiro-Soriano, D., & Iturricha-Fernández, A. (2022). Exploring the challenges of remote work on Twitter users' sentiments: From digital technology development to a post-pandemic era. *Journal of Business Research*, *142*, 242–254. doi:10.1016/j.jbusres.2021.12.052

Silva, R. J. R. D., Rodrigues, R. G., & Leal, C. T. P. (2019). Gamification in Management Education: A Systematic Literature Review. *BAR - Brazilian Administration Review*, *16*(2), e180103. doi:10.1590/1807-7692bar2019180103

Valle Arias, A., Sánchez Rodríguez, S. M., Núñez Pérez, J. C., González Cabanach, R., González García, J. A., & Rosário, P. J. S. L. D. (2010). Motivación y aprendizaje autorregulado [Motivation and Self-Regulated Learning]. *Interamerican Journal of Psychology*, *44*(1), 86–97.

Werbach, K., & Hunter, D. (2012). *For the win: How game thinking can revolutionize your business.* Wharton Digital Press.

KEY TERMS AND DEFINITIONS

Competencies: The desired knowledge, skills, and capabilities of a student.

Game Components: The structure of the game: points and leaderboard.

Game Dynamics: The general objective of the gamified system. They refer to the objective of the game.

Gamification: An active teaching and learning methodology that uses the mechanics of game in non-game context.

Gamification Techniques: Its design includes defining dynamics, mechanics, and components of the game.

Genially: A technological tool that enables the creation of interactive content.

Mechanics of the Game: The rules of the game.

Production Management Course: A subject that studies the functional area or production in industrial firms.

Chapter 12
The Effect of Self-Deception on Learning in Higher Education Systems

Elena M Gimenez-Fernandez
https://orcid.org/0000-0002-7234-0296
Universidad Pablo de Olavide, Spain

Vera Gelashvili
https://orcid.org/0000-0001-5951-6392
Rey Juan Carlos University, Spain

ABSTRACT

The current model of higher education uses digital technologies for learning. One of the major applications is their use for online examinations. However, the validity of these exams is questioned, suggesting the commitment of dishonest practices by students. This research analyses whether self-deception behaviours negatively influence the students' learning performance. First, the authors carry out an identical midterm test to the same students in an online environment and in a face-to-face environment, and exam marks are compared. Second, they carry out a regression analysis where they introduce a dummy variable that reflects the changes on the midterm exam mark and analyse how that variable influences on student learning. Data from 230 students from three different courses in business are used. The findings show that students have a higher mark in the online exam than in the face-to-face exam, suggesting for dishonest behaviours. Also, those students who had a dishonest behaviour in the midterm exam have a lower performance in the final exam, suggesting the existence of self-deception.

INTRODUCTION

The importance of economic growth and innovation for our society has led to the development of a knowledge-based economy and society, where technological development has driven innovation towards, business, social, and economic changes (Saura et al., 2022). The Lisbon agenda seeks to make the Eu-

DOI: 10.4018/978-1-6684-4441-2.ch012

Copyright © 2022, IGI Global. Copying or distributing in print or electronic forms without written permission of IGI Global is prohibited.

ropean Union the most competitive and dynamic knowledge-based economy in the world, driven by the application of new technologies and accelerating the shift to high-skilled workers, which is reflected in the expansion of higher education and the key role of higher education in national and European policies (Brown, Lauder, Ashton, Yingje, & Vincent-Lancrin, 2008). The Bologna Declaration on the European Space for higher education in 1999 meant a change in the higher education system. It directed the creation of the 'European Higher Education Area' by 2010, which aimed more transparency in higher education institutions and the removal of obstacles to students and staff mobility, as well as an improvement on the training quality. In response of these objectives, higher institutions are implementing changes in teaching methods (Fidalgo-Blanco, Sein-Echaluce, & García-Peñalvo, 2014; Monteiro, Leite, & Lima, 2013), such as the introduction of educational information and communication technologies (ICT). These advances have therefore enabled the development of strategies for data management, predicting user behaviour or analysing user actions, emong others (Saura et al., 2021). The ICT policy in higher education aims at preparing young people to participate creatively in the establishment, sustainment and growth of a knowledge society that leads the development of nations and global competitiveness (Toro & Joshi, 2012).

The importance of ICT in times of COVID-19 should be emphasized, since in several countries of the world, universities have opted for remote education (Crawford et al., 2020), as well as companies had to adapt to new technologies and platforms to continue to operate efficiently during the pandemic (Saura et al., 2022a). The correct use of the ICT mostly depends on elements such as the training and profile of the teaching staff and the resources available, both technological and pedagogical (Fernández Cruz, Fernández Díaz, & Rodríguez Mantilla, 2018). Therefore, the situation of COVID-19 has highlighted the improvement of ICTs in the whole educational area since it has allowed traditional teaching method to be transformed in its entirety (Parra, Regalado, & Poma, 2020; Saura et al., 2021a).

ICT have acted as an important driver for change (Kirkup & Kirkwood, 2005), becoming an important component of learning as it provides additional opportunities to support the learning process (Agrawal & Mittal, 2018). The current model of higher education takes advantage of the potential of diverse digital technologies in different areas. ICT have been introduced into courses to support distributed or part-time learners, or simply to supplement classroom-based teaching (Kirkup & Kirkwood, 2005). Hence, not only are these technologies used for distance or blending learning, but they are also applied to conventional courses. There is considerable variability in adoption patterns in higher institutions when it comes to the activities and purposes for which ICT are being used (Kirkup & Kirkwood, 2005; Suara et al., 2022b). One of the major applications is the use of ICT for online examinations at any modality of teaching.

However, the introduction of ICT also has a dark side since it is characterized by the separation between learner and instructor, emerging some threats to the transparency and honesty, such as contract cheating (Rundle, Curtis, & Clare, 2019) or exam cheating (Watson & Sottile, 2010). In particular, the validity of online exams is questioned since the lack of vigilance might lead students to commit dishonest practices, emerging a debate about the prevalence of dishonest behaviours in online examinations vs face-to-face examinations (Stuber-McEwen, Wiseley, & Hoggatt, 2009; Watson & Sottile, 2010). Measures that assure quality teaching and learning in these contexts are paramount as learning quality has been identified as a trait of the Higher Education Area (Andrade, 2014).

Nonetheless, the existence of dishonest behaviours is not the only concern. Closely related to learning quality in technology-enhanced learning environments is the concept of self-regulating learning, which means that, to be successful, students must recognize their strengths and weaknesses, apply learning strategies, monitor their learning and make needed adjustments (Andrade, 2014). As a particular problem of self-regulating learning applied to online examinations is the phenomenon of self-deception. It means that students might distort misbehaviour to reflect positively on themselves, so students who cheat on a test might wrongly believe that their performances reflect their knowledge and skills (Chance, Gino, Norton, & Ariely, 2015; Chance, Norton, Gino, & Ariely, 2011). Debate around the benefits and detriments of self-deception has been discussed in psychology literature (Bachkirova, 2016; Martocchio & Judge, 1997), but to our knowledge, it has not been linked to the current model of education. To accomplish with the principles of Bologna Declaration, it is key to analyse the phenomenon of self-deception on learning, so higher education systems are able to assure the transparency and competitiveness of human capital. Our goal is therefore to analyse whether self-deception behaviours negatively influence the students' learning performance (Saura et al., 2022b).

To test for the existence of self-deception on learning, we follow a two-step methodology, using data from 230 students. First, we analyse whether there are dishonest behaviours in online exams vs face-to-face exams by comparing firstly setting an online midterm exam to the students and, some days later, setting the same exam to the same students, but in a face-to-face written format. The differences between the marks of those exams determine the existence of dishonest behaviours. Second, we generate a dummy variable with the differences on the exam and introduce it in a multiple regression to test whether that variable is negatively related to learning. The findings show that students who had a dishonest behaviour in the midterm exam have a lower performance in the final exam, suggesting for the existence of self-deception (Saura et al., 2022c).

Our contribution is threefold. First, the study promotes the competences of the learning European framework by analysing the ability to be an effective learner to assure the quality in technology-enhanced learning environments. Second, we contribute to the debate on dishonest behaviours on online examinations, which is one of the main problems for educational institutions, especially for those with limited technological surveillance resources. Third, we deepen on the analysis of self-deception through its application to learning. We also provide several implications of self-deception behaviours and technology-enhanced learning environments. Therefore, this book chapter has a great importance in academic literature, since the literature on dishonest behaviours on online examinations and self-deception for higher education learners is scare.

The paper is structured as follows. First, we review the theoretical background of academic honesty and self-deception and then, we develop our hypotheses. After that, we explain the methodology followed in our study and we present our findings. Finally, we discuss our results and conclude with implications and future research lines.

THEORETICAL BACKGROUND AND HYPOTHESES

Honesty on Online Evaluation

One of the main concerns of professors when implementing online evaluation is the students' honesty. Scholars on distance learning have analysed the tendency to cheat on online evaluation related to face-to-face. It is generally believed that cheating on online examination is easier than on face-to-face examination (Gimenez-Fernandez & Gelashvili, 2019; Watson & Sottile, 2010), but other scholars argue that academic misconduct on online courses may not be as prevalent as believed, existing no differences between online and face-to-face examination (Grijalva, Nowell, & Kerkvliet, 2006; McNabb & Olmstead, 2009; Spaulding, 2009), or even being lower the dishonesty on online examination (Peled, Eshet, Barczyk, & Grinautski, 2019; Saura et al., 2022d).

Between the reasons that lead to the belief that deception on online evaluation is higher than on conventional evaluation is the lack of proctor supervision of online activities (Harmon & Lambrinos, 2008). On that scenario, one of the most common misconduct of students is collusion, so students exchange responses or help each other during the exam (Watson & Sottile, 2010). Students might also consult books, electronic resources or class notes while taking the examination (Bawarith, Basuhail, Fattouh, & Gamalel-Din, 2017). Another reason for the tendency to cheat on online evaluation is the lack of social interaction between students and teachers since closeness to teachers is seen as a stimulus to be honest, while indifference or lack of concern is seen as a driver of students' dishonest behaviours (Stuber-McEwen et al., 2009). Additionally, literature on social communication argues that computer mediated communication is more deceptive than face-to-face communication (O'Rourke, Eskritt, & Bosacki, 2018), so it might be expected that students cheat more when taking online examinations since they are thought to be less likely to be caught in online examinations than in face-to-face examinations. This fact is reinforced by the lack of familiarity of professors on detection online exams tools (Stuber-McEwen et al., 2009).

The European Higher Education Area has meant the introduction on digital educational ICT, transforming the conventional methods of learning and evaluation, and leading teachers to the search of integrated solutions that gather the specific competences of the course and technological tools (Cáceres, Esteban, Gálvez, & Rivas, 2019). As a result, face-to-face courses are introducing the use of new technologies in class as well as outside the class (Kirkup & Kirkwood, 2005). In particular, learning examination through digital platforms is one of the most used resources of the new era, so even students enrolled in conventional courses are taking online examinations. Hence, similar dishonest online behaviours might happen on both conventional and distance courses since both of them make use of ICT where teachers and learners are separated.

To contribute to this debate, we propose that students' dishonest behaviours will be higher in online environments than in face-to-face environments.

- **Hypothesis 1 (H1):** Students have more dishonest behaviours in online exams related to face-to-face exams.

Self-deception on Learning

Nowadays we live in a digital era where data provides for users advantages and added value (Saura et al., 2021b). ICT encourage students to take responsibility for their own learning (Toro & Joshi, 2012), but as we have previously mentioned, dishonest behaviours might exist on technology-enhanced learning environments. Dishonest behaviours on online evaluation without proctoring result in a deceptive situation where the student does not show the real knowledge level and blows the course's mark (Alessio, Malay, Maurer, Bailer, & Rubin, 2017). It poses the question if the student is only deceiving the teacher or that student is deceiving themselves. To answer that question, we should first understand the motivation to deceive.

Literature have highlighted that students might behave dishonestly to gain a personal need (Watson & Sottile, 2010), for example, to get greater grades, to overcome fear of failure, or as a response to lack of confidence and motivation (Cebrián-Robles, Raposo-Rivas, Cebrián-de-la-Serna, & Sarmiento-

Campos, 2018; Mensah, Azila-Gbettor, & Asimah, 2018; Özbek & Çeyiz, 2017). It is also pointed out that some students might not understand the scope of deception, and cheat on assessments because the chances of being caught are low or because it is a behaviour done by other colleagues (Mensah et al., 2018). In those contexts, the role of self-regulation is key for the success of learning and the avoidance of misbehaviour. Indeed, a study carried out by Rundle, Curtis, and Clare (2019) about the contract cheating has shown that students with high self-control were unlikely to engage in contract cheating, even when the opportunity was available; whereas students with low self-control have replied that they could cheat if the opportunity was available. On this basis, some scholars have emphasized the role exerted by self-regulation in different learning contexts, including higher education (Andrade, 2014), and how some initiatives that require self-regulation support the development of technology-enhanced learning environment (Steffens, 2006). The extent to which learners are capable of regulating their own learning greatly enhances their learning outcomes (Steffens, 2006), but when students cheat on their evaluations, they might not foresee to engage in self-deception (Chance et al., 2011).

The concept of self-deception has been argued along the history, offering different perspectives and views of the consequences of it. Although there is not a unanimous criterion to define self-deception, there are some common features that literature has highlighted. On this basis, Bachkirova (2016) pointed out five conditions of self-deception: 1) holding a belief regardless the truth; 2) that belief has to be persistent; 3) motivation to keep that belief; 4) the person should be active; and 5) a consideration of the self of self-deceivers. Hence, to be considered as self-deceiver on a learning context, students should consider that dishonest behaviours on learning evaluation are not relevant since their knowledge on that subject is not determined by an examination or they thoroughly believe on their performance. Although honesty is central to self-concept, it would exist a room for moral acceptance (Chance et al., 2015) since self-deception implies a tendency to have honestly held, but biased views of oneself (Martocchio & Judge, 1997). Self-deception therefore becomes an instrumental element in the process of ethical fading (Rees, Tenbrunsel, & Bazerman, 2018).

There are two main streams on literature regarding the consequences of self-deception. On one hand, some authors justify the use of self-deception as they see some benefits on it. Self-deception has the potential of getting people ahead, acquiring benefits such as enhanced self-image or avoiding distress (Bachkirova, 2016). Self-deception can be used either as a defensive mechanisms or as an offensive one. When self-deception is used as a defensive mechanism, the individual protects oneself from the threats of the environment (Freud, 1989). On this basis, students avoid the moral implications of their behaviours since they would hold the conviction that they might have acquired that knowledge. On the contrary, evolutionary psychologist literature has posited that self-deception might be used as an offensive mechanism (von Hippel & Trivers, 2011), so it has evolved to in assist other-deception (Chance et al., 2015). It becomes a sustained strategy of individuals where people focus on the positive outcome and neglect the dishonest process that led to it (Chance et al., 2015). Indeed, it has been evidenced that self-deception is positively related to success in competitive environments as it is associated to stress reduction and pain tolerance, enhancing motivation and performance during competitive tasks (Starek & Keating, 1991).

On the other hand, some authors point out the negative consequences of self-deception. By definition, self-deception implies the rationalization and conviction to the self that a lie is true (von Hippel & Trivers, 2011). Hence, it commits the integrity of reality. The loss of information therefore would be one of the main costs of self-deception (Bachkirova, 2016). As a consequence, self-deceivers distort the reality. In a learning context, self-deception is used to avoid failure, generating an external fake appearance of knowledge. In an experiment conducted by Chance et al. (2011) it was found that people who chose to self-deceive believed that their performance was due to themselves rather than to their answers, so students who exploited the opportunity to cheat on an examination were likely to infer that their elevated performance is a sign of intelligence. However, that external attribution avoids cognitive learning, drawing attention away from training and diminishing the individual learning (Martocchio & Dulebohn, 1994). In fact, it has been evidenced that self-deception is negatively related to learning (Martocchio & Judge, 1997). Additionally, if students perceive that they might have the opportunity to cheat, they would spend less time preparing for their examinations, and so diminishing students' learning (Chance et al., 2015). Another cost of self-deception is the repetition since the good previous performance would lead the student to increase the likelihood of cheating again (Chance et al., 2015).

Balancing the arguments about the pros and cons of self-deception, Chance et al. (2011) concluded that there is a temporal view for benefits and costs of self-deception, so the benefits of self-deception often accrue in the short-term, whereas its costs accrue on the long-term. That temporal perspective of self-deception should be taken into consideration when analysing the effect of self-deception on learning. Apart from the introduction of ICT in learning, the 'Bologna process' has facilitated the combination of face-to-face, distance, and blended learning in academic degrees through the transformation of the unit of academic measurement, the credit, shifting from tuition hours to student effort hours (Duran, Moon, & Giraldo, 2009). As a consequence, current higher education programmes take into consideration the number of hours that student dedicate to a subject, rather than the number of hours that students are actually in class. It offers the opportunity to introduce distance evaluations on conventional courses, but it is also associated to the emergence of risks and more dishonest behaviours since student might behave differently in an online context than in a face-to-face context (Fask, Englander, & Wang, 2014), and subsequently, it might generate an increase of self-deception behaviours. In particular, while midterm exams and other activities might be scrolled to distance evaluations, the final exam is commonly taken in a face-to-face proctored environment. Thus, students might tend to cheat on distance evaluations while they have to face the reality in the final exam. The previous self-deceived positive results might lead them to believe that they have acquired the knowledge and skills required in the module (Chance et al., 2015, 2011), but students might not have acquired them.

Taking into account the temporal perspective and the difference in behaviours of students in different learning environments, we believe that if the student cheats on an exam, in the short-term, that student might have a higher mark, so he/she has an enhanced self-image, reduces the stress or avoid the negative consequences of failure. However, in the long-term, students who has previously cheated in an exam have not acquired the cognitive competences required to pass that course, so they have a false appearance of knowledge that leads to a lower mark on the final exam and subsequently to a diminishing of learning. We therefore propose that self-deception is negatively related to learning.

- **Hypothesis 2 (H2):** Self-deception is negatively related to learning.

MATERIALS AND METHODS

Sample and Setting

In our study, we used data from undergraduate students from three different courses and degrees at Rey Juan Carlos University in Spain: 1) Introduction to Business I from the double Degree in Business and Law; 2) Economic and Financial Analysis in Marketing I, from the Degree in Marketing; and 3) Financial Accounting I from the Degree in Business. All of them were taught during the first semester of the academic year 2018/2019. The first two subjects are first year subjects, while the latter is a second year subject. Two professors were in charge of the courses, one of them for the Introduction to Business I course, and the other professor for the two other courses.

The total number of students enrolled in these courses were 72, 93, and 97, respectively, but not all students completed the courses. Since we are testing the effect of self-deception through dishonest behaviours on learning, our sample is restricted to those students who did both the midterm exam and the final exam. In total 230 students were considered, 59 from Introduction to Business I; 88, from Financial Accounting I; and 83, from Economic and Financial Analysis in Marketing I.

Measures

Online and Face-to-Face Midterm Exam

Following Gimenez-Fernandez & Gelashvili's (2019) methodology, to analyse if dishonest behaviours are higher in online environments than in face-to-face exam we conducted an identical midterm exam to the same students but in two scenarios, first, online and, then face-to face. Students did not know that they were to take the same exam. In the case of Introduction to Business I, students were said that they will continue with the content examination on class; and in the other two courses, students attendance was said to be compulsory to review the exam. The midterm exam, with a possible maximum mark of 10 points, used a multiple-choice question format. We therefore used the students' marks to build the variables online midterm exam and face-to-face midterm exam. If the mark of the online midterm exam is statistically higher than the face-to-face midterm exam, then there are dishonest behaviours.

Learning

Students' scores have previously been used in literature as a measure of learning (Lee & Klein, 2002; Martocchio & Judge, 1997). We used students' final exam mark to test the effect of self-deception on students' knowledge about the course. The final exam of each course, with a possible maximum mark of 10 points, used a multiple-choice question format. We therefore used the students' marks to build the variable final exam.

Self-deception

Two streams of literature can be distinguished when measuring self-deception. On the one hand, psychology literature has referred to subjective measures to identify self-deception (Martocchio & Judge, 1997). On the other hand, there are some attempts to measure self-deception using two samples, one of them has access to answers key, while the other sample does not (Chance et al., 2011), so in absence of self-deception there should be no difference between groups in predicted performance of a future test. However, considering two different group of students would not allow to actually consider the key component of self-deception, the 'self'. Giving the methodological limitations of previous studies, we measure self-deception in an objective way, based on the analysis of dishonest behaviours. We consider the difference in marks in the midterm exam carried out by the same students in the two scenarios (online and face-to-face), and we create a dummy variable that takes the value 1 if the mark for the online exam was higher than the mark of the face-to-face exam, and 0 otherwise. We called that variable self-deception. If this variable is negative and significant in our regression with learning as dependent variable, it means that students are not only deceiving the teachers, but they are deceiving themselves.

Control Variables

Number of Examinations

Literature has stated that the impact of self-deception on learning might change over time (Lee & Klein, 2002). To control for the time that a student has been enrolled on a course, we include a variable that accounts for the number of examinations.

Exchange Student

Introduction to Business I was taught in Spanish language, while the other two courses were in English-taught. As a consequence, a higher number of Erasmus students could be enrolled on English-taught courses. Since there might exist cultural differences on training programs, we considered to include a dummy variable to account whether the student is an exchange student or not.

Gender

Research has shown that gender may play a role in making ethical decisions (Watson & Sottile, 2010). To control for the gender of the student we included a dummy variable, coded as 1 female, and 0 male.

Subject

Since our sample of students are from three different courses (Introduction to Business I, Economic and Financial Analysis in Marketing I and, Financial Accounting I), we included two dummy variables to control the effect of the different courses. Introduction to Business I was the benchmark.

RESULTS

Table 1 reports the annual descriptive statistics (mean and standard deviation) of the variables used in the analysis. The average of students' final exam performance is 6.8. However, it is worth to notice that the average mark for the online midterm exam was around two and a half points higher (8.4) than the average mark for the face-to-face midterm exam (5.7). Only 14% of the students were Erasmus students;

and 59.1% were female. Correlation coefficients of the variables used in the estimations are reported in Table 2. As expected, the variable self-deception is negatively correlated to the learning variable. None of the correlations are sufficiently strong to suggest multicollinearity problems. We conducted variance inflation factor (VIF) tests, and all the VIFs were lower than 2, suggesting that multicollinearity is not a problem in our results.

Table 1. Descriptive statistics

Variable	Mean	Std. Dev.	Min	Max
Online midterm exam	8.396	1.626	3.75	10
Face-to-face midterm exam	5.671	3.966	0	10
Learning	6.796	1.933	2	10
Self-deception	0.587	0.493	0	1
N. examinations	1.061	0.424	1	5
Exchange	0.143	0.351	0	1
Gender	0.591	0.493	0	1
Intr. Business	0.257	0.438	0	1
Accounting	0.383	0.487	0	1
Economic Analysis	0.361	0.481	0	1

Table 2. Correlation coefficients

	Learning	Online Midterm exam	Face-to-Face Midterm Exam	Self-Deception	N. Examinat.	Exchange	Gender	Intr. Business	Accounting
Online midterm	0.440								
exam	*0.000*								
Face-to-	0.224	0.154							
face midterm exam	*0.000*	*0.196*							
Self-deception	-0.146	0.135	-0.645						
exam	*0.027*	*0.041*	*0.000*						
N.	-0.194	-0.128	-0.046	0.160					
examinat.	*0.003*	*0.052*	*0.490*	*0.805*					
Exchange	0.277	0.168	0.005	-0.110	-0.059				
	0.000	*0.011*	*0.942*	*0.096*	*0.374*				
Gender	0.129	0.268	-0.036	0.129	-0.048	0.088			
	0.052	*0.000*	*0.591*	*0.051*	*0.472*	*0.184*			
Intr.	-0.392	-0.472	0.143	-0.154	0.057	-0.212	-0.018		
Business	*0.000*	*0.000*	*0.031*	*0.019*	*0.392*	*0.001*	*0.786*		
Accounting	0.176	-0.043	-0.015	-0.175	0.035	0.367	-0.164	-0.462	
	0.008	*0.516*	*0.824*	*0.008*	*0.600*	*0.000*	*0.013*	*0.000*	
Economic	0.178	0.472	-0.115	0.318	-0.087	-0.178	0.183	-0.441	-0.592
Analysis	*0.007*	*0.000*	*0.082*	*0.000*	*0.190*	*0.007*	*0.005*	*0.000*	*0.000*

Note: Numbers in italics are the p-value.

The first hypothesis proposed that students have more dishonest behaviours on online environments than on face-to-face ones. To test for the existence of dishonest behaviours we statistically compare whether the variable online midterm exam is higher than the variable face-to-face midterm exam, so if there statistical differences we conclude that there are dishonest behaviours. To conduct the mean difference test, we first run the Shapiro-Wilk test to check the normal distribution of the variables. The test shows that our variables are not normally distributed ($z=5.434$, $p<0.001$), so we have to use non-parametrical statistical techniques to test H1. Hence, we ran a Wilcoxon test to compare whether the online and face-to-face midterm exam mean ranks differ (Table 3). The difference between them is significant ($z = 7.819$, $p < 0.01$), being higher the average mark for the online exam, supporting H1 and suggesting the existence of dishonest behaviours in online environments.

Table 3. Wilcoxon Test with sink ranks

Sign	Obs	Sum Ranks	Expected
positive	135	20579.5	12718.5
negative	48	4857.5	12718.5
zero	47	1128	1128
all	230	26565	26565

The second hypothesis proposed that self-deception is negatively related to learning, so our equation determines that learning depends on the existence of self-deception and a series of control variables (see equation #1). To test H2, we employed Ordinary Least Square (OLS) regressions. First, we estimated Model 1, which contains the control variables; and then Model 2 adds the direct effect of self-deception. However, the assumption of normality of residuals in the model was not satisfied, so we employed a logarithm transformation of our dependent variables. The results of the OLS regressions can be found in Table 4.

$$Learning = \beta_0 + \beta_1 Self\text{-}deception + \beta_2 N.examinations + \beta_3 Exchange + \beta_4 Gender + \beta_5 Subject + \varepsilon \quad (1)$$

Results show that the coefficient for the variable self-deception is negative and significant in Model 2, confirming Hypothesis 2. It means that, when having dishonest behaviours, students are not only deceiving the teachers, but they are deceiving themselves.

Regarding the control variables, no differences were found regarding to gender. Students who are on exchange have a higher learning. Students who have previously taken the exam have a lower learning.

Table 4. OLS regressions

	Model 1	**Model 2**
N. examinations	-0.110***	-0.105***
	[0.038]	[0.037]
Exchange	0.141***	0.128**
	[0.050]	[0.049]
Gender	0.054	0.065*
	[0.034]	[0.033]
Accounting	0.190***	0.197***
	[0.044]	[0.043]
Economic Analysis	0.195***	0.985***
	[0.057]	[0.057]
Self-deception		-0.122***
		[0.034]
Constant	1.941***	1.984***
	[0.057]	[0.057]
R-squared	0.208	0.252
No of Obs	230	230
F test	11.78***	12.51***

Note: Standard errors in bracket. *p<0.10; **p<0.05; ***p<0.01

To test the robustness of our findings, we ran different estimates. First, we ran the sing test to test Hypothesis 1. This test is similar to the Wilcoxon test, but it does not assume any asymmetry in the distribution (not reported for the sake of brevity). Results show that students' online marks are higher than the face-to-face marks (p<0.01), confirming H1. Second, we created an alternative variable to measure self-deception. That variable was assessed as the difference between the face-to-face and the online exam marks, and we ran our models again. Results (see table 5, Model 1) are similar to those found in Table 4, supporting H2. Third, we used an alternative measure for our dependent variable. We created a measure of learning based not only on the final exam mark, but also on students' performance that accomplish their grades. Grades were based on class activities, midterm exams, and the final exam, being the latter the predominant variable to assess the final grade. The variable learning is therefore measured as the compositional assessment of the different class activities and exams. The maximum value of the variable is 10. Findings show that not only self-deception is negatively related to learning measured as the final exam mark, but it is also negatively related to learning, understood as a composition of different activities and exams (see Table 5, Model 2), supporting H2. It means that students who cheated on the online midterm exam did not acquire the full competences and knowledge required for the course, having a temporary higher mark, but diminishing their final performance.

Table 5. OLS regressions robustness check

	Model 1	**Model 2**
N. examinations	-0.106***	-0.144***
	[0.037]	[0.042]
Exchange	0.148***	0.109**
	[0.049]	[0.055]
Gender	0.067**	0.061
	[0.033]	[0.037]
Accounting	0.223***	0.394***
	[0.044]	[0.048]
Economic Analysis	0.252***	0.472***
	[0.044]	[0.047]
Self-deception	-0.015***	-0.166***
	[0.004]	[0.038]
Constant	1.936***	1.891***
	[0.055]	[0.063]
R-squared	0.252	0.417
No of Obs	230	230
F test	12.49***	26.53***

Note: Standard errors in bracket. *p<0.10; **p<0.05; ***p<0.01

DISCUSSION

This study raised the question whether students who have dishonest behaviours in learning only deceive to teachers or they deceive themselves.

Regarding the dishonest behaviours, given that the exam questions were the same, the lack of deception would mean that the students would get the same mark on both exams, while a dishonest behaviour would imply a higher mark on the online exam since the online exam was firstly taken and it was done in an unproctored environment. However, we found that students' marks were higher in the online midterm exam than in the face-to-face exam, which suggests for the existence of dishonest behaviours as suggested by previous literature (Fask et al., 2014; Harmon & Lambrinos, 2008) and contributing to the empirical debate.

We expected that if no self-deception occurred, the fact of having cheated on the midterm exam would not have impact on future examinations, and, conversely, if self-deception occurred, students would have lower grades in their future examinations. Findings point out that students who had a dishonest behaviour in the midterm exam have a lower performance in both the final exam and the final grade, suggesting for the existence of self-deception. Those results are in line with previous literature that has argued the negative role of self-deception on learning (Hirschfeld, Thomas, and McNatt 2008; Lee and Klein 2002; Martocchio and Judge 1997). Students with dishonest behaviours might have a higher mark in an exam, but they do not learn the content of the course modules.

CONCLUSION

Theoretical Implications for Education

This study contributes to literature in different ways. First, we revisit the debate on honesty on online evaluation, and contribute to empirical literature by testing students' honesty on a sample of students who took both the face-to-face and the online exam. On this way, we do not consider two different samples of students, but the same students, as well as we use objective measures for deception. We also introduce the use of ICT on conventional courses, whereas previous literature has frequently analysed the phenomenon in distance vs face-to-face courses. Second, we contribute to literature on self-deception on learning through the analysis of self-deception on learning online evaluation. New technologies are introduced in learning strategies in the current context of higher education in Europe. Some students take advantage of the possibilities to get around of control on learning evaluations under these technologies, aspiring for a better performance. However, our study evidences that those students are deceiving themselves since they subsequently have a lower performance. Third, the study sheds light on the development of a knowledge-based society, promoted by the European Higher Education Area, through the analysis of the efficiency of the technology-enhanced learning environments. The European framework highlights the importance of quality learning, and this study reflects on the ability to be an effective learner and the negative effects of self-deception. Taking all of this into account the main contribution of this book chapter is in academic literature on such important issues as dishonest behaviours on online examinations and self-deception for higher education learners.

Practical Implications for Education

Our study has several implications. First, the use of educational ICT has advantages and drawbacks. Although we have evidenced dishonest behaviours on online evaluations, those evaluations were taken on an unproctored environment. We do not advise against online examinations, but we warn about their risks, and recommend taking advantage of technological tools to monitor students' activities. We also recommend increasing efforts to reduce students' unethical behaviours. Second, self-deceivers do not perceive the reality as it is, having a false image of themselves. As a result, self-deception might undermine critical thinking. Third, in a learning context, self-deception implies no acquiring the knowledge, competences and skills related to that topic. Those students are prospected employees in risk of not passing the trial period. In addition, when those attitudes are translated to a work environment, self-deceivers might have a low productivity level. From a policy perspective, our study helps to build a solid higher education system that invests on the transparency and competitiveness of human capital.

Limitations and Future Practices

Although this study reveals some interesting points of view, it has some limitations, which not only represent the boundaries of its insights but also provide opportunities for future research. First, psychology literature measures self-deception using scales and several items. Our measure has tried to overcome some of the previous problems regarding subjective data, and we have only based on objective data from exam marks. However, that measure might lose some psychological components of self-deception. Future research could create a construct that combines subjective and objective elements, or compare results from both perspectives. Linking to that, the explanatory power of our model is low. However, Harmon and Lambrinos (2008) argued that low R-squared statistic might support the existence of cheating on exams since test scores should be explained by human capital variables. We therefore encourage future research to include more variables related to students' skills to test for the existence of self-deception. Additionally, future research could analyse the consequences of self-deception in learning on the work environment as we have outlined that self-deception might have negative consequence on productivity or on the opportunities to get a job.

Self-deception might therefore be a problem for the future of the current model of knowledge-based society as the study has evidenced that self-deceivers do not completely acquire the knowledge and competences specified in the course module syllabus. The findings of this study applies specifically to higher education system in European countries, but it could be extended to other countries as knowledge-based economies are spreading over the world.

REFERENCES

Agrawal, D. A. K., & Mittal, D. G. K. (2018). The Role of ICT in Higher Education for the 21st Century: ICT as A Change Agent for Education. Multidisciplinary Higher Education, Research, Dynamics & Concepts: Opportunities & Challenges For Sustainable Development, 1(1), 76–83.

Alessio, H. M., Malay, N., Maurer, K., Bailer, A. J., & Rubin, B. (2017). Examining the Effect of Proctoring on Online Test Scores. *Online Learning*, *21*(1), 146–161. doi:10.24059/olj.v21i1.885

Andrade, M. S. (2014). Dialogue and Structure: Enabling Learner Self-Regulation in Technology-Enhanced Learning Environments. *European Educational Research Journal*, *13*(5), 563–574. doi:10.2304/eerj.2014.13.5.563

Bachkirova, T. (2016). A new perspective on self-deception for applied purposes. *New Ideas in Psychology*, *43*, 1–9. doi:10.1016/j.newideapsych.2016.02.004

Bawarith, R., Basuhail, A., Fattouh, A., & Gamalel-Din, S. (2017). E-exam cheating detection system. *International Journal of Advanced Computer Science and Applications*, *8*(4), 176–181. doi:10.14569/IJACSA.2017.080425

Brown, P., Lauder, H., Ashton, D., Yingje, W., & Vincent-Lancrin, S. (2008). Education, Globalisation and the Future of the Knowledge Economy. *European Educational Research Journal*, *7*(2), 131–156. doi:10.2304/eerj.2008.7.2.131

Cáceres, C., Esteban, N., Gálvez, M. del C., & Rivas, B. (2019). *Competencia digital docente: una perspectiva de futuro en la Educación Superior [Teaching digital competence: a future perspective in Higher Education]*. Dykinson.

Cebrián-Robles, V., Raposo-Rivas, M., Cebrián-de-la-Serna, M., & Sarmiento-Campos, J. A. (2018). Percepción sobre el plagio académico de estudiantes universitarios españoles [Perception about academic plagiarism of Spanish university students]. *Educación XX1, 21*(2). doi:10.5944/educxx1.20062

Chance, Z., Gino, F., Norton, M. I., & Ariely, D. (2015). The slow decay and quick revival of self-deception. *Frontiers in Psychology*, *6*. Advance online publication. doi:10.3389/fpsyg.2015.01075 PMID:26347666

Chance, Z., Norton, M. I., Gino, F., & Ariely, D. (2011). Temporal view of the costs and benefits of self-deception. *Proceedings of the National Academy of Sciences of the United States of America*, *108*(Supplement 3), 15655–15659. doi:10.1073/pnas.1010658108 PMID:21383150

Crawford, J., Butler-Henderson, K., Rudolph, J., Malkawi, B., Glowatz, M., Burton, R., ... Lam, S. (2020). COVID-19: 20 countries' higher education intra-period digital pedagogy responses. *Journal of Applied Learning & Teaching*, *3*(1), 1–20. doi:10.37074/jalt.2020.3.1.7

Duran, A., Moon, Y. B., & Giraldo, E. (2009). Work in progress - the European Higher Education Area ("Bologna process") in Engineering Education in Spain. *2009 39th IEEE Frontiers in Education Conference*, 1–2. 10.1109/FIE.2009.5350475

Fask, A., Englander, F., & Wang, Z. (2014). Do Online Exams Facilitate Cheating? An Experiment Designed to Separate Possible Cheating from the Effect of the Online Test Taking Environment. *Journal of Academic Ethics*, *12*(2), 101–112. doi:10.100710805-014-9207-1

Fernández Cruz, F. J., Fernández Díaz, M. J., & Rodríguez Mantilla, J. M. (2018). El proceso de integración y uso pedagógico de las TIC en los centros educativos madrileños [The process of integration and pedagogical use of ICT in educational centers in Madrid]. *Educación XX1, 21*(2). doi:10.5944/educxx1.17907

Fidalgo-Blanco, Á., Sein-Echaluce, M. L., & García-Peñalvo, F. J. (2014). Knowledge spirals in higher education teaching innovation. *International Journal of Knowledge Management*, *10*(4), 16–37. doi:10.4018/ijkm.2014100102

Freud, S. (1989). The Ego And The Id (1923). *TACD Journal*, *17*(1), 5–22. doi:10.1080/1046171X.1989.12034344

Gimenez-Fernandez, E. M., & Gelashvili, V. (2019). La honestidad de los estudiantes en los exámenes online. Una comparativa de la realización de exámenes online y presenciales [The honestity of students in online exams. A comparison of taking online and face-to-face exams]. In C. Cáceres, N. Esteban, M. C. Gálvez, & B. Rivas (Eds.), *Competencia digital docente: una perspectiva de futuro en la educación superior [Teaching digital competence: a future perspective in Higher Education]* (pp. 297–307). Dykinson.

Grijalva, T. C., Nowell, C., & Kerkvliet, J. (2006). Academic Honesty and Online Courses. *College Student Journal*, *40*(1), 180–185.

Harmon, O. R., & Lambrinos, J. (2008). Are Online Exams an Invitation to Cheat? *The Journal of Economic Education*, *39*(2), 116–125. doi:10.3200/JECE.39.2.116-125

Hirschfeld, R. R., Thomas, C. H., & McNatt, D. B. (2008). Implications of Self-Deception for Self-Reported Intrinsic and Extrinsic Motivational Dispositions and Actual Learning Performance: A Higher Order Structural Model. *Educational and Psychological Measurement*, *68*(1), 154–173. doi:10.1177/0013164406299129

Kaware, S. S., & Sain, S. K. (2015). ICT application in education: An overview. *International Journal of Multidisciplinary Approach & Studies*, *2*(1), 25–32.

Kirkup, G., & Kirkwood, A. (2005). Information and communications technologies (ICT) in higher education teaching—A tale of gradualism rather than revolution. *Learning, Media and Technology*, *30*(2), 185–199. doi:10.1080/17439880500093810

Lee, S., & Klein, H. J. (2002). Relationships between conscientiousness, self-efficacy, self-deception, and learning over time. *The Journal of Applied Psychology*, *87*(6), 1175–1182. doi:10.1037/0021-9010.87.6.1175 PMID:12558223

Martocchio, J. J., & Dulebohn, J. (1994). Performance Feedback Effects in Training: The Role of Perceived Controllability. *Personnel Psychology*, *47*(2), 357–373. doi:10.1111/j.1744-6570.1994.tb01729.x

Martocchio, J. J., & Judge, T. A. (1997). Relationship between conscientiousness and learning in employee training: Mediating influences of self-deception and self-efficacy. *The Journal of Applied Psychology*, *82*(5), 764–773. doi:10.1037/0021-9010.82.5.764 PMID:9337608

McNabb, L., & Olmstead, A. (2009). Communities of Integrity in Online Courses: Faculty Member Beliefs and Strategies - ProQuest. *Journal of Online Learning and Teaching*, *5*(2), 208.

Mensah, C., Azila-Gbettor, E. M., & Asimah, V. (2018). Self-Reported Examination Cheating of Alumni and Enrolled Students: Evidence From Ghana. *Journal of Academic Ethics*, *16*(1), 89–102. doi:10.100710805-017-9286-x

Monteiro, A., Leite, C., & Lima, L. (2013). Quality of Blended Learning within the Scope of the Bologna Process. *Turkish Online Journal of Educational Technology*, *12*(1), 108–118.

O'Rourke, S., Eskritt, M., & Bosacki, S. (2018). Communication, compassion, and computers: Adolescents' and adults' evaluations of online and face-to-face deception. *Journal of Adolescence*, *65*(1), 133–140. doi:10.1016/j.adolescence.2018.03.010 PMID:29597102

Özbek, O., & Çeyiz, S. (2017). University students' opinions on cheating and plagiarism. *European Journal of Education Studies*. Advance online publication. doi:10.46827/ejes.v0i0.900

Parra, C. N. E., Regalado, G. A. M., & Poma, C. J. R. (2020). Los desafíos de la inclusión en tiempos de COVID-19 (The challenges of inclusion in times of COVID-19). *Revista Scientific*, *5*(17), 221–239. doi:10.29394/Scientific.issn.2542-2987.2020.5.17.11.221-239

Peled, Y., Eshet, Y., Barczyk, C., & Grinautski, K. (2019). Predictors of Academic Dishonesty among undergraduate students in online and face-to-face courses. *Computers & Education*, *131*(1), 49–59. doi:10.1016/j.compedu.2018.05.012

Rees, M. R., Tenbrunsel, A. E., & Bazerman, M. H. (2018). Bounded Ethicality and Ethical Fading in Negotiations: Understanding Unintended Unethical Behavior. *The Academy of Management Perspectives*, *33*(1), 26–42. doi:10.5465/amp.2017.0055

Rundle, K., Curtis, G. J., & Clare, J. (2019). Why Students Do Not Engage in Contract Cheating. *Frontiers in Psychology*, *10*, 2229. Advance online publication. doi:10.3389/fpsyg.2019.02229 PMID:31636584

Saura, J. R., Palacios-Marqués, D., & Iturricha-Fernández, A. (2021). Ethical Design in Social Media: Assessing the main performance measurements of user online behavior modification. *Journal of Business Research*, *129*(May), 271–281. doi:10.1016/j.jbusres.2021.03.001

Saura, J. R., Palacios-Marqués, D., & Ribeiro-Soriano, D. (2022). Exploring the boundaries of Open Innovation: Evidence from social media mining. *Technovation*, 102447. Advance online publication. doi:10.1016/j.technovation.2021.102447

Saura, J. R., Ribeiro-Soriano, D., & Iturricha-Fernández, A. (2022). Exploring the challenges of remote work on Twitter users' sentiments: From digital technology development to a post-pandemic era. *Journal of Business Research*, *142*(March), 242–254. doi:10.1016/j.jbusres.2021.12.052

Saura, J. R., Ribeiro-Soriano, D., & Palacios-Marqués, D. (2021). From user-generated data to data-driven innovation: A research agenda to understand user privacy in digital markets. *International Journal of Information Management, 60*. doi:10.1016/j.ijinfomgt.2021.102331

Spaulding, M. (2009). Perceptions of Academic Honesty in Online vs. Face-to-Face Classrooms. *Journal of Interactive Online Learning*, *8*(3), 183–198.

Starek, J. E., & Keating, C. F. (1991). Self-Deception and Its Relationship to Success in Competition. *Basic and Applied Social Psychology*, *12*(2), 145–155. doi:10.120715324834basp1202_2

Steffens, K. (2006). Self-Regulated Learning in Technology-Enhanced Learning Environments: Lessons of a European peer review. *European Journal of Education*, *41*(3–4), 353–379. doi:10.1111/j.1465-3435.2006.00271.x

Stuber-McEwen, D., Wiseley, P., & Hoggatt, S. (2009). Point, Click, and Cheat: Frequency and Type of Academic Dishonesty in the Virtual Classroom. *Online Journal of Distance Learning Administration*, *12*(3).

Toro, U., & Joshi, M. (2012). ICT in Higher Education: Review of Literature from the Period 2004-201 1. *International Journal of Innovation, Management and Technology*, *3*(1), 20–23.

von Hippel, W., & Trivers, R. (2011). *The evolution and psychology of self-deception*. doi:10.1017/S0140525X10001354

Watson, G., & Sottile, J. (2010). Cheating in the Digital Age: Do Students Cheat More in Online Courses? *Educational Foundations and Technology*. Retrieved from https://mds.marshall.edu/eft_faculty/1

KEY TERMS AND DEFINITIONS

Higher Education: Education at a college or university where subjects are studied in great detail and at an advanced level.

Honesty on Online Evaluation: The honesty of the students not to cheat in the online exams as it is easier to access the resources or to cheat than in the face-to-face exam.

ICT: A combination of technological tools and resources that are used to manipulate and communication the information (Kaware & Sain, 2015).

Online Learning: Method of learning used by educational institutions where students learn in a virtual environment. No face-to-face learning.

Chapter 13
Service-Learning as a Teaching Methodology

Lidia Iniesta Bernabé
University of Murcia, Spain

Francisco Javier S. Lacárcel
University of Alicante, Spain

Jose Antonio Rabadán Rubio
University of Murcia, Spain

ABSTRACT

Educational methodology evolves over time in search of an improvement in the student's learning process, taking into account a practical aspect in its path towards teaching. This chapter presents the service-learning methodology in which, while the learner offers a service to the community in order to improve it, the student learns moral values as well as the basic competences of the educational field. Service-learning is a method for linking educational success and social commitment, since learning brings quality to the service provided and service gives meaning to learning. This study analyses the case of the Sagrado Corazón of Pamplona School as a result of the application of the service-learning methodology within the school's educational programme.

INTRODUCTION

Educational methods have been innovated and modified throughout history with the aim of improving student learning with new teaching methodologies (Gaete, 2011). Teaching methodology is the process by which teachers are able to deliver instruction using a variety of strategies to achieve the desired learning outcomes for students (Ortiz, 2003).

Innovation is directly associated with terms such as change and improvement (Ibáñez, 2008). In the education sector, innovation plays a key role through the promotion of Information and Communications Technology (ICT) (Saura et al., 2022). The teaching and learning processes in educational environments

DOI: 10.4018/978-1-6684-4441-2.ch013

Copyright © 2022, IGI Global. Copying or distributing in print or electronic forms without written permission of IGI Global is prohibited.

have been exposed for years to the use of technological media to promote and encourage students to an environment in which these supports benefit them in their learning process (Ibáñez, 2008).

An essential part of the learning process for the learner is the practical approach that the learner takes throughout their formative years (Ganger, 2020). In this article, the application of the Service-Learning teaching methodology, henceforth referred to in the study as SL, is highlighted (Saura et al., 2022a).

The need for this study is based on the need to apply new educational methodologies in teaching. This research tests a new methodology with a practical emphasis applied in a public school for several years (Saura et al., 2022b). The originality of the research stems from the application of practical methods in a school where both teachers and students face new teaching challenges.

The structure of the research will start with the theoretical framework in which the importance of education in history and its application with practical methods will be reviewed and a comparison with current methodological processes will be addressed. The methodology is then presented through the project of the Sagrado Corazón of Pamplona School: *"Education in the Service of the Community"*. Then, the results obtained through the programme will be analyzed. Finally, the theoretical and practical implications of the importance of SL as a learning methodology in teaching will be addressed (Saura et al.,2022b).

THEORETICAL FRAMEWORK

The learning process takes place throughout life and during this process the individual acquires a series of knowledge that generates both his or her behavior and personal development (Tapia, 2006) (Padrós et al. 2003).

The SL methodology is essential in order for the project to be effective and valid for its educational evolution. In the field of teaching, the experience and participation of those involved will be relevant for the implementation of the project (Tapia, 2006; Saura et al., 2022c).

The learning is adaptable to any social area that understands it, i.e. it embraces all groups regardless of their social and economic situation (Puigdellívol & Flecha, 2003). Learning in SL methodology is relevant as it increases students' motivation and participation in the service offered to the community. This methodology directly involves the student with the people to whom the service is being offered. This is why, by learning in this way in a different reality to that existing in the classroom, its impact is greater, thus making students more aware (Bertomeu & Vivot, 2009).

The community service offered through the SL methodology is important since its realization benefits both the students and the different groups that can receive such a service. The service can be offered to any group, i.e. it can be addressed to the elderly, infants, people with functional diversity, environment, etc (Padrós et al. 2003).

Carrying out this type of methodology in the different teaching courses is fundamental for fostering skills and values in students, such as: solidarity, empathy, companionship, equality, respect, honesty, humility, patience, gratitude, among other essential values. In addition, learning through community service increases students' motivation (Bertomeu et al. 2013; Saura et al., 2022d).

The beginning of SL was in the early 1900s with the academic Dewey (1938) who advocated practical education above all else, so he investigated the role they had in academic institutions. Research on SL methodology continued and it was Kolb (1984) who extended the concept by developing an experiential learning cycle.

However, older data can be observed, as the first manifestations of this practice can be found in the late 19th and early 20th century with the "university extension" movement, which motivated the development of social actions from Higher Education (Pedroza, 2009).

The SL combines on the one hand, traditional teaching, i.e. a purely academic and theoretical learning with the aim that students learn and use research methodologies, thus getting to know the reality, and on the other hand, the active participation of students by developing dynamics and/or solidarity activities (Tapia, 2008).

Continuing with the history of SL we can see the existing interest in creating initiatives that offer in the different educational environments a development of both a democratic and participative culture. This has the aim of fostering in students an interest in coexistence in a multicultural society, promoting group cohesion and thus fighting against the social exclusion that persists in today's society (Pedroza, 2009).

It is important to promote this methodology in different educational settings as it enhances students' learning through their participation, thus fostering their social responsibility (Gaete, 2011) (Saura et al., 2021)

The vision of this methodology is quite broad as it includes students, community partners, teachers and even the educational institution itself. It has been found that by implementing this methodology, students' academic performance and non-academic outcomes have been improved (Garger, 2020).

Nowadays, SL is known as a methodology that gives importance and protagonism to students, thus showing very significant changes in academic and civic results. Likewise, throughout history it has been observed that when students lack protagonism and are not listened to, quality decreases notably, on the other hand, if the methodology is carried out correctly, it can be an effective tool that can help to form a better society (García & García, 2015; Saura et al., 2021a).

This proposal is nowadays applied at all levels of education and in many countries, although its name varies. For example: "curricular social service" in Mexican universities; "university community work" in Costa Rica; "pre-professional community practice", etc. Even in the same country, each author has given it a different concept and connotation (Pedroza, 2009).

Finally, research has confirmed that SL can be integrated into any curriculum, as it could be adapted to the academic year in various ways. But what is clear is that by incorporating this methodology in educational centers, the combination of academic learning with the service offered to the community improves students' knowledge and motivation (Salam, 2019) (Saura et al., 2021b).

Application of Teaching Innovation Methodology: Service-Learning

This research has analyzed a real case in a school located in the capital of the province of Navarra, the city of Pamplona. The aim of the school was to make a situational change within its classrooms to improve the learning of its pupils, as set out in its Annual Innovation Plan. The long-term goal for the school is that through the results, schools in the province and the country will apply this methodology in their teaching process (Colegio Sagrado Corazón de Pamplona, 2020).

CASE STUDY: APPLICATION OF SERVICE-LEARNING IN THE SAGRADO CORAZÓN OF PAMPLONA SCHOOL

The Sagrado Corazón school in Pamplona has been teaching in the city for more than eighty years, offering its pupils training and innovating in line with the demands of society. The participation and voluntary nature of its initiatives have been promoted on other occasions together with organizations such as Oxfam Intermón, Manos Unidas, Banco de Alimentos, Voluntariados, etc.

In the 2017-2018 academic year, the school pedagogically introduced a new way of teaching in which the main objective was to promote the practical side of its students and to promote the Service-Learning methodology. Then, the first step to start with the first projects involving the students was to provide the teaching staff with the methodology to be implemented in the school, reviewing and training with the teaching staff to coordinate and promote the first SL projects to be implemented in the school, both for Preschool, Primary Education, GCSE and GCE students.

Secondly, an educational innovation team was introduced in the school led by a teacher with years of experience in the school in order to be able to draw up a calendar of actions to be carried out during the academic year to promote SL-related projects.

In order to correctly develop the projects in which the pupils would be involved, the school's educational innovation team was committed to a leading role for the pupils, which is why each project is adapted to the interests of the pupils according to the age and size of the group. In addition, the teachers had to connect with their interests and gather opinions for the dynamics to be carried out. Through this intervention, the effort and enthusiasm of the students was greater, making the student a participant in the different projects to be carried out.

During the first year, 16 SL projects were carried out with more than half of the school's student body participating in at least one project, each of which is analyzed in depth in table 1 and for which students it was aimed.

Table 1. Service-learning projects

Service-Learning	Preschool	Primary Education	GCSE	GCE
Buttons Projects: The 3rd year Infant pupils show their 1st year classmates where to put their dressing gowns and lunch.	X			
Robotics for all: Primary school pupils together with people with functional diversity develop computational thinking.		X		
***Colecaminos*:** Participation in areas of pollution, sustainability, data collection and interpretation by primary school pupils.		X		
The theatre is for all of us: Primary 6 pupils prepare a theatre script and dramatise it.		X		
We multiply our help: Students in 5th grade learn the programming language with Scratch.		X		
Storytelling: Pupils in Year 3 Primary listen to their peers in Year 2 Infants to find out what stories they like.		X		
Ephemeral gardens: From the subjects of Plastic Arts, Mathematics and Biology, they think, design and build a garden that will improve a part of the city.			X	
Age does not matter: Elaboration of a series of activities and "gifts" to prepare for their visit to the residents of Ammavir Aragaray.			X	
Women with History: They develop alternative proposals and produce a script. Finally, they record and edit videos in order to disseminate them and remedy this deficiency.			X	
Sport brings us closer together: Didactic units of juggling and dance (merengue) to teach a group with functional diversity.				X
Pamplona, an open city: From the subject of history, they learn about the situation of conflicts in the world today and the violation of human rights.				X
Different but the same: Computer tools for working with pictograms.				X
***Colecaminos*:** Development of a personal project with video editing for their Primary School classmates.				X
Mobile phones that connect: The ICT subject is preparing a programme for the use of mobile phones and tablets.				X
***Ubuntu*:** Debate entitled: "Can citizens transform politics?				X
Fair Trade: Consequences of the unequal distribution of wealth in the world				X

Note. Own elaboration.

Benefits and Possibilities for the Application of Service-Learning

The evaluation of the projects carried out at the school each year was carried out in accordance with the peculiarities of each educational stage in which self-evaluation rubrics, hetero-evaluation, co-evaluation and self-evaluation forms were used.

In general terms, the participants in the projects, including both teachers and students, were satisfactory for their learning process. The following table 2 shows in more detail the results of the application of the SL as an educational methodology in the Sagrado Corazón of Pamplona School.

Table 2. Improvements to the Implementation of Service-Learning Methodology

Benefits Identified	Explanation
Adaptability	Service-Learning has been perfectly adapted to the educational style of the school.
Participation and Involvement	More than 50% of the school has been involved in at least one project that has been carried out, taking into account pupils from pre-primary, primary, GCSE and CGE.
Internal and External Coordination	Coordination has been present in the different educational stages, acting as a link between the centre's management, social entities, families and teachers.
Accessibility	The support of the management team to both teachers and students has been vital in facilitating accessibility to work teams, resources and support in the development of projects.
Teacher Motivation	Implicación del profesorado en cuanto a la formación y efusividad en la ayuda para llevar adelante
Social Outreach	The reach through the different publications on social networks increased significantly with the exposure of the different projects carried out.

Note. Own elaboration

The application of the SL methodology has achieved multiple benefits both in the student's learning process and in the social environment in which they find themselves. In addition, table 3 shows different possibilities for improvement extracted as an analysis of the results of the application of SL.

Table 3. Possibilities for Improvement in Service-Learning

Improvement Possibilities	Explanation
Project Boosting	Implementation of a larger number of projects involving a higher number of participants.
Increase in Teacher Training	Specific training for teachers.
Social External Involvement	Involvement of family members and social organizations.
Quality Improvement Practice	Opt for more time to plan projects.
Internal and External Communication	Improve communication and coordination between the different stages of the project.

Note. Own elaboration.

Once the different projects carried out have been completed, the Sagrado Corazón of Pamplona School specifically lists the parameters to be taken into account as fundamental aspects when considering the addition of SA as an active learning methodology.

CONCLUSION

Service-Learning provides a new approach to the current educational system, as it is an innovative methodology in which the learner offers a service to the community while acquiring the basic competences of the educational course. (Tapia, 2006).

For this reason, it is essential to include this teaching methodology based on ES in the educational environment, as it significantly improves both learning and the autonomy of the learner. After applying this methodology, it has been proven that by learning from reality, students, on the one hand, acquire better knowledge of compulsory subjects, and on the other hand, by offering a service to the community, they develop values such as empathy, solidarity, respect, humility and responsibility (Garger et al. 2020).

As has been shown, when an SL project is carried out in the educational sector, relevant aspects can be achieved, both for the students and for the educational and social community. A social sense of education is generated; a democratic and participative concept is developed by citizens; the ethics of justice is compensated with the ethics of care; cognitive aspects are integrated with attitudinal and moral aspects of learning; social capital and cohesion in neighborhoods and populations are increased; the learning achieved is much more effective; and the learning process is much more efficient.; the issue of volunteering is increased; the social image is improved and the social perception of adolescents is enhanced.

Just as it has been confirmed which are the most relevant aspects when implementing an SL project, four basic elements have also been detected, these are: the social need that exists; the service to the community that is offered; the learning acquired by the learner and the networking with the actors of the environment.

Finally, after carrying out several SLs, it has been possible to verify which are the most common and notable advantages: developing critical thinking, increasing the learner's leadership and decision-making; fostering communication and conflict resolution carried out in a more appropriate and assertive way; generating more positive relationships with the community; relating the experience to academic competences, thus improving their learning; enhancing their understanding of themselves and increasing empathy and respect for others; increasing their knowledge of social problems, i.e. they become aware of Third Sector collectives and finally, cooperative work is increased.

Theoretical and Practical Implications for Education

This research will foster theoretical implications for future studies on the inclusion of new practical methodologies in education. It will also serve for other researchers to analyze how this methodology has been implemented. Therefore, the practical implications are evident because the results of this research will help universities and other educational institutions to better understand how this methodology has been applied in practice and thus avoid possible errors or mistakes.

Limitations and Future Practices

The results of this research will help future practices as it will be possible to carry out preventive actions that were not carried out in this study and, as a justification, did not turn out as well as originally planned.

The limitations in this study were noted in the little information that could be obtained from the participants, not only from the teachers, but also, in order to have more successful results, the students should have been analyzed with a more in-depth study. Even so, the research has borne fruit in terms of educational improvements and enhancing the application of SL as an educational methodology.

REFERENCES

Colegio Sagrado Corazón de Pamplona. (2020). *Educate at the Service of the Community. Pamplona: Spanish Network of Learning - Service* [Educar al Servicio de la Comunidad. Pamplona: Red Española de Aprendizaje - Servicio]. Recuperado de: https://www.aprendizajeservicio.net/wp-content/uploads/2020/11/PROYECTO-EDUCAR-AL-SERVICIO-DE-LA-COMUNIDAD.pdf

Dewey, J. (1938). *Experience and education*. MacMillan.

Folgueiras Bertomeu, P., Luna González, E., & Puig Latorre, G. (2013). Learning and service: Study of the degree of satisfaction of university students [Aprendizaje y servicio: estudio del grado de satisfacción de estudiantes universitarios]. *Review of Education, 362*, 159–185.

Folgueiras Bertomeu, P., & Martínez Vivot, M. (2009). The development of competencies in the university through Solidarity Learning and Service [El desarrollo de competencias en la universidad a través del Aprendizaje y Servicio Solidario]. *Revista Interamericana de Educacion para la Democracia (RIED), 2*(1), 55–76.

Gaete-Ouezada, R. A. (2011). Role play as a strategy for evaluating university learning [El juego de roles como estrategia de evaluación de aprendizajes universitarios]. *Educación y educadores, 14*(2), 289-307.

García García, M. D. C., & Cotrina García, M. J. (2015). *Learning and service in initial teacher training: from critical educational practices to curricular institutionalization* [El aprendizaje y servicio en la formación inicial del profesorado: de las prácticas educativas críticas a la institucionalización curricular]. Academic Press.

Garger, J., Vracheva, V. P., & Jacques, P. (2020). A tipping point analysis of service-learning hours and student outcomes. *Education + Training*, *62*(4), 413–425. doi:10.1108/ET-09-2019-0210

Kolb, D. A. (1984). *Experiential learning: Experience as the source of learning and development.* Prentice Hall.

Morgan, W., & Streb, M. (2003). First do no harm: The importance of student ownership in servicelearning. *Metropolitan State Universities*, *14*(3), 36–52.

Padrós, M., Puigdellívol, I., & Flecha, R. (2003). Learning Communities: transforming the school organization at the service of the community [Comunidades de Aprendizaje: transformar la organización escolar al servicio de la comunidad]. *Organización y gestión educativa, 5*, 4.

Parra Ortiz, J. M. (2003). *Education in values and their practice in the classroom* [La educación en valores y su práctica en el aula]. Academic Press.

Pedroza, G. A. de (2005). The Mexican Social Service: design and construction of models [El Servicio Social Mexicano: diseño y construcción de modelos]. Ministerio de Educacion, Ciencia y Tecnologia. Unidad de Programas Especiales. Programa Nacional Educación Solidaria. Aprendizaje y servicio solidario en la Educación Superior y en los sistemas educativos latinoamericanos.

Salam, M., Iskandar, D. N. A., Ibrahim, D. H. A., & Farooq, M. S. (2019). Service learning in higher education: A systematic literature review. *Asia Pacific Education Review*, *20*(4), 573–593. doi:10.100712564-019-09580-6

Salinas Ibáñez, J. (2008). *Educational innovation and use of ICT* [Innovación educativa y uso de las TIC]. Universidad Internacional de Andalucía.

Saura, J. R., Dwivedi, Y. K., & Palacios-Marqués, D. (2022d). Online User Behavior and User-Generated Content. *Frontiers in Psychology*, *13*, 895467. Advance online publication. doi:10.3389/fpsyg.2022.895467 PMID:35548513

Saura, J. R., Palacios-Marqués, D., & Ribeiro-Soriano, D. (2021). How SMEs use data sciences in their online marketing performance: A systematic literature review of the state-of-the-art. *Journal of Small Business Management*, 1–36. doi:10.1080/00472778.2021.1955127

Saura, J. R., Palacios-Marqués, D., & Ribeiro-Soriano, D. (2022a). Exploring the boundaries of Open Innovation: Evidence from social media mining. *Technovation*, 102447. Advance online publication. doi:10.1016/j.technovation.2021.102447

Saura, J. R., Ribeiro-Soriano, D., & Iturricha-Fernández, A. (2022). Exploring the challenges of remote work on Twitter users' sentiments: From digital technology development to a post-pandemic era. *Journal of Business Research*, *142*(March), 242–254. doi:10.1016/j.jbusres.2021.12.052

Saura, J. R., Ribeiro-Soriano, D., & Palacios-Marqués, D. (2021a, July 15). Setting privacy "by default" in social IoT: Theorizing the challenges and directions in Big Data Research. *Big Data Research*, *25*, 100245. doi:10.1016/j.bdr.2021.100245

Saura, J. R., Ribeiro-Soriano, D., & Palacios-Marqués, D. (2021b). Using data mining techniques to explore security issues in smart living environments in Twitter. *Computer Communications*, *179*, 285–295. doi:10.1016/j.comcom.2021.08.021

Saura, J. R., Ribeiro-Soriano, D., & Palacios-Marqués, D. (2022b). Assessing behavioral data science privacy issues in government artificial intelligence deployment. *Government Information Quarterly*, *101679*. Advance online publication. doi:10.1016/j.giq.2022.101679

Saura, J. R., Ribeiro-Soriano, D., & Palacios-Marqués, D. (2022c). Adopting digital reservation systems to enable circular economy in entrepreneurship. *Management Decision*. doi:10.1108/MD-02-2022-0190

Tapia, M. N. (2006). *Learning and solidarity service: some basic concepts* [Aprendizaje y servicio solidario: algunos conceptos básicos]. Programa Nacional Educación Solidaria.

Tapia, M. N. (2008). *Learning and solidarity service in the mission of higher education* [Aprendizaje y servicio solidario en la misión de la educación superior]. El Aprendizaje-Servicio En la Educación Superior.

Chapter 14
TBS:
Giving Case Studies a Twist

Antonio Montero-Navarro
Rey Juan Carlos University, Spain

José-Luis Rodríguez-Sánchez
Rey Juan Carlos University, Spain

Rocio Gallego-Losada
Rey Juan Carlos University, Spain

Thais González-Torres
Rey Juan Carlos University, Spain

ABSTRACT

The European higher education area (EHEA) aims at creating a climate of less traditional learning through higher levels of interaction between the professors and the students. In that context, the use of participative tools, such as case study discussions, can be especially useful. Nevertheless, the attempt of a group of professors to implement that methodology in their classes had to face some difficulties, with the the high number of students with different goals and needs the main one. In order to deal with this situation, the students were given the possibility to choose amongst three different evaluation methods: non-continuous evaluation, continuous evaluation, and business school – the last one focused on the discussion of freshly prepared case studies about business management. The results can be considered positive, both in terms of academic progress and competencies achievement, and led to the creation of an online version of this "business school."

INTRODUCTION

The studies of Business Management and Administration are expected to provide the students with the knowledge, tools and abilities to be able to face a professional environment. So, the acquisition of management competencies is one of the critical aspects that should be learnt.

DOI: 10.4018/978-1-6684-4441-2.ch014

Copyright © 2022, IGI Global. Copying or distributing in print or electronic forms without written permission of IGI Global is prohibited.

According to Katz (1974), there are three main kinds of management abilities: technical skills, which include having specialized knowledge about specific activities, as well as being able to analyse problems related with the area of specialization and the capability to use tools and techniques related with a particular discipline; human or interpersonal skills, related with groupwork and the ability to join collective efforts to achieve common goals; and conceptual skills, which enable a manager to see the corporation as a whole, being able to understand the interrelations between the different functional areas and business units of the company and the crossed impacts of the actions taken by any of them. Koontz and Weihrich (1994) added a fourth kind, design skills, which include the abilities to diagnose problems and deliver solutions. These groups of managerial abilities can also be related with the management roles stated by Mintzberg (1990).

The European Higher Education Area (EHEA) was born as “a unique international collaboration on higher education and the result of the political will of 48 countries with different political, cultural and academic traditions, which, step by step during the last twenty years, built an area implementing a common set of commitments: structural reforms and shared tools”.

The authors of this chapter are a group of professors of a Spanish University who have shown a permanent interest in implementing innovative educational tools in their subjects, which has led them to design and use gamifications, create specific seminaries and use the social media in order to open additional channels to get in touch with the students. Nevertheless, they found an important difficulty when trying to use case-based learning, as long as the high number of students, with different goals and backgrounds, could undermine the effectiveness of this technique.

This paper analyses how they overcame this barrier, creating a specific group inside the class called *Business School*, devoted to the discussion of case studies. All the students were offered the possibility to join it. The ones who did achieved a better average academic performance and showed a higher level of involvement in the subject, which resulted in a demand to expand the experience after the classroom. This led to the birth of Together Business School (TBS), a LinkedIn group created to discuss cases and stories about Strategic Management, which has resulted to be an interesting meeting point of students, *alumni* and professionals.

Though the positive impacts of case-based learning have been previously analysed by the literature, this chapter shows some differential aspects. Firstly, in the vast majority of the situations in which this methodology is used the conditions are close to be ideal, dealing with small groups of highly motivated students whose engagement can be easily achieved. The generation of a Business School inside a regular big group of degree students gave the authors the opportunity to build from scratch such favourable environment, even increasing the suitability of this tool (as the students themselves chose their learning itinerary), while it created an adequate control group to test the potential differences in the academic performance between the student who chose case-based learning and those who didn’t.

Additionally, the creation of TBS was a pre-pandemic experience of specialized case study discussion which gathered voluntarily students, alumni and management professionals, something relatively rare in 2019, that has become more frequent due to the mobility restrictions caused by COVID-19. This experience gave the authors some helpful insights to improve the adoption of remote and blended learning methodologies.

BACKGROUND

Since its very origin, the different task groups of the EHEA fostered a competence-based learning approach instead of a pure knowledge-based one, aiming at providing the students with the tools, techniques and skills that would enable them to develop successful professional careers.

The exclusive use of traditional teaching techniques and methodologies has been frequently deemed to be a wrong approach to acquire competencies. Behrman and Levin (1984) suggested that traditional methodologies are focused on quantitative analysis, theoretical explanations and the use of tools and models that enable the acquisition of specialized knowledge, related with the technical skills proposed by Katz (1974), which can hardly help to develop interpersonal or design skills. Glasser (1998) stated that the learning process should not be focused on memorizing, as many of the concepts would be forgotten immediately after the evaluation. The results of his study show how a higher degree of participation of the student in the learning process will improve the acquisition of both knowledge and skills.

Therefore, the EHEA has defended the generation of a less traditional learning climate, in which more interactive tools and techniques can propitiate the participation and involvement of the students in their learning process (Castaño-Perea et al., 2012; Gómez, 2013), through a pedagogical approach based on the acquisition of competencies and/or new evaluation models oriented to productive learning (Gil-Flores, 2012). This new framework can be considered an adequate way to overcome some old-school practices associated with a linear and hierarchical teacher-student relationship (López-Navas, 2014), focused on memorizing.

The participation of the professors is critical to reach such goals, as the educational approach used becomes one of the main variables, if not the critical one, which determine the degree of learning achieved by the students (Guardia et al., 2019). Professors must evolve from a traditional role of sole knowledge transmitters to a new one of guiding and mentoring (Wang, 2015), helping the students to develop their own learning process adapted to their needs and requirements (Marín-García, 2018). Swartz et al. (2010), developers of a methodology called *Thinking Based Learning*, stress the need to provide the students with tools that require them to face problems and think, which will not just help them to get specific knowledge, but also to acquire skills that will help them along their entire professional careers.

Amongst these tools, many authors agree about the different advantages of the use of case-based learning, stressing the participation of the students in the process of learning, as they get involved in the solution of real problems about a specific subject (Carlson & Schodt, 1995; Tillman, 1995; Erskine et al., 1998). As the title of his paper stated clearly, Bonney (2015) found out that "case study teaching method improves student performance and perceptions of learning gains". This effect has been proved in several disciplines, such as Engineering Biotechnology (Alani et al., 2020), Nursing (Seshan et al., 2021) or Business Management (Song et al., 2022).

Nevertheless, within the use of such tool, some researchers have stressed the importance of the configuration of the discussion groups in the achievement of the learning goals (Flynn and Klein, 2001). When discussing case studies about business management, the students have to cooperate with their colleagues in order to reach agreements about the situations analysed and the solutions proposed, which may lead to conflicting situations. The dynamics of intragroup conflict have been frequently studied by the scientific literature. A first research stream, which can be considered more classical, stated that conflict was negative for a group, as it eroded the commitment of its members with the decisions made, reducing the quality of such decisions (Mintzberg et al., 1976; Wilson et al., 1986). These authors considered conflict mainly a single construct.

Nevertheless, later research found out that conflict could have an apparently paradoxical effect over decisions, as it could simultaneously improve their quality and complicate the relationship between the members of the group (Schweiger et al., 1986). This led some authors (Amason, 1996; Jehn, 1994; Pelled et al., 1999; Tidd et al., 2004) to suggest the existence of different kinds of conflict, which had different impacts over the quality of decisions. Specifically, they distinguished between a cognitive conflict, task related, which is considered to be functional because of its positive effect on the dynamics of the group, as it contributes to the generation of new ideas and alternatives, strengthening the alignment of the members of the group with the decisions adopted; and an affective conflict, fundamentally emotional, which should be considered dysfunctional, as it reduces the efficiency of the group, generating personal issues and unsatisfaction (Amason et al., 1995; Amason, 1996; Pelled et al., 1999).

Ideally, some degree of cognitive conflict should be considered positive in order to improve the dynamics of a group. The academic literature has found out some antecedents of this kind of conflict, such as the composition and heterogeneity of the group (Pelled, 1996; Pelled et al., 1999) or the kind of task they face (Jehn et al., 1997). In the context of the discussion of a case study, the use of structured techniques, such as devil's advocacy, dialectic inquiry, brainstorming (Schweiger et al., 1986), or more competitive models, like Elevator Pitch (Rusko et al., 2016), can be specially interesting in order to generate some degree of cognitive conflict, pushing the presentation of fresh ideas and the debate amongst the students.

This experience also deals with the generation of a virtual learning environment, Together Business School, stemming from the original one but including also alumni and management professionals. Social media have proved to be adequate channels to break both geographic and temporal communication barriers (Kaplan & Haenlein, 2010), being a bunch of tools with a nearly unlimited potential to put people in touch. Digital platforms have several advantages, potentially helping to improve the work-life balance and reducing the environmental impact of many activities (Saura, Ribeiro-Soriano and Zegarra-Saldaña, 2022), as well as boosting open innovation (Saura, Palacios-Marqués and Ribeiro-Soriano, 2022).

THE USE OF CASE STUDIES IN TBS

The Subject of Strategic Management in The Subject of Strategic Management at Rey Juan Carlos University

Strategic Management can be considered one of the main subjects included in the Degree in Business Management at the University where the authors work as Professors, due to the number of academic credits (12, which means 120 hours, divided into two different parts, Strategic Management I and Strategic Management II), its core character and its natural relationship with the main contents, and even the name, of the Degree. It is placed in the third year (first and second term), as long as it requires a previous background of both instrumental subjects and basic knowledge. The subject deals with the main strategic decisions that managers face, starting from the strategic analysis and getting through strategic formulation and implementation. Most of the recipes of the subject, and the majority of the theoretical developments, stem from real life.

In the academic year 2017/2018, the subject was taught to 28 different groups, combining four different campuses (A, B, C and D), two modalities (face to face and on-line), two languages (Spanish and English) and the aforementioned division between Strategic Management I and II. As all the students of the subject were expected to achieve a similar knowledge regardless these aspects, some coordination mechanisms had been developed:

- **The teaching guide** is a common document that must be used by all the groups. It states many aspects of the subject, including its goals, its contents, the evaluation methodology, the references that must be used...
- **The coordinator**, one of the most experienced Professors, who is in charge of coordinating the different Professors, helping them to solve the potential problems that may arise.
- **At least two coordination meetings per year**, where common problems are analysed, and Professors are invited to present their experiences and insights about the development of the subject.
- **Additional resources**, such as case studies, examples, short stories and a collection of slides, which are available to all the Professors who teach the subject.

The evaluation of the students is divided into three different parts, as specified in Table 1. Each of the parts has to be passed in order to get over the entire subject.

Table 1. Evaluation methodology of Strategic Management

Activities	% of Final Marks	Minimum Marks
Multiple choice theoretical questions	30%	1.5 out of 3 points
Practical part: individual assignments, groups assignments, case study discussions and/or practical exam	30%	1.5 out of 3 points
Individual theoretical exam	40%	2 out of 4 points

Source: Teaching guide of the subject (2017)

In the academic year 2017/2018 there were two main ways to take the subject, called CONTINUOUS ASESSMENT and NON-CONTINUOUS ASESSMENT, amongst which students had to choose at the beginning of each term. In the CONTINUOUS ASESSMENT path, both the multiple-choice tests and the practical activities take place along the term, while there is a date for the individual theoretical exam at the end of the term. In the NON-CONTINUOUS ASESSMENT mode, especially intended for students who cannot attend classes regularly, the three parts of the evaluation take place in the final exam.

Each professor has some flexibility to adapt the methodology to the specific needs of the different groups. For instance, the number of students included in each of them varied from less than 10, in the smallest group, to more than 150 in some of them. This requires different approaches to deal with the practical part, involving combinations of individual and group assignments, and specific ways to deal with the case studies.

Some of the professors, who worked with especially large groups, realized that there was a malfunctioning of the methodology when it came to case study discussions. A huge number of students of each group, who had chosen CONTINUOUS ASESSMENT, had to prepare each discussion, but the individual probability of participating in a debate was close to zero, due to the limited time: in a session of 120 minutes, it is impossible to let more than 100 students take part in any kind of discussion. So, opportunistic free-riding behaviours of some students lived together with the frustration of some others who wanted to, but couldn't, get a deeper knowledge of, and even participate in, real-life management decisions.

A first solution to that situation consisted of dividing the class into small work groups to prepare and discuss the case studies. Though it could solve part of the drawbacks, giving a longer average time to each of the groups to express and discuss their opinions, it did not help to solve the potential problems of free riding: some of the students did not participate in class discussions, hiding behind other members of the group, so it was not easy, or even possible, to know if they had even read the text of the case studies.

The teaching materials created another difficulty. The case studies came from a collection shared by all the professors which is updated each 3/4 years. This gives birth to two different problems. Firstly, some of the case studies got obsolete the very first year after they were published, even if new info was added to them, as the matter of discussion (e.g., the international expansion of a company) had frequently finished in real life. Also, after a case study had been discussed in a class, the comments and solutions quickly spread through social media, so many students never analysed the story, but just learnt and repeated the conclusions that had been reached in previous classes, which was far from being the goal of case study discussion.

In the summer coordination meeting of that academic year, a professor expressed the need to adapt the evaluation methodology in the case of the large groups, where the expectations of the majority of the students weren't being satisfied. So, either the teaching methodology or the evaluation, and maybe both, had to be changed in order to improve the learning experience of the students. Nevertheless, if a new model was going to be created, it had to fulfil some conditions:

- **It had to be universal and voluntary**, offered to all the students included in a group, so each one could choose between the different options available, and so different needs could be met at the same time.
- **It had to follow the teaching guide.** This meant that it had to be a specific kind of CONTINUOUS ASESSMENT, including the partial multiple-choice tests, where the practical part would consist of case study discussions.
- **It couldn't be massive,** so every student could personally participate.
- **Both the materials and the dynamics of the group had to prevent from the use of previously established solutions**. If possible, the use of fresh materials would be the best option.

As the solution had some aspects in common with a case study discussion in business schools, the professors who decided to get into this experience called it Business School mode.

The Business School Mode Inside the Class

Rules and Settings

At the beginning of the academic year 2018/2019, two groups of students, which clearly outnumbered the hundred, were offered three different ways to take the subject. The evaluation of the theoretical part of the subject was not different from previous years. As for the practical part, three different options, detailed in Table 2, were offered.

Table 2. Evaluation methods offered since 2018/2019

Practical Part	Date	Specifications
Non-continuous assessment	Final exam	1 to 3 questions about a case study proposed, with limited time and length
Continuous assessment	The specific rules of each assignment are published two weeks before the deadline	The student has to send the professor four individual assignments, prepared according both to the GENERIC RULES (for all the assignments) and the SPECIFIC RULES (for each one of them)
Business School	The set-up of each case study is published two days before its discussion	Public discussion of five case studies

Source: Authors

Some additional specifications, published at the beginning of the term, completed the description of the Business School Mode:

- **It was available for any student,** though it required a regular attendance to the classes and a continuous work on the subject, including the attendance to the BUSINESS SCHOOL CASE STUDY DISCUSSIONS, set on a sessions' schedule which was published at the beginning of the term along with the rules. The students who chose this evaluation method could only miss only one of the case study discussions, due to an acceptable reason.
- **The case studies would be brand new** and would be published at Aula Virtual just three days before their discussion. So, the students were not expected to handle complete solutions, but to search for information that would enable them to take part in the debate.
- **Free-riding would not be admitted:** In case a student would not participate adequately in the discussions, s/he could be expelled from the Business School Mode, becoming a NON-CONTINUOUS ASESSMENT student, losing all the marks achieved before in previous cases and/or partial multiple-choice tests.

The Pilot Experience

Two groups of students, taught in English and Spanish respectively, participated in the pilot experience, which took place in the academic year 2018/2019.

The group taught in English was composed by 156 people, most of them being exchange students coming from foreign universities. This circumstance resulted in an unfrequently high percentage of choice of the non-continuous assessment, selected by 69 students, a 44,2% of the class. The Business School Mode was chosen by 11 students, which meant a 7,1% of the group, respecting the condition of allowing personal discussions and fostering participation.

The group taught in Spanish was composed by 112 students. The division between continuous and not continuous evaluation was more balanced, with a majority of the students choosing the continuous assessment. The Business School mode was selected by 20 students, a 17,9% of the total, a group that could be easily controlled in a case study discussion.

The term took place between the 3rd of September and the 14th of December of 2018. The schedule of all the sessions was published before the start of the classes. As it had been established, the specific rules for the Business School case studies were published just two days before each discussion. The rules for the assignments of the Continuous Assessment mode were published two weeks in advance of the deadline of each one. For each of the case study discussions, the students were given a set-up, some references and a breakdown of the aspects that would be discussed. They were asked to look for additional information in order to be ready to debate about that facts. An example of these initial case studies is provided in Appendix 1.

The general dynamics of the discussion started with a first talk in small groups of 5-6 people randomly chosen, followed by a pooling of the ideas and conclusions reached. Brainstorming, devil's advocacy, elevator pitch and dialectic inquiry were used in the case study discussions to foster the generation of structured conflict.

Academic Results Achieved

In order to evaluate the results of this methodology, the professors compared the marks achieved in the four partial multiple-choice tests by the students who chose the Business School mode with those who took the traditional continuous assessment, as multiple-choice tests are normally considered a purely objective way to measure the performance of the students. The results of the group that studied in English are shown in table 3.

Two aspects can be remarked. Firstly, as the average marks show, business school students outperformed by more than 1 point above 10 their colleagues who took traditional continuous assessment. Though there could be different origins of this difference, they can be summed up in two main causes: either the students who chose case-study discussion were more interested in the subject beforehand, and so they studied harder; or the methodology generated a higher degree of engagement in the subject to be able to discuss the case studies.

Table 3. Average marks achieved by the students in multiple choice tests. English group

Evaluation	Test #1	Test #2	Test #3	Test #4	Average
Continuous	5,69	7,02	7,41	9,17	6,32
Business School	5,75	8,38	8,25	9,00	7,45

Source: Authors

A deeper look at the data can drop additional insights. The first test, which shows the smallest difference between the two groups (0,06 points), took place before any of the case studies had been discussed. From then on, though the average marks of both groups increased clearly, the gap between Business School students and Continuous Assessment ones enlarged to 1,36 points (Test #2) and 0,84 points (Test#3). Carrying out an average difference test, there is a statistically significant difference just for Test #2.

Nevertheless, the average marks of Business School students in Test#4 were 0,17 points lower than their colleagues'. Table 4, which includes the number of students who took each exam, can help to explain this apparent contradiction. The evaluation system establishes that a student who fails two partial multiple-choice tests must face a global multiple-choice retake in the final exam, leaving the partial ones. As the table shows, just one of the Business School students failed or missed more than one partial test

(9,1%), while 20 students (30,3%) under continuous assessment did. So, the group of continuous assessment finally equalled the average marks of the business school students, but it happened after a hard self-selection process along which one third of the students were sent to a global multiple-choice retake.

Table 4. Number of students who took each partial test. English group

Evaluation	Test #1	Test #2	Test #3	Test #4
Continuous	66	58	48	46
Business School	11	10	7	10

Source: Authors

The data about the group taught in Spanish lead to similar conclusions. In this case, the initial difference in favour of the Continuous Assessment students in tests #1 and #2 is clearly reverted in Test#3: probably the methodology helped the students to understand the subject and/or encouraged them to give their best. In fact, carrying out an average difference test, the differences are only statistically significant for Test #3.

Table 5. Average marks achieved by the students in multiple-choice tests. Spanish group

Evaluation	Test #1	Test #2	Test #3	Test #4	Average
Continuous	5,74	6,36	6,86	8,65	6,48
Business School	5,47	6,06	8,21	8,58	6,87

Source: Authors

Finally, accounting for the early failure ratio, reflected in table 6, it was clearly lower in the case of Business School students (15%) than in the Continuous Assessment ones (29,9%).

Table 6. Number of students who took each partial test. Spanish group

Evaluation	Test #1	Test #2	Test #3	Test #4
Continuous	74	77	70	61
Business School	19	20	18	18

Source: Authors

Additional Qualitative Feedback

To get some additional feedback, two focus groups (one in each language) were conducted amongst the students after they were given their final marks of the subject. All the Business School students of both groups were invited to take part in them, and in both cases six of them were selected randomly amongst the volunteers. Some of the ideas expressed were the following:

- **The students were unanimously satisfied with the methodology:** They consider they have achieved a deeper theoretical knowledge and learnt practical skills.
- **The role of the professor is critical** to foster the debate and control possible free riding attitudes. Nevertheless, the professor needs to keep a balance between helping the students and explaining the solution of the case study.
- **The higher the number of students included in the Business School Mode, the more difficult to achieve the goals:** In case many students decided to choose it, they should be divided into smaller sub-classes to enable an adequate discussion.

Together Business School: Taking the Experience Out of the Classroom

One of the purposes of the Business School mode was increasing the interest of the students in a subject, Strategic Management, which is a natural part of the core of the Degree. The students that participated in the focus groups unanimously agreed that after discussing case studies, they were more concerned by the news related with management. More than half of the students that joined the Business School in the academic year 2018/2019 asked their professors of Business Management to be their tutors in their End of Degree Theses. Also, some Exchange students got in touch with the professors along the second term, stating that they would like to take part in the new discussions if there was a chance to do so.

It was not possible to satisfy this demand in a traditional way. Firstly, the schedule of the classes made any kind of presential or virtual attendance incompatible with taking other subjects or working in an internship or a job. Also, the participation in the debates of people that were not part of the subject could undermine the role of the current students. Finally, the virtual campus of the University, as it is conceived, is not an ideal space to gather students with alumni and professionals.

Social media could be an adequate meeting point to generate a permanent debate about Strategic Management, enabling the contact between current students, alumni and management professionals. Amongst the different options, probably LinkedIn could be the most adequate vehicle, due to its professional orientation.

Together Business School (TBS), a LinkedIn group oriented to the discussion of business management cases, was created in April of 2019, with the publication of an initial case study, Leadership Stories (Annex 2), which had been previously discussed in the development of Strategic Management II.

Since then, the activity of the group has been intense, currently gathering 94 members. Some of the events that have taken place are the following:

- **Discussion of nine case studies in English,** as well as two additional ones in Spanish.
- **A Summer School Edition,** including short stories to be discussed presented in ad hoc videos. One of the Summer School case studies was proposed by a former top executive of a Silicon Valley company, which increased the attractiveness and participation of the members.
- **The courtyard**, a section created to discuss stories not directly related with Strategic Management that caught the attention of some participants (e.g., the possible creation of Libra by Facebook).
- **Stay Home Business School,** an edition of this experience which took place along the lockdown derived from the pandemic of COVID-19.

CONCLUSION

Theoretical Implications for Education

The role of the professor as the only responsible for knowledge transmission in higher education has been frequently criticized, as it does not foster an apprenticeship oriented to the acquisition of competencies by the students. So, innovative teaching tools and techniques, such as case-based learning, are gaining weight and importance in the programs and plans of most of the Faculties integrated in the EHEA.

The majority of the literature dealing with the use of case-based learning in different educational levels reaches very positive conclusions, confirming its favourable impact in both the acquisition of knowledge and the development of useful competencies. Nevertheless, some facts can complicate the implementation of this tool. Large groups, including more than one hundred students, have some positive traits, as they increase the variety of backgrounds and points of view: size and diversity can help to create functional conflict, based on ideas and solutions. Meanwhile, these groups mean a major challenge when trying to manage a class. Both the number of students and the heterogeneity in goals and behaviours can also be at the origin of dysfunctional conflict, related with personal matters.

The experience explained in this chapter shows that case-based learning can also be used in environments and conditions that are, originally, far from being ideal. The creation of what has been called *Business School mode* has given the students an additional alternative, so that each one can, based on his/her own goals and experience, choose the more precise methodological path to fulfil her/his personal needs. Giving the students the chance to choose between different alternatives reinforces the importance of putting them in the centre of their own learning experience.

The analysis of the academic results and the opinions expressed by the students shows how Business School mode has satisfied the expectations of a group of students without reducing the attention paid to the rest of the class. The evolution of the differences in performance between the cohorts confirms the evidence reached by the previous literature: the methodology, and not just the selection, creates a difference along the time, improving the engagement of the students and, therefore, their performance in the subject.

So, two main theoretical consequences can be reached from this study. Firstly, as the previous literature had stated, comparing similar cohorts of students, case-based methodology leads to a better average academic performance. And secondly, allowing the students to decide their own methodological path can reinforce the usefulness of this tool, as each person knows better the abilities and resources s/he has.

Practical Implications for Education

This experience also has some practical implications. Both the original formulation of the Business School mode and TBS arose from difficulties. The huge number of students, and the intention to gather different profiles (students, alumni, professionals) challenged the traditional use of case-based learning, within an entire group of students and inside the walls of a classroom. Probably, flexibility has been the critical asset to develop specific solutions for these situations.

Business School mode considered the possibility of letting the students choose a methodology, which increased both their responsibility and involvement in their own learning experience. The students were offered a flexible approach, where they could decide their educational path based on their own self-knowledge, resulting in a better performance.

TBS profited from the potential of Information and Communications Technologies, in this specific case Social Media, to build a unique learning experience, demanded by the students but profited by different profiles of people. The lessons learned from the development of TBS have been very useful for the Professors who got involved in its development when the mobility restrictions derived from COVID-19 suddenly and dramatically changed the panorama of higher education, moving it initially to fully remote learning, and currently to the use of blended methodologies. Flexibility has been, again, the key to achieve a quick adaptation to this new environment.

A new relevant challenge could be related with the diffusion of what has been learnt along this experience. The insights and ontologies described by Fidalgo-Blanco, Sein-Echaluce and García-Peñalvo (2014) about the transformation of specific experiences into organisational knowledge can be especially helpful to reach this goal.

Limitations

Though the initial results were positive and interesting, the experience of both the Business School mode and Together Business School has not been long yet. So, there is still a need to pay attention to some issues that might create problems. As the students stressed in the focus groups, the role of the professor is critical, not allowing free riding behaviours that could complicate the achievement of the goals proposed and not providing the students with solutions, but just hints and resources to help them reach personally to that solutions, which would be management decisions in real life.

The experience analysed can be considered a pilot program. It must be the accumulation of years and data which confirms the results achieved in this first year of use. Until this moment, only academic results have been analysed, not considering some other performance measures that could have resulted very interesting, especially those related with the acquisition of individual and group competencies and abilities.

Future Practices

Currently, the professors who integrate this teaching innovation working group are getting more involved in the use of this methodology, starting to analyse which are the reasons why the students decide to choose a specific methodological path, as well as the degree of achievement of competencies and abilities, specially focusing on those related with groupwork.

TBS, in turn, has turned into a solid and stable discussion group about Strategic Management, a critical subject in the degree, but also a relevant topic in the professional life of anyone working as a manager. TBS has created a space for networking, where current students meet alumni and managers, receiving a vision that completes their training in the classrooms. Enlarging the experience along the years will generate additional data that can help to profit from all the potential opportunities that it can generate.

This research received no specific grant from any funding agency in the public, commercial, or not-for-profit sectors.

REFERENCES

Alani, F. (2020). Development of Case-Based Learning (CBL) in Engineering Technology Education. *International Journal of Engineering Education, 36*(3), 896–900.

Amason, A. C. (1996). Distinguishing the effects of functional and dysfunctional conflict on strategic decision making: Resolving a paradox for top management teams. *Academy of Management Journal, 39*(1), 123–148.

Amason, A. C., Thompson, K. R., Hochwarter, W. A., & Harrison, A. W. (1995). Conflict: An important dimension in successful management teams. *Organizational Dynamics, 24*(2), 20–35. doi:10.1016/0090-2616(95)90069-1

Behrman, J. N., & Levin, R. I. (1984). Are business schools doing their job. *Harvard Business Review, 62*(1), 140.

Bonney, K. M. (2015). Case study teaching method improves student performance and perceptions of learning gains. *Journal of Microbiology & Biology Education, 16*(1), 21–28. doi:10.1128/jmbe.v16i1.846 PMID:25949753

Carlson, J. A., & Schodt, D. W. (1995). Beyond the lecture: Case teaching and the learning of economic theory. *The Journal of Economic Education, 26*(1), 17–28. doi:10.1080/00220485.1995.10844853

Castaño-Perea, E., Fernández, A. B., & Castañeda, E. A. (2012). Competencias para la tutoría: experiencia de formación con profesores universitarios [Competencies for tutorials: training experience with university professors]. *REDU. Revista de Docencia Universitaria, 10*(2), 193–210. doi:10.4995/redu.2012.6103

Erskine, J. A., Leenders, M. R., & Mauffette-Leenders, L. A. (2018). *Teaching with cases* (2nd ed.). Ivey Publishing.

Fidalgo-Blanco, Á., Sein-Echaluce, M. L., & García-Peñalvo, F. J. (2014). Knowledge spirals in higher education teaching innovation. *International Journal of Knowledge Management, 10*(4), 16–37. doi:10.4018/ijkm.2014100102

Flynn, A. E., & Klein, J. D. (2001). The influence of discussion groups in a case-based learning environment. *Educational Technology Research and Development, 49*(3), 71–86. doi:10.1007/BF02504916

Gil-Flores, J. (2012). La evaluación del aprendizaje en la universidad según la experiencia de los estudiantes [The evaluation of the learning process in the University based on the experience of the students]. *Estudios sobre educación, 22*, 133-153.

Glasser, W. (1998). *Choice Theory*. Harper Collins.

Guardia, J. J., Del Olmo, J. L., Roa, I., & Berlanga, V. (2019). Innovation in the teaching-learning process: The case of Kahoot! *On the Horizon, 27*(1), 35–45. doi:10.1108/OTH-11-2018-0035

Jehn, K. A. (1994). Enhancing effectiveness: An investigation of advantages and disadvantages of value-based intragroup conflict. *International Journal of Conflict Management, 5*(3), 223–238. doi:10.1108/eb022744

Jehn, K. A., Chadwick, C., & Thatcher, S. M. (1997). To agree or not to agree: The effects of value congruence, individual demographic dissimilarity, and conflict on workgroup outcomes. *International Journal of Conflict Management*, *8*(4), 287–305. doi:10.1108/eb022799

Kaplan, A. M., & Haenlein, M. (2010). Users of the world, unite! The challenges and opportunities of Social Media. *Business Horizons*, *53*(1), 59–68. doi:10.1016/j.bushor.2009.09.003

Katz, R. L. (1974). Skills of an effective administrator. *Harvard Business Review*, *52*(5), 90–102.

Koontz, H., & Weihrich, H. (1994). *Administración. Una perspectiva Global* [Administration. A Global perspective]. McGraw Hill.

López-Navas, C. (2014). Educación superior y TIC: conceptos y tendencias de cambio/Higher education and ITC: concepts and changing trends. *Historia y Comunicación Social*, *19*, 227–239.

Marín García, J. (2018). Focos de investigación sobre aprendizaje universitario en el área de dirección de operaciones [Research focus about university learning in the area of operations management]. In *IN-RED 2018. IV Congreso Nacional de Innovación Educativa y Docencia en Red* [IN-RED 2018. IV National Coference on Teaching innovation and On-line Teaching] (pp. 922-932). Universitat Politècnica de València.

Mintzberg, H. (1990). The manager's job: Folklore and fact. *Harvard Business Review*, *68*(2), 163–176.

Mintzberg, H., Raisinghani, D., & Theoret, A. (1976). The structure of "unstructured" decision processes. *Administrative Science Quarterly*, *21*(2), 246–275. doi:10.2307/2392045

Pelled, L. H. (1996). Demographic diversity, conflict, and work group outcomes: An intervening process theory. *Organization Science*, *7*(6), 615–631. doi:10.1287/orsc.7.6.615

Pelled, L. H., Eisenhardt, K. M., & Xin, K. R. (1999). Exploring the black box: An analysis of work group diversity, conflict and performance. *Administrative Science Quarterly*, *44*(1), 1–28. doi:10.2307/2667029

Rusko, R., Härkönen, K., & Liukkonen, S. (2016). Coopetition at elevator pitch events? A case study of micro-activities at a business innovation event. *Journal of Innovation Management*, *4*(3), 79–100. doi:10.24840/2183-0606_004.003_0007

Saura, J. R., Palacios-Marqués, D., & Ribeiro-Soriano, D. (2022). Exploring the boundaries of open innovation: Evidence from social media mining. *Technovation*, 102447. doi:10.1016/j.technovation.2021.102447

Saura, J. R., Ribeiro-Soriano, D., & Saldaña, P. Z. (2022). Exploring the challenges of remote work on Twitter users' sentiments: From digital technology development to a post-pandemic era. *Journal of Business Research*, *142*, 242–254. doi:10.1016/j.jbusres.2021.12.052

Schweiger, D. M., Sandberg, W. R., & Ragan, J. W. (1986). Group approaches for improving strategic decision making: A comparative analysis of dialectical inquiry, devil's advocacy, and consensus. *Academy of Management Journal*, *29*(1), 51–71.

Seshan, V., Matua, G. A., Raghavan, D., Arulappan, J., Al Hashmi, I., Roach, E. J., Sunderraj, S. E., & Prince, E. J. (2021). Case Study Analysis as an Effective Teaching Strategy: Perceptions of Undergraduate Nursing Students From a Middle Eastern Country. *SAGE Open Nursing*, *7*, 23779608211059265. doi:10.1177/23779608211059265 PMID:34869864

Song, B. L., Lee, K. L., Liew, C. Y., Ho, R. C., & Lin, W. L. (2022, April 26). Business students' perspectives on case method coaching for problem-based learning impacts on student engagement and learning performance in higher education. *Education + Training*, *64*(3), 416–432. doi:10.1108/ET-03-2021-0106

Swartz, R. J., Costa, A. L., Beyer, B. K., Reagan, R., & Kallick, B. (2010). *Thinking-Based Learning: Promoting Quality Student Achievement in the 21st Century*. Teachers College Press.

Tidd, S. T., McIntyre, H. H., & Friedman, R. A. (2004). The importance of role ambiguity and trust in conflict perception: Unpacking the task conflict to relationship conflict linkage. *International Journal of Conflict Management*, *15*(4), 364–380. doi:10.1108/eb022918

Tillman, B. A. (1995). Reflections on case method teaching. *Action in Teacher Education*, *17*(1), 1–8. doi:10.1080/01626620.1995.10463225

Wang, A. I. (2015). The wear out effect of a game-based student response system. *Computers & Education*, *82*, 217–227. doi:10.1016/j.compedu.2014.11.004

Wilson, D. C., Butler, R. J., Cray, D., Hickson, D. J., & Mallory, G. R. (1986). Breaking the bounds of organization in strategic decision making. *Human Relations*, *39*(4), 309–331. doi:10.1177/001872678603900402

KEY TERMS AND DEFINITIONS

Brainstorming: A technique to drop new ideas about a matter, where the participants propose briefly their suggestions which are discussed afterwards.

Case Study: A recreation, or a partial description, of a real-life professional situation, that the students have to evaluate, analyse, and try to solve.

Competencies: Technical or generic abilities that a person (student) can acquire, which will enable that person to develop many possible tasks and jobs.

Conflict: A divergence in the goals, needs, ideas or means between different people.

Devil's Advocacy: A technique which tries to improve the ability to defend a position, where a devil's advocate sets different objections to that position or idea.

EHEA: The European Higher Education Area is an initiative which tries to create a series of commitments and agreements between different countries in order to generate some degree of homogeneity between their Educational Systems.

Elevator Pitch: A technique that gives a person or a group a very short time, usually 30 seconds, in order to present and summarize ideas about a business project.

Functional Conflict: It is a kind of conflict that may have positive effects when facing a decision, increasing the number and quality of the alternatives drawn and facilitating the decision-making process.

Strategic Management: An academic subject that deals with some of the main decisions of a firm, mainly those ones related with their corporate (range of activities) and competitive (achieving an advantage from rivals) levels

Teaching Innovation: It includes designing and putting into practice tools and techniques different from traditional one-directional lectures, with the goal of putting the student in the centre of the learning process.

ENDNOTE

1 The name of the University is omitted for the purpose of anonymity.

APPENDIX A

Business School. Case 4. Frozen

In 2009, Pedro Espinosa, heir of a lineage of ice cream makers, decided to start producing frozen ice cream, after tasting it for the first time in the United States. So, he opened the first establishment of his firm in Dénia (Alicante). Soon the business rocketed sky high in spite of working in a city with a strong competence in the ice cream industry. In just one year, Llao Llao opened its first franchise. Currently the firm is present in more than thirty countries, through more than 200 establishments.

In spite of its huge success, some clouds have appeared in the horizon of the company. Both the national franchisees, who created in 2013 an association in order to defend their common interests, and the international ones have started to drop on the table some complains and have even presented some legal suits.

Bearing in mind the information available in the following links, as well as what can be found at the media and industry reports, the students have to get ready to debate the following aspects:

1. Evaluate the suitability of creating a franchise network for the national expansion of the firm, considering its advantages and disadvantages in the specific case of this firm
2. Evaluate the suitability of creating a franchise network for the international expansion of the firm, considering its pros and cons, as well as the alternative options available for the company
3. Propose solutions to the conflicts that have arisen between the franchiser and the franchisees

Some links related with the case:

https://www.muypymes.com/2018/10/24/una-historia-de-exito-llaollao
https://www.elespanol.com/economia/empresas/20170602/220728425_0.html
https://elpais.com/economia/2015/09/03/actualidad/1441302735_794142.html
https://www.elconfidencial.com/consumo/2015-12-13/el-yogur-helado-que-nacio-en-denia-fue-primero-llao-llao-o-smooy_1114086/
https://www.elconfidencial.com/empresas/2016-09-24/llaollao-pedro-espinosa-yogurt-helado-franquicias-demanda_1257921/

APPENDIX B

Together Business School, Case Study #1. Leadership Stories

Roald Amundsen had everything to be the first man to step the North Pole. Nansen, the most successful Arctic explorer until that moment, had let him use the mythic Fram, a perfect ship to sail across the dangerous ice. He had selected the perfect crew, which fit his needs like a glove, with mushers and man with expertise in Nordic ski. His years with the Inuit and his own training in Winter sports should be the key to his success… but when his expedition was about to be ready, the Americans Cook and Peary claimed separately to have reached the North Pole. Thousands of Norwegian Crowns would have been just wasted… or maybe not.

Robert Falcon Scott got really mad with his compatriot Ernest Shackleton when he wanted to use the Antarctic area of McMurdo in order to reach the South Pole. In fact, as Wilson stated, the whole Ross Sea should be considered an exclusive working area for Scott and his crew, something that Schackleton tried to respect, but failed, due to the circumstances. Nevertheless, the failure of his rival in his attempt to reach the 90º latitude point renewed Scott's determination to claim personally the glory of reaching the South Pole for the British Empire. In October of 1910, a cable from Roald Amundsen let him know that what was initially intended as a scientific adventure had become a race... and Scott was not the kind of a loser.

Ernest Shackleton was facing difficulties. In fact, he had never surrendered easily. In Nimrod expedition, he had to turn back home when he was just 180 kms away from the South Pole, saving the life of all his crew, including his right-hand man Frank Wild. Now, after both Amundsen and the sorely missed Scott had reached the South Pole, he had a new ambition: crossing the Antarctic. The expedition had very adequate material and human means, but the Antarctic is an inhospitable place and his ship, the Endurance, got trapped in the ice the 19th of January of 1915. That very day, he knew the ship was history, as it was going to be smashed into pieces by the ice. Once more, adversity was present in his expedition.

It couldn't be. It had no sense. He, Mr. Apple, **Steve Jobs**, had been fired by the firm he founded. The Board of Directors had backed John Sculley, who entered the Company just two years before, in 1983. Offended by the situation, Jobs decided to sell all the shares of the firm but one and start new projects. Moretheless, he knew the reasons why Apple was headed for disaster in a not so far future. And, who knows, maybe one day they would knock his door again claiming for a solution.

Satya Nadella held a hot potato in his hands. A burning hot one. That 27th of March of 2014, when he was about to make his first public appearance as the CEO of Microsoft, succeeding the popular Steve Ballmer, the company had many problems to solve. One of the latest corporate decisions, buying Nokia, had been taken against the criterium of Nadella, who did not agree the need of a third OS for smartphones. Now, they probably were dealing with a bit more than they could chew. But Nadella had new plans and ideas in order to generate additional value for the company. Competing? Maybe… just that?

It was easy to say **Mark Zuckerberg** was a lucky guy. Facebook, which started as a brilliant idea, had turned into a gold mine, and its creator had become one of the wealthiest and most relevant people in the world. This might be the reason why even some media criticized severely the purchase of WhatsApp made by Facebook in 2014. Even some media suggested a funny explanation for the purchase of WhatsApp. Zuckerberg neither agreed nor denied, but published a letter explaining this was part of a plan.

We are intended to discuss the following questions

1. Main capabilities of these leaders, which were especially relevant in order to face the main difficulties along their way and/or which drove them to success
2. How these leaders, both Antarctic explorers and businessmen, performed their organizational tasks
3. Looking for the perfect leader: what were the leaders studied missing? Which other strengths could they have had?

Chapter 15
"Case" as "Text" in the Class:
Plethora of Pedagogical and Structural Nuances

D. Radhakrishnan Nair
Christ University, India

Justin Joy
Christ University, India

ABSTRACT

The research work undertakes to examine "case," "case study," and "case pedagogy." As the first step, the chapter explores the feel of the Case. This leads to a further investigation and lets out certain malfunctions: gross lapses, loopholes, casualties, and shortcomings. Case then has been subjected to further investigations. Keeping intact the primary concerns of case scan and its explications thereupon, the study takes up the interpretations and intricacies involved in understanding the case. These expose the puzzles involved in the pedagogical exercises in educational institutions. The research with astute expedience does the operation with logical reasoning. The work leads to proper remedial measures and redefines case and case grasp. Using theory of ontology, case is subjected to closer examination. Theory of epistemology further deepens research pursuits to unravel a few more case mysteries. From these, the authors evolve a few keys and tips to study case more effectively. All help readers build up exemplary teaching methods and effective learning concepts.

INTRODUCTION

Prolegomena: Teaching Innovation in Education

Innovation in education is about new technology used in pedagogy, but it is even more than that. It's about solving a real problem in a fresh, better way to improve and promote the quality of learning. Innovation in education takes place in many forms. Programs, services, processes, products, and partnerships can all enhance education outcomes in innovative ways (Fidalgo-Blanco, Sein-Echaluce, & García-Peñalvo,

DOI: 10.4018/978-1-6684-4441-2.ch015

Copyright © 2022, IGI Global. Copying or distributing in print or electronic forms without written permission of IGI Global is prohibited.

2014). Many innovators are already at work in classrooms and communities. It is in this context that UNICEF collaborates with partners to identify, incubate, and scale promising innovations that help fulfill everyone's right to learn (UNICEF, 2019). Teaching innovation alone can improve the standard of every stage of formal education from kindergarten. As the world has been progressing, there has been a continuum in educational innovation (Saura, Ribeiro-Soriano, & Iturricha-Ferná, 2022), though the process has always been there, but has been snail-paced till date. But the present time teeming with technological and cybernetic growth demands fast changes. The child in the new ambience is much ahead of the child in the past in acquiring knowledge. The student in a school maintains a higher ampere in receiving knowledge. College atmosphere facilitates students to be better than ever in knowledge building. Research strives at reaching higher levels than ever before. Communication skills development now has reached high peaks. Under these congenial conditions, a faster innovation is absolutely mandatory. The topic Innovation in education, therefore, cannot be limited to only any single special level of education. That is why we propose a thorough examination of education system.

Asynchronous Online Teaching

Today the new pandemic conditions have created many changes in education all over. One of them is online teaching. In asynchronous teaching online, materials are posted online, and learners work through them in their own time. They communicate with one another and with the teacher via discussion boards or forums, or even by email. Good asynchronous teaching includes a variety of media, including audio and video clips. With an asynchronous mode of teaching, the learners can work at their own pace and at times of day convenient for them. The teacher may find that the pattern of their input is very different from the synchronous environment, with many shorter visits to the discussion boards or forums being more valuable to the learners than one single, longer session. There may still be deadlines for work to be submitted for feedback, and there may be a recommended schedule for students to follow so that they have some idea of what they should be doing and when. As we discover later in the week, a 'blended' approach can help teachers bring together the advantages of synchronous and asynchronous teaching and online and face-to-face teaching into a single experience.

Importance of Collaboration

Collaboration between students on one side and between students and teachers is an important factor in both synchronous and asynchronous online teaching, helping to create a sense of connection between all participants and building a sense of community and shared purpose. Collaboration in a synchronous environment is as good as face-to face-classroom. In the asynchronous environment, collaboration can be trickier. But it is still very important in reducing the sense of isolation learners may feel when working online. Discussions and group tasks can work just as well asynchronously as synchronously. Indeed, because of the lack of time constraints, learners can spend time composing a quality response when contributing to an asynchronous online discussion. Digital programs and videos well responded with prompt feedback demand teaching innovation.

Key Concepts

The following are the key concepts discussed in innovation in education (Saura, Palacios-Marqués, & Ribeiro-Soriano, 2022): education shall move from 'project education' to 'project based learning' education and shall teach concepts also, not mere facts. Education shall distinguish concepts from critical information. Education shall treat pedagogic skills as important as knowledge components. Education shall form teams to explore innovative possibilities in knowledge dissemination. Both teachers and students shall, in learning and teaching, use thinking and creativity tools.

Torching the Contents of the Research

We perceive a common process in pedagogical applications in case method. But, we conceive the concept of the case as wanting in essentialities in its function. We note with grave concern the common proverbial concern "the blind leading the blind" syndrome in the approach as the faculty in many educational institutions are not fully equipped to deal with this method in curriculum. The faculty are not trained to teach the way a case shall be handled. Proper pedagogy has not yet been developed for using case strategy. We work as faculty. We take classes. Proper sharing does not take place. One among the various approaches in teaching is case, where we share with all others. We say we prefer outcome-based learning. But we fail to deliver the goods. Neither the faculty nor the students prepare themselves for a proper case study. That leads us to discuss issues involved in case as pedagogy. We never leave or discard any study material as untouchable, inaccessible, unintelligible, and indigestible. The 'crystal clear' quality of the text is solicited. No text is simple. Our zero proximity wipes off the case and its distancing from us. It dilutes the coagulation. It adds to its visibility. It helps to discover or internalize everything concealed in the text. All these thoughts have steered us to think about case study in this present study.

Hypothesis: Nair's Hermeneutic Keys and Joy's Pedagogic Tips

Here, author Dr. Joy provides pedagogic tips to Dr. Nair's hermeneutic keys in "Education Innovation" (Nair, 2017). Using pedagogic tips, communication process in learning is made feasible and with hermeneutics generating a wide range of meanings and interpretations, good comprehension process is made easily possible. These mutual complementary strengthening factors help pedagogy wed hermeneutics into a perfect harmony. In addition, all these vindicate the work undertaken by a joint venture of two authors to take up this subject in this chapter. Dr. Nair thinks that a case study shall invite the student to understand the text from different angles and sources, and the text shall be known well with close look at the case. Case content is in language. The content can be interpreted using many linguistic and semantic explanations. These explanations need to be communicated to the students. For that, strategies in pedagogy are required. Dr. Joy's work in pedagogy is complementary to Dr. Nair's work in hermeneutical manifestations.

CASE: ONTOLOGICAL CONCERNS

Every case shall be properly grasped and learned. The process demands great insight and understanding. This part raises ontological questions. Readers need to know the contents of the case, such as their existence, being, becoming, and reality. It includes the questions of how entities are grouped into different basic categories and their answers.

Case and Ontological Perspectives

Ontological perspectives establish different categories to divide case that exists into in order to better understand those things and how they fit together in the broader world. In the process, the authors retrieve many hidden meanings and explanations from the case using the following yardsticks.

Ontological Perspectives: 'What' of the Case?

The readers shall ask: what, in truth, is a case? Where does it exist? Is it real life-like experience? Is it fact? Is it fiction? Is it a mixing up of fact and fiction? Is it a format in language only? Is case a description or a narration? How shall we substantiate its veracity? Will the person, perspective, and mode in narration influence the case? How far will the case bear faithfully the manifestation of what the case composer proposes? How far what the participating students can comprehend really matter in case study? Ontologically what do we mean by the 'what 'of the case? It is ultimately the subject matter. Initially, it is not fully disclosed at the very outset of the case. Slowly in a process of knowing the case and using as many readings using all possible means, modes, and methods we stir and stir and get the full meaning of what the case exposes. This is the difficult process the class will undertake with the participation of both the teacher and the student as the case may be.

Ontological Perspectives: 'Who' of the Case?

Ontologically what do you mean by the who of the case? The case has the involvement of several persons. These persons may be termed the persona of the case. Personas in the case are the characters in the narrative. As the case develops, owing to the development, the persona may be subjected to changes. Persona will influence the case and the case will influence the persona. Will the students get a real learning experience through a case?

Ontological Perspectives: 'Where' Does the Case Exist?

Where does the case exist? It has to find a place to occur. It has to indicate location. It will occupy space. Whether is it about real life-like experience, or is it fact, is it fiction, or is it a mixing up of fact and fiction? It shall be structured in language. Is it a format in language only? How shall we substantiate its veracity? How far will the case bear faithfully the manifestation of what the case composer proposes in the form of the location? The answers to all these questions provide us the ontological where of the case.

Ontological Perspectives: 'Why' of the Case?

What do we mean by the 'why' of the case? In the process of examining the case, we ask ourselves so many questions, and we struggle hard to elicit all possible ways and means to get all whys answered. The why will mainly relate to the content of the case? The whys will probe into a parallel rational relay of content links?

Ontological Perspectives: 'How' of the Case?

Ontologically what do you mean by the 'how' of the case? The how of the case depends on the way the narrative process proceeds? It also is about how the events proceed in the narrative. It depends mainly on the art of the narrator of the case.

Ontological Perspectives: 'When' of the Case?

The 'when 'of the case is a derivation from the text on the configuration of time employed in the case content. Time of the narrative used may give many permutations and combinations. Even an iota of variation in the temporal strategy, can upset meaning. Therefore in the elucidation of meaning, the temporal possibilities and probabilities can have several roles? It creates several levels of time: the time followed in the events and their trajectory, it can mean the time of enunciation, the time of their happening, and it can mean the time of case analysis.

Case on Platforms: Kindergarten

The word kindergarten (Frobel, 1899) was coined by Friedrich Froebel (1782-1852), an educator who believed in self-activity and hands-on learning for children with love for nature, science, and mathematics. He felt children needed to be nurtured and caringly tended to like plants and called it kindergarten. The occupations provided material such as clay, sand, paper, and string to build skills such as sculpting, lacing, weaving, and folding, and to stimulate imagination, creativity, and ingenuity. According to Froebel Web, Froebel's philosophy of education rested on four basic ideas: free self-expression, creativity, social participation and motor expression. As the first step, we examine the phrase 'case' study and how it fits in kindergarten education. Understanding the nature of communication process, we love to call the helping hand for a child in kindergarten, a nurse. The nurse (here, the person in a nursery school) does not teach but he/she in a kindergarten institution uses case method. Here the level of pedagogy relates to creating and whetting human skills of comprehension in the child's infancy. We say that the case in kindergarten suggests 'object/s' around the child. The child undergoes the process of perceiving things in a garden using senses to know how to learn through senses. The nurse facilitates ambience required for seeing and understanding objects or cases and this is kindergarten case study. The pedagogy used is nurse's bringing the child to cases (objects) around and sharing the experience together using language.

Case on Platforms: School

Now we can handle the second phase. In contrast to the earlier one explained, a teacher in a school takes the child to objects through either spoken or written means of communication. Here the pedagogy used in teaching in contemporary terminology, is applicable. These oral communication skills reinforced with demonstration skills will be used to make children learn. Demonstration skills comprise laboratory and library.

Case on Platforms: College

Further, faculty member in a college or university suggests to the student and helps the student how to know things and objects using wit and wisdom in addition to mere perception. Here pedagogy is related to and reinforced with research prop up. As a prime prior requirement of this approach to case study, we need to know our definition of some critically relevant words: class, case, text, module, experiment, and test. A case is meant a collection of arguments, facts, and reasons in support of or against something. A module is one of the separate parts of a course taught at a college or university. Cases are texts/stories (not fictional, but narratives) of how research projects were conducted. The collection of texts/stories provides a few tracks of case studies, showing the challenges and successes of doing research, written by the researchers themselves.

Case in Research

The researchers use case asking questions themselves and generating answers with different layers of meanings. They explain why they chose the methods they did choose, how they overcame problems in their research goal and what they might have done differently with hindsight: the realities of research that are missing from journal articles and textbooks. Cases are peer-reviewed and come with pedagogical tools, including learning objectives and discussions. They can be used as a teaching tool to demonstrate a particular method and how it is applied in their research, or as inspiration to students who are for their own research project.

EPISTEMOLOGICAL PERSPECTIVES

Case research requires the study of knowledge; theory of knowledge, asking such questions as "What is knowledge?", "How is knowledge acquired?", "What do people know?", "How do we know what we do not know?

Perspectives: Case Is Subject and Predicate

Case is, now, the subject and predicate of a class module in any type of class. It is the subject as it is the subject matter in the class. When case becomes the subject matter/text in the class, it is called the subject in the class. It is the predicate also as and when whatever happens in a class is about the subject and about nothing else. How far it is treated as the subject and how far it is treated as the predicate, is an issue that demands assiduous attention. For example, when the case is presented, as the faculty brings to the class copies of a case and distributes them among the participants of the class, the case is a pedagogic tool, and it communicates with the class. It is then the subject of the class. Students can read the case copy, the subject, the class module. The class takes it as the direct information. On the presentation of the case, it turns out to be another different pedagogic tool with the potential to generate many more interpretations. It communicates with the class as the interpretations about the subject (Genette G., 1976). It becomes the predicate of the class; the class takes it as the indirect information. The case is then something about the subject. It is spoken about the subject is predicate.

Perspectives: Case as Meta-text

Case may appear to be meta-text and we can relate the proposed meaning to it. Meta-textuality is a form of inter-textual discourse in which one text makes critical commentary on itself or another text. This concept is related to Gérard Genette's concept of trans-textuality (Genette G., 1997) (Genette G., 1983) in which a text changes or expands on the content of another text (Genette G., 1982).

Perspectives: Case as Simulacrum

Case will deem itself a simulacrum. A simulacrum means likeness, semblance and it is a representation or imitation of a person or thing. The word was first recorded in the English language in the late 16th century, used to describe a representation, such as a statue or a painting, especially of a god. By the late 19th century, it had gathered a secondary association of inferiority through an image without the substance or qualities of the original. Literary critic Fredric Jameson offers photorealism as an example of artistic simulacrum, in which a painting is created by copying a photograph that is itself a copy of the real thing. Here, in teaching, in many case study materials, a case is built on such a model.

Perspectives: Case Pandora's Box

Case, in some context, is taken as Pandora's Box. Pandora's box is an artefact in Greek mythology connected with the myth of Pandora in Hesiod's Works and Days. He reported that curiosity led her to open a container left in care of her husband, thus releasing physical and emotional curses upon mankind.

Perspectives: Case as Temporal Construct

Knowledge of the realms of theories of time will be essential for understanding a case. The event in a case presented in the class has to be evaluated on the strength of the spatial and temporal existence of the event as represented in the case.

Perspectives: Case a Spatial Construct

Knowledge of the theories of space will be essential for understanding a case. The event in a case presented in the class has to be evaluated on the strength of the spatial and temporal existence of the event as represented in the case.

Perspectives: Case as Chronotope

Chronotope is a term taken over by Mikhail Bakhtin 1920 to describe the manner in which literature represents time and space. In different kinds of writing there are differing chronotopes, by which changing historical conceptions of time and space are realised.

Narratological Suggestions

Some of the permutations in narratology we can use here. We can consider the case as narrative and we will examine the case using the possibilities in narratological analyses and interpretations. A narrative comprises fabula and suzhet. The narrator transforms fabula into suzhet. The narrative therefore can be understood only if the fabula is derived from suzhet which we get as text. The role of the narrator is also equally significant. Another permutation is that we can take case as puzzle and we may expose some of its valid interpretations. A reader takes all possible tracks to unravel the mystery of the fabula-suzhet configuration, which always remains a puzzle. Every reading will unravel possibilities that slowly lead to opening the puzzle to interpretations. These interpretations will help the reader to know the case/ text deeper.

PEDAGOGICAL CONCERNS

Case and Pedagogical Concerns: What Goes Wrong in Case Study?

The above note on case shows lapses, shortcomings, and casualties in treating case as text in a class in academic institutions and, of course, it denotes a few possible solutions to the issues raised. How do they creep in?, and how we can avoid them? We advocate case study on the strength of its merits and advantages. Our findings are epitomised here under. Today we have a new world where data, information, and knowledge are available aplenty from ready sources in abundance. What we need is the wisdom to utilise our intellectual strength to pick and choose the most appropriate. All our potentials in hermeneutics we will use to know the merit and profundity of each case with our students.

Case Scan and Pedagogy

Dr. Nair undertakes eclectic method in case scan: Case comprises information that can be stirred, unravelled, and released using hermeneutics like cultural analysis, reader response, psychological, feminist, new criticism, structuralism, post structuralism, semantics, linguistics, acoustics, symbolic interpretation and other similar combinations individually as well as in combinations. He uses case as the product of relationships, the relationships among force, matter, and motion. The hermeneutics employed here derives ideas, style, or tastes from a broad and diverse range of sources - wide-ranging, wide, broad, broad-ranging, broad-based, extensive, comprehensive, encyclopedic, general, universal, varied, diverse, diversified, catholic, liberal cross-disciplinary, interdisciplinary, multidisciplinary all-embracing, non-exclusive, inclusive, indiscriminate, many-sided, multifaceted, multifarious, heterogeneous, miscellaneous, assorted, selective, selecting, choosing, picking and choosing, discriminating, discerning, and critical thinking. Eclecticism considers that every work of art represents the combination of a variety of influences. The authors here abide by a style of their own. Their destination is an ideal commonwealth of hermeneutics where study leads to interpretations using tools of their choice and tracks are their choice, and the results are the natural products of these tools and tracks.

Dr. Joy, having noted all these, examines mechanics in pedagogy and application of the mechanics of pedagogy. He conceives eclecticism as a conceptual approach that does not hold rigidly to a single paradigm or set of assumptions but instead relies multiple theories, styles, or ideas to gain complementary insights into a subject, or applies different theories in particular cases. Eclectic processes can sometimes seem inelegant, lacking in simplicity, and eclectics are sometimes criticized for lack of consistency in their thinking. It is, however, common in many fields of study. Here the ultimate goal is to generate meanings and senses. But there is no rigidity followed in the application of a particular theory for all applications alike. Dr. Joy opines that one can pick and choose from among the abundance of opportunities to do so. This case scan and pedagogy is visually demonstrated in Figure 1.

Figure 1. Hermeneutics and pedagogic tips
(Proposed by Authors)

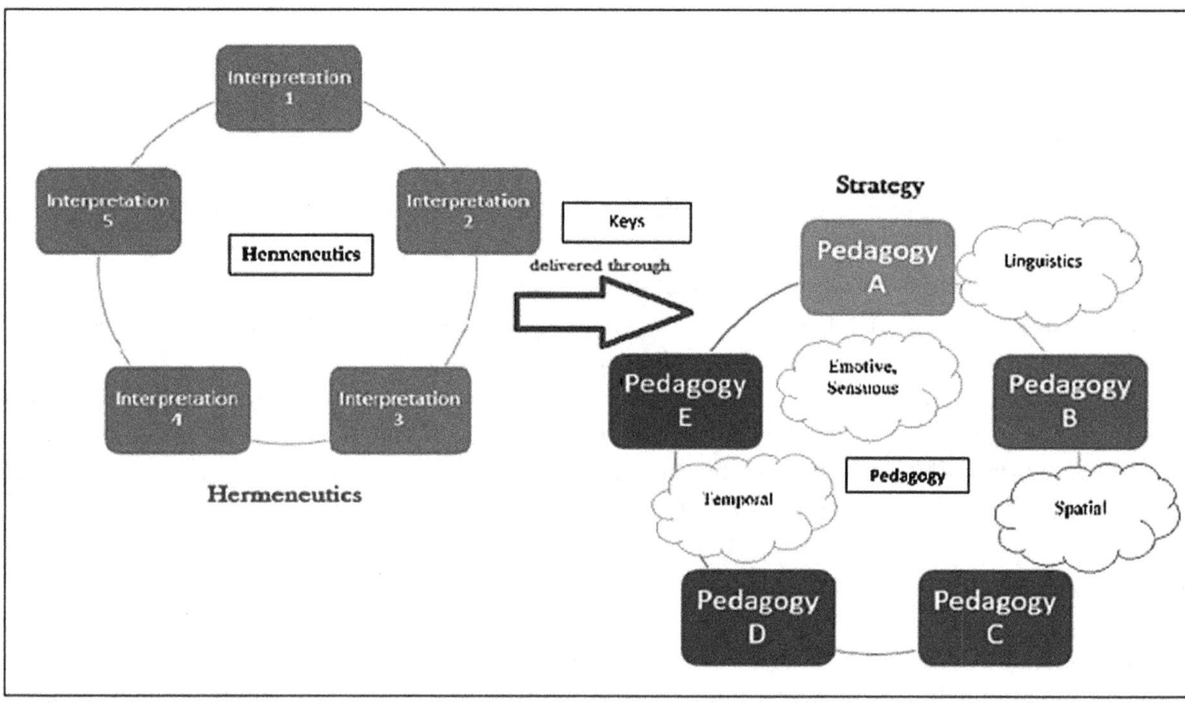

Class Format

Ontologically one has to know what a class really means. Class comprises many students belonging to different cultures and spheres of knowledge. The ontological understanding of these different constituents is essential for the faculty and the students to actively participate in a case discussion.

Case as Text in a Class

Text in a class is a book written, or oral, or printed matter, regarded in terms of its content for learning/ teaching. Pedagogy in a class is the method and practice of teaching, especially as an academic subject or theoretical concept. The quality of the text varies as the class varies. From kindergarten to research the texture of the class is different and also texture of the text.

Challenges and Successes of Research

Cases are texts/stories of how real research projects were conducted. The collection of texts/stories provides a few tracks of case studies, showing the challenges and successes of doing research, written by the researchers themselves. They explain why the researchers chose the methods they did choose, how they overcame problems in their research and what they might have done differently with hindsight: the realities of research that are missing from journal articles and textbooks. Cases are peer-reviewed and come with pedagogical tools including learning objectives and discussion questions. They can be used as a teaching tool to demonstrate a particular method and how it is applied in real research, or as inspiration to students who are preparing for their own research project.

Case Method

The case method is based on a philosophy of professional education which associates knowledge directly with action (Boehrer, 1995). This philosophy rejects the doctrine that students should first learn passively and then, having learned should apply knowledge. Instead, the case method is based on the principle that real education consists of the cumulative and unending acquisition, combination and reordering of learning experiences.

Case Study Preferred to Other Main Pedagogical Practices

Among the various practices, we choose case study and believe that it alone does draw our attention as the best form of learning. We examine case study and its existing outdated obsolete modes and conventional trodden tracks of methods, and we suggest fresh emerging concepts in an attempt at finding faultless strategies. We firmly opine that among main practices we prefer, case study to other main practices irrespective of level differences among all stages from kindergarten to higher education.

Case, the Base in Pedagogy

The pandemic Covid 19, since 2020, has been globally growing. It has been bringing out sea change in all walks of life. The pandemic concerns in the sustenance of education culminated in many transformations. The world accepted hybrid schedules: synchronous teaching and asynchronous classes. The teacher's role in online synchronous teaching might not be so very different from their role in the face-to-face environment. Synchronous learning may feature webinars (live online lessons), group chats, or drop-in sessions where teachers are available to help at a particular time. However, teaching synchronously online requires some new skills to be developed, for example, in managing the faster pace of this form of teaching.

Case Problematic

Case is a problematic term in pedagogy. It has many meanings as given in different dictionaries. Here we are giving a very special meaning to case. It is treated as the text taken up for the subject matter in pedagogy used in teaching. It has many levels and parameters in its ontology and its hermeneutics, and therefore the term though appears very easy to grasp, is not that simple. Case study as a pedagogic strategy has not been properly used in a class room. Care has neither been taken in preparation of the case or its presentation. Nor prior training is imparted to students in comprehending, responding, and addressing the issues related to the case. The competence of a language expert with proficiency in knowledge theories and expertise in case writing and presenting, is desirable. These theories will be used in textual analysis, reader response, psychoanalysis, phenomenology, structuralism, semiology, deconstruction or similar other theories.

Case Study as a Pedagogic Strategy

Case study as a pedagogic strategy has not been properly used in a classroom. Care has neither been taken in preparation of the case or its presentation. Nor prior training is imparted to students in comprehending, responding, and addressing the issues related to the case. The competence of a language expert with proficiency in knowledge theories and expertise in case writing and presenting is desirable. These theories will be used in textual analysis, reader response, psychoanalysis, phenomenology, structuralism, semiotics, deconstruction, or similar other theories. The above note on case brings to light lapses, shortcomings, and casualties in treating case as text in a class in academic institutions, and of course, it denotes a few possible solutions to the issues raised. Propriety demands to investigate the what, the why, the where, the who, the when and the how of the case ontologically. A full understanding of the class, where a case is tried, is also crucial. Ontologically one has to know what a class really means. Class comprises many students belonging to different cultures and spheres of knowledge. The ontological understanding of these different constituents is essential for the faculty and the students to actively participate in a case discussion.

Two Fundamental Principles

There are two fundamental principles underpinning the case method. First, the best-learned lessons are the ones that students teach themselves through their own struggles. Second, many of the most useful kinds of understanding and judgment cannot be taught but must be learned through practical experience. Teaching through the case method allows educators to address specific pedagogical issues and develop higher-order skills in students. Velenchek (1995) highlights four pedagogical issues addressed by the case method: Motivation to learn theory, Application of theory, and Use of evidence and Empirical analysis, guided by theoretical concepts and analytical tools, that is central to many economics modules. Case studies include raw data that students have to manipulate, represent, and comment on in order to solve the problem.

The case method can also be used effectively in order to move students gradually up the cognitive skills ladder from the low skills level of knowledge, comprehension, and application to the higher and more desirable skills of analysis, synthesis, and evaluation. This educational taxonomy was originally proposed by Bloom (Bloom, 1956) and, even if not uncontested, it provides a transparent and structured approach to the development of students' skills. The following list describes this educational taxonomy and then explains how the case method helps in developing each of the skills: Knowledge, Comprehension, Application Analysis, Synthesis and Evaluation. The process is ideal as follows. Students shall analyse and synthesize a particular case, and then engage in an evaluation of alternative policies or strategies available to policy-makers or business leaders. The case method is a rich and powerful approach to the development of cognitive skills in students. It is also a flexible approach in the sense that faculty can use it in alternative ways.

CONCLUSION

Nair's Hermeneutic Keys to Case Knowledge and Joy's Pedagogic Tips to Case Learning

The study and research undertaken in the chapter "Case" as "Text" in the Class: Plethora of Pedagogical and Structural Nuances" lead to keys and tips to get case analysis properly executed. The authors admit that strictures cannot be given for case study as cases cannot be brought under any rigour demanded by strictures. Above all, primary concern of authors in the chapter is case. The basic aim is to illuminate the case, scan it and learn it well. The case is similar to an organism. It grows and expands as conditions are congenial. It slowly shrinks and almost dies out if the conditions are not favourable. Case will be induced to develop as we caress it and fondle it with encouraging questions. Strategies steer it to grow as keys open up strategies. The study discovers umpteen opportunities that provide the student to make choices. The first part of the effort turns fruitful as it releases as many meanings and interpretations to fix their choices using all these possible ways. It's in this context that Nair's following hermeneutic keys become relevant.

Nair's Hermeneutic Keys to Case Knowledge

Spatial-temporal configuration key unravels the world of the text that brings to limelight the spatial-temporal configuration of the text. Spatial key unfolds the spatial features of the event/s. Temporal key unfolds the temporal features of the event/s probed. All these help us understand the text. Spatio-temporal (Chronotope) uses spatial-temporal configuration key unravelling the world of the text that signifies spatial and temporal configurations. Both the spatial and temporal features of the event/s probed will help us understand the text better.

Mediational configuration of keys consists of Mediacy comprising person, perspective, and mode (Stanzel, 1984). Person, perspective, and mode individually or/and together enhance the quality of the text to provide further elaboration in meaning levels.

Among ontological configurations, keys open up the questions: "Who of the case?", "What of the case?", "When of the case?", "Where of the case?", "Why of the case?", "How of the case?". All questions probed and answered will help the students to elicit large number of meaningful answers.

Classes generally range from the lowest to research: level of classes from kindergarten, to school level, to college level, and to research level. The level differences will culminate in proper hatching o meaning.

Text Triplets: text, context, and context under close scan will reveal a lot of interpretations. The text analysis will be accompanied with co-textual parts and reinforced with contextual factors. All these will expand meaning possibilities.

Joy's Tips to Case Pedagogy

Pedagogy, taken as an academic discipline, is the study of how knowledge and skills imparted in an educational context, and it considers the interactions that take place during learning. Both the theories and practices of pedagogy vary greatly, as they reflect different social, political, and cultural contexts. Pedagogic research is a form of self-study and/or action research involving critical reflection and reflexivity on current practice, which gives way to new knowledge. It encourages investigating learning. A central aim of university teaching is to transform students' conceptual understanding of disciplinary knowledge.

The first part of study and research leading to textual expansion and elucidation yearns for a complementary process. The secondary part explains Joy's Tips. The tips are meant to lead the chapter to teaching and learning possibilities. The tips also do not insist on any rigour in pedagogic strictures. It's in this context that Joy's' pedagogic keys become useful. Spatial-temporal configuration unravels the pedagogic world of the text that brings to limelight spatial-temporal configuration in the teaching and learning process of the text. Spatial tip unfolds the spatial features of the event/s. Temporal tip unfolds the temporal features of the event/s probed. Both these help us understand the pedagogic process of text. Spatial-temporal (Chronotope) uses spatial-temporal configuration tips help us unravel the needs of the pedagogy of the text. Ontological Configurations: "Who of the case?", "What of the case?", "When of the case?" " Where of the case?", "Why of the case?", "How of the case?" form different levels of classes from kindergarten to school level, there to college level and to research level Tips are given.

Limitations Noted

The authors admit that despite the infinite number of hermeneutic keys suggested, knowledge is immeasurable and unfathomable and it defies perfect tapping and eliciting meanings. Therefore the study proves imperfect. The study has another limitation: all learning and teaching modes lead to many more yet to take up and therefore unending. The authors hope that the very knowledge of these limitations record successes in their research.

THE FINAL STATEMENT

Case is a narrative. It's a narrative format in language. As the narrative voice changes, the narrative changes and the case changes. As the fabula of narrative changes, the suzhet of the case changes. Case is a chronotope. Case can convey differently as the function of the chronotope changes. Case is an ontological presence which means differently as the ontological questions tilt. Case is a product from issues created naturally from fertile minds. Case is a born out of artifice, then it is a product of fiction. Case is a magical device imprisoned, at times released on invocation by the principles of teaching and learning. The faculty handling students shall be aware of the power and potentials of the case. These all substantiate that case learning increases the power potential of the learner tremendously.

REFERENCES

Bloom, B. S. (1956). Axonomy of educational objectives: The classification of educational goals. Longman Group.

Boehrer, J. (1995). *How to teach a case. Kennedy School of Government Case Programme*. Kennedy School of Government. Retrieved from http://www.ksgcase.harvard.edu

Fidalgo-Blanco, A., Sein-Echaluce, M. L., & García-Peñalvo, F. J. (2014). Knowledge spirals in higher education teaching innovation. *International Journal of Knowledge Management*, *10*(4), 16–37. doi:10.4018/ijkm.2014100102

Frobel, F. (1899). *Friedrich Froebel's Education by Development: The Second Part of the Pedagogics of the Kindergarten*. D. Appleton.

Genette, G. (1976, Autumn). Boundaries of Narrative. *New Literary History*.

Genette, G. (1982). Figures of Literary Discourse. In *Translation*. Columbia University Press.

Genette, G. (1983). Narrative discourse: An essay in method (Vol. 3). Cornell University Press.

Genette, G. (1997). Palimpsests: Literature in the Second Degree. In C. Newman & C. Doubinsky (Eds.), *Translation*. University of Nebraska Press.

Nair, R. (2017). *Case as Text in Class: Business School Pedagogy*. Retrieved from Case as Text in Class: Business School Pedagogy: https://radhakrishnannair.com/

Saura, J. R., Palacios-Marqués, D., & Ribeiro-Soriano, D. (2022). Exploring the boundaries of Open Innovation: Evidence from social media mining. *Technovation*, 102447. Advance online publication. doi:10.1016/j.technovation.2021.102447

Saura, J. R., Ribeiro-Soriano, D., & Zegarra Saldaña, P. (2022, March). Exploring the challenges of remote work on Twitter users' sentiments: From digital technology development to a post-pandemic era. *Journal of Business Research*, *142*, 242–254. doi:10.1016/j.jbusres.2021.12.052

Stanzel, F. K. (1984). *A Theory of Narrative*. Cambridge University Press.

UNICEF. (2019). *Strengthening education systems and innovation*. Retrieved 02 05, 2022, from unicef for every child: https://www.unicef.org/education/strengthening-education-systems-innovation

Velenchik, A. D. (1995). The case method as a strategy for teaching policy analysis to undergraduates. *The Journal of Economic Education*, *26*(1), 29–38. doi:10.1080/00220485.1995.10844854

Compilation of References

Abella, V., Delgado, V., Ausín, V., & Hortigüela, D. (2018). Satisfacción de los estudiantes en una experiencia de ABP mediado por tecnologías [Student satisfaction in a technology-mediated PBL experience]. *Investigación y práctica en la educación superior*, 421-426.

Abuzant, M., Ghanem, M., Abd-Rabo, A., & Daher, W. (2021). Quality of using google classroom to support the learning processes in the automation and programming course. *International Journal of Emerging Technologies in Learning*, *16*(6), 72–87. doi:10.3991/ijet.v16i06.18847

Abykanova, B., Idrissov, S., Saltanova, G., Shazhdekeyeva, N., & Syrbayeva, S. (2017). The problem of practice-oriented instruction in higher education. *Revista*, *38*(56), 2–5.

Adams, D. L. (1998). What works in the non-major's science laboratory: Some practical advice on building a workable and meaningful introductory science laboratory? *Journal of College Science Teaching*, 103–108.

Agrawal, D. A. K., & Mittal, D. G. K. (2018). The Role of ICT in Higher Education for the 21st Century: ICT as A Change Agent for Education. Multidisciplinary Higher Education, Research, Dynamics & Concepts: Opportunities & Challenges For Sustainable Development, 1(1), 76–83.

Aguiar, B., Velazquez, R., & Aguiar, J. (2019). *Teaching innovation and use of ICT in Higher Education* [Innovación docente y empleo de las TIC en la Educación Superior]. Academic Press.

Aksan, N., Kisac, B., Aydin, M., & Demirbuken, S. (2009). Symbolic Interaction Theory. *Procedia: Social and Behavioral Sciences*, *1*(1), 902–904. doi:10.1016/j.sbspro.2009.01.160

Alani, F. (2020). Development of Case-Based Learning (CBL) in Engineering Technology Education. *International Journal of Engineering Education*, *36*(3), 896–900.

Al-Ansi, A., Suprayogo, I. & Abidin, M. (2019). *Impact of Information and Communication Technology (ICT) on Different Settings of Learning Process in Developing Countries*. . doi:10.5923/j.scit.20190902.01

Al-Bahrani, A., & Patel, D. (2015). Incorporating Twitter, Instagram, and Facebook in economics classrooms. *The Journal of Economic Education*, *46*(1), 56–67. doi:10.1080/00220485.2014.978922

Alessio, H. M., Malay, N., Maurer, K., Bailer, A. J., & Rubin, B. (2017). Examining the Effect of Proctoring on Online Test Scores. *Online Learning*, *21*(1), 146–161. doi:10.24059/olj.v21i1.885

Al-Husseini, S., & Elbeltagi, I. (2015). Knowledge Sharing Practices as a Basis of Product Innovation: A Case of Higher Education in Iraq. *International Journal of Social Science and Humanity*, *5*(2), 182–185. doi:10.7763/IJSSH.2015.V5.449

Aliaga, C., & Schalk, A. (2010). E2: Early employability and entrepreneurship. Two major challenges in higher education in Chile [E2: Empleabilidad temprana y emprendimiento. Dos grandes desafíos en la formación superior en Chile]. *Calidad en la Educación*, (33), 319–337. doi:10.31619/caledu.n33.145

Allen, T. J., & Cohen, D. J. (1969). Information flow in research and development laboratories. *Administrative Science Quarterly*, *14*(1), 12–20. doi:10.2307/2391357

Al-Maroof, R. S., Salloum, S. A., Hassanien, A. E., & Shaalan, K. (2020). Fear from COVID-19 and technology adoption: The impact of Google Meet during Coronavirus pandemic. *Interactive Learning Environments*, 1–16. doi:10.1080/10494820.2020.1830121

Almazova, N., Krylova, E., Rubtsova, A., & Odinokaya, M. (2020). Challenges and opportunities for Russian higher education amid COVID-19: Teachers' perspective. *Education Sciences*, *10*(12), 368. doi:10.3390/educsci10120368

Almenara, J. C., & Díaz, V. M. (2014). Educational possibilities of social networks and group work. University students' perceptions. *Comunicar. Media Education Research Journal*, *22*(1), 165–172.

Almulla, M. A. (2020, July). The Effectiveness of the Project-Based Learning (PBL) Approach to Engage Students in Learning. *SAGE Open*, *10*(3). Advance online publication. doi:10.1177/2158244020938702

Aloi, S. L., Gardner, W. S., & Lusher, A. L. (2003). A framework for assessing general education outcomes within the majors. *The Journal of General Education*, *52*(4), 237–252. doi:10.1353/jge.2004.0009

Alonso, M. H., Valles, J. E. G., & Muñoz de Luna, A. B. (2016). Advantages and disadvantages of using electronic devices in the classroom: Perception of undergraduate students in communication sciences. *Revista de Comunicacion de la Seeci*, (41), 136–154. doi:10.15198eeci.2016.41.136-154

Alqahtani, A. Y., & Rajkhan, A. A. (2020). E-learning critical success factors during the covid-19 pandemic: A comprehensive analysis of e-learning managerial perspectives. *Education Sciences*, *10*(9), 216. doi:10.3390/educsci10090216

Alrahlah, A. (2016). How effective the problem-based learning (PBL) in dental education. A critical review. *The Saudi Dental Journal*, *28*(4), 155–161. doi:10.1016/j.sdentj.2016.08.003 PMID:27872545

Amason, A. C. (1996). Distinguishing the effects of functional and dysfunctional conflict on strategic decision making: Resolving a paradox for top management teams. *Academy of Management Journal*, *39*(1), 123–148.

Amason, A. C., Thompson, K. R., Hochwarter, W. A., & Harrison, A. W. (1995). Conflict: An important dimension in successful management teams. *Organizational Dynamics*, *24*(2), 20–35. doi:10.1016/0090-2616(95)90069-1

Amir, L. R., Tanti, I., Maharani, D. A., Wimardhani, Y. S., Julia, V., Sulijaya, B., & Puspitawati, R. (2020). Student perspective of classroom and distance learning during COVID-19 pandemic in the undergraduate dental study program Universitas Indonesia. *BMC Medical Education*, *20*(1), 1–8. doi:10.118612909-020-02312-0 PMID:33121488

Andrade, M. S. (2014). Dialogue and Structure: Enabling Learner Self-Regulation in Technology-Enhanced Learning Environments. *European Educational Research Journal*, *13*(5), 563–574. doi:10.2304/eerj.2014.13.5.563

Angulo, F. (1990). Action research and curriculum: a new perspective in educational research [Investigación-acción y currículum: una nueva perspectiva en la investigación educativa]. *Investigación en la escuela*, *11*, 39-50.

Anlauf, R. (2016). Aspekte anwendungsorientierter Hochschullehre in Deutschland. In J. Cai & H. Lackner (Eds.), *Jahrbuch Angewandte Hochschulbildung* (pp. 201–213). Springer.

Antolí, N. S., Jarauta, B., & Campos, S. (2012). Active methodologies and Facebook in higher education. *International Journal of Technology and Educational Innovation*, 3134–3143.

Apodaca-Orozco, G. U. G., Ortega-Pipper, L. P., Verdugo-Blanco, L. E., & Reyes-Barribas, L. E. (2017). Modelos educativos: un reto para la educación en salud. *Ra Ximhai, 13*(2), 77-86.

Appelbaum, S., & Steed, A. (2005). The critical success factors in the client-consulting relationship. *Journal of Management Development, 24*(1), 68–93. doi:10.1108/02621710510572362

Aranzabal, A., Epelde, E., & Artetxe, M. (2022). Team formation on the basis of Belbin's roles to enhance students' performance in project based learning. *Education for Chemical Engineers, 38*, 22–37. doi:10.1016/j.ece.2021.09.001

Araujo, M., & Campos, M. (2006). La praxis pedagógica en la educación física y los estilos de enseñanza predominantes en los docentes de educación básica. *Revista EDUCARE-UPEL-IPB-Segunda Nueva Etapa 2.0, 10*(3).

Arbaugh, J. B. (2013). Does academic discipline moderate CoI-course outcomes relationships in online MBA courses? *Internet High. Educ, 2013*(17), 16–28. doi:10.1016/j.iheduc.2012.10.002

Arias, E., Barba-Sánchez, V., Carrión, C., & Casado, R. (2018). Enhancing Entrepreneurship Education in a Master's Degree in Computer Engineering: A Project-Based Learning Approach. *Administrative Sciences, 8*(4), 58. doi:10.3390/admsci8040058

Arizabaleta, S. L., & Ochoa, A. F. (2016). Hacia una educación superior inclusiva en Colombia. *Pedagogía y saberes*, (45), 41-52.

Arnal de Rincón, J., & Latorre, M. (1994). *Educational Research Fundamentals and Methodology* [Investigación Educativa Fundamentos y Metodología]. Editorial Labor SA.

Arnold, D. Y., & Yapita, J. D. (2000). *El rincón de las cabezas: Luchas textuales, educacion y Tierras en los Andes*. La Paz, Bolivia: Instituto de Lengua y Cultura aymara IICA.

Aronson, E. (Ed.). (1978). *The Jigsaw Classroom*. Sage Publications.

Auernhammer, J., & Roth, B. (2021). The Origin and Evolution of Stanford University's Design Thinking: From Product Design to Design Thinking in Innovation Management. *Journal of Product Innovation Management, 38*(6), 623–644. doi:10.1111/jpim.12594

Ausubel, D. (1963). *The psychology of meaningful verbal learning*. Grune & Stratton.

Ausubel, D. (1978). *Educational Psychology: A Cognitive View*. Holt, Rinehart and Winston.

Ausubel, D. (1983). Teoría del aprendizaje significativo. *Fascículos de CEIF, 1*, 1–10.

Ausubel, D. P. (1961). In Defense of Verbal Learning. *Educational Theory, 1961*(11), 15–25. doi:10.1111/j.1741-5446.1961.tb00038.x

Ausubel, D. P. (1968). *Educational psychology. A cognitive view*. Holt Rinehart and Winston.

Ausubel, D., Novak, J., & Hanesian, H. (1978). *Educational psychology: A cognitive view*. Holt, Rinehart & Winston.

Aznar, P. (1992). *Constructivismo y educación*. Tirant lo Blanch.

Baase, S. (2012). *A gift of fire*. Pearson Education Limited.

Bachkirova, T. (2016). A new perspective on self-deception for applied purposes. *New Ideas in Psychology, 43*, 1–9. doi:10.1016/j.newideapsych.2016.02.004

Bahner, D. P., Adkins, E., Patel, N., Donley, C., Nagel, R., & Kman, N. E. (2012). How we use social media to supplement a novel curriculum in medical education. *Medical Teacher, 34*(6), 439–444. doi:10.3109/0142159X.2012.668245 PMID:22449268

Bai, X. L. (2017). Research on the Innovation Ability of PE Teaching under the Multi Objective Dynamic Condition. *International Conference on Economics, Management Engineering and Education Technology (ICEMEET)*, 56–61. 10.2991/icemeet-16.2017.11

Baker, R. S., D'Mello, S. K., Rodrigo, M. M. T., & Graesser, A. C. (2010). Better to be frustrated than bored: The incidence, persistence, and impact of learners' cognitive–affective states during interactions with three different computer-based learning environments. *International Journal of Human-Computer Studies, 68*(4), 223–241. doi:10.1016/j.ijhcs.2009.12.003

Baldeón, J., Rodríguez, I., Puig, A., & López-Sánchez, M. (2017). Evaluación y rediseño de una experiencia de gamificación en el aula basada en estilos de aprendizaje y tipos de jugador [Evaluation and redesign of a gamification experience in the classroom based on learning styles and player types]. In R. Contreras & J. Eguia, J.(Eds.), Experiencias de gamificación en aulas [Gamification experiences in classrooms (pp. 95-111). Academic Press.

Balderas, S. V., & Tapia, J. M. (2021). Learning experiences on YouTube, an analysis during the COVID-19 pandemic. *IE Journal of Educational Research of the REDIECH*, (12), 18.

Baliga, S. S., Walvekar, P. R., & Mahantshetti, G. J. (2021). Concept map as a teaching and learning tool for medical students. *Journal of Education and Health Promotion, 10*(1), 35. doi:10.4103/jehp.jehp_146_20 PMID:33688544

Bandura, A. (1986). *Social Foundations of Thought and Action: A Social Cognitive Theory*. Prentice Hall.

Bao, L., & Koenig, K. (2019). Physics education research for 21st century learning. *Discip Interdscip Sci Educ Res, 1*(1), 2. doi:10.118643031-019-0007-8

Barbosa, R., Jófili, Z., & Watts, M. (2004). Cooperating in constructing knowledge: Case studies and citizenship. *International Journal of Science Education, 26*(8), 935–949. doi:10.1080/0950069032000138842

Bartol, K., & Srivastava, A. (2002). Encouraging knowledge sharing: The role of organizational reward systems. *Journal of Leadership & Organizational Studies, 9*(1), 64–76. doi:10.1177/107179190200900105

Baskervill, R. L., & Stage, J. (1996). Controlling Prototype Development Through Risk Analysis. *Management Information Systems Quarterly, 20*(4), 481–502. doi:10.2307/249565

Bawarith, R., Basuhail, A., Fattouh, A., & Gamalel-Din, S. (2017). E-exam cheating detection system. *International Journal of Advanced Computer Science and Applications, 8*(4), 176–181. doi:10.14569/IJACSA.2017.080425

Beck, K. (2004). eXtreme Programming Eagilelained: Embrace change (2nd ed.). Addison-Wesley.

Beck, K., Cockburn, A., Jeffries, R., & Highsmith, J. (2001). *Agile manifesto*. http://www.agilemanifesto.org

Beck, E., Sollbrekke, T., Sutphen, M., & Fremstad, E. (2015). When mere knowledge is not enough: The potential of building as self-determination, co-determination, and solidarity. *Higher Education Research & Development, 34*(3), 445–457. doi:10.1080/07294360.2014.973373

Behrman, J. N., & Levin, R. I. (1984). Are business schools doing their job. *Harvard Business Review, 62*(1), 140.

Ben-Ari, M. (1998). Constructivism in Computer Science. *Proceedings of the 29th SIGCSE Technical Symposium on Computer Science Education*, 257-261.

Benito, Á., & Cruz, A. (2005). *Nuevas claves para la docencia universitaria en el Espacio Europeo de Educación Superior* [New keys to university teaching in the European Higher Education Area]. Narcea Ediciones.

Bergmann, J. & Sams, A. (2012). *Flip your classroom: reach every student in every class every day*. Academic Press.

Berne Manero, C., Lozano Chavarria, P., & Marzo Navarro, M. (2011). Innovation in university teaching through the TTM method. *Revista de Educacion*, (355), 605–619. doi:10.4438/1988-592X-RE-2010-355-117

Blanco, A. V., & Amigo, J. C. (2016). El rol del docente en la era digital [The role of the teacher in the digital age]. *Revista interuniversitaria de formación del profesorado, 30*(2), 103-114.

Bloom, B. S. (1956). Axonomy of educational objectives: The classification of educational goals. Longman Group.

Blosser, P. E. (1993). Using Cooperative learning in Science Education. Clearinghouse for Science, Mathematics, Environmental Science Education. ERIC ED351207.

Blumer, H. (1969). The methodological position of symbolic interactionism. In *Symbolic interactionism: Perspective and Method* (pp. 1–60). Prentice-Hall.

Bodner, G. M. (1986). Constructivism: A theory of knowledge. *Journal of Chemical Education, 63*(10), 873–878. doi:10.1021/ed063p873

Bodner, G. M., Klobuchar, M., & Geelan, D. (2001). The many forms of constructivism. *Journal of Chemical Education, 78*(8), 1107. doi:10.1021/ed078p1107.4

Boehrer, J. (1995). *How to teach a case. Kennedy School of Government Case Programme*. Kennedy School of Government. Retrieved from http://www.ksgcase.harvard.edu

Boh, W. F. (2014). Knowledge Sharing in Communities of Practice: Examining Usefulness of Knowledge from Discussion Forums versus Repositories. *The Data Base for Advances in Information Systems, 45*(2), 8–31. doi:10.1145/2621906.2621908

Bond, M., Bedenlier, S., Marín, V. I., & Händel, M. (2021). Emergency remote teaching in higher education: Mapping the first global online semester. *International Journal of Educational Technology in Higher Education, 18*(1), 1–24. doi:10.118641239-021-00282-x PMID:34778537

Bonilla del Río, M., Diego Mantecón, J. M., & Lena Acebo, F. J. (2018). Estudiantes Universitarios: Prosumidores de recursos digitales y mediáticos en la era de internet [University students: prosumers of digital and media resources in the internet age]. *Aula Abierta, 47*(3), 319–326. doi:10.17811/rifie.47.3.2018.319-326

Bonney, K. M. (2015). Case study teaching method improves student performance and perceptions of learning gains. *Journal of Microbiology & Biology Education, 16*(1), 21–28. doi:10.1128/jmbe.v16i1.846 PMID:25949753

Bonwell, C. C., & Eison, J. A. (1991). Active Learning: Creating Excitement in the Classroom. *ASHE-ERIC Higher Education Report, 1*(1).

Bordogna, J., Fromm, E., & Ernst, E. W. (1993). Engineering education: Innovation through integration. *Journal of Engineering Education, 82*(1), 3–8. doi:10.1002/j.2168-9830.1993.tb00065.x

Borge, M., Ong, Y. S., & Goggins, S. (2020). A sociocultural approach to using social networking sites as learning tools. *Educational Technology Research and Development, 68*(3), 1089–1120. doi:10.100711423-019-09721-z

Borup, J., West, R. E., & Graham, C. R. (2012). Improving online social presence through asynchronous video. *Internet High. Educ., 2012*(15), 195–203. doi:10.1016/j.iheduc.2011.11.001

Boss, S. (2015). *Implementing Project-Based Learning*. Solution Tree.

Bostrom, R. P., & Thomas, B. D. (1983). Achieving Excellence in Communications: A Key to Developing Complete, Accurate and Shared Information Requirements. *Twentieth Annual Computer Personnel on Research Conference*.

Boud, D., Cohen, R., & Walker, D. (1993). Introduction: Understanding learning from experience. In D. Boud, R. Cohen, & D. Walker (Eds.), *Using experience for learning* (pp. 1–17). Lehmanns.

Bourke, B., Bray, N. J., & Horton, C. C. (2009). Approaches to the core curriculum: An exploratory analysis of top liberal arts and doctoral-granting institutions. *The Journal of General Education, 58*(4), 219–240. doi:10.2307/25702445

Bower, G. H. (1992). How might emotions affect learning? In S.-Å. Christianson (Ed.), *The handbook of emotion and memory: Research and theory* (pp. 3–31). Lawrence Erlbaum Associates, Inc.

Bozzi, M., Raffaghelli, J. E., & Zani, M. (2021). Peer Learning as a Key Component of an Integrated Teaching Method: Overcoming the Complexities of Physics Teaching in Large Size Classes. *Education Sciences, 11*(2), 67. doi:10.3390/educsci11020067

Brint, S., Proctor, K., Murphy, S. P., Turk-Bicakci, L., & Hanneman, R. A. (2009). General education models: Continuity and change in the US undergraduate curriculum, 1975–2000. *The Journal of Higher Education, 80*(6), 605–642. doi:10.1080/00221546.2009.11779037

Brown, P., Lauder, H., Ashton, D., Yingje, W., & Vincent-Lancrin, S. (2008). Education, Globalisation and the Future of the Knowledge Economy. *European Educational Research Journal, 7*(2), 131–156. doi:10.2304/eerj.2008.7.2.131

Brown, S. B., Collins, A., & Duguid, P. (1989). Situated Cognition and the Culture of Learning. *Educational Researcher, 18*(1), 32–42. doi:10.3102/0013189X018001032

Brown, T. E., LeMay, E. H., Bursten, B. E., Murphy, C., & Woodward, P. (2008). *Chemistry: The Central Science.* Pearson Education Inc.

Brunsell, E. (2012). *Integrating Engineering and Science in Your Classroom.* National Science Teachers Association.

Bryer, T. A., & Chen, B. (2010). *The use of social media and networks in teaching public administration. Cutting-edge Social Media Approaches to Business Education: Teaching with LinkedIn, Facebook, Twitter, Second Life, and Blogs (HC).* Information Age Publishing.

Buckley, K., Stone, S., Farrell, A. M., Glynn, M., Lowney, R., & Smyth, S. (2021). Learning from student experience: Large, higher education classes transitioning online. *Irish Educational Studies, 40*(2), 399–406. doi:10.1080/03323315.2021.1916566

Burke, K. A., Greenbowe, T. J., & Hand, B. M. (2006). Implementing the Science Writing Heuristic in the chemistry laboratory. *Journal of Chemical Education, 83*(7), 1032–1038. doi:10.1021/ed083p1032

Burke, K. A., Hand, B. M., Poock, J. R., & Greenbowe, T. J. (2005). Using the Science Writing Heuristic: Training chemistry teaching assistants. *Journal of College Science Teaching, 35*, 36–41.

Byrnes, Y. M., Civantos, A. M., Go, B. C., McWilliams, T. L., & Rajasekaran, K. (2020). Effect of the COVID-19 pandemic on medical student career perceptions: A national survey study. *Medical Education Online, 25*(1), 1798088. doi:10.1080/10872981.2020.1798088 PMID:32706306

Cabı, E. (2018). The impact of the flipped classroom model on students'academic achievement. *International Review of Research in Open and Distance Learning, 19*(3), 203–221. doi:10.19173/irrodl.v19i3.3482

Cáceres, C., Esteban, N., Gálvez, M. del C., & Rivas, B. (2019). *Competencia digital docente: una perspectiva de futuro en la Educación Superior [Teaching digital competence: a future perspective in Higher Education].* Dykinson.

Caine, R. N., & Caine, G. (1994). *Making connections. Teaching and the human brain.* Innovative Learning Publication.

Camacho, M. D. M., Urquía, E., Pascual, D., & Rivero Menéndez, M. (2016). Recursos multimedia para el aprendizaje de Contabilidad Financiera en los grados bilingües [Multimedia resources for learning Financial Accounting in bilingual grades]. *Educación XX1, 19*(1), 63-89. doi:10.5944/educxx1.15578

Camacho, M. D. M., & Del Campo, C. (2015). Impacto de la motivación intrínseca en el rendimiento académico a través de trabajos voluntarios: Un análisis empírico [Impact of intrinsic motivation on academic performance through voluntary work: An empirical analysis]. *Revista Complutense de Educación, 26*(1), 67–80. doi:10.5209/rev_RCED.2015.v26.n1.42581

Camiel, L. D., Goldman-Levine, J. D., Kostka-Rokosz, M. D., & McCloskey, W. W. (2014). Twitter as a medium for pharmacy students' personal learning network development. *Currents in Pharmacy Teaching & Learning, 6*(4), 463–470. doi:10.1016/j.cptl.2014.04.008

Cantó-Domenech, J. (2015). Results of the implementation of neurodidactics in early childhood education classrooms [Resultados de la implementación de la neurodidáctica en las aulas de educación infantile]. *Opción, 31*(5), 189–199.

Cao, L., & Ramesh, B. (2007). Agile Software Development: Ad Hoc Practices or Sound Principles? *IT Professional, 9*(2), 41–47. doi:10.1109/MITP.2007.27

Caponetto, I., Earp, J., & Ott, M. (2014). Gamification and education: A literature review. In *European Conference on Games Based Learning* (*vol. 1*, p. 50). Academic Conferences International Limited.

Carlson, J. A., & Schodt, D. W. (1995). Beyond the lecture: Case teaching and the learning of economic theory. *The Journal of Economic Education, 26*(1), 17–28. doi:10.1080/00220485.1995.10844853

Carter, G., & Jones, M. G. (1994). Verbal and nonverbal behavior of ability-grouped dyads. *Journal of Research in Science Teaching, 31*(6), 603–619. doi:10.1002/tea.3660310604

Castaño-Perea, E., Fernández, A. B., & Castañeda, E. A. (2012). Competencias para la tutoría: experiencia de formación con profesores universitarios [Competencies for tutorials: training experience with university professors]. *REDU. Revista de Docencia Universitaria, 10*(2), 193–210. doi:10.4995/redu.2012.6103

Castedo, R., López, L. M., Chiquito, M., Navarro, J., Cabrera, J. D., & Ortega, M. F. (2019). Flipped classroom—Comparative case study in engineering higher education. *Computer Applications in Engineering Education, 27*(1), 206–216. doi:10.1002/cae.22069

Castle, S., Deniz, C. B., & Tortora, M. (2005). Flexible grouping and student learning in a high-needs school. *Education and Urban Society, 37*(2), 139–150. doi:10.1177/0013124504270787

Castro-Schez, J. J., Redondo, M. A., Jurado, F., & Albusac, J. (2014). Experience applying language processing techniques to develop educational software that allow active learning methodologies by advising students. *Journal of Network and Computer Applications, 41*, 65–79. doi:10.1016/j.jnca.2013.10.011

Cebrián-Robles, V., Raposo-Rivas, M., Cebrián-de-la-Serna, M., & Sarmiento-Campos, J. A. (2018). Percepción sobre el plagio académico de estudiantes universitarios españoles [Perception about academic plagiarism of Spanish university students]. *Educación XX1, 21*(2). doi:10.5944/educxx1.20062

Cejas, R., Navio, A., & Barroso, J. (2016). The university teacher's abilities from the tpack model (technological and pedagogical content knowledge). *Pixel-Bit-Revista De Medios Y Educacion, 49*, 105–119.

Chance, Z., Gino, F., Norton, M. I., & Ariely, D. (2015). The slow decay and quick revival of self-deception. *Frontiers in Psychology, 6*. Advance online publication. doi:10.3389/fpsyg.2015.01075 PMID:26347666

Chance, Z., Norton, M. I., Gino, F., & Ariely, D. (2011). Temporal view of the costs and benefits of self-deception. *Proceedings of the National Academy of Sciences of the United States of America*, *108*(Supplement 3), 15655–15659. doi:10.1073/pnas.1010658108 PMID:21383150

Charitopoulos, A., Vassiliadis, S., Rangoussi, M., & Koulouriotis, D. (2017). E-learning and blended learning in textile engineering education: A closed feedback loop approach. *IOP Conference Series. Materials Science and Engineering*, *254*(22), 222002. Advance online publication. doi:10.1088/1757-899X/254/22/222002

Chaturvedi, S., Elmahdi, A. E., Abdelmonem, A. M., Haralur, S. B., Alqahtani, N. M., Suleman, G., Sharif, R. A., Gurumurthy, V., & Alfarsi, M. A. (2021). Predoctoral dental implant education techniques—Students' perception and attitude. *Journal of Dental Education*, *85*(3), 392–400. doi:10.1002/jdd.12453 PMID:33067837

Chen, J., Zhang, L. J., Wang, X., & Zhang, T. (2021). Impacts of Self-Regulated Strategy Development-Based Revision Instruction on English-as-a-Foreign-Language Students' Self-Efficacy for Text Revision: A Mixed-Methods Study. *Frontiers in Psychology*. https://www.frontiersin.org/article/10.3389/fpsyg.2021.670100 DOI=10.3389/fpsyg.2021.670100

Chen, Wang, Zou, Lin, & Xie. (2019). Effects of caption and gender on junior high students' EFL learning from iMap-enhanced contextualized learning. *PLOS ONE Students' challenges and learning strategies.*

Chetty, S. (1996). The case study method for research in small-and medium-sized firms. *International Small Business Journal*, *15*(1), 73–85. doi:10.1177/0266242696151005

Child, J. (1972). Organisation structure, environment, and performance: The role of strategic choice. *Sociology*, *6*(1), 1–22. doi:10.1177/003803857200600101

Chin, G. (2006). *Agile Project Management*. AEW Services.

Choi, A. (2008). *Dissertation: A Study of Student Written Argument Using the Science Writing Heuristic Approach in Inquiry-Based Freshman General Chemistry Laboratory Classes* [Dissertation].

Christensen, C., Hall, T., Dillon, K., & Duncan, D. (2016). Know Your Customers' Jobs to Be Done. *Harvard Business Review*, *2016*(9), 54–62.

Chu, K. K., Lee, C. I., & Tsai, R. S. (2011). Ontology technology to assist learners' navigation in the concept map learning system. *Expert Systems with Applications*, *38*(9), 11293–11299. doi:10.1016/j.eswa.2011.02.178

Clough, M. P. (2003). Using the laboratory to enhance student learning. In R. W. Bybee (Ed.), *Learning science and the essence of learning, 2002 NSTA yearbook*. National Science Teachers' Association.

Cockburn, A. & Williams, L. (2003). Agile software development: It's about feedback and change *IEEE Computer*, *36*(6), 39–43.

Cockburn, A. (2000). *Writing Effective Use Cases*. Addison-Wesley.

Cockburn, A. (2006). *Agile Software Development: The Cooperative Game*. Addison-Wesley.

Cohn, T., & Paul, R. (2001). A Comparison of Requirements Engineering in Extreme Programming (AGILE) and Conventional Software Development Methodologies. *Seventh Americas Conference on Information Systems*.

Colegio Sagrado Corazón de Pamplona. (2020). *Educate at the Service of the Community. Pamplona: Spanish Network of Learning - Service* [Educar al Servicio de la Comunidad. Pamplona: Red Española de Aprendizaje - Servicio]. Recuperado de: https://www.aprendizajeservicio.net/wp-content/uploads/2020/11/PROYECTO-EDUCAR-AL-SERVICIO-DE-LA-COMUNIDAD.pdf

Collard, A., Brédart, S., & Bourguignon, J. P. (2016). Context impact of clinical scenario on knowledge transfer and reasoning capacity in a medical problem-based learning curriculum. *Higher Education Research & Development*, *35*(2), 242–253. doi:10.1080/07294360.2015.1087383

Cooper, B., & Naatus, M. K. (2014). LinkedIn as a learning tool in business education. *American Journal of Business Education*, *7*(4), 299–306. doi:10.19030/ajbe.v7i4.8815

Cooper, M. (1995). Cooperative learning: An approach for large enrollment courses. *Journal of Chemical Education*, *72*(2), 162–164. doi:10.1021/ed072p162

Copeland, B. J., Posy, C. J., & Shagrir, O. (Eds.). (2013). *Computability: Turing, gödel, church, and beyond.* Mit Press. doi:10.7551/mitpress/8009.001.0001

Coram, M., & Bohner, S. (2005). The Impact of Agile Methods on Software Project Management. *Proceedings of the 12th IEEE International Conference and Workshops on the Engineering of Computer-Based Systems (ECBS'05)*, 363-370. 10.1109/ECBS.2005.68

Corbett, F., & Spinello, E. (2020). Connectivism and leadership: Harnessing a learning theory for the digital age to redefine leadership in the twenty-first century. *Heliyon*, *6*(1), e03250. doi:10.1016/j.heliyon.2020.e03250 PMID:31993523

Cordell, R. M. (2013). Indiana University South Bend. In Library Reference Services and Information Literacy: Models for Academic Institutions (pp. 153–170). IGI Global. doi:10.4018/978-1-4666-4241-6.ch011

Corder, G. W., & Foreman, D. I. (2009). *Nonparametric Statistics for non-statisticians: A step-by-step approach.* John-Wiley & Sons Inc. doi:10.1002/9781118165881

Cored, S., Liesa, M., Vázquez, S., Latorre, C., & Anzano, S. (2021). Digital Competence of University Teachers of Social and Legal Sciences from a Gender Perspective. *Education Sciences*, *11*(12), 806. doi:10.3390/educsci11120806

Crawford, J., Butler-Henderson, K., Rudolph, J., Malkawi, B., Glowatz, M., Burton, R., ... Lam, S. (2020). COVID-19: 20 countries' higher education intra-period digital pedagogy responses. *Journal of Applied Learning & Teaching*, *3*(1), 1–20. doi:10.37074/jalt.2020.3.1.7

Crotty, M. (1998). *The foundations of social research: Meaning and perspectives in the research process*. Sage Publications.

Cunningham, W. (2001). *Agile Manifesto.* http://www.agilemanifesto.org

Dabbagh, N., & Kitsantas, A. (2012). Personal Learning Environments, social media, and self-regulated learning: A natural formula for connecting formal and informal learning. *The Internet and higher education*, *15*(1), 3–8. doi:10.1016/j.iheduc.2011.06.002

Dahar, R. W. (2011). *Teori belajar dan pembelajaran.* Erlangga.

Daley, B. J., & Torre, D. M. (2010). Concept maps in medical education: An analytical literature review. *Medical Education*, *44*(5), 440–448. doi:10.1111/j.1365-2923.2010.03628.x PMID:20374475

Damian, D., Lassenius, C., & Paasivaar, M. (2012). Teaching a globally distributed project course using Scrum practices. In *Proceedings of the Second International Workshop on Collaborative Teaching of Globally Distributed Software Development.* IEEE. 10.1109/CTGDSD.2012.6226947

Damodaran, L., & Olphert, W. (2000). Barriers and facilitators to the use of knowledge management systems. *Behaviour & Information Technology*, *19*(6), 405–413. doi:10.1080/014492900750052660

Davenport, T. H., & Prusak, L. (1998). *Working knowledge: How organizations manage what they know, MA*. Harvard Business School Press.

Davila, T., Epstein, M. J., & Shelton, R. (2006). *Making Innovation Work: How to Manage it, Measure it, and Profit from it*. Pearson Education.

de Borges, M. I., Dias, C., & Santos, C. (2020). COVID-19 and online learning in higher education – A case study of students from the Polytechnic Institutes of Portalegre and Beja [COVID-19 y el aprendizaje en línea en la educación superior – Un estudio de caso de alumnos de los Institutos Politécnicos de Portalegre y Beja]. *IJERI: International Journal of Educational Research and Innovation*, (15), 317–325. doi:10.46661/ijeri.5253

de León, P. C. (2005). *Educational innovation* [La innovación educativa]. Ediciones Akal.

De Miguel Díaz, M. (2005). *Teaching modalities focused on the development of competences. Guidelines to promote methodological change in the European Higher Education Area* [Modalidades de enseñanza centradas en el desarrollo de competencias. Orientaciones para promover el cambio metodológico en el Espacio Europeo de Educación Superior] (Proyecto EA2005-0118). Servicio de Publicaciones: Universidad de Oviedo. Recuperado de http://www.mec.es/univ/proyectos2005/EA 2005-0118.pdf

De Miguel Díaz, M. (2006). Methodologies to optimise learning: second objective of the European Higher Education Area [Metodologías para optimizar el aprendizaje: segundo objetivo del Espacio Europeo de Educación Superior]. *Revista interuniversitaria de formación del profesorado, 57*, 71-92.

Del Campo, S. (2000). *Análisis del manejo de la autoevaluación de los alumnos por parte de los profesores que imparten cursos transferidos con el nuevo modelo de rediseño creado en la misión del ITESM para el año 2005 en el campus Cd. Juárez* (Tesis de maestría, Instituto Tecnológico y de Estudios Superiores de Monterrey). https://repositorio.tec.mx/bitstream/handle/11285/628762/EGE00000007633.pdf?sequence=1

Delgado, A. M., & Oliver, R. (2010). Interacción entre la evaluación continua y la autoevaluación formativa: La potenciación del aprendizaje autónomo. *Revista de Docencia Universitaria, 4*, 2-13. https://revistas.um.es/redu/article/view/92581

Denert, E. (2005). Zum Verschwinden des Diploms und zum Verhältnis Fachhochschule/Universität. *Informatik Spektrum, 23*(2), 45–47. doi:10.100700287-004-0464-z

Denzin, N. K., & Lincoln, Y. S. (1998). *Collecting and interpreting qualitative materials*. Sage Publications.

Deterding, S., Dixon, D., Khaled, R., & Nacke, L. (2011). From game design elements to gamefulness: Defining gamification. In *15th International Academic MindTrek Conference: Envisioning Future Media Environments* (pp. 9-15). New York, NY: ACM.

Deterding, S., Dixon, D., Khaled, R., & Nacke, L. (2011). From game design elements to gamefulness: defining "gamification". In *Proceedings of the 15th international academic MindTrek conference: Envisioning future media environments* (pp. 9-15). 10.1145/2181037.2181040

Dewey, J. (1938). *Experience and education*. MacMillan.

Dias, G. P., Barbosa, B., Santos, C. A., Pinheiro, M. M., Simões, D., & Filipe, S. (2021). Between promises and pitfalls: The impact of mobility on the internationalization of higher education. *Journal of Further and Higher Education, 45*(1), 79–94. doi:10.1080/0309877X.2020.1735321

Díaz, J. T., & Gómez, J. I. A. (2009). Professional development of teachers in the face of the new challenges of information and communication technologies in schools [Desarrollo profesional docente ante los nuevos retos de las tecnologías de la información y la comunicación en los centros educativos]. *Pixel-Bit. Revista de medios y educación*, (34), 31-47.

Dinh, L. P., & Nguyen, T. T. (2020). Pandemic, social distancing, and social work education: Students' satisfaction with online education in Vietnam. *Social Work Education, 39*(8), 1074–1083. doi:10.1080/02615479.2020.1823365

Domin, S. D. (1999). A review of Laboratory instruction styles. *Journal of Chemical Education*, *76*(4), 543–547. doi:10.1021/ed076p543

Dumpit, D. Z., & Fernandez, C. J. (2017). Analysis of the use of social media in Higher Education Institutions (HEIs) using the Technology Acceptance Model. *International Journal of Educational Technology in Higher Education*, *14*(1), 1–16. doi:10.118641239-017-0045-2

Duncan, T., & Sandra, E. M. (1998). A Communication Based Marketing Model for Managing Relationships. *Journal of Marketing*, *62*(April), 1–12. doi:10.1177/002224299806200201

Duran, A., Moon, Y. B., & Giraldo, E. (2009). Work in progress - the European Higher Education Area ("Bologna process") in Engineering Education in Spain. *2009 39th IEEE Frontiers in Education Conference*, 1–2. 10.1109/FIE.2009.5350475

Dyganoca, E. A., & Yavgildina, Z. M. (2020). Development of Student Musician's Methodological Competence in Practice-Oriented University Environment. *Utopía y Praxis Latinoamericana*, *25*(5), 113–124.

Eisenhardt, K. M. (2020). Theorizing from cases: A commentary. In *Research methods in international business* (pp. 221–227). Palgrave Macmillan. doi:10.1007/978-3-030-22113-3_10

Ellis, V., & Childs, A. (2019). Innovation in teacher education: Collective creativity in the development of a teacher education internship. *Teaching and Teacher Education*, *77*, 277–286. doi:10.1016/j.tate.2018.10.020

Erceg-Hurn, D. M., & Mirosevich, V. M. (2008). Modern Robust Statistical Methods: An easy way to maximize the accuracy and power of your research. *The American Psychologist*, *63*(7), 591–601. doi:10.1037/0003-066X.63.7.591 PMID:18855490

Erskine, J. A., Leenders, M. R., & Mauffette-Leenders, L. A. (2018). *Teaching with cases* (2nd ed.). Ivey Publishing.

Escamilla-Fajardo, P., Sheriff, M., & López-Carril, S. (2021). Incorporating TikTok in higher education: Pedagogical perspectives from a corporal expression sport sciences course. *Journal of Hospitality, Leisure, Sport and Tourism Education*, *28*, 100302. doi:10.1016/j.jhlste.2021.100302

Espada, M., Rocu, P., Navia, J. A., & Gómez-López, M. (2020). Rendimiento académico y satisfacción de los estudiantes universitarios hacia el método flipped classroom [Academic performance and university students' satisfaction with the flipped classroom method]. *Profesorado. Revista de Currículum y Formación del Profesorado*, *24*(1), 116–135. doi:10.30827/profesorado.v24i1.8710

Espejo Leupin, R. M. (2016). ¿Pedagogía activa o métodos activos? El caso del aprendizaje activo en la universidad. *Revista Digital de Investigación en Docencia Universitaria*, *10*(1), 16. doi:10.19083/ridu.10.456

Espinosa, M. P. P., & Cartagena, F. C. (2021). Advanced technologies to meet the challenge of educational innovation [Tecnologías avanzadas para afrontar el reto de la innovación educativa]. *RIED. Revista Iberoamericana de Educación a Distancia*, *24*(1), 33–53.

Fach Gómez, K. (2012). Ventajas del Problem Based Learning (PBL) como método de aprendizaje del Derecho internacional [Advantages of Problem Based Learning (PBL) as a method of learning international law]. *Bordón. Revista de Pedagogía.*, *64*(1), 59–73.

Fähnrich, B., Vogelgesang, J., & Scharkow, M. (2020). Evaluating universities' strategic online communication: How do Shanghai Ranking's top 50 universities grow stakeholder engagement with Facebook posts? *Journal of Communication Management (London)*, *3*(24), 265–283. doi:10.1108/JCOM-06-2019-0090

Fask, A., Englander, F., & Wang, Z. (2014). Do Online Exams Facilitate Cheating? An Experiment Designed to Separate Possible Cheating from the Effect of the Online Test Taking Environment. *Journal of Academic Ethics*, *12*(2), 101–112. doi:10.100710805-014-9207-1

Fergani, A. (2019). The future persona: A futures method to let your scenarios come to life. *Foresight*, *21*(4), 445–466. doi:10.1108/FS-10-2018-0086

Fernández Cruz, F. J., Fernández Díaz, M. J., & Rodríguez Mantilla, J. M. (2018). El proceso de integración y uso pedagógico de las TIC en los centros educativos madrileños [The process of integration and pedagogical use of ICT in educational centers in Madrid]. *Educación XX1, 21*(2). doi:10.5944/educxx1.17907

Fernández, A., García, B., Verde, Z., & Fernández, D. (2020). Satisfacción, motivación y aprendizaje de los estudiantes de enfermería en prácticas farmacológicas con metodología flipped classroom [Satisfaction, motivation and learning of nursing students in pharmacological internships with flipped classroom methodology]. *La docencia en la Enseñanza Superior: Nuevas aportaciones desde la investigación e innovación educativas,* 1202-1213.

Fernández-Fernández, M., Martínez-Navalón, J. G., & Gelashvili, V. (2021). Sustainability and online classes at the university in times of COVID-19: Has it served as a starting point for a new teaching modality? [La sostenibilidad y las clases online en la universidad en tiempos de COVID-19: ¿Nos ha servido como punto de partida para una nueva modalidad de enseñanza?]. *Espacios*, *42*(5), 127–144. doi:10.48082/espacios-a21v42n05p09

Fernández-Jiménez, C., López-Justicia, M.D., Fernández, M., & Polo, M.T. (2014). Aplicación del aprendizaje basado en problemas para la formación del alumnado de Educación en la atención a la discapacidad [Application of problem-based learning for the training of education students in disability care]. *Revista de Currículum y formación del profesorado, 18*(2), 334-352.

Fernández-Zamora, J. C., & Arias-Aranda, D. (2017). Implementation of a gamification platform in a master degree (master in economics). *WPOM-Working Papers on Operations Management, 8*, 181-190.

Ferreira, A. C., Altamirano, M., Ortega, M. D. L. Á. L., & González, O. A. G. (2019). Learning analytics and educational neurosciences: New challenges in technological integration [Analítica del aprendizaje y las neurociencias educativas: nuevos retos en la integración tecnológica]. *Revista Iberoamericana de Educación, 80*(1), 31–54.

Fiallos, A., Fiallos, C., & Figueroa, S. (2021, July). Tiktok and Education: Discovering Knowledge through Learning Videos. *2021 Eighth International Conference on eDemocracy & eGovernment (ICEDEG)*, 172-176 10.1109/ICEDEG52154.2021.9530988

Fidalgo-Blanco, Á., Sein-Echaluce, M. L., & García-Peñalvo, F. J. (2014). Espirales de conocimiento en la innovación docente en educación superior. *Revista Internacional de Gestión del Conocimiento (IJKM), 10*(4), 16-37. doi:10.4018/ijkm.2014100102

Fletcher, T. & Chróinín, D. N. (2021). Pedagogical principles that support the prioritisation of meaningful experiences in physical education: conceptual and practical considerations. *Physical Education and Sport Pedagogy*. doi:10.1080/17408989.2021.1884672

Flores, G., De Alba, R., & Caicedo, E. (2020). Recomendaciones básicas de competencias docentes para la modalidad no escolarizada en tiempos de la pandemia. *Humanidades, Tecnología y Ciencia, del instituto Politécnico Nacional, 22*(25). http://revistaelectronica-ipn.org/ResourcesFiles/Contenido/23/HUMANIDADES_23_000877.pdf

Flynn, A. E., & Klein, J. D. (2001). The influence of discussion groups in a case-based learning environment. *Educational Technology Research and Development*, *49*(3), 71–86. doi:10.1007/BF02504916

Folgueiras Bertomeu, P., Luna González, E., & Puig Latorre, G. (2013). Learning and service: Study of the degree of satisfaction of university students [Aprendizaje y servicio: estudio del grado de satisfacción de estudiantes universitarios]. *Review of Education, 362*, 159–185.

Folgueiras Bertomeu, P., & Martínez Vivot, M. (2009). The development of competencies in the university through Solidarity Learning and Service [El desarrollo de competencias en la universidad a través del Aprendizaje y Servicio Solidario]. *Revista Interamericana de Educacion para la Democracia (RIED), 2*(1), 55–76.

Forman, E., & Cazen, C. (1985). Exploring Vygotskian perspectives in education: the cognitive value of peer interaction. In Culture, Communication, and Cognition: Vygotskian Perspectives. Cambridge, UK: Cambridge University Press.

Foster, J., & Yaoyuneyong, G. (2016). Teaching innovation: Equipping students to overcome real-world challenges. *Higher Education Pedagogies, 1*(1), 42–56. doi:10.1080/23752696.2015.1134195

Fowler, M. (2002). *AGILE Customer Quotes*. WikiWikiWeb. https://martinfowler.com/articles/agileStory.html

Freud, S. (1989). The Ego And The Id (1923). *TACD Journal, 17*(1), 5–22. doi:10.1080/1046171X.1989.12034344

Freund, R. J., Wilson, W. J., & Mohr, D. L. (2010). *Statistical Methods*. Academic Press, Elsevier Inc.

Frobel, F. (1899). *Friedrich Froebel's Education by Development: The Second Part of the Pedagogics of the Kindergarten*. D. Appleton.

Froment, F., García-González, A. J., & Cabero-Almenara, J. (2022). The relationship of Twitter with teacher credibility and motivation in university students. *Communicate (High Wycombe), 30*(71), 131–142. doi:10.3916/C71-2022-10

Fromm, J. (2004). The emergence of complexity. Kassel University Press.

Fullan, M., & Stiegelbauer, S. (1991). *The New Meaning of Educational Change*. Casell.

Gaete-Ouezada, R. A. (2011). Role play as a strategy for evaluating university learning [El juego de roles como estrategia de evaluación de aprendizajes universitarios]. *Educación y educadores, 14*(2), 289-307.

Galdames, V., Walqui, A., & Gustafson, B. (2011). *Enseñanza de la lengua indígena como Lengua Materna*. PROEIB Andes.

Garcez, A., Silva, R., & Franco, M. (2022). Digital transformation shaping structural pillars for academic entrepreneurship: A framework proposal and research agenda. *Education and Information Technologies, 27*(1), 1159–1182. doi:10.100710639-021-10638-5 PMID:34248387

García García, M. D. C., & Cotrina García, M. J. (2015). *Learning and service in initial teacher training: from critical educational practices to curricular institutionalization* [El aprendizaje y servicio en la formación inicial del profesorado: de las prácticas educativas críticas a la institucionalización curricular]. Academic Press.

García Magro, C., Martín Peña, M. L., & Díaz Garrido, E. (2019). Protocol: Gamify a Subject without Advanced Technology. *WPOM-Working Papers on Operations Management, 10*(2), 20-35.

García Magro, C., & Martín Peña, M. L. (2021). Aprendizaje autorregulado y gamificación en educación superior [Self-regulated learning and gamification in higher education: a proposal for an analysis model]. *Revista Española de Pedagogía, 79*(279), 341–362. doi:10.22550/REP79-2-2021-02

García-Alberti, M., Suárez, F., Chiyón, I., & Mosquera Feijoo, J. C. (2021). Challenges and experiences of online evaluation in courses of civil engineering during the lockdown learning due to the COVID-19 pandemic. *Education Sciences, 11*(2), 59. doi:10.3390/educsci11020059

García, C. M. (1996). *Educational innovation, counselling and professional development* (Vol. 124). Ministerio de Educación.

García-Peñalvo, F. J. (2011). La Universidad de la próxima década: La Universidad Digital. In C. SuárezGuerrero & F. J. García-Peñalvo (Eds.), Universidad y Desarrollo Social de la Web (pp. 181-197). Editandum.

García-Peñalvo, F. J. (2015). Map of trends in Educational Innovation [Mapa de tendencias en Innovación Educativa]. *Education in the Knowledge Society, 16*(4), 6-23.

García-Peñalvo, F. J., Johnson, M., Alves, G. R., Minović, M., & Conde-González, M. Á. (2014). Informal learning recognition through a cloud ecosystem. *Future Generation Computer Systems*, *32*, 282–294. doi:10.1016/j.future.2013.08.004

García-Valcárcel, A., Basilotta, V., & López, C. (2014). Las TIC en el aprendizaje colaborativo en el aula de Primaria y Secundaria [ICT in collaborative learning in primary and secondary classrooms]. *Comunicar*, *21*(42), 65–74.

Gargallo, B. (2008). Teaching styles and evaluation of university professors and their influence on the ways of learning of their students [Estilos de docencia y evaluación de los profesores universitarios y su influencia sobre los modos de aprender de sus estudiantes]. *Revista Española de Pedagogía*, *241*, 425–445.

Garger, J., Vracheva, V. P., & Jacques, P. (2020). A tipping point analysis of service-learning hours and student outcomes. *Education + Training*, *62*(4), 413–425. doi:10.1108/ET-09-2019-0210

Garrote Rojas, D., Garrote Rojas, C., & Jiménez Fernández, S. (2016). Factores Influyentes en Motivación y Estrategias de Aprendizaje en los Alumnos de Grado REICE. *Revista Iberoamericana sobre Calidad, Eficacia y Cambio en Educación*, *14*(2), 31-44.

Genette, G. (1983). Narrative discourse: An essay in method (Vol. 3). Cornell University Press.

Genette, G. (1976, Autumn). Boundaries of Narrative. *New Literary History*.

Genette, G. (1982). Figures of Literary Discourse. In *Translation*. Columbia University Press.

Genette, G. (1997). Palimpsests: Literature in the Second Degree. In C. Newman & C. Doubinsky (Eds.), *Translation*. University of Nebraska Press.

Georgios, Z. (2016). *In our own image: Savior or destroyer? The history and future of artificial intelligence*. Pegasus Books.

Gersick, C. J. (1988). Time and transition in work teams: Toward a new model of group development. *Academy of Management Journal*, *31*(1), 9–41.

Gikas, J., & Grant, M. M. (2013). Mobile computing devices in higher education: Student perspectives on learning with cellphones, smartphones & social media. *The Internet and Higher Education*, *19*, 18–26. doi:10.1016/j.iheduc.2013.06.002

Gilby, T. (1988). Principle of Software Engineering Management. Addison-Wesley.

Gil-Flores, J. (2012). La evaluación del aprendizaje en la universidad según la experiencia de los estudiantes [The evaluation of the learning process in the University based on the experience of the students]. *Estudios sobre educación, 22*, 133-153.

Gil-Flores, J., Santero, J. R., & Torres-Gordillo, J.-J. (2017). Factors that explain the use of ICT in secondary-education classrooms: The role of teacher characteristics and school infrastructure. *Computers in Human Behavior*, *68*, 441–449. doi:10.1016/j.chb.2016.11.057

Gil-Galván, R., Martín-Espinosa, I., & Gil-Galvan, F. J. (2021). Percepciones de los estudiantes universitarios sobre las competencias adquiridas mediante el aprendizaje basado en problemas [University students' perceptions of competencies acquired through problem-based Learning]. *Educación XX1, 24*(1), 271-295. doi:10.5944/educxx1.26800

Gimenez-Fernandez, E. M., & Gelashvili, V. (2019). La honestidad de los estudiantes en los exámenes online. Una comparativa de la realización de exámenes online y presenciales [The honestity of students in online exams. A comparison of taking online and face-to-face exams]. In C. Cáceres, N. Esteban, M. C. Gálvez, & B. Rivas (Eds.), *Competencia digital docente: una perspectiva de futuro en la educación superior [Teaching digital competence: a future perspective in Higher Education]* (pp. 297–307). Dykinson.

Giordano, N. A., Compton, P., Joseph, P. V., Romano, C. A., Piano, M. R., & Naylor, M. D. (2020). Opportunities and challenges presented by recent pedagogical innovations in doctoral nursing education. *Journal of Professional Nursing*. Advance online publication. doi:10.1016/j.profnurs.2020.09.003 PMID:33674100

Gittins, R., Hope, S., & Williams, L. (2002). Qualitative Studies of AGILE in a medium-sized Business. In M. Marchesi, G. Succi, D. Wells, & L. Williams (Eds.), *Extreme Programming Perspectives*. Addison-Wesley.

Glasser, W. (1998). *Choice Theory*. Harper Collins.

Gleick, J. (2012). *The information: A history, a theory, a flood*. Vintage.

Global Report on the Digital Environment 2022. (2022). *Hootsuite*. https://hootsuite.com/en/resources/digital-trends-2021

Glynn, S. M., Aultman, L. P., & Owens, A. M. (2005). Motivation to learn in general education programs. *The Journal of General Education, 54*(2), 150–170. doi:10.2307/27798014

Gómes, C., & Gargallo, B. (1993). Las bases de una concepción constructivista de la educación. Implicaciones pedagógicas. In *Construcción humana y procesos de estructuración: propuestas de intervención pedagógica* (pp. 35–65). Quiles Artes Gráficas.

Gómez, A. (Coord.). (2021). Análisis multisectorial de cuentas anuales y sus informes de auditoría [Multisectoral analysis of annual accounts and their audit reports]. Ediciones Pirámide.

Gómez-Aguilar, M., Roses-Campos, S., & Farias-Batlle, P. (2012). The academic use of social networks among university students. *Comunicar: Revista Científica de Comunicación y Educación, 19*(38), 131–138. doi:10.3916/C38-2012-03-04

Gomezelj, D. O. (2016). A systematic review of research on innovation in hospitality and tourism. *International Journal of Contemporary Hospitality Management, 28*(3), 516–558. doi:10.1108/IJCHM-10-2014-0510

Gómez-Martínez, R., & Romero-Rodriguez, L. M. (2021). Coworking spaces and virtual learning communities in Social Networks: Case Study of# ElClaustroDeIG on Instagram. *Open Classroom, 50*(1), 453–464. doi:10.17811/rifie.50.1.2021.453-464

González González, C. S., & Mora Carreño, A. (2015). Técnicas de gamificación aplicadas en la docencia de Ingeniería Informática [Gamification techniques applied in the teaching of Computer Engineering]. *ReVisión, 8*(1).

González, J. (2018). *Uso de la Tecnología en la Educación* [Use of Technology in Education]. México, UNID editorial digital 31. Available at https://bit.ly/2SPRxQw

González-Hernando, C., Martín-Villamor, P., Carbonero-Martín, M. Á., & Lara-Ortega, F. (2013). Evaluación por competencias de los estudiantes de Enfermería a través de Aprendizaje Basado en Problemas [Competency-based assessment of nursing students through Problem-Based Learning]. *Enfermería Universitaria, 10*(4), 120–124. doi:10.1016/S1665-7063(13)72640-X

Gopal, R., Singh, V., & Aggarwal, A. (2021). Impact of online classes on the satisfaction and performance of students during the pandemic period of COVID 19. *Education and Information Technologies*, *26*(6), 6923–6947. doi:10.100710639-021-10523-1 PMID:33903795

Goshevski, D., Veljanoska, J., & Hatziapostolou, T. (2017, September). A review of gamification platforms for higher education. In *Proceedings of the 8th Balkan Conference in Informatics* (pp. 1-6). 10.1145/3136273.3136299

Gowin, D. B. (1990). *Educating* (2nd ed.). Cornell University Press.

Graham, S., Harris, K. R., & Mason, L. (2005). Improving the writing performance, knowledge, and self-efficacy of struggling young writers: The effects of self-regulated strategy development. *Contemporary Educational Psychology*, *30*(2), 207–241. doi:10.1016/j.cedpsych.2004.08.001

Greenbowe, T. J., & Hand, B. M. (2005). Introduction to Science Writing Heuristic. In N. J. Peinta, M. Cooper, & T. J. Greenbowe (Eds.), *Chemists Guide to Effective Teaching* (Vol. 140). Prentice Hall.

Grewal, R., Meyer, R., & Mittal, V. (2022). Education and Marketing: Decision Making, Spending, and Consumption. *JMR, Journal of Marketing Research*, *59*(1), 1–10. doi:10.1177/00222437211068091

Gribbin, J. (2005). *Deep simplicity: Chaos, complexity and the emergence of life.* Penguin UK.

Grijalva, T. C., Nowell, C., & Kerkvliet, J. (2006). Academic Honesty and Online Courses. *College Student Journal*, *40*(1), 180–185.

Grillon, C., Lago, T., Stahl, S., Beale, A., Balderston, N., & Ernst, M. (2020). Better cognitive efficiency is associated with increased experimental anxiety. *Psychophysiology*, *57*(8), 1–10. doi:10.1111/psyp.13559 PMID:32180239

Groen, J., Ghani, S., Germain-Rutherford, A., & Taylor, M. (2020). Institutional Adoption of Blended Learning: Analysis of an Initiative in Action. *The Canadian Journal for the Scholarship of Teaching and Learning*, *11*(3), 3. doi:10.5206/cjsotl-rcacea.2020.3.8288

Grossman, P., Dean, C. G. P., Herrmann, Z., & Schneider Kavanaght, S. (2021). *Core Practices for Project-Based Learning*. Harvard Education Press.

Guardia, J. J., Del Olmo, J. L., Roa, I., & Berlanga, V. (2019). Innovation in the teaching-learning process: The case of Kahoot! *On the Horizon*, *27*(1), 35–45. doi:10.1108/OTH-11-2018-0035

Guerrero Castañeda, A., Rojas Morales, C., & Villafañe Aguilar, C. (2019). Impacto de la Educación Virtual en Carreras de Pregrado del Área de Ciencias de la Salud. Una Mirada de las Tecnologías Frente a la Educación. Trabajo de Grado presentado como requisito parcial para optar al título de: Especialización en Docencia Universitaria Línea de Investigación: Monografía Universidad Cooperativa de Colombia Facultad de Educación Especialización en docencia universitaria.

Guiñez-Cabrera, N., & Mansilla-Obando, K. (2022). Booktokers: Generate and share content about books through TikTok. *Communicate: Scientific Journal of Communication and Education*, *30*(71).

Gunn, C. (2010). Sustainability factors for e-learning initiatives. *ALT-J Research in Learning Technology*, *18*(2), 89–103. doi:10.1080/09687769.2010.492848

Gupta, A., & Katarya, R. (2020). Social media based surveillance systems for healthcare using machine learning: A systematic review. *Journal of Biomedical Informatics*, *108*, 103500. doi:10.1016/j.jbi.2020.103500 PMID:32622833

Gupta, T., Burke, K. A., Mehta, A., & Greenbowe, T. J. (2014). Impact of Guided-Inquiry-Based Instruction with a Writing and Reflection Emphasis on Chemistry Students' Critical Thinking Abilities. *Journal of Chemical Education*, *92*(1), 32–38. doi:10.1021/ed500059r

Gurney, B. (1989). Constructivism and Professional Development: A stereoscopic view. *ERIC Document ED, 305*(259), 1–28.

Haak, L. L., Fenner, M., Paglione, L., Pentz, E., & Ratner, H. (2012). ORCID: A system to uniquely identify researchers. *Learned Publishing, 25*(4), 259–264. doi:10.1087/20120404

Habibi, A., Yaakob, M. F. M., Mukminin, A., Muhaimin, M., Prasojo, L. D., Yusop, F. D., & Muzakkir, M. (2021). Teachers' digital technology access to motivation, skills and use: A structural equation modeling study. *Aslib Journal of Information Management, 4*(73), 543–559. doi:10.1108/AJIM-11-2020-0382

Hair, J. F., Risher, J. J., Sarstedt, M., & Ringle, C. M. (2018). When to use and how to report the results of PLS-SEM. *European Business Review*. Advance online publication. doi:10.1108/EBR-11-2018-0203

Hamdan, R., Ashour, W., & Daher, W. (2021). The role of the e-learning departments in controlling the quality of electronic assessments in Palestinian universities during the COVID-19 pandemic. *Sustainability, 13*(21), 12021. doi:10.3390u132112021

Hamel, G., & Prahalad, C. K. (1993). Strategy as stretch and leverage. *Harvard Business Review, 71*(2), 75–84. PMID:10124635

Hammer, D., Goldberg, F., & Fargason, S. (2012). Responsive teaching and the beginnings of energy in a third-grade classroom. *Review of Science, Mathematics, and ICT Education, 6*(1), 51–72.

Hanani, N. (2020). Meaningful Learning Reconstruction for Millennial: Facing competition in the information technology era. *IOP Conference Series. Earth and Environmental Science, 469*(1), 012107. doi:10.1088/1755-1315/469/1/012107

Händel, M., Stephan, M., Gläser-Zikuda, M., Kopp, B., Bedenlier, S., & Ziegler, A. (2020). Digital readiness and its effects on higher education students' socio-emotional perceptions in the context of the COVID-19 pandemic. *Journal of Research on Technology in Education*, 1–13.

Hansen, M. T. (2002). Knowledge networks: Explaining effective knowledge sharing in multiunit companies. *Organization Science, 13*(3), 232–248. doi:10.1287/orsc.13.3.232.2771

Hanssen, G. K., & Fægri, T. E. (2006). Agile Customer Engagement: A Longitudinal Qualitative Case Study. In *ISESE'06* (pp. 164–173). ACM Press. doi:10.1145/1159733.1159759

Hanushek, E. A., Schwerdt, G., Woessmann, L., & Zhang, L. (2017). General education, vocational education, and labor-market outcomes over the lifecycle. *The Journal of Human Resources, 52*(1), 48–87. doi:10.3368/jhr.52.1.0415-7074R

Harari, Y. N. (2014). *Sapiens: A brief history of humankind*. Random House.

Harmon, O. R., & Lambrinos, J. (2008). Are Online Exams an Invitation to Cheat? *The Journal of Economic Education, 39*(2), 116–125. doi:10.3200/JECE.39.2.116-125

Hattar, S., AlHadidi, A., Sawair, F. A., Alraheam, I. A., El-Ma'aita, A., & Wahab, F. K. (2021). Impact of COVID-19 pandemic on dental education: Online experience and practice expectations among dental students at the University of Jordan. *BMC Medical Education, 21*(1), 1–10. doi:10.118612909-021-02584-0 PMID:33685451

Hawking, S. (2009). *A brief history of time: From big bang to black holes*. Random House.

Herbert, C., Velan, G. M., Pryor, W. M., & Kumar, R. K. (2017). A model for the use of blended learning in large group teaching sessions. *BMC Medical Education, 17*(1), 1–11. doi:10.118612909-017-1057-2 PMID:29121908

Herrero-Diz, P., Conde-Jiménez, J., & Reyes-de-Cózar, S. (2021). Spanish adolescents and fake news: Level of awareness and credibility of information. *Culture and Education, 33*(1), 1–27. doi:10.1080/11356405.2020.1859739

Hertzog, P. E., & Swart, A. J. (2018, April). The use of WhatsApp in design-based modules. In *2018 IEEE Global Engineering Education Conference (EDUCON)* (pp. 445-450). IEEE. 10.1109/EDUCON.2018.8363264

Highsmith, J. (2001). The Great Methodologies Debate, Part I: Opening Statement. *Cutter IT Journal, 14*, 2–4.

Hincapié, D., Ramos, A., & Chirino, V. (2018). Aprendizaje Basado en Problemas como estrategia de Aprendizaje Activo y su incidencia en el rendimiento académico y pensamiento crítico de estudiantes de Medicina de Segundo Semestre [Problem Based Learning as an Active Learning strategy and its impact on the academic performance and critical thinking of second semester medical students]. *Revista Complutense de Educación, 29*(3), 665–681. doi:10.5209/RCED.53581

Hinds, P. J., Patterson, M., & Pfeffer, J. (2001). Bothered by abstraction: The effect of expertise on knowledge transfer and subsequent novice performance. *The Journal of Applied Psychology, 86*(6), 1232–1243. doi:10.1037/0021-9010.86.6.1232 PMID:11768064

Hirschfeld, R. R., Thomas, C. H., & McNatt, D. B. (2008). Implications of Self-Deception for Self-Reported Intrinsic and Extrinsic Motivational Dispositions and Actual Learning Performance: A Higher Order Structural Model. *Educational and Psychological Measurement, 68*(1), 154–173. doi:10.1177/0013164406299129

Hockings, C. (2005). Removing the barriers? A study of the conditions affecting teaching innovation. *Teaching in Higher Education, 10*(3), 313–326. doi:10.1080/13562510500122149

Hodges, C., Moore, S., Lockee, B., Trust, T., & Bond, A. (2020). The difference between emergency remote teaching and online learning. *EDUCAUSE Review*.

Hoffman, J. (2002). Flexible grouping strategies in the multiage classroom. *Theory into Practice, 41*(1), 47–52. doi:10.120715430421tip4101_8

Hofstein, A. (2004). The laboratory in Chemistry Education: Thirty years of experience with developments, implementation, and research. *Chemistry Education Research and Practice, 5*, 247–264.

Hofstein, A., & Lunetta, V. N. (1982). The role of the laboratory in science teaching: Neglected Aspects of Research. *Review of Educational Research, 52*, 201–217.

Hollander, M., & Wolfe, D. A. (1973). *Nonparametric Statistical Methods*. John Wiley & Sons.

Hong, A. J., & Kim, H. J. (2018). College students' digital readiness for academic engagement (DRAE) scale: Scale development and validation. *The Asia-Pacific Education Researcher, 27*(4), 303–312. doi:10.100740299-018-0387-0

Horcher, R. (1998). Fachhochschule oder Universität? In H. W. Stahl & W. W. Stahl (Eds.), *Effizient Studieren: Wirtschaftswissenschaften an Fachhochschulen* (pp. 115–120). Gabler. doi:10.1007/978-3-322-84594-8_8

Hornyak, M., Green, S. G., & Heppard, K. A. (2007). Implementing experiential learning. In M. Reynolds & R. Vince (Eds.), *The handbook of experiential learning and management education* (pp. 137–152). Oxford University Press.

Howland, J. L., Jonassen, D. H., & Marra, R. M. (2011). *Meaningful Learning with Technology* (4th ed.). Pearson.

Hsu, Y. C., & Ching, Y. H. (2012). Mobile microblogging: Using Twitter and mobile devices in an online course to promote learning in authentic contexts. *International Review of Research in Open and Distributed Learning, 13*(4), 211–227. doi:10.19173/irrodl.v13i4.1222

Huber, G. L. (2008). Active learning and methods of teaching [Aprendizaje activo y metodologías educativas]. *Tiempos de cambio universitario en, 59*.

Hunt, J., Brannan, E., & Sexson, S. (2019). Lifelong Learning for Professional Development in Psychiatry: Pedagogy, Innovations, and Maintenance of Certification. *Psychiatria Clinica*, *42*(3), 425–437. doi:10.1016/j.psc.2019.05.014 PMID:31358122

Hüther, O., & Krücken, G. (2018). *Higher education in Germany - Recent developments in an international perspective*. Springer. doi:10.1007/978-3-319-61479-3

Hu, Z., & McGrath, I. (2011). Innovation in higher education in China: Are teachers ready to integrate ICT in English language teaching? *Technology, Pedagogy and Education*, *20*(1), 41–59. doi:10.1080/1475939X.2011.554014

Ifinedo, P., Pyke, J., & Anwar, A. (2018). Business undergraduates' perceived use outcomes of moodle in a blended learning environment: The roles of usability factors and external support. *Telematics and Informatics, 35*(1), 93–102. .10.001 doi:10.1016/j.tele.2017

Iglesias Martínez, M. J., Lozano Cabezas, I., & Roldán Soler, I. (2018). *Educational quality and innovation in continuous teacher training: a qualitative study in two educational centers* [La calidad e innovación educativa en la formación continua docente: un estudio cualitativo en dos centros educativos]. Academic Press.

Islam, A. K. M. N. (2013). Investigating e-learning system usage outcomes in the university context. *Computers and Education, 69*, 387–399. .2013.07.037 doi:10.1016/J.COMPEDU

Islam, A. K. M. N. (2016). E-learning system use and its outcomes: Moderating role of perceived compatibility. *Telematics and Informatics*, *33*(1), 48–55. doi:10.1016/j.tele.2015.06.010

Jehn, K. A. (1994). Enhancing effectiveness: An investigation of advantages and disadvantages of value-based intragroup conflict. *International Journal of Conflict Management*, *5*(3), 223–238. doi:10.1108/eb022744

Jehn, K. A., Chadwick, C., & Thatcher, S. M. (1997). To agree or not to agree: The effects of value congruence, individual demographic dissimilarity, and conflict on workgroup outcomes. *International Journal of Conflict Management*, *8*(4), 287–305. doi:10.1108/eb022799

Johnson, D. W. (1984). *Circles of Learning: Cooperation in the Classroom*. Association for Supervision and Curriculum Development.

Johnson, R. T., & Johnson, D. W. (1985). Student-Student Interaction: Ignored but Powerful. *Journal of Teacher Education*, *36*, 22–26.

Joksimovic, S., Gasevic, D., Kovanovic, V., Adesope, O., & Hatala, M. (2014). Psychological characteristics in cognitive presence of communities of inquiry: A linguistic analysis of online discussions. *Internet High. Educ*, *22*, 1–10. doi:10.1016/j.iheduc.2014.03.001

Jonassen, D. H. (2003). *Learning to Solve Problems with Technology: A Constructivist Perspective* (2nd ed.). Merrill.

Jones, M. G., Rua, M. J., & Carter, G. (1998). Science Teachers' Conceptual Growth within Vygotsky's Zone of Proximal Development. *Journal of Research in Science Teaching*, *35*, 967–985.

Joo, Y. J., Lim, K. Y., & Kim, E. K. (2011). Online university students' satisfaction and persistence: Examining perceived level of presence, usefulness, and ease of use as predictors in a structural model. *Computers & Education*, *2011*(57), 1654–1664. doi:10.1016/j.compedu.2011.02.008

Joshi, A., Vinay, M., & Bhaskar, P. (2020). Impact of coronavirus pandemic on the Indian education sector: Perspectives of teachers on online teaching and assessments. *Interactive Technology and Smart Education*.

Julca, F. (2000). *Uso de las lenguas quechua y castellano en la escuela urbana: Un estudio de caso* (Tesis de maestría). Cochabamba: Universidad Mayor de San Simón – Bolivia. Recuperado de http://bvirtual.proeibandes.org/bvirtual/docs/tesis/proeib/Tesis_Felix_Julca.pd

Jurado-Navas, A., & Munoz-Luna, R. (2017). Scrum Methodology in Higher Education: Innovation in Teaching, Learning and Assessment. *International Journal of Higher Education*, *6*(6), 1–18. doi:10.5430/ijhe.v6n6p1

Kagan, S. (1989). The structural approach to cooperative learning. *Educational Leadership*, *47*, 12–15.

Kanuru, S. L., & Priyaadharshini, M. (2020). Lifelong Learning in higher education using Learning Analytics. *Procedia Computer Science*, *172*, 848–852. doi:10.1016/j.procs.2020.05.122

Kaplan, A. M., & Haenlein, M. (2010). Users of the world, unite! The challenges and opportunities of Social Media. *Business Horizons*, *53*(1), 59–68. doi:10.1016/j.bushor.2009.09.003

Kapp, K. M. (2012). Games, gamification, and the quest for learner engagement. *T+D, 66*(6), 64-68.

Katwala, A. (2021). *Quantum computing: How it works and how it could change the world.* Random House.

Katz, R. L. (1974). Skills of an effective administrator. *Harvard Business Review*, *52*(5), 90–102.

Kaware, S. S., & Sain, S. K. (2015). ICT application in education: An overview. *International Journal of Multidisciplinary Approach & Studies*, *2*(1), 25–32.

Kay, D., & Kibbl, J. (2016). Learning theories 101: Application to everyday teaching and scholarship. *Advances in Physiology Education*, *40*(1), 17–25. doi:10.1152/advan.00132.2015 PMID:26847253

Ke, F. (2010). Examining online teaching, cognitive, and social presence for adult students. *Computers & Education*, *2010*(55), 808–820. doi:10.1016/j.compedu.2010.03.013

Kelley, T. (2016). *The art of innovation: Lessons in creativity from IDEO, America's leading design firm.* Profile.

Kendon, A. (1995). Gestures as illocutionary and discourse structure markers in Southern Italian conversation. *Journal of Pragmatics*, *23*(3), 1–31. doi:10.1016/0378-2166(94)00037-F

Kessler, M. M. (1963). Bibliographic coupling between scientific papers. *American Documentation*, *14*(1), 10–25. doi:10.1002/asi.5090140103

Khalaf, K., El-Kishawi, M., Moufti, M. A., & Al Kawas, S. (2020). Introducing a comprehensive high-stake online exam to final-year dental students during the COVID-19 pandemic and evaluation of its effectiveness. *Medical Education Online*, *25*(1), 1826861. doi:10.1080/10872981.2020.1826861 PMID:33000704

Kidder, L. H. (1982). *Face validity from multiple perspectives.* New Directions for Methodology of Social & Behavioral Science.

Kim, J., Kwon, Y., & Cho, D. (2011). Investigating factors that influence social presence and learning outcomes in distance higher education. *Computers & Education*, *2011*(57), 1512–1520. doi:10.1016/j.compedu.2011.02.005

Kirkup, G., & Kirkwood, A. (2005). Information and communications technologies (ICT) in higher education teaching—A tale of gradualism rather than revolution. *Learning, Media and Technology*, *30*(2), 185–199. doi:10.1080/17439880500093810

Kitchenham, B., & Charters, S. (2007). Guidelines for conducting systematic literature reviews in software engineering [Pautas para realizar revisiones sistemáticas de literatura en ingeniería de software]. *Ingeniería*, *2*, 1051–1052. doi:10.1145/1134285.1134500

Kivunja, C. (2015). Using De Bono's Six Thinking Hats Model to Teach Critical Thinking and Problem Solving Skills Essential for Success in the 21st Century Economy. *Creative Education*, *2015*(6), 380–391. doi:10.4236/ce.2015.63037

Kolb, D. A. (1984). *Experiential learning: Experience as the source of learning and development.* Prentice-Hall.

Komljenovic, J. (2019). Linkedin, platforming labour, and the new employability mandate for universities. *Globalisation, Societies and Education*, *17*(1), 28–43. doi:10.1080/14767724.2018.1500275

Koontz, H., & Weihrich, H. (1994). *Administración. Una perspectiva Global* [Administration. A Global perspective]. McGraw Hill.

Korchinskaya, O., Ivanova, I., Shchukina, N., & Mendziv, M. (2019). Business Games as a Teaching Strategy for Delivering a Practice-Oriented Course in Mathematics at Agricultural University. In *Proceedings of the International Scientific Conference The Fifth Technological Order - Prospects for the Development and Modernization of the Russian Agro-Industrial Sector.* Atlantis Press.

Korkmaz, G., & Kalayci, N. (2019). Theoretical foundations of project based curricula in higher education. *Çukurova University. Faculty of Education Journal*, *48*(1), 236–274. doi:10.14812/cufej.479322

Koromzay, T. (2021). *Integrative Leadership.* Springer. doi:10.1007/978-3-662-62973-4

Kostaris, C., Sergis, S., Sampson, D. G., Giannakos, M. N., & Pelliccione, L. (2017). Investigating the potential of the flipped classroom model in K-12 ICT teaching and learning: An action research study. *Journal of Educational Technology & Society*, *20*(1), 261–273.

Kostiainen, E., Ukskoski, T., Ruohotie-Lyhty, M., Kauppinen, M., Kainulainen, J., & Mäkinen, T. (2018). Meaningful learning in teacher education. *Teaching and Teacher Education*, *2018*(71), 66–77. doi:10.1016/j.tate.2017.12.009

Koulikov, M. (2011). Emerging Problems in Knowledge Sharing and the Three New Ethics of Knowledge Transfer. *Knowledge Management & E-Learning. International Journal*, *3*(2), 237–250.

Kounenou, K., Roussos, P., Yotsidi, V., & Tountopoulou, M. (2015). Trainee Teachers' Intention to Incorporating ICT Use into Teaching Practice in Relation to their Psychological Characteristics: The Case of Group-based Intervention. *Procedia: Social and Behavioral Sciences*, *190*, 120–128. doi:10.1016/j.sbspro.2015.04.925

Kozan, K., & Caskurlu, S. (2018). On the Nth presence for the Community of Inquiry framework. *Computers & Education*, *2018*(122), 104–118. doi:10.1016/j.compedu.2018.03.010

Krueger, D., & Kumar, K. B. (2004). Skill-specific rather than general education: A reason for US–Europe growth differences. *Journal of Economic Growth*, *9*(2), 167–207. doi:10.1023/B:JOEG.0000031426.09886.bd

Kuhn, M. H. (1964). Major Trends in Symbolic Interaction Theory in the past Twenty-Five years. *The Sociological Quarterly*, *5*, 61–84.

Kujala, S. (2007). Effective user involvement in product development by improving the analysis of user needs. *Behaviour & Information Technology, Taylor & Francis*, *2007*, 1–16.

Kumar, A., Sarkar, M., Davis, E., Morphet, J., Maloney, S., Ilic, D., & Palermo, C. (2021). Impact of the COVID-19 pandemic on teaching and learning in health professional education: A mixed methods study protocol. *BMC Medical Education*, *21*(1), 1–7. doi:10.118612909-021-02871-w PMID:34412603

Lachman, V. D., Glasgow, M. E. S., & Donnelly, G. F. (2009). Teaching innovation. *Nursing Administration Quarterly*, *33*(3), 205–211. doi:10.1097/NAQ.0b013e3181acca9a PMID:19546739

Lal, P., Kumar, A., Kumar, S., Kumari, S., Saikia, P., Dayanandan, A., Adhikari, D., & Khan, M. L. (2020). The dark cloud with a silver lining: Assessing the impact of the SARS COVID-19 pandemic on the global environment. *The Science of the Total Environment*, *732*, 139297. doi:10.1016/j.scitotenv.2020.139297 PMID:32408041

Lamia, T., Ashouri, H., & Sarra, T. (2017). Lesson via the e-learning platform MOODLE. In *2017 Joint International Conference on Information and Communication Technologies for Education and Training and International Conference on Computing in Arabic*. IEEE. . 809530410.1109/ICCA-TICET.2017

Lantz, M. E. (2010). The use of 'clickers' in the classroom: Teaching innovation or merely an amusing novelty? *Computers in Human Behavior*, *26*(4), 556–561. doi:10.1016/j.chb.2010.02.014

Larionova, I., Kapysheva, G., Chzhan, Y., Fedossova, S., & Rovnyakova, I. (2021). Modelling of Teaching Korean as a Second Foreign Language in Higher Education using CLIL (An Example of Educational Program Disciplines). *International Journal of Society, Culture & Language*, *9*(2), 98–113.

Larmer, J., Mergendoller, J., & Boss, S. (2015). *Setting the Standard for Project Based Learning*. ASCD.

Lašáková, A., Bajzíková, Ľ., & Dedze, I. (2017). Barriers and drivers of innovation in higher education: Case study-based evidence across ten European universities. *International Journal of Educational Development*, *55*, 69–79. doi:10.1016/j.ijedudev.2017.06.002

Laserna, M. S. S., & Miguel, M. C. (2018). Social media as a teaching innovation tool for the promotion of interest and motivation in higher education. *SIIE 2018 - 2018 International Symposium on Computers in Education, Proceedings*. 10.1109/SIIE.2018.8586752

Laurillard, D. (2002). *Rethinking University Teaching: a framework for the effective use of educational technology*. Academic Press.

Lazarowitz, R., & Tamir, P. (1997). Research on using laboratory instruction in science. In Handbook of Research on Science Teaching. Routledge Publishers.

Lederer, M., & Schott, P. (2020). Business Process Management. In M. Khosrow-Pour (Ed.), *Encyclopedia of Organizational Knowledge, Administration, and Technologies* (pp. 2287–2302). IGI Global.

Leech, N. L., & Onwuegbuzie, A. J. (2002). *A Call for Greater Use on Non-Parametric Statistics* (ERIC Document Reproduction Service No. ED 471346). Paper Presented at the annual meeting of the Mid-South Educational Research Association, Chattanooga, TN.

Lee, D. Y., & Lehto, M. R. (2013). User acceptance of YouTube for procedural learning: An extension of the Technology Acceptance Model. *Computers & Education*, *61*, 193–208. doi:10.1016/j.compedu.2012.10.001

Lee, J. H., & Segev, A. (2012). Knowledge maps for e-learning. *Computers & Education*, *59*(2), 353–364. doi:10.1016/j.compedu.2012.01.017

Lee, S., & Klein, H. J. (2002). Relationships between conscientiousness, self-efficacy, self-deception, and learning over time. *The Journal of Applied Psychology*, *87*(6), 1175–1182. doi:10.1037/0021-9010.87.6.1175 PMID:12558223

Liebana-Cabanillas, F., Martinez-Fiestas, M., & Rejon-Guardia, F. (2012). Analysis of microblogging applications as university teaching tools. *INTED2012 Proceedings*, 6309–6314.

Lillo, V. (2014). Salud Y Educación: Dos Vocaciones Al Servicio De Los Derechos Humanos. *Revista Médica Clínica Las Condes*, *25*(2), 357–362. doi:10.1016/S0716-8640(14)70047-1

Lim, J. S. Y., Agostinho, S., Harper, B., & Chicharo, J. (2014). The engagement of social media technologies by undergraduate informatics students for academic purpose in Malaysia. *Journal of Information. Communication and Ethics in Society*, *3*(12), 177–194.

Lin, K. Y. (2020). Application of a blended assessment strategy to enhance student interest and effectiveness in learning: case study with information security literacy. *CIN: Computers, Informatics, Nursing, 38*(10), 508–514.

Lin, L., & Han, Y. (2017). Innovation of Teaching Method for Improvement of Higher Education Teaching Quality. *International Conference on Education, Sports, Arts and Management Engineering (ICESAME)*, 1854–1857. 10.2991/icesame-17.2017.393

López-Carril, S., Sheriff, M., & Anagnostopoulos, C. (2022). LinkedIn in sport management education: Developing the students' professional profile boosting the teaching-learning process. *International Journal of Management Education, 20*(1), 100611.

López-Meneses, E., Sirignano, F. M., Vázquez-Cano, E., & Ramírez-Hurtado, J. M. (2020). University students' digital competence in three areas of the DigCom 2.1 model: A comparative study at three European universities. *Australasian Journal of Educational Technology*, *36*(3), 69–88.

López-Navas, C. (2014). Educación superior y TIC: conceptos y tendencias de cambio/Higher education and ITC: concepts and changing trends. *Historia y Comunicación Social, 19*, 227–239.

Loyens, S. M. M., & Gijbels, D. (2008). Understanding the efects of constructivist learning environments: Introducing a multi-directional approach. *Instructional Science*, *36*(5-6), 351–357. doi:10.100711251-008-9059-4

Lui, A. M., & Bonner, S. M. (2016). Preservice and inservice teachers' knowledge, beliefs, and instructional planning in primary school mathematics. *Teaching and Teacher Education*, *56*, 1–13. doi:10.1016/j.tate.2016.01.015

Lundgren, L., Curcio, R., & Schroeder, S. E. (2021). Are you a team player or a personal pinner? situating pinterest as part of teachers' online and offline professional learning networks. *Innovación Educativa (México, D.F.)*, *3*(1), 1–13.

Lunetta, V. N., Hofstein, A., & Clough, M. P. (2007). Learning and Teaching in the School Science Laboratory: An analysis of Research, Theory & Practice. In Handbook of Research in Science Education. Routledge Publishers.

Luo, T., Shah, S. J., & Cromptom, H. (2019). Using Twitter to support reflective learning in an asynchronous online course. *Australasian Journal of Educational Technology*, *35*(3). Advance online publication. doi:10.14742/ajet.4124

MacArthur, C. A. (2015). Instruction in evaluation and revision. In Handbook of Writing Research. New York, NY: Guilford Publications.

MacArthur, C. A. (2018). Evaluation and revision. In S. Graham, C. A. Charles, M. Hebert, & J. Fitzgerald (Eds.), *Best Practices in Writing Instruction* (pp. 287–308). Guilford Publications.

Machado, M. S. P., Sepúlveda, G. C. T., & Montoya, M. S. R. (2016). Educational innovation and digital competencies: The case of OER in a private Venezuelan university. *International Journal of Educational Technology in Higher Education*, *13*(1), 1–10.

Macías, A., Sánchez, M. A., & Prado, M. (2018). Evaluación de la implantación de aprendizaje basado en proyectos como herramienta para el estudio de la economía de la empresa [Evaluation of the implementation of project-based learning as a tool for the study of business Economics]. *Journal of Management and Business Education*, *1*(3), 190–209. doi:10.35564/jmbe.2018.0014

Magaña, J. R., Ferreirapinto, J., Blair, M., & Mata, A. (1992). Pedagogy of consciousness taking for the prevention of HIV/AIDS. *Revista Latinoamericana de Psicología*, *24*(1-2), 97–108.

Mahnic, V. (2015). Scrum in software engineering courses: An outline of the literature. *Global Journal of Engineering Education*, *17*(2), 77–83.

Maines, D. R. (1997). Interactionism and Practice. *Applied Behavioral Science Review*, *5*, 1–18.

Maltseva, O. A., Khovanskaya, E. A., Martynova, N. A., & Karpova, I. V. (2020). The Digitalization of Education in Higher Education: Methodological and Practice-Oriented Aspects. In *Proceedings of the International Scientific Conference Digitalization of Education - History, Trends and Prospects*. Atlantis Press. 10.2991/assehr.k.200509.152

Manca, S. (2020). Snapping, pinning, liking or texting: Investigating social media in higher education beyond Facebook. *The Internet and Higher Education*, *44*, 100707.

Manca, S., & Ranieri, M. (2016). Facebook and the others. Potentials and obstacles of social media for teaching in higher education. *Computers & Education*, *95*, 216–230.

Manca, S., & Ranieri, M. (2016). Yes for sharing, not for teaching!": Social Media in academic practices. *The Internet and Higher Education*, *29*, 63–74.

Manzanares, M. C. S., & Arreba, A. B. (2014). Aprendizaje basado en la evaluación mediante rúbricas en educación superior [Learning based on evaluation through rubrics in higher Education]. *Suma Psicologica*, *21*(1), 28–35. doi:10.1016/S0121-4381(14)70004-9

Marcelo Garcia, C., & Marcelo Martinez, P. (2021). Educational influencers on Twitter: Hashtag analysis and relational structure. *Comunicar: Ibero-American Scientific Journal of Communication and Education, 29*(68), 73-83.

Marín García, J. (2018). Focos de investigación sobre aprendizaje universitario en el área de dirección de operaciones [Research focus about universitary learning in the area of operations management]. In *IN-RED 2018. IV Congreso Nacional de Innovación Educativa y Docencia en Red* [IN-RED 2018. IV National Coference on Teaching innovation and On-line Teaching] (pp. 922-932). Universitat Politècnica de València.

Martiañez, N. L., Rubio, M., Terrón, M. J., & Gallego, T. (2015). Diseño de una rúbrica para evaluar las competencias del Prácticum del Grado en Fisioterapia. Percepción de su utilidad por los estudiantes [Design of a rubric to assess the competences of the Practicum of the Degree in Physiotherapy. Students' perception of its usefulness]. *Fisioterapia*, *37*(2), 83–95. doi:10.1016/j.ft.2014.06.005

Martín-Blas, T., & Serrano-Fernández, A. (2009). The role of new technologies in the learning process: Moodle as a teaching tool in physics. *Computers & Education*, *52*(1), 35–44. doi:10.1016/j.compedu.2008.06.005

Martínez & Piedad. (2006). The case study method: methodological strategy of scientific research [El método de estudio de caso: estrategia metodológica de la investigación científica]. *Pensamiento & Gestión, 20*, 165-193.

Martocchio, J. J., & Dulebohn, J. (1994). Performance Feedback Effects in Training: The Role of Perceived Controllability. *Personnel Psychology*, *47*(2), 357–373. doi:10.1111/j.1744-6570.1994.tb01729.x

Martocchio, J. J., & Judge, T. A. (1997). Relationship between conscientiousness and learning in employee training: Mediating influences of self-deception and self-efficacy. *The Journal of Applied Psychology*, *82*(5), 764–773. doi:10.1037/0021-9010.82.5.764 PMID:9337608

Matthies, C. (2018). Scrum2Kanban: Integrating Kanban and Scrum in a University Software Engineering Capstone Course. In *Proceedings of the International Workshop on Software Engineering Education for Millennials*. IEEE/ACM. 10.1145/3194779.3194784

Mayer, R. E. (2004). Should there be a three-strikes rule against pure discovery learning? *The American Psychologist*, *59*(1), 14–19. doi:10.1037/0003-066X.59.1.14 PMID:14736316

May, J., York, J., & Lending, D. (2016). Teaching Tip Play Ball: Bringing Scrum into the Classroom. *Journal of Information Systems Education*, *27*(2), 87–92.

Mayo-Cubero, M. (2021). Teaching innovation experience for COVID-19 times: A case study on blended learning of television journalism courses with moodle. *Asia Pacific Media Educator*, *31*(2), 178–194. doi:10.1177/1326365X211048619

Mazer, J. P., Hunt, S. K., & Kuznekoff, J. H. (2008). Revising general education: Assessing a critical thinking instructional model in the basic communication course. *The Journal of General Education*, *56*(3-4), 173–199. doi:10.2307/27798079

McKenny, C. (2006). *The World's Newest Profession. Management Consulting in the Twentieth Century*. Cambridge University Press. doi:10.1017/CBO9780511511622

McNabb, L., & Olmstead, A. (2009). Communities of Integrity in Online Courses: Faculty Member Beliefs and Strategies - ProQuest. *Journal of Online Learning and Teaching*, *5*(2), 208.

McSeeney, M., & Katz, B. M. (1978). Nonparametric Statistics: Use and nonuse. *Perceptual and Motor Skills*, *4*, 1023–1032.

Mead, G. H. (1962) Mind, self, and society from the standpoint of a social behaviorist. Chicago, IL: University of Chicago Press.

Méndez Peón, C. Á., Herrera Avilés, M., Toriz Palacios, A., & González Pérez, M. (2016). Estudio de la brecha Empresario-Investigador. La Percepción del Investigador [Study of the Entrepreneur-Researcher Gap. The Researcher's Perception]. *European Scientific Journal, ESJ*, *12*(28), 28. doi:10.19044/esj.2016.v12n28p109

Mensah, C., Azila-Gbettor, E. M., & Asimah, V. (2018). Self-Reported Examination Cheating of Alumni and Enrolled Students: Evidence From Ghana. *Journal of Academic Ethics*, *16*(1), 89–102. doi:10.100710805-017-9286-x

Mikki, S., Zygmuntowska, M., Gjesdal, Ø. L., & Al Ruwehy, H. A. (2015). Digital presence of Norwegian scholars on academic network sites—Where and who are they? *PLoS One*, *10*(11), e0142709.

Mintzberg, H. (1990). The manager's job: Folklore and fact. *Harvard Business Review*, *68*(2), 163–176.

Mintzberg, H., Raisinghani, D., & Theoret, A. (1976). The structure of "unstructured" decision processes. *Administrative Science Quarterly*, *21*(2), 246–275. doi:10.2307/2392045

Mintzes, J., & Wandersee, J. (2000). Reforma e Inovação no Ensino da Ciência: uma visão construtivista. In Ensinando Ciência para a compreensão – uma visão construtivista. Plátano Edições Técnicas.

Miraglia, K. M. (2008). Attitudes of preservice general education teachers toward art. *Visual Arts Research*, •••, 53–62.

Monteiro, A., Leite, C., & Lima, L. (2013). Quality of Blended Learning within the Scope of the Bologna Process. *Turkish Online Journal of Educational Technology*, *12*(1), 108–118.

Montes, C. P., & Andrés, S. M. (2021). The teaching modalities in the new normal for the 2020-21 academic year in Spanish public universities [Las modalidades de enseñanza en la nueva normalidad para el curso 2020-21 en las universidades públicas españolas]. *IJERI: International Journal of Educational Research and Innovation*, (15), 273-290.

Montico, S. (2004). Motivation in the university classroom: A pedagogical need? [La motivación en el aula universitaria: ¿una necesidad pedagógica?]. *Ciencia, Docencia y Tecnología*, *15*(29), 105–112.

Morales-Cevallos, M. B. (2020). Trends in Educational Research about e-Learning: A Systematic Literature Review (2009–2018). *Sustainability*, *12*(12), 5153. doi:10.3390u12125153

Moravcová, L., & Maďarová, L. (2016). *Neurodidactics and its utilization in the field of language teaching*. International Scientific Days.

Moreira, M. A. (2011). Why Concepts, Why Meaningful Learning, Why Collaborative Activities and Why Concept Maps? *Aprendizagem Significativa em Revista/Meaningful Learning Review*, *6*(3), 5.

Moreira, M. A., & González, C. S. G. (2015). De la enseñanza con libros de texto al aprendizaje en espacios online gamificados [From Teaching with Textbooks to Learning on Online Gamified Spaces]. *Educatio Siglo XXI*, *33*(3), 15–38. doi:10.6018/j/240791

Moreno-Correa, S. M. (2020). Educational innovation in the times of the Coronavirus [La innovación educativa en los tiempos del Coronavirus]. *Salutem Scientia Spiritus*, *6*(1), 14–26.

Morgan, W., & Streb, M. (2003). First do no harm: The importance of student ownership in servicelearning. *Metropolitan State Universities*, *14*(3), 36–52.

Moses, L. A. (1952). Non-Parametric Statistics for Psychological Research. *Psychological Bulletin*, *49*, 122–143.

Mpungose, C. B. (2020). Is Moodle or WhatsApp the preferred e-learning platform at a South African university? First-year students' experiences. *Education and Information Technologies*, *25*(2), 927–941.

Mujiyanto, J., Nurkamto, J., & Hartono, R. (2021). The impact of online instruction integrated with Brain Based Teaching to EFL Students with Different Motivation Level. *Journal of e-Learning and Knowledge Society*, *17*(2), 66-73.

Müller, A. M., Goh, C., Lim, L. Z., & Gao, X. (2021). Covid-19 emergency elearning and beyond: Experiences and perspectives of university educators. *Education Sciences*, *11*(1), 19. doi:10.3390/educsci11010019

Mwalumbwe, I., & Mtebe, J. S. (2017). Using learning analytics to predict students' performance in moodle learning management system: A case of Mbeya University of science and technology. *The Electronic Journal on Information Systems in Developing Countries*, *79*(1), 1–13. doi:10.1002/j.1681-4835.2017.tb00577.x

Mystakidis, S. (2019). Motivation Enhanced Deep and Meaningful Learning with Social Virtual Reality. University of Jyväskylä.

Mystakidis, S., Berki, E., & Valtanen, J.-P. (2019). The Patras Blended Strategy Model for Deep and Meaningful Learning in Quality Life-Long Distance Education. *Electron. J. e-Learning*, *17*, 66–78.

Mystakidis, S. (2021). Deep Meaningful Learning. *Encyclopedia*, *2021*(1), 988–997. doi:10.3390/encyclopedia1030075

Nair, R. (2017). *Case as Text in Class: Business School Pedagogy.* Retrieved from Case as Text in Class: Business School Pedagogy: https://radhakrishnannair.com/

Nesbit, J. C., & Adesope, O. O. (2013). Concept maps for learning: Theory, research, and design. In G. Schraw, M. T. McCrudden, & D. Robinson (Eds.), *Current perspectives on cognition, learning, and instruction. Learning through visual displays* (pp. 303–328). Information Age Publishers.

Newman, F. M., Marks, H. M., & Gamoran, A. (1996). Authentic pedagogy and student performance. *American Journal of Education*, *104*(4), 280–312. doi:10.1086/444136

Newmann, F. M., and Thomson, J. A. (1987). *Effects of cooperative learning on achievement in secondary schools: A summary of research.* ERIC Document Reproduction Service No. ED 288 853.

Ní Shé, C., Farrell, O., Brunton, J., Costello, E., Donlon, E., Trevaskis, S., & Eccles, S. (2019). *Teaching online is different: critical perspectives from the literature.* Dublin City University. 10.

Nicoleta, C. (2005). Agile Software Project Management Methodologies. *Economy Informatics*, 1-4.

Nielsen, L. (2011). *Personas - User Focused Design.* Springer.

Niyazov, Y., Vogel, C., Price, R., Lund, B., Judd, D., Akil, A., & Shron, M. (2016). Open access meets discoverability: Citations to articles posted to Academia. edu. *Plos One, 11*(2), e0148257.

Nonaka, I. (1991). The knowledge-creating company. *Harvard Business Review*, *69*(6), 96–104.

Nonaka, I., & Takeuchi, H. (1995). *The Knowledge-Creating Company*. Oxford University Press.

Novak, J. (1990). Human Construtivism: A Unification of Psychological and Epistemological Phenomena in Meaning Making. *Dalam Fourth North American Conference on Personal Construct Psychology*, 15.

Novak, J. D. (1993). A view on the status of Ausubel's assimilation theory of learning. In *Proceedings of the third international seminar on misconceptions and educational strategies in science and mathematics*. Misconceptions Trust.

Novak, J. D., & Cañas, A. J. (2008). *The theory underlying concept maps and how to construct them*. Technical report IHMC CmapTools 2006-01 Rev 01-2008.

Novak, J. D., & Gowin, D. (2006). *Learning How to Learn*. Cambridge University Press.

O'Banion, T. (2016). A brief history of general education. *Community College Journal of Research and Practice*, *40*(4), 327–334. doi:10.1080/10668926.2015.1117996

O'Brien, W., Adamakis, M., O'Brien, N., Onofre, M., Martins, J., Dania, A., Makopoulou, K., Herold, F., Ng, K., & Costa, J. (2020). Implications for European Physical Education Teacher Education during the COVID-19 pandemic: A cross-institutional SWOT analysis. *European Journal of Teacher Education*, *43*(4), 503–522. doi:10.1080/02619768.2020.1823963

O'Byrne, W. I., & Pytash, K. E. (2015). Hybrid and blended learning: Modifying pedagogy across path, pace, time, and place. *Journal of Adolescent & Adult Literacy*, *59*(2), 137–140. doi:10.1002/jaal.463

O'Donnell, A. M., Dansereau, D. F., & Hall, R. H. (2002). Knowledge maps as scaffolds for cognitive processing. *Educational Psychology Review*, *14*(1), 71–86. doi:10.1023/A:1013132527007

O'Rourke, S., Eskritt, M., & Bosacki, S. (2018). Communication, compassion, and computers: Adolescents' and adults' evaluations of online and face-to-face deception. *Journal of Adolescence*, *65*(1), 133–140. doi:10.1016/j.adolescence.2018.03.010 PMID:29597102

Ocampo, R. D. L. S. (2016). Aplicación de juegos digitales en educación superior [Application of digital games in higher education]. *Revista San Gregorio, 11*, 82–91.

Okebukola, P. A. (1986). An investigation of some factors affecting students' attitudes towards laboratory chemistry. *Journal of Chemical Education*, *63*, 531–532.

Oliva, H. A. (2016). Gamification as a methodological strategy in the university educational context [La gamificación como estrategia metodológica en el contexto educativo universitario]. *Realidad y Reflexión, 16*(44), 108-118.

Oliva, H. A. (2016). La gamificación como estrategia metodológica en el contexto educativo universitario [The gamification as a methodological strategy in the university educational context]. *Realidad y Reflexión*, *16*(44), 108–118.

Oliva, M. F. R., Fernández, R. J., & Ponce, H. H. (2019). Analysis of the implementation of an educational program based on the mobile learning methodology [Análisis de la implementación de un programa educativo basado en la metodología mobile learning]. *Texto Livre. Linguagem e Tecnologia*, *12*(2), 172–201. doi:10.17851/1983-3652.12.2.172-201

Oostdam, R. J., Peetsma, T. T. D., & Blok, H. (2007). *Het nieuwe leren in basisonderwijs en voortgezet onderwijs nader beschouwd* [New learning in primary and secondary education reconsidered]. SCO-Kohnstamm Instituut.

Orduña-Malea, E., Martín-Martín, A., & Delgado-López-Cózar, E. (2016). ResearchGate as a source of scientific evaluation: Revealing its bibliometric applications. *Information Professional*, *25*(2), 303–310.

Ovadia, S. (2014). ResearchGate and Academia. edu: Academic social networks. *Behavioral & Social Sciences Librarian*, *33*(3), 165–169.

Owston, R., York, D. N., & Malhotra, T. (2019). Blended learning in large enrolment courses: Student perceptions across four different instructional models. *Australasian Journal of Educational Technology*, *35*(5), 29–41. doi:10.14742/ajet.4310

Özbek, O., & Çeyiz, S. (2017). University students' opinions on cheating and plagiarism. *European Journal of Education Studies*. Advance online publication. doi:10.46827/ejes.v0i0.900

Öztürk, M., & Çakıroğlu, Ü. (2021). Flipped learning design in EFL classrooms: Implementing self-regulated learning strategies to develop language skills. *Smart Learn. Environ.*, *8*(1), 2. doi:10.118640561-021-00146-x

Paar, C., & Pelzl, J. (2009). *Understanding cryptography: A textbook for students and practitioners*. Springer Science & Business Media.

Padrós, M., Puigdellívol, I., & Flecha, R. (2003). Learning Communities: transforming the school organization at the service of the community [Comunidades de Aprendizaje: transformar la organización escolar al servicio de la comunidad]. *Organización y gestión educativa, 5*, 4.

Pal, K. (2019). Markov Decision Theory Based Crowdsourcing Software Process Model. In Crowdsourcing and Probabilistic Decision-Making in Software Engineering: Emerging Research and Opportunities. IGI Global.

Pal, K. (2020). Framework for Reusable Test Case Generation in Software Systems Testing. In Software Engineering for Agile Application Development. IGI Global

Pal, K. (2021). A Case Study of Knowledge Management and Organizational Culture in an Undergraduate Software Development Team Project. In Contemporary Challenges for Agile Project Management. IGI Global.

Pal, K., & Karakostas, B. (2021). Software Testing Under Agile, Scrum, and DevOps. In Agile Scrum Implementation and its Long-Term Impact on Organization. IGI Global.

Pal, K., & Williams, I. (2021). Global Software Development Knowledge Management Using Semantic Web Technology. IGI Global.

Palos-Sanchez, P., Saura, J. R., & Martin-Velicia, F. (2019). A study of the effects of programmatic advertising on users' concerns about privacy overtime. *Journal of Business Research*, *96*, 61–72. https://doi.org/10.1016/j.jbusres.2018.10.059

Panfeng & Zhao. (2015). *Discussion on Teaching Method of Electronic Technology based on MOOC*. Academic Press.

Parente, D. (2016). Gamificacion en la educación. *Gamificación en aulas universitarias*, 11.

Parra Ortiz, J. M. (2003). *Education in values and their practice in the classroom* [La educación en valores y su práctica en el aula]. Academic Press.

Parra, C. N. E., Regalado, G. A. M., & Poma, C. J. R. (2020). Los desafíos de la inclusión en tiempos de COVID-19 (The challenges of inclusion in times of COVID-19). *Revista Scientific*, *5*(17), 221–239. doi:10.29394/Scientific.issn.2542-2987.2020.5.17.11.221-239

Parrado-Martínez, P., & Sánchez-Andújar, S. (2020). Development of competences in postgraduate studies of finance: A project-based learning (PBL) case study. *International Review of Economics Education*, *35*, 100192. doi:10.1016/j.iree.2020.100192

Patrick, S., & Sturgis, C. (2015). *Maximizing competency education and blended learning: Insights fromexperts.* Vienna: iNACOL.

Pavlova, O., Chirkova, N., & Burlakova, I. (2020). Building a practice-oriented model of preservice teacher education. In *Proceedings of the SHS Web of Conferences*. EDP Sciences.

Pedroza, G. A. de (2005). The Mexican Social Service: design and construction of models [El Servicio Social Mexicano: diseño y construcción de modelos]. Ministerio de Educacion, Ciencia y Tecnologia. Unidad de Programas Especiales. Programa Nacional Educación Solidaria. Aprendizaje y servicio solidario en la Educación Superior y en los sistemas educativos latinoamericanos.

Pele, A. (2012). Twitter as a teaching technique? *INTED2012: International Technology, Education and Development Conference*, 4481–4485.

Peled, Y., Eshet, Y., Barczyk, C., & Grinautski, K. (2019). Predictors of Academic Dishonesty among undergraduate students in online and face-to-face courses. *Computers & Education*, *131*(1), 49–59. doi:10.1016/j.compedu.2018.05.012

Pelled, L. H. (1996). Demographic diversity, conflict, and work group outcomes: An intervening process theory. *Organization Science*, *7*(6), 615–631. doi:10.1287/orsc.7.6.615

Pelled, L. H., Eisenhardt, K. M., & Xin, K. R. (1999). Exploring the black box: An analysis of work group diversity, conflict and performance. *Administrative Science Quarterly*, *44*(1), 1–28. doi:10.2307/2667029

Perez, A., Omar, B., & Velazquez, R. (2019). Innovación docente y empleo de las TIC en la Educación Superior. *Revista Espacios*, *40*(2), 8.

Pérez-Aldeguer, S. (2017). Las artes escénicas como metodología educativa en la educación superior. *Foro de Educación*, *15*(22). Advance online publication. doi:10.14516/fde.587

Perifanou, M., Tzafilkou, K., & Economides, A. A. (2021). The Role of Instagram, Facebook, and YouTube Frequency of Use in University Students' Digital Skills Components. *Education in Science*, *11*(12), 766.

Petzold, C. (2000). *Code: The hidden language of computer hardware and software*. Microsoft Press.

Phi, G. T., & Clausen, H. B. (2020). Fostering innovation competencies in tourism higher education via design-based and value-based learning. *Journal of Hospitality, Leisure, Sport and Tourism Education*, *100298*. Advance online publication. doi:10.1016/j.jhlste.2020.100298

Polman, J., Hornstra, L., & Volman, M. (2021). The meaning of meaningful learning in mathematics in upper-primary education. *Learning Environments Research*, *24*(3), 469–486. doi:10.100710984-020-09337-8

Poock, J. R., Burke, K. A., Greenbowe, T. J., & Hand, B. M. (2007). Using the Science Writing Heuristic in the general chemistry laboratory to improve student's academic performance. *Journal of Chemical Education*, *84*, 1371–1379.

Prieto, A., Díaz, D., & Santiago, R. (2014). Inductive Methodologies: The challenge of teaching through questioning and challenges [Metodologías Inductivas: El desafío de enseñar mediante el cuestionamiento y los retos]. *Innovations in Education and Teaching International*, *56*(1), 46–56. doi:10.1080/14703297.2017.1399808

Prince, M. S., Tenorio, G. C., & Ramirez, M. S. (2016). Educational innovation and digital competencies: The case of OER in a private Venezuelan university. *International Journal of Educational Technolgy in High Education*, *13*(10), 10. Advance online publication. doi:10.118641239-016-0006-1

Prosalova, V. S., & Nikolaeva, A. A. (2020). Implementation of Practice-Oriented Training as the Basis of University Competitiveness. In *Proceedings of the International Scientific Conference Far East Con.* Atlantis Press. 10.2991/aebmr.k.200312.054

Puljak, L., Čivljak, M., Haramina, A., Mališa, S., Čavić, D., Klinec, D., Aranza, D., Mesarić, J., Skitarelić, N., Zoranić, S., Majstorović, D., Neuberg, M., Mikšić, Š., & Ivanišević, K. (2020). Attitudes and concerns of undergraduate university health sciences students in Croatia regarding complete switch to e-learning during COVID-19 pandemic: A survey. *BMC Medical Education*, *20*(1), 1–11. doi:10.118612909-020-02343-7 PMID:33167960

Pun, J., & Jin, X. (2021, May 7). Student challenges and learning strategies at Hong Kong EMI universities. *PLoS One*, *15 / 16*(5), e0251564. Advance online publication. doi:10.1371/journal.pone.0251564

Raff, R. A. (2012). *The shape of life: Genes, development, and the evolution of animal form.* University of Chicago Press.

Rapp, A. K., Healy, M. G., Charlton, M. E., Keith, J. N., Rosenbaum, M. E., & Kapadia, M. R. (2016). YouTube is the most frequently used educational video source for surgical preparation. *Journal of Surgical Education*, *73*(6), 1072–1076.

Ratcliff, J. L., Johnson, D. K., La Nasa, S. M., & Gaff, J. G. (2001). *The status of general education in the year 2000: Summary of a national survey.* Association of American Colleges & Universities.

Redondo, R. D. R., Ktena, A., Kunicina, N., Zabasta, A., Patlins, A., & Mele, D. E. (2020). Advanced practices: micro learning, practice oriented teaching and gamified learning. In *Proceedings of the International Scientific Conference on Power and Electrical Engineering of Riga Technical University.* IEEE. 10.1109/RTUCON51174.2020.9316555

Rees, M. R., Tenbrunsel, A. E., & Bazerman, M. H. (2018). Bounded Ethicality and Ethical Fading in Negotiations: Understanding Unintended Unethical Behavior. *The Academy of Management Perspectives*, *33*(1), 26–42. doi:10.5465/amp.2017.0055

Remesal, A., Colomina, R. M., Mauri, T., & Rochera, M. J. (2017). *Online questionnaires use with automatic feedback for e-innovation in university students.* doi:10.3916/C51-2017-05

Renz, A., & Hilbig, R. (2020). Prerequisites for artificial intelligence in further education: Identification of drivers, barriers, and business models of educational technology companies. *International Journal of Educational Technology in Higher Education*, *17*(1), 1–21. doi:10.118641239-020-00193-3

Resnick, L. B. (1988). Learning in School and out. *Educational Researcher*, *16*, 13–20.

Ribeiro-Navarrete, S., Saura, J. R., & Palacios-Marqués, D. (2021). Towards a new era of mass data collection: Assessing pandemic surveillance technologies to preserve user privacy. *Technological Forecasting and Social Change*, *167*, 120681. doi:10.1016/j.techfore.2021.120681 PMID:33840865

Rippa, P., & Secundo, G. (2019). Digital academic entrepreneurship: The potential of digital technologies on academic entrepreneurship. *Technological Forecasting and Social Change*, *146*, 900–911. doi:10.1016/j.techfore.2018.07.013

Rodriguez Valerio, D. (2020). Beyond instant messaging: WhatsApp as a mediation and support tool in the teaching of Library Science. *Información, Cultura y Sociedad*, (42), 107–126.

Rodríguez, C. A. C. (2018). Gamificación en educación superior: experiencia innovadora para motivar estudiantes y dinamizar contenidos en el aula [Gamification in higher education: innovative experience to motivate students and stimulate content in the classroom]. *Edutec. Revista Electrónica de Tecnología Educativa*, *63*, 29–41.

Rodríguez, D. V., Mezquita, J. M. M., & Vallecillo, A. I. G. (2019). Innovative methodology based on educational gamification: Test type evaluation with the Quizizz tool. Teaching staff [Metodología innovadora basada en la gamificación educativa: evaluación tipo test con la herramienta Quizizz. Profesorado]. *Revista de Currículum y Formación del Profesorado*, *23*(3), 363–387. doi:10.30827/profesorado.v23i3.11232

Rodriguez, R. (2017). A case of reflexive and critical interaction in a campaign about Twitter in the course of Legal Theory. *IJERI-International Journal of Educational Reasearch and Innovation*, (7), 186–201.

Rodríguez, S., Núñez, J. C., Valle, A., Blas, R., & Rosario, P. (2009). Teacher self-efficacy, teacher motivation and teaching strategies [Auto-eficacia docente, motivación del profesor y estrategias de enseñanza]. *Escritos de Psicología (Internet)*, *3*(1), 1–7.

Roederer, J. G. (2006). *Information and its role in nature*. Springer Science & Business Media.

Roelofs, E., & Terwel, J. (1999). Constructivism and authentic pedagogy: State of the art and recent developments in the Dutch national curriculum in secondary education. *Journal of Curriculum Studies*, *31*(2), 201–227. doi:10.1080/002202799183232

Roelofs, E., Visser, J., & Terwel, J. (2003). Preferences for various learning environments: Teachers' and parents' perceptions. *Learning Environments Research*, *6*(1), 77–110. doi:10.1023/A:1022915910198

Roffe, I. M. (1998). Conceptual problems of continuous quality improvement and innovation in higher education. *Quality Assurance in Education*, *6*(2), 74–82. doi:10.1108/09684889810205723

Rogado, A. B. G., Conde, M. J. R., Migueláñez, S. O., Riaza, B. G., & Peñalvo, F. J. G. (2010, May). Efficiency assessment of a blended-learning educational methodology in engineering. In *International Conference on Technology Enhanced Learning* (pp. 148-155). Springer. 10.1007/978-3-642-13166-0_22

Roig-Vila, R., Antolí Martínez, J. M., Blasco Mira, J. E., Lledó Carreres, A., & Pellín Buades, N. (2017). *Collaborative networks around university teaching* [Redes colaborativas en torno a la docencia universitaria]. Academic Press.

Romero Juárez, M. G. (2020). *Enseñanza de programación de estructuras de datos aplicando estrategias didácticas basadas en la teoría de carga cognitiva.* Tesis de maestría en informática y tecnologías computacionales-Universidad Autónoma de Aguascalientes. Centro de Ciencias Básicas. Repositorio bibliográfico. http://hdl.handle.net/11317/1857

Romero López, M. A. (2017). European higher education area-driven educational innovation. *Procedia: Social and Behavioral Sciences*, *237*, 1505–1512. doi:10.1016/j.sbspro.2017.02.237

Romero-Rodríguez, L. M., De-Casas-Moreno, P., & Caldeiro-Pedreira, M. C. (2018). Desinformación e infoxicación en las cuartas pantallas [Disinformation and infoxication on the fourth screens]. In I. Aguaded & L.M. Romero-Rodríguez (Coord.), Competencias mediáticas en medios digitales emergentes (pp. 73-90). Comunicación Social Ediciones y Publicaciones.

Rosano, S. (2007). *La cultura de la diversidad y la educación inclusiva*. Recuperado de http://benu. edu.mx/wp-content/uploads/2015/03/La_cultura_de_la_diversidad_y_la_educacion_inclusiva.pdf

Roses, S., Aguilar, M.G., & Farias, P. (2013). the academic use of social networks: a comparative analysis between Science students and social science students / Academic use of social networks: comparative analysis between science and literature students. *History and Social Communication*, 667-679.

Rowe, M. P., Gillespie, B. M., Harris, K. R., Koether, S. D., Shannon, L. J. Y., & Rose, L. A. (2015). Redesigning a general education science course to promote critical thinking. *CBE Life Sciences Education*, *14*(3), ar30. doi:10.1187/cbe.15-02-0032 PMID:26231561

Rowntree, D. (1994). *Preparing materials for open, distance and flexible learning: an action guide for teachers and trainers.* Academic Press.

Royce, W. W. (1970). Managing the Development of Large Software Systems. *Proceedings of IEEE WESCON, 26*(August), 1–9.

Rubin, B., Fernandes, R., & Avgerinou, M. D. (2013). The effects of technology on the Community of Inquiry and satisfaction with online courses. *Internet High. Educ, 2013*(17), 48–57. doi:10.1016/j.iheduc.2012.09.006

Rubio, E. P. (2014). Juegos como elemento docente en un entorno TIC [Games as an educational element in an ICT environment]. *Revista Aequitas: Estudios sobre historia, derecho e instituciones, 4,* 407-416.

Rudd, J. A. II, Greenbowe, T. J., & Hand, B. M. (2001). Recrafting the general chemistry lab report. *Journal of College Science Teaching, 31,* 230–234.

Rué, J., Font, A., & Cebrian, G. (2011). El ABP, un enfoque estratégico para la formación en Educación Superior. Aportaciones de un análisis de la formación en Derecho [PBL, a strategic approach to training in Higher Education. Contributions from an analysis of training in law]. *Revista de Docencia Universitaria, 9*(1), 25–44. doi:10.4995/redu.2011.6178

Ruiz Garrido, A., Vélez Rivera, R., Leal Orellana, P., & Quintiliano Scarpelli, D. (2021). *Characterization of the Educational Innovation Process: Teaching Concerns and Results in the Teaching and Learning Process in a Chilean University Over 5 Years.* doi:10.33423/jhetp.v21i15.4892

Rundle, K., Curtis, G. J., & Clare, J. (2019). Why Students Do Not Engage in Contract Cheating. *Frontiers in Psychology, 10,* 2229. Advance online publication. doi:10.3389/fpsyg.2019.02229 PMID:31636584

Rush, D. E., & Connolly, A. J. (2020). An Agile Framework for Teaching with Scrum in the IT Project Management Classroom. *Journal of Information Systems Education, 31*(3), 196–207.

Rusko, R., Härkönen, K., & Liukkonen, S. (2016). Coopetition at elevator pitch events? A case study of micro-activities at a business innovation event. *Journal of Innovation Management, 4*(3), 79–100. doi:10.24840/2183-0606_004.003_0007

Russell, A. A. (1994). A rationally designed General Chemistry Diagnostic Test. *Journal of Chemical Education, 71,* 314–317.

Ryder, B., Zhang, T., & Hua, N. (2021). The Social Media "Magic": Virtually Engaging Visitors during COVID-19 Temporary Closures. *Administrative Sciences, 11*(2), 53.

Sadiq, F., Rasa, S. I., Shami, N., Seemadaud, S., & Bhatti, S. (2018). Comparing Effectiveness of Collaborative Blended Learning and Traditional Teaching Using Students Final Test Scores. *Pakistan Journal of Medical & Health Sciences, 12*(4), 1428–1431.

Salam, M., Iskandar, D. N. A., Ibrahim, D. H. A., & Farooq, M. S. (2019). Service learning in higher education: A systematic literature review. *Asia Pacific Education Review, 20*(4), 573–593. doi:10.100712564-019-09580-6

Salihoğlu, Y. (2001). *User Involvement in Software Project Development: A Review of Models.* Software Project Management Research Paper.

Salinas, J. (2004). Teaching innovation and use of ICT in university education. Journal of University and Knowledge Society (RUSC) [Innovación docente y uso de las TIC en la enseñanza universilavtaria. Revista de Universidad y Sociedad del Conocimiento (RUSC)]. *UOC, 1*(1).

Salinas, J. (2008). *Educational innovation and use of ICT* [Innovación educativa y uso de las TIC]. Universidad Internacional de Andalucía.

Salmerón-Pérez, H., Rodríguez-Fernández, S., & Gutiérrez-Braojos, C. (2010). Methodologies to improve communication in virtual learning environments. *Comunicar, 17*(34), 163–171. doi:10.3916/C34-2010-03-16

Sánchez, F. J. S., & Sarabia, F. (1999). *Methodology for research in marketing and business management* [Metodología para la investigación en marketing y dirección de empresas]. Ediciones Pirámide.

Satorre Cuerda, R. (2021). *New educational challenges in higher education in the face of the COVID-19 challenge* [Nuevos retos educativos en la enseñanza superior frente al desafío COVID-19]. Academic Press.

Saura, J. R., Ribeiro-Soriano, D., & Palacios-Marqués, D. (2021). From user-generated data to data-driven innovation: A research agenda to understand user privacy in digital markets. *International Journal of Information Management, 60.* doi:10.1016/j.ijinfomgt.2021.102331

Saura, J. R., Ribeiro-Soriano, D., & Palacios-Marqués, D. (2022c). Adopting digital reservation systems to enable circular economy in entrepreneurship. *Management Decision.* doi:10.1108/MD-02-2022-0190

Saura, J. R., Dwivedi, Y. K., & Palacios-Marqués, D. (2022d). Online User Behavior and User-Generated Content. *Frontiers in Psychology, 13,* 895467. Advance online publication. doi:10.3389/fpsyg.2022.895467 PMID:35548513

Saura, J. R., Palacios-Marqués, D., & Iturricha-Fernández, A. (2021). Ethical Design in Social Media: Assessing the main performance measurements of user online behavior modification. *Journal of Business Research, 129*(May), 271–281. doi:10.1016/j.jbusres.2021.03.001

Saura, J. R., Palacios-Marqués, D., & Ribeiro-Soriano, D. (2021). How SMEs use data sciences in their online marketing performance: A systematic literature review of the state-of-the-art. *Journal of Small Business Management*, 1–36. doi: 10.1080/00472778.2021.1955127

Saura, J. R., Palacios-Marqués, D., & Ribeiro-Soriano, D. (2022a). Exploring the boundaries of Open Innovation: Evidence from social media mining. *Technovation*, 102447. Advance online publication. doi:10.1016/j.technovation.2021.102447

Saura, J. R., Ribeiro-Soriano, D., & Iturricha-Fernández, A. (2022). Exploring the challenges of remote work on Twitter users' sentiments: From digital technology development to a post-pandemic era. *Journal of Business Research, 142*(March), 242–254. doi:10.1016/j.jbusres.2021.12.052

Saura, J. R., Ribeiro-Soriano, D., & Palacios-Marqués, D. (2021a, July 15). Setting privacy "by default" in social IoT: Theorizing the challenges and directions in Big Data Research. *Big Data Research, 25*, 100245. doi:10.1016/j.bdr.2021.100245

Saura, J. R., Ribeiro-Soriano, D., & Palacios-Marqués, D. (2021b). Using data mining techniques to explore security issues in smart living environments in Twitter. *Computer Communications, 179*, 285–295. doi:10.1016/j.comcom.2021.08.021

Saura, J. R., Ribeiro-Soriano, D., & Palacios-Marqués, D. (2022b). Assessing behavioral data science privacy issues in government artificial intelligence deployment. *Government Information Quarterly, 101679*. Advance online publication. doi:10.1016/j.giq.2022.101679

Schaupp, L., & Vitullo, E. (2020). Implementing experiential action learning in the MBA: Use of an international consulting experience. *International Journal of Educational Management, 34*(3), 505–517. doi:10.1108/IJEM-04-2019-0154

Schroeder, J. D. (2007). The lab-lecture correlation: From the science writing heuristic to the traditional organic chemistry laboratory. In B. M. Hand (Ed.), *Science Inquiry, Argument and Language: A case for the Science Writing Heuristic.* Sense Publishers.

Schwaber, K. (2004). *Agile Project Management with Scrum.* Microsoft Press.

Schwaber, K., & Beedle, M. (2001). *Agile Software Development with Scrum.* Prentice-Hall.

Schwartz, S., & Pollishuke, M. (1995). *Active Learning: A Student-Centered Classroom Organization* (Vol. 134). Narcea Ediciones.

Schwarz, B. B., & Asterhan, C. S. (2011). E-Moderation of Synchronous Discussions in Educational Settings: A Nascent Practice. *Journal of the Learning Sciences*, *20*(3), 395–442. doi:10.1080/10508406.2011.553257

Schweiger, D. M., Sandberg, W. R., & Ragan, J. W. (1986). Group approaches for improving strategic decision making: A comparative analysis of dialectical inquiry, devil's advocacy, and consensus. *Academy of Management Journal*, *29*(1), 51–71.

Scott, D., & Friesen, S. (2013). Inquiry-Based Learning: A Review of the Research Literature. *Alberta Education*, *1*, 1–29.

Scull, J., Phillips, M., Sharma, U., & Garnier, K. (2020). Innovations in teacher education at the time of COVID19: An Australian perspective. *Journal of Education for Teaching*, *46*(4), 497–506. doi:10.1080/02607476.2020.1802701

Seife, C. (2007). *Decoding the universe: How the new science of information is explaining everything in the cosmos, from our brains to black holes*. Penguin.

Şentürk, C. (2021). Effects of the blended learning model on preservice teachers' academic achievements and twenty-first century skills. *Education and Information Technologies*, *26*(1), 35–48. doi:10.100710639-020-10340-y PMID:33020691

Sepúlveda, P., Cabezas, M., García, J., & Fonseca-Salamanca, F. (2019). *Aprendizaje basado en problemas: percepción del proceso enseñanza aprendizaje de las ciencias preclínicas por estudiantes de Kinesiología* [Problem-based learning: Kinesiology students' perception of the teaching-learning process in pre-clinical sciences]. Educación Médica., doi:10.1016/j.edumed.2019.01.004

Seshan, V., Matua, G. A., Raghavan, D., Arulappan, J., Al Hashmi, I., Roach, E. J., Sunderraj, S. E., & Prince, E. J. (2021). Case Study Analysis as an Effective Teaching Strategy: Perceptions of Undergraduate Nursing Students From a Middle Eastern Country. *SAGE Open Nursing*, *7*, 23779608211059265. doi:10.1177/23779608211059265 PMID:34869864

Shapin, S. (2018). *The scientific revolution*. University of Chicago Press.

Sharan, Y. (2015). *Meaningful Learning in the Co-operative Classroom. Education 3-13: International Journal of Primary, Elementary and Early Years Education, 43(1), 83-94.*

Sharan, Y., & Sharan, S. (1989). Training teachers for cooperative learning. *Educational Leadership*, *45*, 20–25.

Sharma, S. K., Joshi, A., & Sharma, H. (2016). A multi-analytical approach to predict the Facebook usage in higher education. *Computers in Human Behavior*, *55*, 340–353.

Shaw, E. (1999). A guide to the qualitative research process: Evidence from a small firm study. *Qualitative Market Research*, *2*(2), 59–70. doi:10.1108/13522759910269973

Shea, P., & Bidjerano, T. (2009). Community of inquiry as a theoretical framework to foster "epistemic engagement" and "cognitive presence" in online education. *Computers & Education*, *2009*(52), 543–553. doi:10.1016/j.compedu.2008.10.007

Shea, P., & Bidjerano, T. (2012). Learning presence as a moderator in the community of inquiry model. *Computers & Education*, *2012*(59), 316–326. doi:10.1016/j.compedu.2012.01.011

Sheng, W., & Noe, R. A. (2010). Knowledge sharing: A review and directions for future research. *Human Resource Management Review*, *20*(2), 115–131. doi:10.1016/j.hrmr.2009.10.001

Siegel, S. (1956). *Nonparametric Statistics for the behavioral Sciences*. Mc Graw-Hill.

Silva, J., & Maturana, D. (2017). Una propuesta de modelo para introducir metodologías activas en educación superior [A proposed model for introducing active methodologies in higher Education]. *Revista Innovación Educativa, 17*(73), 117–131.

Silva, R. J. R. D., Rodrigues, R. G., & Leal, C. T. P. (2019). Gamification in Management Education: A Systematic Literature Review. *BAR - Brazilian Administration Review, 16*(2), e180103. doi:10.1590/1807-7692bar2019180103

Slavin, R. E. (1988). Cooperative learning and student achievement. *Educational Leadership, 46*, 31–33.

Slavin, R. E. (1988). *Student team learning: An overview and practical guide*. National Education Association.

Smirnova, Z. V., Vaganova, O. I., Loshkareva, D. A., Konyaeva, E. A., & Gladkova, M. N. (2018). Practice-oriented approach implementation in vocational education. In *Proceedings of the Materials Science and Engineering Conference*. IOP.

Sobaih, A. E. E., Moustafa, M. A., Ghandforoush, P., & Khan, M. (2016). To use or not to use? Social media in higher education in developing countries. *Computers in Human Behavior, 58*, 296–305.

Song, B. L., Lee, K. L., Liew, C. Y., Ho, R. C., & Lin, W. L. (2022, April 26). Business students' perspectives on case method coaching for problem-based learning impacts on student engagement and learning performance in higher education. *Education + Training, 64*(3), 416–432. doi:10.1108/ET-03-2021-0106

Spain, I. (2018). *Estudio Anual Redes Sociales*. Retrieved from https://iabspain.es/wp-content/uploads/estudio- redes-sociales-2018_vreducida.pdf

Spaulding, M. (2009). Perceptions of Academic Honesty in Online vs. Face-to-Face Classrooms. *Journal of Interactive Online Learning, 8*(3), 183–198.

Sriraman. (2010). *Theories of Mathematics Education*. Springer-Verlag Berlin Heidelberg.

Stanzel, F. K. (1984). *A Theory of Narrative*. Cambridge University Press.

Starek, J. E., & Keating, C. F. (1991). Self-Deception and Its Relationship to Success in Competition. *Basic and Applied Social Psychology, 12*(2), 145–155. doi:10.120715324834basp1202_2

Steffens, K. (2006). Self-Regulated Learning in Technology-Enhanced Learning Environments: Lessons of a European peer review. *European Journal of Education, 41*(3–4), 353–379. doi:10.1111/j.1465-3435.2006.00271.x

Stegink, G., Pater, J., & Vroon, D. (n.d.). Computer science and general education: Java, graphics, and the web. In *Proceedings of the 13th SIGCSE Technical Symposium on Computer Science Education* (pp. 146–149). Academic Press.

Stewart, G. (2006). Praxisbezug als profilbildendes Element in Bachelorstudiengängen an bayerischen Fachhochschulen. *Beiträge zur Hochschulforschung, 2*(28), 90–114.

Stone, J. V. (2015). *Information theory: A tutorial introduction*. Sebtel Press.

Stuber-McEwen, D., Wiseley, P., & Hoggatt, S. (2009). Point, Click, and Cheat: Frequency and Type of Academic Dishonesty in the Virtual Classroom. *Online Journal of Distance Learning Administration, 12*(3).

Suyatno. (2009). *Menjelajah Pembelajaran Inovatif*. Bumi Aksara.

Swartz, R. J., Costa, A. L., Beyer, B. K., Reagan, R., & Kallick, B. (2010). *Thinking-Based Learning: Promoting Quality Student Achievement in the 21st Century*. Teachers College Press.

Tacca, D. R., Tacca, A. L., & Alva, M. A. (2019). Estrategias neurodidácticas, satisfacción y rendimiento académico en estudiantes universitarios [Neurodidactic strategies, satisfaction and academic performance in university students]. *Cuaderno de Investigacion en la Educacion: Serie Especial de Temas Especiales. University of Puerto Rico. Recinto de Rio Piedras. Centro de Investigaciones Educativas, 10*(2), 15–32. doi:10.18861/cied.2019.10.2.2905

Tapia, M. N. (2006). *Learning and solidarity service: some basic concepts* [Aprendizaje y servicio solidario: algunos conceptos básicos]. Programa Nacional Educación Solidaria.

Tapia, M. N. (2008). *Learning and solidarity service in the mission of higher education* [Aprendizaje y servicio solidario en la misión de la educación superior]. El Aprendizaje-Servicio En la Educación Superior.

Tello, O. W., & Ruiz, D. (2016). Didactic use of Web 2.0 tools for teachers in subject of Communication. *Campus Virtuales, 5*(1), 48–61.

Tess, P. A. (2013). The role of social media in higher education classes (real and virtual)–A literature review. *Computers in Human Behavior, 29*(5), A60–A68.

Thelwall, M., & Kousha, K. (2015). ResearchGate: Disseminating, communicating, and measuring Scholarship? *Journal of the Association for Information Science and Technology, 66*(5), 876–889.

Thomas, R. A., West, R. E., & Borup, J. (2017). An analysis of instructor social presence in online text and asynchronous video feedback comments. *Internet and Higher Education, 2017*(33), 61–73. doi:10.1016/j.iheduc.2017.01.003

Tidd, S. T., McIntyre, H. H., & Friedman, R. A. (2004). The importance of role ambiguity and trust in conflict perception: Unpacking the task conflict to relationship conflict linkage. *International Journal of Conflict Management, 15*(4), 364–380. doi:10.1108/eb022918

Tillman, B. A. (1995). Reflections on case method teaching. *Action in Teacher Education, 17*(1), 1–8. doi:10.1080/01626620.1995.10463225

Toding, M., & Venesaar, U. (2018). Discovering and developing conceptual understanding of teaching and learning in entrepreneurship lecturers. *Education + Training, 60*(7/8), 696–718. doi:10.1108/ET-07-2017-0101

Torío López, S., Peña Calvo, J. V., & Fernández García, C. M. (2010). Evaluación de una experiencia de innovación docente para el aprendizaje significativo en pedagogía: Un marco para la reflexión a partir de la percepción de los estudiantes [Evaluation of a teaching innovation experience for meaningful learning in pedagogy: a framework for reflection based on student perceptions]. *ESE. Estudios sobre Educación, 18*, 229–254.

Toro, U., & Joshi, M. (2012). ICT in Higher Education: Review of Literature from the Period 2004-201 1. *International Journal of Innovation, Management and Technology, 3*(1), 20–23.

Torres-Barzabal, L. M., Martínez-Gimeno, A., & Hermosilla-Rodríguez, J. M. (2020). Twitter social network in university teaching. Digital innovation strategy for social responsibility. *Sustainability (Switzerland), 12*(8), 3350. Advance online publication. doi:10.3390u12083350

Traux, D. D. (2007). Restructuring the undergraduate laboratory process. *Journal of Professional Issues in Engineering Education and Practice*, 192–198.

Trujillo, F. (2015). *Project-based learning. Infant, Primary and Secondary* [Aprendizaje basado en proyectos. Infantil, Primaria y Secundaria]. MECD & INTEF.

Tseng, F.-C., & Kuo, F.-Y. (2014). A study of social participation and knowledge sharing in the teachers' online professional community of practice. *Computers & Education, 72*, 37–47. doi:10.1016/j.compedu.2013.10.005

Tsimane, T. A., & Downing, Ch. (2019). Transformative learning in nursing education: A concept analysis. *International Journal of Nursing Sciences, 7*(1), 91-98, https://www.sciencedirect.com/science/article/pii/S2352013219301760

Tur, G., Marín-Juarros, V., & Carpenter, J. (2017). Using Twitter in higher education in Spain and the USA. Comunicar. *Media Education Research Journal, 25*(1).

Ukut, I. I. T., & Krairit, D. (2019). Justifying students' performance: A comparative study of both ICT students' and instructors' perspective. *Interactive Technology and Smart Education, 16*(1), 18–35. doi:10.1108/ITSE-05-2018-0028

Umer, W. (2020). *Agile Scrum Crash Course*. Amazon Digital Services.

UNESCO. (2021). *AI and education: Guidance for policy-markers*. UNESCO publishing.

UNESCO. (n.d.). *International Bureau of Education. Competency-based approach* [Oficina Internacional de educación. Enfoque por competencias]. Consultado el 2 de abril de 2018 en http://www.ibe.unesco.org/es/temas/enfoque-por-competencias

UNICEF. (2019). *Strengthening education systems and innovation*. Retrieved 02 05, 2022, from unicef for every child: https://www.unicef.org/education/strengthening-education-systems-innovation

Uziak, J., & Kommula, V. P. (2019). Application of problem based learning in mechanics of machines course. *International Journal of Engineering Pedagogy.*, *9*(1), 68–83. doi:10.3991/ijep.v9i1.9673

Valerio Ureña, G., & Rodríguez Martínez, M. C. (2017). Perfil del profesor universitario desde la perspectiva del estudiante [Profile of the university lecturer from the student's perspective]. *Revista Innovación Educativa*, *17*(74), 109–124.

Valle Arias, A., Sánchez Rodríguez, S. M., Núñez Pérez, J. C., González Cabanach, R., González García, J. A., & Rosário, P. J. S. L. D. (2010). Motivación y aprendizaje autorregulado [Motivation and Self-Regulated Learning]. *Interamerican Journal of Psychology*, *44*(1), 86–97.

Van den Ende, J. (2021). *Innovation Management*. Macmillan Education.

Van Deursen, A. (2001a). *Customer Involvement Experiences in a Software Product Line*. XP2001 workshop on customer involvement, Italy. Available online at https://homepages.cwi.nl/~arie/wci2001/vandeursen.pdf

Van Deursen, A. (2001b). Customer Involvement in Extreme Programming, XP2001 Workshop Report. *XP2001 Workshop on Customer Involvement*, 70-73.

Van Eck, N., & Waltman, L. (2010). Software survey: VOSviewer, a computer program for bibliometric mapping. *Scientometrics, 84*(2), 523-538.

Van Oers, B. (1998). From context to contextualizing. *Learning and Instruction*, *8*(6), 473–488. doi:10.1016/S0959-4752(98)00031-0

Van Oers, B. (2009). Developmental education: Improving participation in cultural practices. In M. Fleer, M. Hedegaard, & J. Tudge (Eds.), *Childhood studies and the impact of globalization: Policies and practices at global and local levels* (pp. 213–229). Routledge.

Van Rijk, Y., Volman, M., de Haan, D., & van Oers, B. (2017). Maximizing meaning: Creating a learning environment for reading comprehension of informative texts from a Vygotskian perspective. *Learning Environments Research*, *20*(1), 77–98. doi:10.100710984-016-9218-5

Velenchik, A. D. (1995). The case method as a strategy for teaching policy analysis to undergraduates. *The Journal of Economic Education*, *26*(1), 29–38. doi:10.1080/00220485.1995.10844854

Vergara, I., Travieso, N., & Crespo, M. (2014). Dinámica del proceso enseñanza-aprendizaje de la Química en tecnología de la salud. *Educación Médica Superior, 28*(2), 272–281.

Verschafel, L., & Greer, B. (2013). Mathematics education. In J. M. Spector, M. D. Merrill, J. Elen, & M. J. Bishop (Eds.), *Handbook of research on educational communications and technology* (pp. 553–563). Springer. doi:10.1007/978-1-4614-3185-5_43

VersionOne. (2011). *State of Agile Survey 2011 - The State of Agile Development*. Author.

Vincent-Lancrin, S., Urgel, J., Kar, S., & Jacotin, G. (2019). *Measuring Innovation in Education 2019: What Has Changed in the Classroom? Educational Research and Innovation*. Paris: OECD Publishing. Recuperado de https://www.oecd-ilibrary.org/docser ver/9789264311671-en.pdf ?expires=1586359992yid=idyaccname=guestychecksum=83713685B45347B501719B47ABFBEB4D

Virdun, C., Gray, J., Sherwood, J., Power, T., Phillips, A., Parker, N., & Jackson, D. (2013). Working together to make Indigenous health care curricula everybody's business: A graduate attribute teaching innovation report. *Contemporary Nurse, 46*(1), 97–104. doi:10.5172/conu.2013.46.1.97 PMID:24621295

Volman, M., & Ten Dam, G. (2015). Critical thinking for educated citizenship. In M. Davies & R. Barnett (Eds.), *The Palgrave handbook of critical thinking in higher education* (pp. 593–603). Palgrave Macmillan. doi:10.1057/9781137378057_35

vom Brocke, J., Simons, A., Riemer, K., Niehaves, B., Plattfaut, R., & Cleven, A. (2015). Standing on the shoulders of giants: Challenges and recommendations of literature search in information systems research. *Communications of the Association for Information Systems, 37*(1), 9. doi:10.17705/1CAIS.03709

Von Glaserfeld, E. (1984). *The Invented Reality: How do we know what we believe we know?* (P. Waltzlawick, Ed.). W. W. Norton & Co Inc.

von Hippel, W., & Trivers, R. (2011). *The evolution and psychology of self-deception*. doi:10.1017/S0140525X10001354

Von Thienen, J., Clancey, W., Corazza, G., & Meinel, C. (2017). Theoretical foundations of design thinking. Part I: John E. Arnold's creative thinking theories. In H. Plattner, C. Meinel, & L. Leifer (Eds.), *Design thinking research. Making distinctions: Collaboration versus cooperation* (pp. 13–40). Springer.

Von Thienen, J., Clancey, W., & Meinel, V. (2019). Theoretical Foundations of Design Thinking. Part II: Robert H. McKim's Need-Based Design Theory. In C. Meinel & L. Leifer (Eds.), *Design thinking research. Looking Further: Design Thinking Beyond Solution-Fixation* (pp. 13–40). Springer. doi:10.1007/978-3-319-97082-0_2

Von Thienen, J., Clancey, W., & Meinel, V. (2021). Theoretical Foundations of Design Thinking. Part III: Robert H. McKim's Visual Thinking Theories. In C. Meinel & L. Leifer (Eds.), *Design thinking research. Interrogating the Doing* (pp. 9–23). Springer. doi:10.1007/978-3-030-62037-0_2

Wakefield, J. S., Warren, S. J., & Alsobrook, M. (2011). Learning and teaching as communicative actions: A mixed-methods twitter study. *Knowledge Management and E-Learning, 3*(4), 563–584. doi:10.34105/j.kmel.2011.03.038

Wang, A. I. (2015). The wear out effect of a game-based student response system. *Computers & Education, 82*, 217–227. doi:10.1016/j.compedu.2014.11.004

Wang, A. I., Zhu, M., & Sætre, R. (2016). The effect of digitizing and gamifying quizzing in classrooms. In *Proceedings of the 10th European Conference on Games Based Learning*. University of the West of Scotland.

Wang, H., Tlili, A., Lehman, J. D., Lu, H., & Huang, R. (2021). Investigating feedback implemented by instructors to support online competency-based learning (CBL): A multiple case study. *Int J Educ Technol High Educ, 18*(1), 5. doi:10.118641239-021-00241-6

Wang, J., Mendori, T., & Xiong, J. (2014). A language learning support system using course-centered ontology and its evaluation. *Computer Education*, *78*, 278–293. doi:10.1016/j.compedu.2014.06.009

Wang, J., Ogata, H., & Shimada, A. (2017). A meaningful discovery learning environment for e-book learners. *IEEE Global Engineering Education Conference*, 1158–1165. 10.1109/EDUCON.2017.7942995

Wang, J., Shimada, A., Oi, M., Ogata, H., & Tabata, Y. (2020). Development and evaluation of a visualization system to support meaningful e-book learning. *Interactive Learning Environments*, 1–18. Advance online publication. doi:10.1080/10494820.2020.1813178

Wardekker, W., Boersma, A., Ten Dam, G., & Volman, M. (2012). Motivation for school learning: Enhancing the meaningfulness of learning in communities of learners. In M. Hedegaard, A. Edwards, & M. Fleer (Eds.), *Motives in children's development: Cultural–historical approaches* (pp. 153–170). Cambridge University Press.

Warner, D. B., & Koeppel, K. (2009). General education requirements: A comparative analysis. *The Journal of General Education*, *58*(4), 241–258. doi:10.2307/25702446

Wastell, D. (1999). Learning Dysfunctions in Information Systems Development: Overcoming the Social Defences with Transitional Objects. *Management Information Systems Quarterly*, *23*(4), 581–600. doi:10.2307/249490

Watermeyer, R., Crick, T., Knight, C., & Goodall, J. (2021). COVID-19 and digital disruption in UK universities: Afflictions and affordances of emergency online migration. *Higher Education*, *81*(3), 623–641. doi:10.100710734-020-00561-y PMID:32836334

Watson, G., & Sottile, J. (2010). Cheating in the Digital Age: Do Students Cheat More in Online Courses? *Educational Foundations and Technology*. Retrieved from https://mds.marshall.edu/eft_faculty/1

Weatherly, L. A. (2003). The value of people: The challenges and opportunities of human capital measurement and reporting. *Research Quarterly*, *123*, 1–11.

Wei, S., Wang, X., & Liu, Z. (2016). Teaching Research on the University Practical Course Based on Taxonomy of Educational Objectives. *Management Science*, *66*, 108.

Werbach, K., & Hunter, D. (2012). *For the win: How game thinking can revolutionize your business*. Wharton Digital Press.

Westmeyer, P. (1985). *A History of American Higher Education*. Charles C. Thomas, Publisher.

Whitworth, A. (2012). Invisible success: Problems with the grand technological innovation in higher education. *Computers & Education*, *59*(1), 145–155. doi:10.1016/j.compedu.2011.09.023

Wickham, L., & Wilcock, J. (2012). *Management Consulting. Delivering an effective project*. Pearson.

Wilson, D. C., Butler, R. J., Cray, D., Hickson, D. J., & Mallory, G. R. (1986). Breaking the bounds of organization in strategic decision making. *Human Relations*, *39*(4), 309–331. doi:10.1177/001872678603900402

Wrenn, J., & Wrenn, B. (2009). Enhancing Learning by Integrating, Theory and Practice. *International Journal on Teaching and Learning in Higher Education*, *21*(2), 258–265.

Wu, W. C. V., Hsieh, J. S. C., & Yang, J. C. (2017). Creating an online learning community in a flipped classroom to enhance EFL learners' oral proficiency. *Journal of Educational Technology & Society*, *20*(2), 142–157.

Xiao-Li, L., Wei, G., Xin-Li, C., & Ke-Gang, H. (2006). Designing a test case library system of supporting sharing and reusing. *Journal of Computational Science*, *33*, 290–291.

Xie, Y., & Zhang, Y. L. (2013). Research on Extracurricular Teaching System Based on Twitter Mode. In Applied Mechanics and Materials. Trans Tech Publications Ltd. doi:10.4028/www.scientific.net/AMM.409-410.1624

Yin, R. K. (2011). *Applications of case study research*. Sage.

Yock, P. G., Brinton, T. J., & Zenios, S. A. (2011). Teaching biomedical technology innovation as a discipline. *Science Translational Medicine, 3*(92). doi:10.1126/scitranslmed.3002222

Zautorova, E.V., & Bodrova, E.V. (2021). Practice-Oriented Training in Higher Education Institutions of the Federal Penitentiary Service of Russia. *Penitentiary science, 15*(55), 575–584.

Zempoalteca, B., González, J., Barragán, J., & Guzmán, T. (2018). Factors influencing incorporation of Information and Communication Technologies in public universities: Approach based on teacher self-perception. *Revista de la Educación Superior*, *47*(186), 51–74. doi:10.36857/resu.2018.186.348

Zhang, Y., Liang, R., & Ma, H. (2012). Teaching innovation in computer network course for undergraduate students with packet tracer. *IERI Procedia*, *2*, 504–510. doi:10.1016/j.ieri.2012.06.124

Zhang, Y., & Mi, Y. (2010, September). Another look at the language difficulties of international students. *Journal of Studies in International Education*, *14*(4), 371–388. doi:10.1177/1028315309336031

Zhan, Z., & Mei, H. (2013). Academic self-concept and social presence in face-to-face and online learning: Perceptions and effects on students' learning achievement and satisfaction across environments. *Computers & Education*, *2013*(69), 131–138. doi:10.1016/j.compedu.2013.07.002

Zhu, J., Liao, Z., Yam, K., & Johnson, R. (2018). Shared leadership: A state-of-the-art review and future research agenda. *Journal of Organizational Behavior*, *39*(7), 834–852. doi:10.1002/job.2296

Zientek, L. R., Werner, J. M., Campuzano, M. V., & Nimon, K. (2018). The use of Google Scholar for research and research dissemination. *New Horizons in Adult Education and Human Resource Development*, *30*(1), 39–46.

Zupic, I., & Čater, T. (2015). Bibliometric methods in management and organization. *Organizational Research Methods*, *18*(3), 429–472. doi:10.1177/1094428114562629

About the Contributors

Jose Ramon Saura research has focused on the theoretical and practical insights of various aspects of User Generated Content (UGC), with a specific focus around three major research approaches applied to business and marketing: data mining, knowledge discovery and information sciences. International Ph.D. in Business Economics at the Rey Juan Carlos University, London South Bank University (LSBU) and Harvard University (RCC). He is a Marketing Lecturer of the Department of Business Economics at the Rey Juan Carlos University, lecturing at the Faculty of Social Science and Law of Madrid. He has published articles focused on areas such as Business, Management, Computer Sciences, Multidisciplinary or Information Sciences, among others. His research has appeared in leading international journals such as the Journal of Business Research, International Journal of Information Management, Journal of Business & Industrial Marketing, Review of Managerial Sciences, Journal of Innovation and Knowledge, Journal of Mobile Communication, IJERPH or IEEE Access. Jose Ramon Saura serves on editorial and reviewer boards of a number of business and information sciences journals.

* * *

K. A. Burke is an Associate Professor of Teaching at Iowa State University. She brings experience from teaching in both two-year and four-year undergraduate chemistry programs. Past research work includes statewide and nationwide curriculum enhancement projects. Research interests include student metacognitive strategies, strategies for guided inquiry and active learning, especially the Science Writing Heuristic approach, and curriculum development.

Ignacio Danvila del Valle is Researcher and Associate Professor of Human Resources Management and Business Administration and Organizational Theory at the Complutense University of Madrid (Spain).

Eloísa Díaz Garrido is an Associate Professor at Rey Juan Carlos University. She earned her doctorate in Economic and Business Sciences at Rey Juan Carlos University. Lecturer on management and operations management at the graduate and postgraduate level. Her line of research focuses on operations strategy, environmental management, servitization, and gamification. Has presented various papers in congresses at the national and international level. Author of various publications in national and international journals and books.

Silke Finken is a professor of innovation management at the International School of Management in Munich. Her current research interests include innovation, ecosystems, and open banking. Silke was previously head of the innovation and consulting management for the transaction banking at DZ Bank, as well as a project leader in the financial service practice at Bain & Company. She holds a PhD in finance from Frankfurt University.

Rocío Gallego-Losada holds a PhD in Economics and Business Administration. Her research work has focused mainly on issues related to educational innovation, financial literacy and public-private pensions. Gallego-Losada is an associate professor at Universidad Rey Juan Carlos in the Department of Financial Economics. She has previously worked at Marsh & McLennan, Natwest Bank, Ford Spain and El Corte Inglés. She has received several grants (Harvard, 2011; Atlanta, 2009; Mapfre 2003). She has written several articles in academic journals. Finally, she belongs to a gamification educational innovation group of Universidad Rey Juan Carlos.

Cristina García-Magro obtained her doctorate in Administration and Logistics for Security and Defence Systems at the Universidad Rey Juan Carlos. She is Associate Professor in the Faculty of Legal and Social Sciences of the Universidad Rey Juan Carlos. Her principal research interests are servitisation, design of services, and gamification. She is the author of various publications in indexed journals.

Vera Gelashvili is an Assistant Professor at Universidad Rey Juan Carlos.

Elena M. Gimenez-Fernandez, PhD in Business Administration, is an Assistant Professor in the Business Administration and Marketing Department at Pablo de Olavide University (Seville, Spain). She has been a visitor student at Garwood Corporate Innovation Center. Her research focuses on open innovation and entrepreneurship. Her research has been published in academic journals such as Research Policy, Industry & Innovation, International Small Business Journal, and Creativity and Innovation Management among others.

Paula González-Padilla researches Digital Marketing and the use of Digital Technology in the Interaction with Customers. She is specialized in Marketing of Services and Business. Paula González-Padilla held positions of project manager and made consultancy at a number of other private companies.

Thais González-Torres is Lecturer in Business Administration and Organization at Rey Juan Carlos University, Spain. She is the author and co-author of several works dealing with business management and education innovation. Numerous publications have been involved in the development of all this research activity.

Thomas Greenbowe is a Senior Instructor II and chemical educator at the University of Oregon and a Morrill Professor of Chemistry Emeritus at Iowa State University. He has received numerous awards and honors for his contributions to the development and advancement of computer simulations in chemistry education and active-student centered teaching and learning pedagogy and practices. Over the course of his 50-year career, Prof. Greenbowe has taught 90,000 students in six universities. He has facilitated numerous workshops for AP Chemistry teachers and college faculty. He has served on various ACS exam committees and served on the AP Chemistry Test Development Committee. During the two years of the COVID-19 pandemic, the chemistry demonstration and educational resources website at the University of Oregon was used by over 2,000 chemistry instructors.

Tanya Gupta is an instructor in the department of Chemistry & Biochemistry at the University of Oregon. She is also an established chemical education researcher with peer-reviewed publications in leading journals and books. Dr. Gupta's area of expertise includes guided-inquiry, active learning and integration of technology for student-centered teaching and learning.

Justin Joy is an Assistant Professor at School of Business and Management, Christ (Deemed to be University). He has taken his B.Tech in Mechanical Engineering from Govt. Engineering College, Thrissur, Masters (MSc in Business Information Technology) from Newcastle Business School, University of Northumbria, U.K. and a second Masters (M.Tech in Manufacturing Management) from BITS Pilani, Rajasthan. He did his PhD in Management from the Department of Management Studies, Pondicherry University. Before joining Christ University, he was working as Assistant Professor in SCMS Cochin School of Business, Kerala. With a total of 19 years of experience, he was the Business Area Manager of Educomp Solutions Ltd. and Web and Business Development Manager cum Head of Computer Applications of IFCR India - a Canadian based Research Organization in Cochin. Apart from his corporate experience in India, he has also experience working abroad in Newcastle Upon Tyne, UK. He has also published several articles in Scopus indexed and UGC Recognised Journals.

Francisco J. S. Lacárcel is a doctoral student in Tourism from the University of Alicante. Relating tourism with digital communication.

Matthias Lederer is Full Professor of Information Systems at the Technical University of Applied Sciences Amberg-Weiden. Prior to this, he was a professor at the ISM International School of Management Munich and at the same time Chief Process Officer at the IT Service Center of the Bavarian justice system. His previous positions include research assistant at the University of Erlangen-Nuremberg and strategy consultant at the German industrial company REHAU. His research and studies focus on business process management and IT management. Prof. Lederer holds a doctorate as well as a master's degree in international information systems and is the author of over 70 scientific publications in this field.

Almudena Macías-Guillén is a Lecturer and Researcher in the Department of Enterprise Economy at Rey Juan Carlos University in Madrid since 2004. She is doctor in Enterprise and Accountancy Economy. She is member of ASEPUC group since 2005, and also in AEDEM since 2007 and she has four qualifications/sections in Docentia by the URJC. She was involved in the Commission for the design and degree adaptation of the "Contabilidad y Finanzas" in the same University. She has participated in six projects which dealt with innovative education, obtained in 2005, 2008, 2011, 2018, 2019, 2020 and 2021 calls in the URJC, heading three of them. She is member of the recognition commission in ADE, 2012-2015. She has participated preparing educational books, joined with lecturers of Commercial and Business Management Faculty and Innovative Education as well. Almudena has been member of organizing and scientific committee of national and international conferences. Equally, she presented innovative education results in Congresses dealing with Innovation Teaching and Information and communication Technology congresses, national as well as international. She has published several articles in high impact journals. Almudena actively collaborate in innovation education conferences in different Spanish Universities.

María Luz Martín-Peña is an Associate Professor at Rey Juan Carlos University of Madrid. She earned her doctorate in Business Administration (cum laude and Extraordinary Prize for doctoral thesis) at Complutense University of Madrid. She is lecturer on management and operations management. Her current research interests include operations strategy, servitization and gamification in the firm. She is Head of Openmanuserv R&D Group. She has published her research in leading journals such as International Journal of Production Research, International Journal of Operations and Production Management, International Journal of Sustainable Transportation, European Journal of Operational Research, Journal of Business and Industrial Marketing, among others.

Juan Gabriel Martínez Navalón is an Assistant professor in Rey Juan Carlos university in the Finance area. PhD student in Rey Juan Carlos University in Social Sciences. Master's in Management in Rey Juan Carlos University and training in Digital Marketing and E-commerce. Bachelor's in Business Administration in the University of Castilla la Mancha. Current collaborator in Fundación Camilo Prado for the Research in Business Economy. Member of the European Academy of Management and Business Economics. Participation in national and international congresses obtaining mentions for the developed research. Professional experience as manager and consultant in the tourism sector.

Antonio Montero-Navarro holds a PhD in Business Administration. His research has focused mainly in the fields of corporate reputation, educational innovation, financial literacy and digital transformation. Montero-Navarro is an Associate Professor at Universidad Rey Juan Carlos. He has been recognised both by his students and his Institution as one of the most innovative and valuable professors. He has written several articles in academic journals. He belongs to a gamification educational innovation group of Universidad Rey Juan Carlos.

Alexandra Mora-Cruz is a Bachelor of Business Administration and Master of Business Administration with an Emphasis in Finance. Currently a student in the Doctoral Program in Business Administration at the Technological Institute of Costa Rica. More than 15 years of experience, including management positions, finance consulting, human talent management, business strategy, and administrative data analysis (job profiles, procedure manuals, budgets, financial models, among others). In addition, 9 years of experience as a teacher in different programs in the areas of General Administration, Human Talent Management, Business Strategy, Administrative Analysis, Finance and Organizational Behavior.

D. Radhakrishnan Nair is a faculty member who has a long, distinguished career as Professor of English Language, Literature, Cultural studies, and English Communication, he is the author of award winning book on Narratology, and author of other seminal books and papers. His latest book: Academic Journal: Editing and Publishing has been published by Notion Press. He has presented papers in international conferences, on narratology and literary comparatistics. Besides being a speaker for many academic and social causes he was the editor of a double blind peer reviewed, scientific/academic journal in business and management studies, embedded in databases: Cabell's, ICI, Index Copernicus, J-Gate, EBSCO, ProQuest, Ulrich's, and Scopus. One of the leaders of popular movements like "Against Establishment of Atomic Reactor in Kerala" (1982-90), he is a teacher with five decades of experience in teaching English. He has attended workshop: "Train the trainers" organized by the British Council, Refresher Course in ELT at CIEFL, and training in English teaching given by CUP. He has organized many UGC Seminars, Refresher courses for University and College teachers, and academic conferences.

Alba Gómez-Ortega has a degree in Business Administration and Management from the Rey Juan Carlos University, 2010, with an extraordinary award. PhD in Business Economics, 2015, from Rey Juan Carlos University, with distinction cum laude and extraordinary doctorate award. Master's Degree in Financial and Risk Auditing from the Instituto de Estudios Bursátiles, 2013. She is currently a professor in Accounting and Finance in Department of Business Economics at the Rey Juan Carlos University. She has six years of professional experience in the well-known multinational KPMG, having worked specifically in auditing in the financial sector, reaching the position of Audit Manager. She is Co-Director of the Master's Degree in Auditing and Senior Accounting at Rey Juan Carlos University since 2019. She is a member of the Observatory of Costs and Financing of Collective Urban Transport, which produces regular reports for companies in the sector. He was a member of the Chair of Ecotransport, Technology and Mobility, funded by the Municipal Transport Company of Madrid, from 2009 to 2012. She is also a member of the European Academy of Management and Business Economics and the Spanish Association of University Professors of Accounting. She is the author of several publications in journals, books and papers, both nationally and internationally, in the areas of accounting, auditing and urban transport. She also carries out research work on teaching innovation in the subjects she teaches at the University.

Kamalendu Pal is with the Department of Computer Science, School of Science and Technology, City, University of London. Kamalendu received his BSc (Hons) degree in Physics from Calcutta University, India, Postgraduate Diploma in Computer Science from Pune, India, MSc degree in Software Systems Technology from the University of Sheffield, Postgraduate Diploma in Artificial Intelligence from the Kingston University, MPhil degree in Computer Science from the University College London, and MBA degree from the University of Hull, United Kingdom. He has published over seventy international research articles (including book chapters) widely in the scientific community with research papers in the ACM SIGMIS Database, Expert Systems with Applications, Decision Support Systems, and conferences. His research interests include knowledge-based systems, decision support systems, teaching and learning practice gamification, blockchain technology, software engineering, service-oriented computing, sensor network simulation, and edge computing. He is on the editorial board of an international computer science journal and is a member of the British Computer Society, the Institution of Engineering and Technology, and the IEEE Computer Society.

Pedro Palos-Sanchez received the Bachelor of Science degree in computer science from Extremadura University, Spain, the master's degree in marketing from UOC, Spain, MBA from Camilo Jose Cela University, Spain and the Ph.D. degree in business administration from University of Sevilla, Spain. He served as a Professor with the University of Extremadura, Pablo de Olavide University and International University of La Rioja, Spain. Nowadays, he is Associate Professor of University of Seville, Spain. Experience includes direction of numerous postgraduate courses and collaborations with private and public organizations. He has participated in research projects and different courses and articles in various conferences and programs on digital economy, entrepreneurship and management both nationally and internationally, being his lines of research Digital Marketing, Business Organization and Information Systems. He has been guest editor of several international scientific publications.

Jose Rabadán Rubio is a professor at the University of Murcia of the Department of Theory and History of Education Doctor in CC. of Education and doctoral student in Psychology with Master in

Personnel Management and HR Management, Early Care, Psychology and Health, in The Directorate of Social Services Centres and in Psychopedagogy and in Clinical Psychology.

José-Luis Rodríguez-Sánchez is PhD and Professor of Management at the Rey Juan Carlos University, Spain. His research interest includes strategic alliances, cooperative agreements, merger and acquisitions and human resources management. His research has been published in International Journal of Hospitality Management, Finance Research Letters, International Journal of Environmental Research and Public Health, International Journal of Manpower, Journal of Organizational Change Management and Frontiers in Psychology among others journals. https://orcid.org/0000-0001-7913-874.

José G. Vargas-Hernández, M.B.A., Ph.D., Member of the National System of Researchers of Mexico and a research professor at Tecnológico Mario Molina Unidad Zapopan formerly at University Center for Economic and Managerial Sciences, University of Guadalajara. Professor Vargas-Hernández has a Ph. D. in Public Administration and a Ph.D. in Organizational Economics. He has undertaken studies in Organisational Behaviour and has a Master of Business Administration, published four books and more than 200 papers in international journals and reviews (some translated to English, French, German, Portuguese, Farsi, Chinese, etc.) and more than 300 essays in national journals and reviews. He has obtained several international Awards and recognition.

Liguo Yu received his PhD degree in Computer Science from Vanderbilt University in 2004. He is an associate professor at Indiana University South Bend. He received his MS degree from Institute of Metal Research, Chinese Academy of Science in 1995. He received his BS degree in Physics from Jilin University in 1992. Before joining IUSB, he was a visiting assistant professor at Tennessee Tech University. During his sabbatical of Spring 2014, he was a visiting faculty at New York Institute of Technology-Nanjing. His research interests include software coupling, software maintenance and software evolution, empirical software engineering, and open-source development.

Index

Q

R

S

T

U

W

Recommended Reference Books

IGI Global's reference books are available in three unique pricing formats: Print Only, E-Book Only, or Print + E-Book.

Shipping fees may apply.

www.igi-global.com

ISBN: 9781522589648
EISBN: 9781522589655
© 2021; 156 pp.
List Price: US$ **155**

ISBN: 9781799840756
EISBN: 9781799840763
© 2021; 282 pp.
List Price: US$ **185**

ISBN: 9781799855989
EISBN: 9781799856009
© 2021; 382 pp.
List Price: US$ **195**

ISBN: 9781799864745
EISBN: 9781799864752
© 2021; 271 pp.
List Price: US$ **195**

ISBN: 9781799875710
EISBN: 9781799875734
© 2021; 252 pp.
List Price: US$ **195**

ISBN: 9781799857709
EISBN: 9781799857716
© 2021; 378 pp.
List Price: US$ **195**

Do you want to stay current on the latest research trends, product announcements, news, and special offers?

Join IGI Global's mailing list to receive customized recommendations, exclusive discounts, and more.

Sign up at: **www.igi-global.com/newsletters.**

Publisher of Timely, Peer-Reviewed Inclusive Research Since 1988

IGI Global
PUBLISHER of TIMELY KNOWLEDGE

www.igi-global.com Sign up at www.igi-global.com/newsletters facebook.com/igiglobal twitter.com/igiglobal linkedin.com/igiglobal

Ensure Quality Research is Introduced to the Academic Community

Become an Evaluator for IGI Global Authored Book Projects

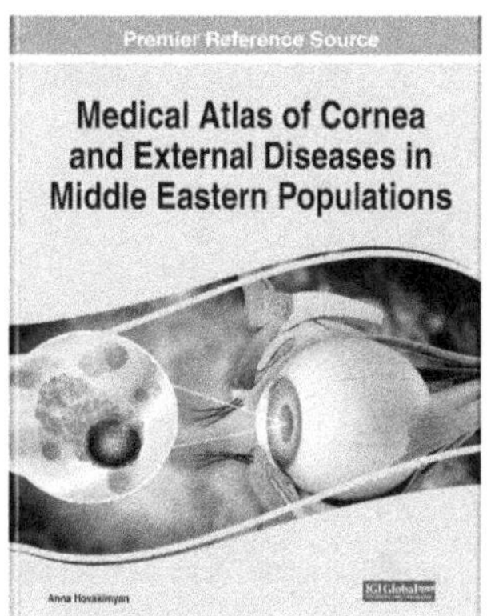

The overall success of an authored book project is dependent on quality and timely manuscript evaluations.

Applications and Inquiries may be sent to:
development@igi-global.com

Applicants must have a doctorate (or equivalent degree) as well as publishing, research, and reviewing experience. Authored Book Evaluators are appointed for one-year terms and are expected to complete at least three evaluations per term. Upon successful completion of this term, evaluators can be considered for an additional term.

If you have a colleague that may be interested in this opportunity, we encourage you to share this information with them.

Increase Your Manuscript's Chance of Acceptance

IGI Global Author Services

Copy Editing & Proofreading

Professional, native English language copy editors improve your manuscript's grammar, spelling, punctuation, terminology, semantics, consistency, flow, formatting, and more.

Scientific & Scholarly Editing

A Ph.D. level review for qualities such as originality and significance, interest to researchers, level of methodology and analysis, coverage of literature, organization, quality of writing, and strengths and weaknesses.

Figure, Table, Chart & Equation Conversions

Work with IGI Global's graphic designers before submission to enhance and design all figures and charts to IGI Global's specific standards for clarity.

- **Professional Service**
- **Quality Guarantee & Certificate**
- **Timeliness**
- **Affordable Pricing**

What Makes IGI Global Author Services Stand Apart?

Services/Offerings	IGI Global Author Services	Editage	Enago
Turnaround Time of Projects	*3-5 Business Days*	6-7 Busines Days	6-7 Busines Days
Pricing	Fraction of our Competitors' Cost	Up to **2x Higher**	Up to **3x Higher**

Learn More or Get Started Here:

For Questions, Contact IGI Global's Customer Service Team at cust@igi-global.com or 717-533-8845

IGI Global
PUBLISHER of TIMELY KNOWLEDGE
www.igi-global.com

6,600+ E-BOOKS. ADVANCED RESEARCH. INCLUSIVE & ACCESSIBLE.

IGI Global
PUBLISHER of TIMELY KNOWLEDGE

IGI Global e-Book Collection

- **Flexible Purchasing Options** (Perpetual, Subscription, EBA, etc.)
- Multi-Year Agreements with **No Price Increases** Guaranteed
- **No Additional Charge** for Multi-User Licensing
- No Maintenance, Hosting, or Archiving Fees
- Transformative **Open Access Options** Available

Request More Information, or Recommend the IGI Global e-Book Collection to Your Institution's Librarian

Among Titles Included in the IGI Global e-Book Collection

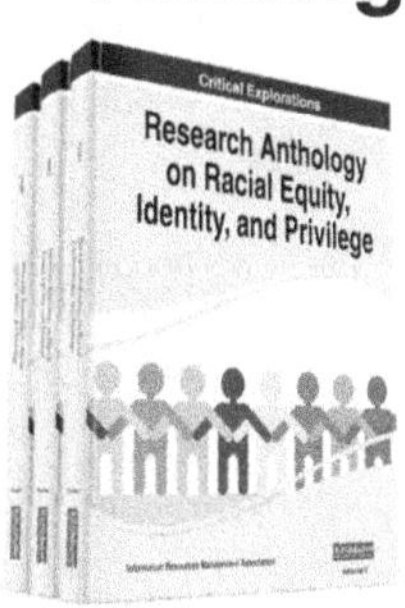

Research Anthology on Racial Equity, Identity, and Privilege (3 Vols.)
EISBN: 9781668445082
Price: US$ 895

Handbook of Research on Remote Work and Worker Well-Being in the Post-COVID-19 Era
EISBN: 9781799867562
Price: US$ 265

Research Anthology on Big Data Analytics, Architectures, and Applications (4 Vols.)
EISBN: 9781668436639
Price: US$ 1,950

Handbook of Research on Challenging Deficit Thinking for Exceptional Education Improvement
EISBN: 9781799888628
Price: US$ 265

Acquire & Open

When your library acquires an IGI Global e-Book and/or e-Journal Collection, your faculty's published work will be considered for immediate conversion to Open Access *(CC BY License)*, at no additional cost to the library or its faculty *(cost only applies to the e-Collection content being acquired)*, through our popular **Transformative Open Access (Read & Publish) Initiative**.

For More Information or to Request a Free Trial, Contact IGI Global's e-Collections Team: eresources@igi-global.com | 1-866-342-6657 ext. 100 | 717-533-8845 ext. 100

www.ingramcontent.com/pod-product-compliance
Lightning Source LLC
LaVergne TN
LVHW060422300926
849162LV00006B/1503